WOMEN OF EM

WOMEN OF EMPIRE

Nineteenth-Century Army Officers' Wives in India and the U.S. West

Verity McInnis

UNIVERSITY OF OKLAHOMA PRESS : NORMAN

Some material from "'Ladies' of the Frontier Forts," *Military History of the West* 35 (2005): 35–56, appears in chapters 2, 3, and 4 in much altered form and is used here by permission.

Material originally published in "Indirect Agents of Empire: Army Officers' Wives in British India and the American West, 1830–1875," *Pacific Historical Review* 83, no. 3 (August 2014): 378–406, appears, in altered form, in chapters 4 and 8.

Library of Congress Cataloging-in-Publication Data

Name: McInnis, Verity, 1957– author.
Title: Women of empire : nineteenth-century army officers' wives in India and the U.S. west / Verity McInnis.
Description: Norman : University of Oklahoma, 2017. | Includes bibliographical references and index.
Identifiers: LCCN 2017007064 | ISBN 978-0-8061-5774-0 (hardcover : alk. paper)
Subjects: LCSH: Officers' spouses—Great Britain—History—19th century. | Officers' spouses—United States—History—19th century. | Great Britain. Army—Military life—History—19th century. | United States. Army—Military life—History—19th century. | Army spouses—Great Britain—History—19th century. | Army spouses—United States—History—19th century.
Classification: LCC U767 .M38 2017 | DDC 355.1089/21054—dc23
LC record available at https://lccn.loc.gov/2017007064

1 2 3 4 5 6 7 8 9 10

For my sons
Tristan, Joshua, and Tobias

Contents

Illustrations

Preface

My fascination with the exercise of female authority began when researching the experiences of Southern women during the American Civil War. I found the gendered power play between military husbands and their wives absorbing. Many of these women took complete and capable charge of all domestic and business affairs during their husbands' absence. Such discovery prompted an investigation of nineteenth-century officers' wives posted in the U.S. West. Here, it became clear that these historical actors constructed an empowered role that held legitimacy across the male terrain of the army garrison. Military wives enjoyed no officially recognized status, so how was power and influence constructed? Rather than simply accepting the prescribed domestic role, many women defied such limitations and glowingly recorded episodes that demonstrated the development of more nuanced codes of female behavior. They sensationally recorded "packing" pistols, commanding garrisons, and enjoying unaccompanied lunch dates with lightly clad American Indian chiefs. These women significantly altered traditional gender, race, and social attitudes and behaviors by designing and maintaining a distinct social reality. In utilizing the ranking structure within the military communities, officers and their wives created a distinct hierarchical class, within which women demonstrated authority and influence. My curiosity with the construction of female identity and spaces of gendered power fueled a considerably larger research project. In broadening the field of study to include the British officers' wives stationed in India, I decided to undertake a comparative analysis to examine female autonomy within the imperial sites. To scaffold the undertaking, I complicated the foundational questions to ask: Does the rank of officer husbands provide status for wives in both peripheries? Do the American and British core societies signify class status using similar values, symbols, and social rituals? How does this model translate/operate in both peripheries? What are the similarities/differences in the two territories? In answering these questions, a previously obscured dimension of imperialism became visible, revealing that military wives held key roles, both in India and the U.S. West, in designing, directing, and maintaining national ambitions.

My archival research for this project extended from Fort Davis, situated within the rugged mountainous landscape of West Texas, to the Centre of South Asian Studies, which was then located in Laundress Lane, Cambridge, UK. The experiences of the British military wives unfolded amidst the ambient sounds of punters spending leisurely afternoons on the River Cam. Despite the idyllic surroundings, my visit would not have been so productive without the professional support extended and vast knowledge kindly shared by Kevin Greenbank and Barbara Roe—a sincere thank you. I am extremely grateful for research grants provided by the Texas A&M University History Departments at Corpus Christi and College Station, and for the following TAMU awards: Melbern G. Glasscock Center for Humanities Research Graduate Travel to Archives Grant, DeLoach and Amelia Martin Graduate Dissertation Research Fellowship, College of Liberal Arts Dissertation Research Award, and a Dissertation Completion Fellowship.

I owe a huge debt of gratitude to three people. R. J. Q. Adams, Joseph G. Dawson III, and David Vaught all played major roles in shaping and improving my work—thank you, so very much, for your unfailing support, advice, and encouragement. Much appreciation also goes to Sylvia Hoffert, Claudia Nelson, and Adam Siepp. In addition, I would like to take this opportunity to thank Sherry Smith for her insightful comments and suggestions, which have made this study far more robust. Robert Wooster, Texas A&M University–Corpus Christi, deserves a special mention. He both recognized and encouraged development of abilities and skills that prompted a change in major to history. I thank him, sincerely, for his guidance, enduring patience, and continuing friendship. Thanks also go to Susan Wladaver-Morgan for her perceptive observations, counsel, and unfailing encouragement. In addition, thanks go to Adam Kane, Stephanie Evans, and Jehanne Moharram at the University of Oklahoma Press, for their kind assistance and direction. I, however, acknowledge that the largest debt of gratitude is owed to my three sons, Tristan, Joshua, and Tobias, and my husband, Damon. As my very best friends, they patiently supported my academic goals, tolerated (unflinchingly) many long-winded academic conversations, and proudly celebrated my successes; thank you.

Colonel [Joseph N. G.] Whistler's
Rules for Wife Behavior

1
You will see that all meals are served on time.

2
You will come to the table in a wrapper.

3
You will smile at breakfast.

4
If possible, you will serve meat at least four times a week.

5
You will not move the furniture without my permission.

6
You will present the household accounts to me by the fifth of each month.

7
You will examine my uniforms each Tuesday and if they need repair
you will take the necessary action.

8
You will do no work in the evenings. You will entertain me.

9
You will not touch my desk.

10
You will remember you are not in command of anything except the cook.[1]

WOMEN OF EMPIRE

1

Introduction

[F]or the upholding of British prestige in the East, far more credit
is due to the individual men and women who have carried out
in their lives the loftiest conceptions of English truth and virtue,
than to the collective wisdom of the office in Downing Street.

—*Maud Diver*

In considering the men and women stationed in India as active agents of empire,
nineteenth-century novelist Maud Diver attempted to dispel contemporary
understandings of feminine weakness and caprice by portraying military wives
as ambassadors of English civilization. Officers' wives stationed in British India
understood this expectation to represent, and undertake duties for, the empire.
Despite the availability of journals, letters, and travelogues, scant scholarly
attention has been paid to these personal accounts. Similarly, despite increasing
numbers of attempts to interpret the role of the American officers' wives stationed
in the West, these women, thus far, have not been fully examined as major power
holders.[1]

At a time when women held no authority outside the home, the impact of
nineteenth-century army officers' wives stationed in British India and the U.S.
West adds a new perspective to studies of empire. In centralizing and comparing
the female experiences of army officers' wives during the period 1818–1910, and
by incorporating interdisciplinary approaches, it becomes clear that imperialism
is not simply a masculine preserve. In constructing a distinct role these military
women, who shared their husbands' sense of mission, generated power to design
and project an imagined imperial landscape. By transferring, adopting, and

adapting middle-class cultural values and customs they fashioned a new social reality within the military installations, influencing the development of imperial formations by cutting across and restructuring race, gender, and class boundaries. In feminizing military practices and by designing, reproducing, and policing social representations of empire, officers' wives held distinct, pivotal roles. By appropriating male spaces and applying an adaptive model of sociability, these women controlled markers and modalities to scaffold and maintain an imperial class—within which they became power holders.[2]

But what constitutes imperialism? John Buchan attempted to answer this question in his novel *A Lodge in the Wilderness*. Hugh, a central character, argued, "We need a definition. . . . I call myself an Imperialist . . . I can give no summary statement of my creed." "Is not the reason because it is not a creed but a faith?" Lady Lucy responded, "You cannot carve an epic on a nutshell or expound Christianity in an aphorism. If I could define Imperialism satisfactorily in a sentence I should be very suspicious of its truth." A third contributor proffered, "No . . . we don't want a definition. By its fruits ye shall know it. It is a spirit, an attitude of mind, an unconquerable hope. You can phrase it in a thousand ways without exhausting its content. It is a sense of the destiny of England. It is the wider patriotism which conceives our people as a race and not as a chance community." This spirit of destiny and patriotic rhetoric provides an ideological ideal, and explicitly underscores the intangible nature of "empire."[3]

Traditional imperial history, however, recounts global rivalry, benevolent assimilation, cultural conflict, and economic advantages to justify territorial conquest. Hence, as Linda Colley observes, imperial studies were a "comprehensively masculine enterprise. . . . [T]aught by chaps. . . . [S]tudied overwhelmingly by chaps . . . [and] centrally concerned with what chaps in the past, mainly of the pale variety, did to, or for, yet more chaps who were often not pale." To further advance emerging cross-disciplinary scholarship, however, she suggests that researchers adopt a comparative approach, and explore connections in power systems and actors. Patricia Nelson Limerick equally charges that "Western historians can play a central role in comparative studies of processes of colonialism and imperialism, locating the region in the big picture of world history." Indeed, she argues that similarities between the British and American imperial experience are "underdeveloped, neglected, even concealed." Considering "indirect rule as a device of colonialism," she suggests that "the process we have called 'westward expansion' or 'the frontier' or even 'conquest,' the devices, techniques, strategies, and justifications used by the Unites States bear an unsettling resemblance to the practices used by European countries as they wielded power around the planet." Limerick adds that a logical comparative analysis would be of nineteenth-century army officers' wives who accompanied their husbands to the U.S. West with similar women of a European power. This study, in part, represents an answer to these calls.[4]

In comparing the American and British officers' wives' experiences, a global analysis identifies similarities and differences to argue that both sets of women understood they held an imperial role. To be sure, written by a small number of women, the accounts tell nothing of those who returned home disillusioned with the dislocation of military life, nor of the enlisted soldiers' wives. This study does not seek to challenge existing methodologies or gender, race, and class interpretations, but makes visible a set of women who, thus far, remain generally underappreciated. In raising the profile of these historical actors, and by comparing two global locations, a compelling narrative emerges from this group of women writers that needs to be added to the historical record. Officers' wives influenced and sustained national prestige and legitimacy, as the designers and arbiters of a distinct imperial sociability.

There is no dispute concerning the description of Great Britain as an empire. With regard to the American experience, however, Richard Van Alstyne states, "In the United States it is almost a heresy to describe the nation as an empire. [Yet] the founders so regarded it . . . and the word continued to be accepted usage through the middle of the nineteenth century." Julian Go suggests that the word "empire" acts as a conceptual scaffolding to prompt an analytical schematic. Empire, then, is a "sociopolitical formation wherein a central political authority (a king, a metropole, or an imperial state) exercises unequal influence and power over the political (and in effect the sociopolitical) processes of a subordinate society, peoples, or space." Imperialism, Go argues, is the processes through which empires are "established, extended, or maintained," and includes formations that "deploy multiple tactics, techniques, or modalities—sometimes unstated or unofficial—to realize their policies and extend or sustain themselves." Indeed, Richard Immerman examines the various scholarly debates "over whether the United States is an empire, is not an empire, or is something very similar to an empire." He concludes his investigation with a clear "America is and has always been an empire" and during the nineteenth century "was most ruthless in creating" the same. Immerman's views are supported by Linda Colley, who traces the existence of American imperialism to the continent-wide westward expansion beginning in the late eighteenth century.[5]

Adding to the discussion, Paul Kramer provides a rich interpretive review of the scholarship of American "empire" and "imperialism," to argue that "despite claims to the contrary . . . the imperial is a necessary tool for understanding the United States' global history." Instead of questioning "what the imperial 'is'—we should instead emphasize what it does." Kramer underscores the importance of utilizing "the imperial" to facilitate critical inquiry, and as a methodological tool, making "the use or non-uses of the words 'imperial' and 'empire'" redundant. He stresses, however, that "imperial" relates to dimensions of power, and encourages the investigation of comparative models and connections, not as "whole" systems, but selective elements. In accepting that multiple processes construct and maintain an empire, the intracontinental U.S. military-social complex of the frontier fort system, and the communities that evolved around the garrisons, represent an important variation of an imperial formation. Kramer insists that during the nineteenth century the United States was "an empire-building nation in which state and settler colonial conquest and the territorializing of the continent were fundamental to an increasingly confident national self-definition." Concerning the U.S. West, which he considers a continental empire, Kramer delineates the development of frontier urbanization as the imperial formation of settler colonialism. Here, as elsewhere in North America, towns and cities rivaled "for control of regional markets, resources, prestige, and labor power." Frontier fort towns, as hubs of such enterprise, generated the "dividing lines between civilization and savagery, modernity and backwardness," thus demark friends from foes, and "register the relative power or weakness of the imperial formations that they express and anchor."[6]

In offering an additional perspective, Walter Hixson advises that the Spanish-American War and post-1898 overseas annexations are normally connected to a clearly recognized American colonial empire. Yet Hixson advises that "postcolonial analysis illuminates a much longer process of colonialism and empire building, long preceding the American Revolution and rooted in settler colonization." Settler colonialism, however, is just one manifestation of national expansionist practices utilized to produce, legitimize, and sustain power. Indeed, Nancy Shoemaker defines twelve such processes that often coexisted or fused, creating multifaceted structures. In considering the differences between the British and American imperial formations, Julian Go usefully offers an analysis to suggest that both empires began with state expansion. The acquisition of land, however, does not indicate an empire. Yet, in both the British (1688–1815) and American (1776–1945) experiences, both nations introduced imperial processes and practices identified by population of new areas by settlers, economic and administrative control by the governing bodies, military operations of policing and protection, and creation of imperial identities and ideologies.[7]

"The absence of empire in studies of American culture," led Amy Kaplan to argue that "multiple histories of continental and overseas expansion, conquest, conflict, and resistance . . . have shaped the cultures of the United States." She suggests that the encounter between diverse identities attests to the inseparability of imperialism and cultural discourses of gender, race, class, and ethnicity. Donald Pease builds on this interpretation by acknowledging that American imperialist ambitions were predicated on military superiority, economic wealth, and political organization, yet he notes that the efficacy of these imperial encounters depended upon "cultural technologies" to succeed. Building on this holistic view of imperialism, Ranajit Guha provides a point of entry to examine the military wives as imperial agents. He advises: "There is something uncanny about Empire. The entity known by that name is, in essence, mere territory. . . . As such, it *requires* no homes, if only because the authority, the imperium, from which it derives its form, function, and purpose, is easily sustained by forts and barracks." He concludes, "Yet as history shows, empire is not reconciled for long to this abstracted condition. Caravans seek the shade of camps, markets their custom in the garrisons. . . . [S]ettlements grow, as empire too is seized by the urge to make a home of its territory." This interpretation is explored by Joan M. Mickelson, whose study of British women in India argues that an exaggerated model of English domestic virtues developed in India. Even though a wife's status relied upon her husband's rank, this "cult of home" provided the dislocated spouse with a sense of purpose and authority. In identifying domestic space as a location of imperialism, a landscape emerges within which to view military wives as active agents of empire.[8]

To frame the discussion of officers' wives' behavior, the parameters of the "Cult of Domesticity" and "Separate Spheres" provide a baseline from which to explore the British and American female experiences. The existence of fluid domestic, gender, and class boundaries at the military outposts, however, facilitated the creation of a distinct imperial reality. Barbara Jeanne Fields offers a useful analysis that explores cultural construction as the negotiation of a social terrain through ritualistic discourse. She argues, "Ideology is best understood as the descriptive vocabulary of day-to-day existence, through which people sought to make sense of the social reality that they live and create from day to day. . . . Human beings live in human societies by negotiating a certain social terrain, whose map they keep alive in their minds by the collective, ritual repetition of the activities they must carry out in order to negotiate the terrain, if the terrain changes, so must their activities, and therefore so must the map." The "terrain" of the isolated military garrison presented an unknown environment. The officers' wives, therefore, constructed an embellished model of Victorian domesticity to accommodate and remap the very different landscape. Rigid class distinctions and divisions were forged from military rank. For example, the wife of a garrison commander gained an inordinate level of power to control the sociability of, and access to, the imperial class. She vetted aspiring members and was afforded deference at all official and unofficial events. On some occasions, this senior lady exercised substantial power to command a garrison, effectively issuing orders to enlisted men that were immediately obeyed and, in one recorded episode, acted as a magistrate in a military-civilian affair.[9]

In both the U.S. West and India, American and British imperial formations required a notable military presence, which operated from an infrastructure of distinct installations. The British utilized benevolent imperialism to control the indigenous populations through discipline and example. In the American experience, the army acted as the vanguard of white settlement, enforcing and maintaining the social order to answer the needs of an expanding nation through indigenous removal. Statistical analysis indicates that approximately 70 to 80 percent of the U.S. Army populated the garrisons located in the West. This high percentage may suggest that many informal military traditions and processes would have been developed and implemented in the garrisons, thus setting standards throughout the entire institution.[10]

In comparing the experiences of the British and American army officers' wives, who lived within the walls of the American forts and the British cantonments, this study contributes to the discussion of imperial sociability. It responds to Kramer's suggestion to explore "the dynamics of legitimacy . . . the creation of buy-in . . . the politics of production values, the radiance and prestige that attach to asymmetric power and wealth." In mapping experiences, it becomes clear that these women designed, directed, and maintained the social and cultural dimensions of imperialism, and constructed a distinct identity from so doing. For example, American Helen Chapman, writing from Fort Brown, Texas, declared, "I have seen women thrown upon this frontier under most trying circumstances, and I know they look with envy upon us who are sheltered within the walls of a garrison. There is this difference between being *in* the Army and *out* of it." In accepting and balancing the "slight annoyances" of life in the military West, with chivalric "care and kindness" proffered by soldiers, she understood her military status as quite different from that of a civilian. Living on the peripheries of empire, both groups of wives understood their roles, status, and identities were radically changed, now inseparably entwined to the mission and responsibilities of their officer husbands.[11]

In considering the American experience, scholars suggest that officers' wives played central roles in the creation of a unique military culture. Women brought refinement and stability to their husbands' lives by creating comfortable homes in sometimes primitive conditions. They attempted to transport social values and cultural artifacts from core locations to the peripheries, to tame what appeared to some as a feral landscape. In the peripheral environments, then, the women and their husbands held a joint responsibility to adhere to military practices and support national aims, thus placing the military wife as an active contributor to imperial history.[12]

American and British officers' spouses came to terms with the dislocation and isolation of life in distant locations by reconstructing familiar class hierarchies through social rituals. Communal activities offered an avenue to forge bonds of friendship and encouraged the formation of practical and emotional support mechanisms. Generally from middle-class families, officers' wives sought one another's company through many forms of leisure activities, and utilized standardized markers of identity to establish a class hierarchy striated by rank. Dinner parties, masked balls, picnics, billiards, and croquet offered polite entertainment in the U.S. West. Engaging in similar events, the women in British India likewise acted as Victorian hosts, and designed a social life that reflected the ambience of home. Stationed at the military cantonments and garrisons, both sets of women redefined their social realities to construct an imperial class that paralleled the military ranking system. Expected to attend countless social functions, they generated authority by utilizing such rituals to gain access to, broker information from, and manipulate male power holders. Working within the military system, however, required the women to live highly regulated lives, and to observe codes of conduct appropriate to their partners' position in the imperial hierarchy.[13]

In comparing these female experiences, it becomes clear that imperialism is not simply a masculine preserve. To illustrate participation and empowerment, chapter 2, "Imperial Esprit de Corps: Nineteenth-Century British and American Army Officers and Wives," captures the development of imperial communities, generated by matriculation at the military academies of Sandhurst, Addiscombe, and West Point. Here, the results of discipline and rigorous instruction replaced green cadets with the ultimate male—an officer and gentleman. This role transition from civilian to military masculinity facilitated the development of a distinct imperial class. After receiving commissions to British and American outposts, former Academy graduates dominated the nineteenth-century British, Indian, and United States military forces. Many wives who accompanied their husbands admired and connected with this model of respectability, voicing pride and admiration for their dashing officer husbands and colleagues. By fusing core gentility with military etiquette they constructed a hybrid female counterpart—an imperial lady who shared the mission to further the ambitions of empire.

Chapter 3, "Imperial Journeys and Arrivals: Couriers, Circuits, and Connections," contends that during travel to join military husbands, and after immediate arrival, women blue-printed roles as imperial ambassadors. Officers' wives expressed a sense of disorientation and dislocation en route—via rail, steamship, and stagecoach journeys—to the imperial holdings. To allay fears and establish identity, they voiced extreme patriotic nationalism and racial prejudice. They overlaid familiar national qualities and values on alien landscapes. yet discriminated against the indigenous peoples and their locales, thus providing a foil upon which Anglo identity could be forged and solidified. To restore stability amid such discombobulation, these women crafted a unique imperial reality, and designed purpose and distinctiveness by connecting into national processes and ambitions.

Indeed, with no official claim to imperial status, the women who joined their husbands nonetheless played a central role in designing and maintaining an empire. Chapter 4, "Imperial Women: Military Adjuncts, Station Sisterhoods, and Senior Ladies," argues that officers' wives appropriated male practices, artifacts, and rituals to design a powerful female identity. In so doing, they crossed conventional gender boundaries to occupy masculine spaces of power. Adopting military language, titles, and attire, they forged a new social reality by constructing identities that paralleled the ranking system. By incorporating and feminizing military markers, they forged a sisterhood, hierarchically arranged and supervised by a commanding officer's wife. Each woman understood herself to be duty-bound to uphold and sustain prestige; thus the women generated social power as arbiters, promoters, and enforcers of an imperial class. Chapter 5, "Imperial Pageantry: Officers' Wives as Public Actors and Ceremonial Performers," asserts that in such social roles, these women maneuvered and power-bargained within formal spaces. As organizers and dutiful attendees of soirées, dinner parties, and balls these women acted as imperial ambassadors. The thrilling, or sometimes dull and unpleasant, duty as representatives and documenters of ceremonial pageantry both solidified female identity and sustained imperial aims and prestige.

Chapter 6, "Imperial Gender Crossings: Officers' and Wives' Dress and Home-making on the Edges of Empire," considers the intimate selections of dress and home décor, by the officers and their wives, as historical texts. The women utilized these cultural features and artifacts to bridge male and female spaces and to negotiate authority. In so doing, they generated an imperial identity that mirrored yet modified conventional gender models. Female efforts to construct and enforce dress codes and standards of interior design became commandeered to symbolize national power and status. Going native (assimilation of indigenous cultural dress), within limits, became incorporated into the British male dress as a component of benevolent imperialism. Both British and American military wives, however, as the embodiment of civilization, were forbidden to adopt indigenous garments. These female representatives, nonetheless, flexed authority as image makers and regulators. The military male retaliated by acting as a fashion watchdog, coercing through ridicule, a male-determined style of female respectability. Hence, a fluidity of gender boundaries provided for the construction and maintenance of distinct imperial styles and behaviors.

Chapter 7, "Imperial Gatekeepers: Officers' Wives as Social Arbiters of Empire," moves the discussion from the cultural artifacts of dress and décor to social events in the home. These women, through the practices of calling and domestic rituals, policed the imperial landscape. In controlling the process of introduction, and by determining standards of suitability, they awarded admittance to whom they deemed fit, thus providing access to the social currency of power and respect. In refusing to accept a caller they, sometimes damagingly, rejected applicants they considered unsuitable. This power was not obtained without consequences. An institutional and national backlash of censure targeted and tarnished the reputa-tion of the imperial woman, specifically in British India, leading to accusations of female culpability in the downfall of empire. Staying within the intimate space, Chapter 8, "Imperial Intimacy: Race, Ethnicity, and Class Relationships within the Home," examines the attitudes of officers' wives toward, and the relation-ship with, their domestic staff. These women subordinated Indian, American Indian, Mexican American, African American, and Chinese servants, and in utilizing class and ethnocentricity similarly denigrated Anglo employees. By such discrimination the constructed female identity and status would remain socially elevated, thus reinforcing notions of imperial authority and control at the most intimate contact point.

Despite many similarities between the British and American experiences, however, differences existed as to how the imperial formations developed—largely based on dissimilar levels of formality. The British Army operated under a vast quagmire of official red tape that regulated both military and social conventions. Public performances, such as the fantastical durbar, provided an official vehicle to display authority to an indigenous audience. Controlled dress codes indicated identity and status, regulated rituals of sociability, and forged an imperial class who legitimized benevolent imperialism. In the U.S. West, similar strictures existed but in far less prescribed forms. These practices and devices supported an imperial formation that required removal, not co-option, of the indigenous peoples. The American processes, nevertheless, operated to sustain and promote internal identity and class status, targeting the military community and the local Anglo civilian centers. In both the British and American holdings, however, lay mechanisms to create and sustain an imperial class that upheld the nations' ambitions.

A noticeable discrepancy between the two groups of women also deserves mention: that of cultural absorption. Within peripheral locations—contact zones—Mary Pratt identified a process of transculturation that afforded a two-way adoption of material, social, and cultural processes by both the subordinated and dominant communities. Indeed, the British military wives absorbed cultural practices, such as language, to make sense of new locations and forge identity through "imperial meaning-making." This incorporation is less evident in the American experience. To illustrate this variation, most British officers' wives' narratives naturally interjected Indian vocabulary (spelled in various ways) when writing home or to one another, indicating common use. For example, the word *ayah* is consistently used for an indigenous woman employed as a lady's maid or a child's nurse. With regard to the female task of dressmaking and alterations, wives employed a *durzee*; they called officer housing *dak* bungalows; the cooling fans *punka*; and most referred to one another as *memsahib*. Another adoption was the everyday incorporation of the local diet that included *nans* and *chupatties*, and breakfast was routinely recorded as *chota-hazree*. This level of assimilation is not highly evident in the American women's narratives, although officers' wives stationed in the Southwest utilized Spanish terms, such as *camisa*, *tamale*, and *tortillas*. This vocabulary, however, does not appear to have been co-opted into everyday use.[14]

The British wives clearly understood their role as operatives within the empire. The American spouses, however, would not have considered themselves as imperialists. They clearly understood, nonetheless, that they lived in a different world beyond the boundaries of American civilization. Their narratives frequently indicated a complete separation from the "States." Yet several women recorded that they acted during, as Ellen Biddle recorded, "the days of empire." For example, Frances Carrington's narrative included the verse "Westward the course of empire takes its way, the first four acts already past, a fifth shall close the drama with the day, time's noblest offering is the last." In returning to Sheridan, Wyoming, in 1908 she reflected on its history to comment, "The rival civilizations of Spanish, French, and English must be considered; and surely, as the good Bishop Berkley sang so many years ago of the westward course of empire, 'Time's noblest offering is the last, the native type, the American citizen.'" Additionally, she recorded a memorial address given by her husband during this public visit. Col. Henry B. Carrington clearly underscored the imperial role of the U.S. Army in the West with: "My countrymen and friends . . . I know that you cannot regret that the Eighteenth United States Infantry, through their arrival in 1866, made it possible for your later enjoyment in the largest fruition of its rich soil, its fertile valleys, its magnificent mountains, abundant timber, adequate streams, and indeed of all other blessings on or beneath the surface, within the power of nature to place at your disposal." Thus both Mrs. and Colonel Carrington considered the military vanguard of the Eighteenth U.S. Infantry as active agents in an imperial formation.[15]

Additionally, Elizabeth Custer reminded her readers of the fact that "hordes of settlers are sweeping into the western States and Territories, quite unmindful of the soldiers and frontiersmen, who fought, step by step, to make room for the coming of the overcrowded population of the East. . . . [B]eyond the pale of civilization." In understanding her role as an officer's wife, she penned the following vignette: "How well I remember the long wait we made on one of the staircases of the Capitol at Washington, above which hung then the great picture by Leutze, 'Westward the Course of Empire Takes its Way.' We little thought then . . . that our lives would drift over the country which the admirable picture represents. . . . The picture made a great impression on us. How much deeper the impression, though, had we known that we were to live out the very scenes depicted!" Thus, Biddle, the Carringtons, and the Custers understood their experiences in the West as directly contributing to national aims and ambitions.[16]

An officer's wife then, held an influential position in imperial affairs. An 1838 article published in the *Asiatic Journal* identified that "[e]very [British] lady has a direct participation in her husband's advancement. . . . For, as he rises step by step . . . he imparts to her that enviable distinction . . . .[T]he glittering toy, called rank!" Although this published essay satirized the British rigid adherence to a social hierarchy and practices commuted by rank, it confirmed considerable female power. A military wife in British India and the U.S. West, dismissed limitations imposed by traditional gender roles to determine and promote the values and behaviors of a distinct imperial class. In exercising such social power she legitimized internal and external representations of imperial authority, superiority, and prestige.[17]

2

Imperial Esprit de Corps

Nineteenth-Century British and American
Army Officers and Wives

I made the acquaintance . . . of Capt. [Louis] Carpenter of the 10th, who now is in command of the post. He is a gentleman by birth and training. He is not a narrow minded 'routinier' but a broad minded student of his profession.

—*Lt. John Bigelow, Tenth U.S. Cavalry*

"It has been said that India was to Britain what the Frontier was to America—a land of limitless opportunity, a testing ground, a place of romance and adventure," declared Captain Albert Hervey of the Fifth and later the Fortieth Regiment Madras Native Infantry. He opened his memoirs with "India! India! India! Is now all the vogue. That land of the sun, with her swarthy millions, now occupies the attention of our own country, and attracts the eyes of the whole civilized world. Year after year witnesses the sons of Britain land on its burning shores, to join the ranks and follow the banners of her gallant armies." On reaching his first posting at Palaveram, he recalled, after a night's sleep, "I was roused out my bed very early indeed, and had to put on my uniform for the first time. . . . I buckled on my sword (an immense long one too, it was) and sallied forth to the barracks and parade." Following his introduction to his "brother officers," he advised, "An officer carries with him an air of gentility (if I may say so) and, by associating with his comrades, obtains a degree of polish, so ornamental in the circles of society, and so creditable to the rank he holds."[1]

This idea of male gallantry echoed in the 1896 novel *Posie; or, From Reveille to Retreat*, written by Mrs. M. A. Cochran, whose dedication illustrated the role of the American military spouse. She poetically penned:

> Who have ever been the inspirators and guiding stars
> To their dauntless heroes; and as the magnet
> Attracts the steel, so the educated, brave
> And brilliant young officer woos,
> Wins, and brings to our midst,
> The cultivated and fair
> -est women [*sic*] of the
> land.

This tribute to the "Ladies of the Army" romantically articulated that an officer's wife's role was to guide and inspire her warrior husband. Indeed, acting in tandem with their husbands, these women fully embraced the rigors of military life as imperial ambassadors—among "the cultivated and fairest women of the land."[2]

In utilizing memoirs written by British and American "dauntless heroes" and "fairest women," this chapter will capture their commitment to military duty, discuss the evolution of an esprit de corps, and illustrate how they understood an overriding sense of imperial purpose. By examining the military academies of Sandhurst, Addiscombe, and West Point, whose graduates would come to dominate the nineteenth-century British, Indian, and United States armies, I will explain how a distinct imperial mindset developed within the cadres of gentlemen cadets undergoing training, and how the prescribed requirement to display "an air of gentility" reflected middle-class values. Similarities in capturing the idealized officer and gentleman existed within the imperial forts and stations in British India and the U.S. West, yet the level of formality differed. The British officer, fettered by tradition and regulations, created an imperial class of gentlemen who displayed honesty, honor, and morality. The American officer, however, sought a commission in the army as a professional, a "republican machine," who upheld virtues of honor, obedience, and selflessness as a genteel gentleman. Despite indoctrination in the military academies, violations of the behavioral model frequently occurred. Yet, after transfer to the outreaches of the British and American territorial holdings, most graduates and their wives attempted to articulate and display a code of respectability that befitted imperial ambassadors.[3]

Military training played a central role in molding male behavior and instilling a strong sense of imperial duty. Indeed, the badge of honor of the officer corps of the British Army, "Serve to Lead," implicitly conceptualizes the ideas of family, purpose, unity, and dedication. In the eighteenth century, military schools already existed in France, Germany, and Russia, and the nascent English institution, the Royal Military Academy, Woolwich (established in 1741), trained cadets as Royal Artillery and Royal Engineer line officers. The Staff School evolved from a series of lectures presented at High Wycombe to regimental officers in December 1792 by General François Jarry, a distinguished French officer and *émigré*. In 1798, following Lord Nelson's victory on the Nile, and with Britain still deeply embattled against revolutionary France, Colonel John Gaspard Le Marchant presented an innovative officer training scheme to the Duke of York. He argued that martial success depended on the education of army officers in the arts of war. Up until this point, commissions were purchased by sometimes indifferent aristocrats and the rank and file consisted of mostly ne'er-do-wells. Recognizing the need for a professional and efficient officer corps, Le Marchant's proposal, "A Plan for Establishing Regimental Schools for Officers throughout the Service," received Royal approval and led to the opening of the Royal Military College, High Wycombe, in 1800 to train staff officers. The Royal Military Academy Sandhurst evolved from the Royal Military Academy and the Royal Military College, and opened its doors in 1812, combining staff and line cadets. In 1860 (following the establishment of the Raj) Addiscombe, the British East India Company's military seminary, merged with the prestigious academy. Following the abolition of the commission purchase system in 1870, all officers had to graduate from Sandhurst before taking up duty in the empire.[4]

The original educational system design provided for a class of two hundred, consisting of one hundred gentlemen's sons, fifty East Indian Company cadets (who paid yearly fees of one hundred guineas), and fifty orphans of men who died in military service, or in reduced circumstances (who paid thirty-one guineas). Despite initial low enrollment and early discharge of junior officers to fight on the Continent, cadets who passed examinations in history, German or French, Vauban systems of fortification, and military drawing received commissions. Officers who entered the Junior Department for a four-year course (which they had to complete by their nineteenth birthday) received a balanced, but military-focused, education. Le Marchant recommended the additional qualifications of geography, history, and Persian or Hindustani for those destined to serve in the East India Company ranks. Church services on Sundays and, in summer, cricket, boating, and swimming kept the young men occupied. In winter, they mandatorily participated in hockey, skating, and "fives (hand-tennis)."[5]

Major Augustus Mockler-Ferryman provides a history of Sandhurst, and in useful appendices he presents the entrance qualifications, syllabi, and Standing Orders of the college. The regulations governing admission required the cadet to be unmarried, pass a rigorous set of entrance examinations, pass a full physical check, and pay fees according to his entrance category. The course of instruction included military engineering, topography, tactics, administration, law, languages, exercises, and electives. The assigned textbook, *Manual of Military Law*, helpfully instructed the cadets on their imperial role. Chapter 1 reminds pupils that members of Her Majesty's Armed Forces are governed by military and civil law. Indeed, Item 5 states, "A commander of troops in time of war, and in occupation of a foreign country, or any part thereof, acts in two absolutely distinct categories. First, he governs his troops by military law only; secondly, he stands temporarily in position as governor of the country, or part of the country, he governs." The item continued, "In this latter capacity he imposes such laws on the inhabitants he thinks expedient for the security, on the one hand, the safety of his army, and, on the other, the good government of the district which, by reason of his occupation, is for the time being deprived of its ordinary rulers." Such unilateral power clearly indicates absolute imperial authority.[6]

Every officer in Her Majesty's Service owned a copy of, and was expected to strictly observe, all orders delineated in *The Queen's Regulations*. This lengthy handbook covered an array of military concerns including ranks, duties, precedence, uniforms, salutes, and marriage. Indeed, every noncommissioned officer and private required his commanding officer's consent to marry, knew that his future wife must be "of good character," and his marriage would be recorded in a regimental register. Thus a choice of wife was not simply a personal decision but one made with the needs of the empire clearly in view. A section titled "Interior Economy" addressed the behavior and performance of every military man. Item 56 admonished "The *Dress* and *Appearance*, as well as the *Conduct*, of the soldier, are, on all occasions, and in all situations, to be such as to create respect for the military service. His demeanour and bearing are to be such as to distinguish the effects of Order and Discipline from the habits of the untrained Rustic." The section continued, "He is to avoid being mixed in broils or disturbances . . . which lead to no useful result, but too frequently end in breaches of the public peace."

An additional clause insisted upon unfashionably short haircuts to ensure "the cleanliness, and the military appearance of the soldier," thus requiring imperial men to model and display the vitality of British masculinity.[7]

According to an editorial published in *The United Service Journal* in 1830, cadets faced twice-yearly examinations, a severe process of written, practical, and oral testing. The examining board included "Gen. the Hon. Sir Edward Paget, the Governor-Lieutenant General the Hon. Sir Alexander Hope; Sir Herbert Taylor, the Adjutant-General of the Army; Lord Edward Somerset, the Lieutenant-General of the Ordnance; and Sir George Scovell, the Lieutenant-Governor of the institution," a panel that surely intimidated the most confident of students. The examinations on the first day covered geometry and interviews in French and German, and continued the next day with assessments on field fortifications, offensive and defensive tactics, horsemanship, and fort construction. The reporter advised that sixteen out of seventeen cadets passed all examinations satisfactorily. One can only imagine the ridicule inflicted upon, and the shame experienced by, the lone failure. At least his name did not appear in the published report.[8]

Immediately following the article on Sandhurst, a similar survey provided information on the mid-year, pre-merger examinations at Addiscombe. These cadets completed a two-year course for an engineering commission in British India, majoring in mathematics. Fortification, however, held a close second place, and the reporter noted, "The cadets commence it from their entrance, beginning with two simple outlines of the bastion system, containing a full detail of the names of the various lines and angles forming a front of fortification." Supplemental offerings included courses on gunnery, surveying, Latin, and French, and twenty lectures offered to the senior year in chemistry and geology. With regard to the foreign language requirement, the diligent reporter advised that the 1830 examination results were highly satisfactory and concluded, "The general air and demeanour of the corps confirmed in every respect our first impression, that the claim of its members was more than nominal to the title of *Gentlemen*-Cadets."[9]

All was not, however, studious behavior and the polite sportsmanship of the cricket eleven. The physical excesses of young males needed to be tightly controlled, both formally and informally. Swift and severe reprimands, but not corporal punishment, lay in store for any violation of Sandhurst's rules. Extra guardroom duties and close or open arrest rewarded minor infringements. Insubordination resulted in a diet of bread and water or solitary confinement in the "Black Hole." Drinking alcohol (a prohibition operated on campus grounds) and more serious cases of disobedience placed the cadet in front of the lieutenant governor. Guilty cadets would find their summer holidays cancelled, commissions suspended, bunking imposed (public expulsion), or for the worst offenders—rustication (being barred from serving for a two-to four-year period). Captains of the cadet companies instilled discipline by supervising parades, monitoring class attendance, and acting as vigilant watchdogs. To avoid bullying, first-year "Johns" (from Johnny Raw) "fagged" for senior classmen known as "Regs." Fagging included making beds, running messages, and smuggling contraband.[10]

Indeed, Major-General Thomas Bland Strange's irreverent autobiography spoke of the cadet's experience in the military college. He declared, "Formerly it was *de rigeur* for a cadet to join at Woolwich in an evening dress-coat and a tall hat, 'a claw-hammer coat and a stove-pipe,' as the Yankees call it, and woe betide the boy who did not comply with the custom. *Mos pro lege* [custom as law]. The disciplinary process at the hands of the senior cadets, rough but effectual, commenced at once." The general continued, "Cadet Jingo's [Strange's college moniker] first disciplinary lesson was severe, and he did not require a second. Going downstairs from the halls of study, his descent was accelerated by a kick between the swallow tails from an old but diminutive cadet." For failing to acknowledge the senior in the expected manner, Jingo was "severely belted" by four corporals of his division. Strange concluded, "With seniors of bad disposition discipline occasionally degenerated into cruelty. The prevailing spirit was, however, more of fun than deliberate cruelty, though many a severe and sometimes salutary lesson was conveyed." Thus, informal sanctions performed by the cadets created a cadre of "tough fellows," who could endure hazing, dress impeccably, and offer polite deference to rank. Indeed, in *Dombey and Son*, Charles Dickens offers a social commentary on the conditions at the Military Academy with, "None but the tough fellows could live through . . . Sandhurst. . . . But it made us what we were, Sir. . . . We were iron, and it forged us."[11]

The officers trained at Sandhurst and Addiscombe upheld the military esprit de corps of honor and duty fused with the Victorian ideal of a gentleman. The term "gentleman" implied certain values and codified behavior. According to Philip Mason, the Victorians "needed an imperial class, men who were accustomed to giving orders and to see they were obeyed, and to do this with a minimum of force, and with a consideration for the governed that would inspire a minimum of resentment." An honorable gentleman displayed chivalric notions of loyalty and courage combined with civic virtues of thoughtfulness and unselfishness. A true gentleman, according to William Burn, was required "to use his position for good ends, never to abuse it; he ought to be as much afraid of seducing a girl as of cheating at cards, or running away from battle . . . the conception of the gentlemen was being enlarged to give more weight to virtue, to education, and to a sense of social obligation." Even so, the unwritten law in obtaining a commission, according to Hew Strachan, required an applicant to be "a man of education, manners, honor, and other qualities acquired by the education which English Gentlemen receive."[12]

Similarly, Sir John MacDonald's address to the Eleventh Hussars (Light Dragoons), printed in the October 1840 editions of both the *Times* and *The United Service Journal*, delineated the connection between the civilian and military masculine code—the ideal of an officer and gentleman. In reminding the men of their obligation to be an "honour" to Her Majesty's service, he reiterated, "the rules, articles, and regulations for the government of the British Army require that the officers thereof should conduct themselves as ought gentlemen, men of truth, honour, and morality. It is, then, the proud characteristic of the British Army, that its officers are gentlemen by education, manners, and habits; that some are men of the first families in the country, and some of large property, but the rules and regulations of the Service require strictly from all, that they should conduct themselves as ought gentlemen in every situation in which they may be placed." Confirming this sense of imperial representation, Albert Hervey delineated the indoctrination of the gentlemanly code on arrival at his new posting. He declared, "[A] mess well-regulated serves to keep up the respectability of the body of officers." He added, "[T]he British soldier is a paragon of excellence as a soldier; he is a very type of an Englishman in his military spirit; he is brave as a lion before the enemy, and has a heart, with energy as indomitable as the country from whence he sprang." Hence, the gentlemen officers operating within the military institution answered the economic and territorial needs of the empire, reflected moral and behavioral ideals of the parent society, and acted as guardians of these values.[13]

Hew Strachan and Peter Stanley offer an examination of British military men in nineteenth-century British India. Strachan finds that regular officer commissions depended somewhat on birth, but mainly on the ability to purchase a commission. He determines that in 1830, 21 percent were aristocrats, 32 percent landed gentry, and the remaining 47 percent from middle-class families. A growing shift to a professional, middle-class occupation becomes clear by 1847 when, out of five thousand infantry officers, only 103 held a title. Stanley compares the enlistment in the Regular and Company armies to find that the Queen's officers were generally from aristocratic families, but wealth increasingly played a role. Simple economics determined whether young men would join the Queen's or Company's service, with schooling, commissions and outfitting in the Regular Army costing *double* that of a Company contract. "Pretensions to gentility," Stanley argues, existed in both services, although the Queen's men considered the Indian Army officers as "distinctly inferior." In 1840, 92 percent of Sandhurst cadets were sons of "gentlemen" and military officers, who upheld their aspirations to genteel status, but the officers in the Company's employ could not match these birth or wealth conditions.[14]

This understanding of a rigid class division, however, does not find support by two contemporary military men: Field-Marshal Garnet Viscount Wolseley and Captain Sydney Jones-Parry. Wolseley hailed from a military background. His father, he remarked, "was by no means clever ... [he was] badly educated ... [and] very poor and very proud ... [yet] he was chivalry itself in thought, word, and action." Wolseley followed his father's example and received his first commission on 12 March 1852 as an ensign in the South Staffordshire (Queen's) Regiment. He received an immediate posting to India with a company consisting of Irish "boy recruits" all under the age of nineteen. While awaiting embarkation orders at "Pongo [Chatham] Mess," the newly qualified ensign described his fellow tyros. "I confess," he stated, "we were an uninteresting lot. The great bulk of the young men who then usually went to India were socially not of a high order. Of course, though very poor, many were the sons of old officers of good families, whose poverty compelled their sons to serve in India, if serve they would in the Army." He noted that most posted were "wanting in good breeding, and all seemed badly educated. For many and many a year, this depot had been similarly emptied each summer of its beardless ensigns to fill up the annual vacancies in the Queen's regiments serving in India." He summarized, nonetheless, "However, as I look back at my early contemporaries ... I feel a pride in thinking and knowing that one and all, good and bad together, did England righteous service ... they fought hard for her honour ... they loved their country, and never shrank from death when her interests required them to face it."[15]

While Wolseley denigrated the Queen's men, Captain Jones-Parry promoted the Company men. In 1849, he arrived in British India to take up his commission with the Fifty-Second Madras Native Infantry. On arriving at Vellore, he described his fellow officers in glowing terms: "I was extremely lucky in my regiment. The 52nd was a good one, officered by a set of well-educated gentlemen. I was more than lucky in my Adjutant ... [he] was not only a good soldier, but pre-eminently a gentleman." With regard to rivalry between the Company's and Queen's and officers, he commented, "I do not think that there is any difference in the class from which our officers and those of the Queen's army are selected; every man in the Company's service has brothers, father, or relations in the Queen's, but I think the constant active service make them the better soldiers of the two. They are not so agreeable or polished, owing to the long absence from home and its associations." Thus, Company men understood themselves equal in class, yet accepted that they, perhaps, lacked social grace.[16]

Despite their lack of refinement, Jones-Parry added, "We were very sociable amongst ourselves, the married officers often asking us youngsters to dine. We were singularly fortunate in our officers' wives: they were charming." But what did the "charming" military spouses think of the men? Minnie Blane, the wife of Captain Archibald Wood of the Bengal Army, suffered an unhappy marriage, mired in debt. In a letter to her mother dated 2 April 1857, however, she included an inspection report of her husband's men conducted by Major General Sir Thomas Reed. The "flattering account" announced, "[B]est thanks be offered to the European Officers, Native Officers, Staff Sergeants and Non Commissioned Officers and Sepoys of the Fourteenth Regiment Native Infantry for their united exertions which combined to ensure their success." The report continued that the general was satisfied with "the cleanly appearance of the accoutrements" and "steadiness of the men," with only one criticism—that "the Light Infantry was performed too steadily." Mrs. Blane ended her missive with, "Dearest Mama, is that not pleasing!" Hence, the conditions of an unhappy and debt-ridden marriage did not deter this officer's wife from enthusiastically upholding the imperial reputation of the Fourteenth Native Infantry.[17]

Rivalry between the British Army and the Native Infantries imposed a concomitant divide between the wives. Florence Marryat (the wife of Major-General T. Ross-Church of the Madras Army) bridled at "the conduct of some of the wives of officers in English corps, who used, on account of their own supposed superiority, to affect greatly to *look down* upon the married ladies of the 'N. I.' (as the Native Infantry regiments are technically termed), as well as upon their husbands." Rising to the defense of the Madras Army, she enlightened her readers with: "After a period of seven years spent continuously in the presence of both . . . I most emphatically affirm that, as a rule, I have never met with gentlemen anywhere to surpass in breeding and manners the officers of the Native Infantry regiments in Madras, Bengal, and Bombay." This officer's wife was aware of manufactured divisions not only between the Regular and Native armies, but also within the commission and promoted ranks. She explained, "There may be a great deal of Lords' blood drafted into the European corps, but there is also a vast amount of shopkeepers', and one is not quite certain on an introduction upon which one may fall; besides, men holding the position of officers in our home [British] regiments have often risen from the ranks, and raised their wives with them." Thus, this officer's wife refused to accept the premise that the Native Armies were less socially polished than the Queen's companies, thus asserting equality of the imperial men, taking care to reveal the presence of commissioned shopkeepers' sons, and promotion through the supposed elitist ranks.[18]

Supporting Mesdames Blane's and Marryat's positive view, Frances Parkes, daughter of Captain William Archer of the Sixteenth Lancers and married to a civil servant, wrote romantically of the military personages with whom she came in contact. She found Colonel William L. Gardner, who commanded an Irregular Horse Regiment (Twenty-Eighth Native Infantry), an attractive man who "naturally made a strong impression. . . . Colonel Gardner's tall, commanding figure, soldier-like countenance, and military air, render his appearance very striking." Mrs. Parkes's admiration was typical. In contrast, Emma Roberts provided an extraordinary, alternative view that admired the sepoy and denigrated the Company men. The Native Infantries of all three presidencies she credited with qualities of equality "in the field, in strength, vigour, and good conduct. . . . But the Bengal sepoy has the advantage of a finer person and a more military air. . . . [and] are principally composed of high-caste men." Of the officers she complained, "The lounging, dishevelled habits, produced by the climate, have assuredly a deteriorating effect upon the style and bearing of European officers in the Company's service. These gentlemen have certainly . . . none of the upright, ramrod stiffness, which disciplinarians consider so essential, and which in Europe usually distinguishes a soldier from his fellow-citizens." Her disdain became even more blatant with her comment that "the officer of the Madras army is known by the deranged or dilapidated state of his attire . . . it is not uncommon to see him lounging about in a jacket so much the worse for wear as not to possess its full complement of buttons. Women, who are very quick-sighted in such matters, perceive at a glance the least violation of military proprieties." Miss Roberts's dim view of the Madras Army officers appears to be an isolated observation of bias expressed for her brother-in-law's regiment, or perhaps she recorded the reality more truthfully than her contemporaries. Implicit within her female response, nonetheless, was the expectation that military men would uphold, at all times, the imperial masculine ideal.[19]

In shifting the imperial female role from mere observer to participant, Elizabeth, the wife of Captain Dunbar Muter of the Sixtieth (The King's Royal) Rifle Corps, stationed at Meerut, opened her memoirs on 10 May 1857, the day when, and the place where, the Sepoy Mutiny began. She narrated: "A dull sound . . . came over the stillness of nature . . . it was the commencement of saturnalia destined to take a place in history, and to revolutionize the great empire which we had founded in the East." She immediately returned home and hid, recording: "To conceal myself in my own home, in the lines held by a regiment that had reckoned up a century of renown! And from what? That was the question. Was the native army in revolt? Had the threatened storm come so soon, and was the instrument, so carefully sharpened by our Government, at its own throat?" In describing those first fearful moments the captain's wife, by using "we founded," included herself in the dutiful ranks of the Queen's soldiers and disclosed a political awareness of imperial devices. In so doing she revealed that military wives understood themselves to be knowledgeable and active agents of empire.[20]

Frances, wife of Major Henry Duberly, paymaster for the Eighth (King's Royal Infantry) Hussars, speaks naturally throughout her narratives of being an active member of the regiment. She became quite a public hero when she daringly accompanied her husband to Crimea, and witnessed the infamous charge of the Light Brigade. She published her experiences, both in Crimea and during the suppression of the Sepoy Mutiny in British India, as a way to earn a personal income. Her accounts speak knowledgably of military orders and results, and she often placed herself in the midst of action by utilizing such terms as "our fighting instincts." For example, she recorded: "Our regimental orders of this day contain a notification that on arrival at Jehazpoor a communication will be received from General [Frederick] Roberts, which will probably hurry us to the front. We are therefore ordered to hold ourselves in readiness for forced marches." On routing a rebel force, she determined, "I thought it advisable to stop until the artillery and infantry came up. . . . I was then sent on after the enemy with cavalry and Horse Artillery. . . . We skirmished."[21]

In confirming the inclusion of women as integral members of the imperial class, Isabella Fane, daughter of the Indian commander-in-chief General Sir Henry Fane, mentioned, "[W]e went for a few minutes to our Almack's. Here the ladies were able to showcase their latest gowns to one another." Fane noticed that "the Nepaul [sic] General [Martabar Singh Thapa] was there, much disgusted I am told, with so much female exhibition . . . he is said to have fixed his eyes most intently on . . . [Isabella, wife of Colonel Marcus Beresford]. . . . So we think he might have been turning over in his mind that she would make him a good *nautch* girl!" The general, who would become prime minister of Nepal in 1843, disapproved of the British female fashion. Yet Miss Fane dismissed his attitude with "we were doing nothing contrary to our habits and if he could not reconcile his mind to it he had better have staid [*sic*] at home." As a female representative of empire, operating within a British club, this private musing of indifference and disrespect suggest an arrogant confidence in her ambassadorial status.[22]

Also acting as imperial representatives, the Sherwoods attended a function at the palace of the *nawab* in Moorshedabad, to celebrate the annual rising of the river waters. The couple's discussion provides a glimpse at the self-regulation of the officer corps. Dressed in their finest evening attire the couple enjoyed the entertainments. Their "politeness was put to the test," however, when the regimental assistant surgeon and his wife made their appearance. Mary, the wife of Captain Henry Sherwood of the Fifty-Third (Second Yorkshire, West Riding, The King's Own Light Infantry) Regiment, described the Scottish surgeon as having the "physiognomy of a horse" and his spouse as a "short, round, slovenly person . . . [and] he [her husband] had caused her to dress in all imaginary finery." Apparently Captain Sherwood whispered "Don Quixote and Sancho Panza! and the whisper was never forgotten." Although dress could be imitated, manners could not. Captain and Mrs. Sherwood clearly decided that the Scottish surgeon and his "slovenly" wife could only imagine, as did the Spanish protagonist and his companion, that they belonged to an august community.[23]

Equally telling, an encounter with a Mrs. V, a "Dutch lady," caused Mary Sherwood to comment on the exclusivity of the British contingent stationed in India. The woman who prompted unveiled disdain from the officer's wife "spoke very broken English [and] in utter fearlessness . . . said everything that came uppermost, though she was always covered with fine muslin and jewels when she appeared abroad." Despite wearing "fine" clothing, Mrs. V lacked verbal circumspection, which excluded her from the imperial set. Sherwood announced, "I never could, and indeed I never tried to assimilate with that sort of person, to be found, I fear, in all ranks, who lowers the standard of society by coarseness, as did this Dutch lady, though she was otherwise without taint to her reputation." The slovenly attire of the surgeon's wife and Mrs. V's careless speech did not harmonize with the image of an officer and gentleman's wife, a central actor of the imperial class.[24]

In ways similar to the British officers, the American officer clique demonstrated an imperial purpose, duty, and military spirit. Despite contentions of national exceptionalism, there can be no question that the American military system evolved from the British model. Russell Weigley, considering the origins of the American "respectable" Army, concludes that "essentially, the British Regular Army transplanted European methods of war to America, and did so success-fully." The imperial regiments fighting in America during the Seven Years War, he adds, "took on the brunt of fighting, won the war, and set a standard of expert soldiering for Americans to emulate." Indeed, in the midst of Revolutionary fervor twenty years later, George Washington asserted that mere militia could *not* win against the British fighting force. He advocated that a regular army should be raised, led by commissioned gentlemen officers to create a "respectable army, and such as will be competent to every exigency." The newly created Continental Army utilized a modified version of the British Articles of War, and patterned its military companies on British organization, thus emulating the respected men with whom Washington had served.[25]

America achieved independence, but the problem of a peacetime army remained. Despite public skepticism, Alexander Hamilton initially led the effort to create a professional standing army, established by Congress in 1784. Following the apparent settling of conflict with the American Indians in the Northwest, Congress disbanded the "Legion of the United States" in 1796, and authorized in its place a much smaller institution, renamed the "United States Army." Congress expanded the army in 1798, and appointments for 532 officers were invited, with the overrid-ing qualification a highly political one: the candidate must be a Federalist. With the removal of the French threat, this nascent military force experienced sharp reductions during the first administration of the new Democratic-Republican president, Thomas Jefferson. The possibility of another conflict with England, however, combined with the government-sponsored explorations of the Louisiana Purchase, witnessed an increase in the army to more than 5,700 by 1802. Despite the cost of a professional army, Jefferson authorized the establishment of a national military academy, West Point. By creating commissioned men who graduated with a sense of honor, duty, and loyalty, this officer training school purposely developed a cadre of highly skilled engineers who would assist national expansion.[26]

The early curriculum concentrated on preparing a cadre of twenty officers to perform technical services within the Corps of Engineers and, with Jefferson's patronage, the United States Military Philosophical Society became established to broaden the mental horizons of its students. Membership expanded, and the society's motto *Scientia in bello pax* (Science in war is the guarantee of peace) became synonymous, according to Jennings L. Wagoner, with the aim of the academy itself, that of "military preparedness, the advancement of engineering sciences, and western exploration." The cadets gained training in areas suitable to assist westward expansion by incorporating, Wagoner explains, "exploration, mapping, building canals, bridges, roads, and railways." Thus, West Point graduates answered the practical needs of the American imperial formation.[27]

In seeking to clarify "the significance of the early academy in contingency and evolution, process and outcome," Samuel J. Watson argues that West Point contributed to "the reconciliation of individual and community through the self-discipline and self-regulation of . . . 'republican machines.'" President Jefferson's ideals of combining military and scientific training for West Point graduates would inspire public servants to socialize broadly, to gain a "civil vision of their future accountability to the public . . . [as] leaders of character to serve the nation." The academy, according to Watson, produced a graduate accomplished as an engineer, scientist, well-drilled officer, and cosmopolitan technocrat, a man who held genteel manners and self-discipline "fostered by the precepts of duty, honor, and country." Alongside the academic courses, dancing, fencing, and horsemanship assisted the cadet to achieve social grace and develop a sense of independence and honor. Use of gentrified language and an "aristocratic value system," however, faced criticism. To disabuse such censure, duty became accepted as "committing oneself to serving others," while honor found definition in a cadet's ability to perform his duty with "selfless integrity." The all-encompassing term "country" served to legitimize and motivate personal efforts. Watson concludes that the gradual evolution of this code of honor encouraged a crucial sense of professional ethics, personal responsibility, and accountability. In the process, Jefferson's "republican machines" carried the honorable, brave, obedient, and polite virtues of gentlemanly imperial agents.[28]

Joseph Ellis suggests that early West Point represented "a floundering school for sons of the well-born," though in the later years many cadets were middle class. Responding to such criticism Superintendent Sylvanus Thayer, like his British counterparts, remodeled the school to resemble the French École Polytechnique. With this restructuring, the academy gained a national reputation for engineering and discipline. The cadets, in an atmosphere of strict rules, policies, and prohibitions, became "remade in the image of Thayer himself . . . [understanding] they were privy to archetypal insights denied to others and that the mental training and character traits ostensibly acquired as cadets separated them from other men." Dennis H. Mahan, a former cadet, returned to the academy in 1830 and became professor of civil and military engineering. He taught the capstone course that included "civil and military architecture, field fortification, permanent fortification, and the science of artillery." Learning, according to K. Bruce Gallaway and Robert B. Johnson, revolved around a rigid honor system. The simple wording "a cadet will not lie, cheat, or steal" belied a complex code, which created self-regulation. This sense of personal accountability extended as a collective identity. The graduate protected the "honor of the corps," and according to the authors, "it is a kind of ritualistic participation mystique difficult for those who have not worshipped at the Thayer monument to understand." These values of honor, bravery, obedience, integrity, and reputation encouraged at West Point reflected gentlemanly traditions.[29]

Yet, as at Sandhurst, the transformation of a young cadet into an officer and gentleman did not occur without strict discipline. Virginian Thomas Rowland, the eldest son of Maj. Isaac S. Rowland, wrote letters to his family from his admission to West Point in 1859 until his resignation following secession in 1861. As a cadet, he ranked first in a class of forty-two pupils and would later serve as a Confederate Army major. He excitedly described his daily routine of study, swimming, and dance lessons, yet underscored the strict discipline imposed by the senior students. He remarked, "[T]he cadet officers are very fierce and give their commands with an emphasis that makes a man *tremble in his shoes*, and if a poor 'plebe' in his fright and confusion makes a false step or an awkward or slow movement with his musket, no matter how inexperienced he may be, he is confined to the guard tomb for the offence." This informal discipline among the cadets clearly mirrors British practices. Graduates who successfully navigated the four-year training program dominated the officer corps and often served on the military frontier. There they upheld the principled behavior and imperial purpose instilled at West Point—honor, duty, and country.[30]

Perhaps what the institution considered dishonorable best explains the cadet's quest to be regarded as honorable. Capt. Orsemus B. Boyd, who entered the army in 1861, received his congressman's recommendation to attend West Point two years later. Unfortunately, during his first year his refusal to prove his "courage and ability" by declining a challenge to "battle" with a fellow cadet earned him the label of "coward." A far more serious incident, however, branded Boyd as a thief. His wife recounted, "In the academy at that time were several cadets, sons of very wealthy parents, who, contrary to West Point rules, kept in their rooms at barracks large sums of money. . . . So great was the confidence of the academy classmates in each other that the money was simply placed in a trunk, to which all the clique had free access." Following the disappearance of large amounts from this fund, company cadets formed a committee "to find and punish the thief." Targeted by his cowardly reputation, Mrs. Boyd's husband was found guilty and placed "in confinement until later in the day, when at dress parade they could publicly and brutally disgrace him." Accompanied by the "unearthly harmony" of the fifes and drum playing the "Rogues March" and with a placard affixed on his chest naming him as a coward, liar, and thief, Boyd left the academy in disgrace. On hearing of the informal proceedings, however, Superintendent George W. Cullum ordered Boyd back to the school, and a later official court of inquiry found him "not guilty." His peers, nonetheless, found the charge simply "not proven," and ostracized him throughout his remaining two years at West Point. Determined to "show the world he possessed such bravery as would not allow false charges to ruin his whole career," he continued his studies and graduated as an officer and gentleman in 1867, receiving a commission in the Eighth Cavalry.[31]

Examining the social composition of the American army officer corps, William B. Skelton concludes that by the immediate antebellum period, and reflecting the shift of the British Army identified by Strachan and Stanley, the majority of men hailed from "respectable middle and upper-middle class families with traditions of public service." His analysis of the army registers of 1830 and 1860 confirms that 20 percent of officers' fathers were federal civil or military officeholders, 25 percent held professional occupations, 25 percent had commercial employment, and a further 25 percent were engaged in commerce/manufacturing. As in the British experience, men entered the Army as a family tradition. On entering West Point in 1841, Edmund K. Smith's network of family members in the army included a brother, three uncles, and a brother-in-law. His father had risen to the rank of colonel, and his grandfather had held a Continental Army commission. Despite this family custom of military service, Skelton suggests that, like the British experience, economics played a central role in this career choice. Financial hardship prompted at least 20 percent of officer applications, and outnumbered, four to one, ideological/romantic motivations. Despite, perhaps, the economic motivation to serve, training academies insisted on gentlemanly performances and instilled a real sense of honorable duty to one's country.[32]

Morris Schaff, a cadet during the period 1858–1862, confirmed the ambience at West Point as encouraging "the military spirit in its medieval habit of thought and aristocratic isolation" and the academy itself as the "fountain of truth, its hearth of courage, its altar of duty, and its temple of honor." Such practices promoted the formation of regimental brotherhoods, striated by rank and influenced by notions of gentility installed at West Point. The new professional military man used this code of ethics to support his claim to status. In 1817, 14 percent of the army officer corps were West Point graduates; in 1830, this percentage rose to 63 percent, and in 1860, a staggering 75 percent had completed the four-year officer program. Approximately 60 percent of officers serving in the West graduated from the prestigious academy. This military training, then, produced "nation-builders," whose "strong sense of honor" forged a common identity and professional cohesion at the isolated western garrisons.[33]

This military ethos operational within the officer corps can be best understood, perhaps in the memoirs of Robert H. McKay, who served in several southwestern posts. After passing an Army Medical Board examination he was mustered into service in 1869 as an acting assistant surgeon and ordered to report to the Department of the Missouri at Leavenworth, Kansas. Here, he made his "first impression of the rank and file of the Regular Army. The officers impressed me as very self-important, exceedingly courteous and cordial, and charming. . . . Another thing that impressed me was the absolute separation of the officers and enlisted men. . . . They seemed as distinct as oil and water." Whilst travelling to Fort Craig, New Mexico, he spent time in Santa Fe and recorded his discombobulation with: "The town was utterly strange to me, so different from anything I had ever seen . . . and the people as strange as the houses. . . . I believe if I had been dropped down in some town in the interior of China and had found few Americans to talk to it would not have seemed more strange to me." Yet within a short time both he and his wife quickly adapted to the alien territories. He concluded his narrative with a challenge to public opinion of the elite nature of the army officer community. He advised that both during his time in the army and after retirement "I have had people refer to our army officers and their families with some degree of aspersion, saying they were too proud and would not speak to common folk; that they were aristocrats, and much other nonsense." He acknowledged, "Possibly their isolated condition when I was in the service, gave some color to such accusations, but as far as I can estimate them, if they are an aristocracy, it is an aristocracy of merit; of intellect; of honor; of integrity; of loyalty; of a strong sense of duty and many other worthy qualities." This military community he distinguished from "any other kind of aristocracy we have in this country and I think particularly from our so-called aristocracy of wealth, so often associated with snobbery, and whose daughters so often present the nauseating spectacle, of trading themselves off to some degenerate and profligate descendant of inherited title and giving a million to boot."[34]

Not all officers, however, behaved as McKay's understanding of a respectable gentlemen. Following indefatigable amorous advances made by the married Capt. Andrew Geddes in 1879, Lillie, daughter of Lt. Louis H. Orleman, stationed at

Fort Stockton, unwisely accepted Geddes's protestations of love and acquiesced
to frequent unchaperoned visits. Living in the quarters adjacent to Miss Orleman
and her father, he regularly took advantage of the young woman's naïveté. This
sordid affair ended in an official court-martial. In an attempt to justify his behavior,
Geddes accused Miss Orleman's father of incest, and painted his own visits as
necessary to "champion" a "distressed maiden." The allegation of incest against
Orleman remained unproven. Found guilty of conduct unbecoming a gentleman,
Geddes was cashiered from the army and required to serve a three-year prison
term. Although this sentence was overturned by President Rutherford B. Hayes,
Geddes would be subsequently dismissed on a separate conviction of conduct
unbecoming an officer and gentleman. His argument in court manipulated
widely held codes of honorable respectability in the American army to defend
inappropriate carnal behavior.[35]

The officers' wives who journeyed west to join their husbands, however, built
upon the heritage of the idealized gentleman gentility by applauding and insisting
upon principled behavior. On watching the Seventh Cavalry depart for the 1876
summer campaign, Elizabeth Custer recalled, "The sun . . . took every little bit
of burnished steel on the arms and equipment along the line of horsemen, and
turned them into glittering flashes of radiating light. . . . [M]y husband glanced
back to admire his men, and could not refrain from constantly calling my attention
to their grand appearance. The soldiers, inured to many years of hardship, were
the perfection of physical manhood." She continued admiringly, "Their brawny
limbs and lithe, well-poised bodies . . . their resolute faces, brave and confident,
inspired one with a feeling that they were going out aware of the momentous hours
awaiting them, but inwardly assured of their capability to meet them." To more
fully understand Custer's narrative, however, Shirley Leckie analyzed her published
works to argue that she mythologized her husband as a glorious hero, loving
husband, and diligent commander of men. In protecting and embellishing his
character and actions she successfully produced a national icon. As a middle-class
female writer, Custer's unquestioned public authority and legitimacy was derived
from her role as a model wife and widow, and remained unchallenged until after
her death. Thus, in describing the "grand appearance" of the men as "the perfection
of physical manhood" with "resolute faces," she brokered and manipulated the
historical account to promote her husband as an exemplary commander, imbued
with West Point's virtues of duty, honor, and gentlemanly demeanor. [36]

Similarly, Martha, the wife of Lt. Jack Summerhayes, following twenty-four
years in the West, declared, "I am glad to have known the Army: the soldiers, the

line, and the Staff; it is good to think of honor and chivalry, obedience to duty and the pride of arms; to have lived amongst men whose motives were unselfish and whose aims were high, who stood ready, at the call of their country, to give their lives for a Government which is, to them, the best in the world." Here, as with the Custer narratives, Summerhayes published her experiences for a specific purpose. She tells us that she wrote the book in response to her children's request, and as a guide for younger army wives. Louise Barnett's introduction in the recent second edition of *Vanished Arizona* suggests that the army wife narratives formed a genre that combined the traditional travelogue with a comparison of eastern and western life, revealing "the profound difference between a western army life and the civilized East." Barnett advises that Summerhayes held a romantic view, whilst providing her husband with a conservative masculine role of protection and practicality. This gendered division served perhaps as a foil against which she gained greater freedom of action and expression. In both women's writings, their references clearly portray their husbands, posted in the U.S. West, as genteel representatives of imperialism.[37]

In addition, Alice, the wife of Lt. Frank Baldwin of the Thirty-Seventh U.S. Infantry, twice decorated with the Medal of Honor, romantically cast military men as "lords" and "gallant warriors" who accomplished "brave deeds." She quoted directly from Sir Walter Scott's poem *Marmion: A Tale of Flodden Field* to describe her husband as "My 'Young Lochinvar out of the West.'" In identifying her military spouse with the fictional knight, she portrayed her soldier husband as such a gallant, implicitly casting herself as his lady fair. Similarly, Teresa, the wife of Brig. Gen. Egbert Ludovickus Vielé of the First U.S. Infantry, on moving to her husband's new post at Ringgold Barracks in 1850, reflected this romanticism with "There never was a country more unfitted by nature to the home of civilized man, than this region of lower Rio Grande in Texas. . . . [T]hrough the character of all [the Americans] there runs a tinge of romance and chivalry. . . . Their innate nobility and high-toned sense of honor resemble more the days of Ivanhoe and Richard Cœur-de-Lion." She enthusiastically continued, "No recruit ever entered the service with more enthusiasm than I did or felt more eager to prove himself a soldier. . . . Mars would have gloried in the wonderful female that my imagination loved to paint . . . intercourse with the most savage tribe of Indians was nothing to her! . . . 'The Regiment adored her.'" In this glamorized announcement, Vielé revealed her imagined role as an ambassador. In an uncivilized territory, she would "prove" to be a brave and adorable "soldier," one of the regiment—sharing a noble and honorable esprit de corps. Confirming this understanding of an imperial partnership, an overnight stop at Pond Creek Station, Kansas, while en route to Fort Reno led Mrs. D. B. Dyer to declare that here, "on the dividing line of civilization," she and her husband "were looked upon as 'big chiefs' from Washington."[38]

The American wives, just as their British counterparts, identified themselves as integral members of their husband's units. Many women naturally included the pronouns "we" and "our" to detail day-to-day military activity. Indeed, Forrestine, stationed with her father Lt. Charles Cooper of the Tenth U.S. Cavalry, wrote of a unit who left Fort Concho "for a two-month scout." She described the Tenth's activities as: "[W]e were to make a supply camp. . . . We rested . . . we marched . . . [and] we all endured." Similarly, Jennie, wife of Capt. Albert Barnitz of the Seventh Cavalry, considered an anticipated transfer to Fort Morgan as a "brilliant prospect." Yet, she advised, "if, however, the Indians will not accept the terms offered them, then we are to commence hostilities, and make them do so—and finally, if they break the treaty (provided they agree to one) then of course we will have to ride about and 'expend' a few thousand of them! Which horn of dilemma do you prefer?" Such inclusivity litters the American narratives, suggesting that these officers' wives, just as their corresponding actors in British India, considered themselves fully immersed in, and membership holders of, the military forces.[39]

Despite the "lounging and dishevelled habits" of the Madras Army officers, and the philandering of Lieutenant Geddes, the majority of British and American officers who graduated from the military academies were committed to duty, created an unshakeable esprit de corps, and wholeheartedly furthered imperialist ambitions. The survey of Sandhurst, Addiscombe, and West Point clearly indicates the similarities in training, behaviors, and understandings of imperial roles. After posting to British India and the U.S. West, most commissioned men performed and reinforced nineteenth-century gentlemanly ideals. Indeed, wives who accompanied their military men understood themselves as admirers and partners of their "dauntless warriors." As one such imperial "lady fair," Mrs. Parkes approved of the commanding and striking air of Colonel Gardner. Miss Fane's belittlement of General Martabar Singh Thapa at Almack's, however, and Mrs. Sherwood's ridicule of the "Don Quixote and Sancho Panza" couple, denied such personages any imperial qualities. However, Lieutenant-General Colin Mackenzie, stationed at Lodiana on the North West Frontier in 1847, passed muster. His wife proudly declared, "He succeeded in forming a splendid regiment [Fourth Sikhs]." Despite the primitive conditions and mud-hut housing, he "always impressed upon his men that a soldier was a gentleman, and *therefore* should be foremost in doing whatever had to be done." Similarly, the mid-nineteenth-century cadets enrolled at West Point, according to Cadet Thomas Rowland, developed into a "distinctly military milieu," a "band of brothers" complete with aristocratic airs and imbued with a sense of honor, duty, and loyalty.[40]

A brief examination of these specific communities sheds further light on the differences in the class structure. The British model reflected the rigid practices embedded in the core society. Men who enlisted as soldiers, according to historian T. A. Heathcote, "had no pretensions to respectability," and as one contemporary observer noted represented "the scum of the earth," who joined the nineteenth-century British Army to answer economic need. The regiment provided a uniformed surrogate of village society, with "the colonel as squire and magistrate, his officers as local proprietors. . . . Men whose position gave them respectability, as overseers and stewards." Heathcote advises that "the officers were drawn from an altogether superior class," who acted according to prescribed markers of gentility to demonstrate status, combined with an intense responsibility to lead men into battle under the constant threat of injury and death. Thus, they were competent and respected leaders. These class lines were rigidly drawn, maintained, and legitimized within the imperial "village" society in British India.[41]

Not precisely "scum of the earth," yet enlisted men, according to Kevin Adams "entered an institution that traditionally and legally regarded them as subservient drudges." In considering the nineteenth-century social hierarchy in the American army serving in the West, Adams's study similarly argues that a rigid divide separated the enlisted men from the officers who cultivated "notions of a gentleman aristocracy" to reflect "Gilded Age class attitudes, accentuated by an organization that encouraged the expression of hierarchical distinctions." The officers created an exclusive set of those who either graduated from West Point or utilized the patronage system to obtain commissions. Thus, asserts Adams, "once in the army, officers made perfect bourgeois Victorians, as their salary automatically elevated them to the economic elite," and their role was one of nation-building and to forcibly subdue Native American tribes who resisted subjugation. Adams posits that the majority of postwar officers hailed from wealthy families, and to project their class status, officers and wives utilized education, consumer consumption, and leisure pursuits to create a class divide. Thus they modeled a "gentlemanly gentility."[42]

Both sets of officer groups, then, who graduated from the academies received a liberal education, military instruction, and were expected to be officers and gentlemen, values fostered by concepts such as honor, loyalty, and selfless duty to the nation. Yet Archibald Forbes, a ten-year veteran of the Royal Dragoons and a highly reputable war correspondent, identified differences between the two armies. After visiting the United States, he compared the post–Civil War army to the British force. He commented, "[T]he United States and Great Britain [are] the only two countries of the civilized world whose standing armies are professional. . . . Whose duties . . . must be confined to defensive and police work." Forbes discussed career advancement and economic rationale, however, to highlight differences. In detailing promotion through the ranks he posited that the American enlisted man "may attain any rank." He continued, "[I]t is the common belief in Europe that all officers of the American regular army are graduates of West Point; but this is quite an error. . . . Of the four hundred and thirty-two cavalry officers in the American army, there are no fewer than one hundred and eighteen 'rankers,' as the officers who have risen in the ranks are called in the British army." However, "these 'rankers' do not populate the lower grades, as is mostly the case with the British 'ranker.'"[43]

Forbes also identified a difference in economic incentive. He asserted, "The pay of the British officer is utterly inadequate to his maintenance in any fashion other than a genteel." This is overcome by professional glamor, "to speak colloquially, Britain 'runs' a professional army on what would be a dry crust, but that it is larded with empty honors and some social prestige." The American army, however, "is run on a wholly different basis. . . . Soldiering shall differ from no other calling in being a business-like, adequately remunerated avocation." He listed and compared salaries to advise that the pay in the British army was far less than its American counterpart, and "barely enough to pay the mess bill." Thus, "The spirit pervading the pay-scale of the officerhood [sic] of the American army is that he who selects it as his profession shall have an adequate income on which to live, no matter what his rank, an income yielded by his profession reasonably on a par with the professional incomes of other callings throughout the republic; whereas the key-note to the English scale is that private resources must supplement the inadequate professional pittance."[44]

"Uncle Sam," argued Forbes, "pays a man well enough to do his duty; he holds that duty includes the best and fullest the man can do." Indeed, the American officer's "axiom is roughly a practical one—'Merit and success are synonymous; failure spells incompetence.' In all this he differs utterly from his cousin, Dame

Britannia. Her army is not a business profession; and so she cannot deal with it on business principles." Hence, Forbes detected a significant difference in the recruitment and expectations of the British and American officer class. The British officer, poorly paid in comparison to his American counterpart, served for recognition of honor and duty through promotion and military decoration; the officer serving in the West was akin to a businessman, recompensed financially as a professional with "no store of honors and lavish advancement as the reward for duty-doing."[45]

After considering the differences in motivation and prospects of the officer class, Forbes recounts his observation of a parade in Camp Cumming, New Mexico, to note a difference in attitude to service. He commented, "At the first glance, an English Cavalry officer, accustomed to the polish and trimness of his own command, might be excused for standing aghast in horror at the aspect of such a squadron of horsemen . . . ready in every item for active service." He continued, "[A]s the impression of slovenliness wore off, it became apparent that to the minutest detail everything was contrived for and subordinated to practical utility." He described, "The arms were essentially practical—no saber, a Smith and Weston revolver, a Hotchkiss magazine carbine . . . carried conveniently on the saddle. . . . Men, lean, wiry, tough-looking fellows, wearing clothes there could be no fear of spoiling, adepts by training . . . individually and collectively self-reliant." The officers he viewed displayed initiative, efficiency and self-reliance in adapting their arms and attire to befit a scouting party. Forbes concluded, "In fine, a detachment of American cavalry on march might, to the European conversant with standing armies, bear a suspicious resemblance to banditti, but it is carefully equipped for the kind of service on which it is employed, and possesses a practical adaptability."[46]

In 1860 Sir Richard Burton, who served with the Eighteenth Regiment, Bombay Native Infantry, provided an additional British view. He advised that "[a] tour through the domains of Uncle Samuel without visiting the wide regions of the Far West would be, to use a novel simile, like seeing Hamlet with the part of Prince of Denmark, by desire, omitted." He wished to study "the beginnings of a mighty empire 'in that New World which is the Old,'" observe the Mormon practices, and to "enjoy a little skirmishing with the savages." He arranged for a military escort and met with "Lieutenant Dana, my future *compagnon de voyage*" at Camp Floyd, Utah Territory," to embrace "with pleasure the opportunity of seeing the most of my American brothers in arms." He determined, "As far as I could judge of American officers, they are about as republican in mind and tone of thought as those of the British army. They are aware of the fact that the bundle of sticks requires a tie, but they prefer, as we all do, King Stork to King Log, and King Log to King Mob." He attended "company inspections, and found the men well dressed and tolerably set up, while the bands, being German, were of course excellent." A notable difference between the two armed forces, just as with Forbes, caused comment, "The uniform is a study. The States have attempted in the dress of their army, as in the forms of their government, a moral impossibility. It is expected to be at once cheap and soldier-like, useful and ornamental, light and heavy." But, he concluded, "[i]ts principal merit is a severe republican plainness, very consistent with the prepossessions of the people, highly inconsistent with the customs of military nations. Soldiers love to dress up Mars, not to clothe him like a butcher."[47]

In considering these observations, it becomes clear that despite the similarity in purpose, as professional armies, there are substantial differences. The social background of the men, ranking practices, motivation to seek a commission, and financial entitlements suggest the American officer entered service as a professional, on par with his civilian counterpart. Despite a level of formality required as a genteel gentleman, an officer, unfettered by the demands made by *The Queen's Regulations*, could implement practical, resourceful, and self-reliant initiatives to best conduct his duty.

Both the British and American armies prescribed codes of behavior that insisted an officer be honorable, educated, and display genteel politeness—an idealized officer and gentleman. The British officer corps included many titled and landed men, and offered to the middle class a suitable vocation. These men who graced the hallways of Sandhurst and Addiscombe were expected to adhere to a rigidly formal code of conduct creating an imperial class. The U.S. Army had no titled aristocracy to fill the ranks. Upper- and middle-class men became "republican machines," mirroring many traditions of their European counterparts. These professional soldiers, steeped in values of honor, bravery, and obedience, also created an imperial class, albeit less formalized. These distinct communities, whose very *raison d'être* was that of facilitating national expansion and protection, and who expected to be posted to zones of conflict—usually on the fringes of territorial holdings—adopted and adapted class hierarchies based on prevailing middle-class values and markers.

No matter the degree of formality, British and American officers' wives both admired, and connected to, their husbands' roles as officers and gentlemen.

In joining their husbands on the outposts of empire, these women undertook long and occasionally dangerous journeys, often unaccompanied, to join their husbands. In comparing travel and destination arrivals through a transnational lens, it becomes apparent that the writers attempted to ameliorate a sense of dislocation by declaring an exaggerated attachment to symbols of nationalism, overlaid memories of home on alien landscapes, and espoused extreme racial prejudice. In so doing they created a new social reality by designing a unique identity forged through military commitment, loyalty, and imperial duty.

3

Imperial Journeys and Arrivals

Couriers, Circuits, and Connections

In all this wild West the influence of woman is second only in its benefits to the influence of religion, and where the last unhappily does not exist the first continually exerts its restraining power.

—*Isabella Lucy Bird*

The fair 'ladies of the land' . . . have unbounded influence over [their menfolk] . . . , then why do they not, one and all, rise up and say. . . . "I will have no spitting." . . . American ladies! do this, and you may not only as now be proud of your countrymen as men, but vain of them as gentlemen.

—*Matilda Houstoun*

Writing on board the British merchant vessel *Reliance*, en route to India in 1837, Honoria, the wife of Lt. Henry Lawrence of the Bengal Artillery, noted in her journal, "I sit in my cabin *déshabillée*, that is to say no clothing save a chemise, dressing gown, and a pair of slippers. How am I ever to go clothed like a civilized being in India is more than I can divine." She clearly understood that dress, as an imperial text, would signal British civilization and that she would need to pay close attention to such matters. An earlier entry indicated her understanding of the role as the wife of a minor government official. Thankful that her husband had received a civil secondment, she looked forward to sharing "an influential station where a man can repress wrong and encourage right." Indeed, in keeping the journal for the sole purpose of providing a record for her husband's sight, she continued, "We [women] do and must influence the character of men, and therefore we ought deliberately and conscientiously to form our opinions, that our weight may be thrown into the right scale. I will tell you what I believe to be one of the strongest feelings in me: desire after influence. Not the love of sway, or carrying the point . . . but the power of influencing minds."[1]

In contrast, Frances, the wife of Lt. Fayette Roe of the Third U.S. Infantry Regiment, recorded her "own life [reminiscences] with the Army in the Far West, whether they be about Indians, desperadoes, or hunting." After prefacing her collection of published letters with a claim to their honesty and the omission of "flowery descriptions," Mrs. Roe described her journey to Fort Lyon in 1871. Forced to spend an evening in Kit Carson township, she remarked, "I am thankful enough that our stay is short in this terrible place where one feels there is a danger of being murdered any minute. Not one woman have I seen here, but there are men—dreadful looking men." She then proceeded to describe the town, clearly different from her home in Cincinnati, Ohio. "The houses we saw . . . were worse even than the men," she observed, and decided they were more suited as homes for "spooks and creepy things. . . . The whole place is horrible, and dismal beyond description." She additionally complained that only a small trunk could accompany her directly to the fort; thus she felt "mortified" that she would be introduced to the regiment with "only two dresses."[2]

The juxtaposition of Mrs. Lawrence's eloquent anticipation of greater female authority with Mrs. Roe's disdainful and uneasy account of her physical westward journey exemplifies the polar extremes of expectations and concerns voiced by nineteenth-century British and American officers' wives. Both women expressed concern in presenting themselves through appropriate dress codes as imperial wives. Sea voyages, overland treks, and arrivals, then, acted as spaces within which officers' wives blueprinted roles as imperial ambassadors. In examining private correspondence, travelogues, and published memoirs, a comparative, transnational analysis argues that women who journeyed to reunite with their spouses on the borders of empire donned protective masks of extreme patriotic nationalism and racial prejudice. On arrival, the women sought familiar, reassuring landscapes in British India and the U.S. West. Indigenous peoples and terrains, however, were viewed as different, the "other," and subjected to racial censure. In creating a new social reality the women ameliorated a sense of dislocation and isolation by crafting a new identity forged through military commitment, loyalty, and duty—as intermediaries of empire.[3]

As analysts point out, nineteenth-century female travel accounts offer insights into the worldviews of the authors, and thus a reflection of national norms. Travel writing as a genre provides the reader with a complicated product of imagined geographies. Indeed, in focusing on the journey we see the construction of both a territorial and a human other, and the legitimatization of national authority relies on such fantasized terrains. Wolfgang Iser advised that collective "memory and otherness" are both generated "by a boundary crossing and by a realignment of what has become separate." The officers' wives utilized the journey as a space in which they realigned their past roles to construct an identity as national representatives. By intensifying nostalgia as a collective memory and mythologizing the nation, these women constructed a distinct social reality that elevated all American and British objects, values, and behaviors, whilst generally depicting the indigenous terrain, peoples, and culture in disdainful terms.[4]

Denise Comer utilizes a feminist and postcolonial approach to argue that British women adopted female fictional genres to distance their contributions from traditional "desire" forms of "travel-as-sexual quest or travel-as-scientific" narratives. In so doing, they perpetuated "fiction of empire as a masculine endeavor" and constructed an imagined geography that "maintain[ed] and strengthen[ed] British hegemony in India." She asserts that these women participated in the "British endeavor . . . to create, maintain, and reify" India as an imagined imperial community. For Comer, women "were not merely idle appendages to their husbands . . . existing to organize the household of servants and take naps," but active participants in crafting and maintaining imperialism by creating "fiction[s] of empire." Similarly, Rosemary Raza's investigations of British female writers who published Indian monographs suggest that within the domestic and social realms women "reinforced structures of society, established its cultural and social tone, monitored its standards, and patrolled its boundaries." She questions the negative stereotype of the *memsahib* as prejudicial and isolationist, to underscore the female as a cultural icon, representing "the highest ideals of [British] society . . . and civilization." Scholars who examine nineteenth-century American army wives' narratives agree that their writings offer a social commentary of the nation, revealing more about the female social role than Western landscapes.[5]

Most telling, perhaps, are the published accounts of the officers' wives themselves. Margaret, the first wife of Col. Henry B. Carrington of the Eighteenth U.S. Infantry, offered the following book dedication: "With acknowledgments to Lieutenant-General [W. T.] Sherman, whose suggestions at Fort Kearney [*sic*], in the spring of 1866, were adopted in preserving a daily record of the events of a peculiarly eventful journey." The "peculiarly eventful journey" began in May 1866, when Margaret observed the regimental preparations for travel from Fort Kearny to Absaraka, North Dakota. She echoed the oft-stated sentiment of traveling to a different world by noting, "All contingencies had to be anticipated, so that the day of arrival in the new country should be the day of commencement, and there should then be no delay to wait for anything from the United States." In making the distinction between the East and West, she clearly viewed the continent's interior as a geographical "other." With regard to her writings, she understood herself as tasked by Sherman to act as a representative of a developing imperial formation. She recorded, "At his suggestion some of the ladies began their daily journal of events, and thus laid the basis for the conversion of *one* into this narrative for the eyes of friends who could not share the trip." Frances, at this time the wife of Lt. Col. George Grummond of the Eighteenth U.S. Infantry, recalled that Sherman "urged all army officers' wives to accompany their husbands and to take with them all needed comforts for a pleasant garrison life in the newly opened country, where all would be healthful, with pleasant service, and absolute peace."[6]

Margaret and Frances Carrington, Elizabeth Custer, and by extension other officers' wives deliberately utilized published narratives to both profile and manage historical accounts. In the mid-1800s, according to literary critics, domestic fiction written by women dominated and hence "feminized the literary marketplace." These narratives both connected and underscored domestic agency within national affairs, creating a "gendered nationalism." Shannon Smith investigated the 1866 Fetterman Fight to argue that negative scholarly interpretations of the central actor—Capt. William J. Fetterman—stemmed from the published writings of Colonel Carrington's first and second wives—Margaret and Frances. Carrington had been scapegoated, at the highest military level, for the reckless pursuit of Red Cloud's band of Cheyenne and Sioux Indians, which had led to the ambush and death of U.S. soldiers under the command of Fetterman. In failing to obtain recourse through military channels, his predicament prompted Margaret and Frances to write of their experiences in the U.S. West. As respected middle-class women, their honesty and integrity would be beyond reproach. In publishing acclamatory, but manipulated, accounts of Carrington's gentlemanly character and behavior these women generated power in the public sphere, which according to Smith, provided a vehicle for both women to shape and control history.[7]

Although not writing to exonerate her husband's actions, Maria, the wife of Scottish naval officer Thomas Graham, assumed the mantle of a self-appointed imperial commentator. Although she prefaced her reflections with "they were really and truly written . . . for the amusement of an intimate friend," she bemoaned the fact that all published works on India were "entirely occupied" with military, commercial, and political discussions. This being so, she decided to publish her narrative as a "popular work" for a general audience. She attested that "though aware that, among a people whose laws, whose religion, whose arts, whose habits of reasoning and notions of politeness, all differ from ours, as radically as their language or complexion, it was natural to expect some variation from our standards as to the morals and the charities and decencies of social life, she [Graham] must confess that the difference was greater than she found it easy to reconcile." Notwithstanding her aforementioned popular purpose, she clearly understood her imperial role in seeking "to direct the attention of those in whose hands so much of their [Indian people's] destiny is placed, to the means of improving their moral and intellectual condition, as well as of securing them from political or civil injuries."[8]

In the preface to her narrative, published immediately after the outbreak of the 1857 Sepoy Mutiny, Helen Mackenzie revealed her imperial affiliation in no uncertain terms. She declared, "We conquered India from the *Muhammadan* [Muslim] invaders, who had ruled it with a rod of iron . . . our rule has been a deliverance and an unspeakable benefit to the Hindus . . . we rescued the aged Emperor, whose descendants we have ever since pensioned and protected." Her alarm and outrage reached a crescendo in warning, "we must remember that, as regards morality, the natives are what the heathens of old were—without principle, implacable, [and] unmerciful." She recognized that kindness and courtesy toward them ought to be increased, "yet now that they have polluted the earth with such unspeakable atrocities against not only men, but innocent women and children, we must remember that even a Christian ruler is not to bear the sword in vain." Her travel to escape from the Mutiny's violence clearly prompted an outraged final rejoinder that directed, "[S]ay to our nobles, our rulers, and to the rest of the people, 'Be not ye afraid of them: remember the Lord who is great and terrible, *and fight for your brethren, your sons, your daughters, and your wives.*'—Neh. iv. 14; 'for the *land cannot be cleansed of the blood that is shed therein,* BUT BY THE BLOOD OF HIM THAT SHED IT.'—Num. xxxv. 33."[9]

Although not taking the fire and brimstone approach of Mrs. Mackenzie, the Carrington wives understood, and delighted in the fact, that they were charged by

Sherman to record their imperial experiences. Mrs. Graham and Mrs. MacKenzie, however, became empowered by their roles as officers' wives. Writing in 1814, the former asked for resources to improve the moral, intellectual, and political rights of the Indian peoples. The latter, writing after the initial outbreak of violence in 1857, appropriated quotations from the Old Testament books of Nehemiah and Numbers to call for bloody retaliation. Both urged imperial authorities to take political action.[10]

Although few women issued such a vehement call to arms, Mrs. Mackenzie's stirring preface emphasizes the role of officers' wives as writers. In utilizing published narratives of travel, the authors brokered vast amounts of information to generate a specific narrative for consumption by a national audience. Military spouses felt briefed, duty-bound, as imperial agents to publish their observations. We see the U.S. West and British India polarized, at one end aggrandized with descriptions of noble warrior chiefs and bejeweled, benign rajahs. Opposing this positive view, other women denigrated tribal peoples and members of Indian castes as heathens and savages. These class, race, and cultural markers reflect embedded national understandings. Thus, they underpinned justifications of empire as a benevolent, superior entity, duty-bound to control and civilize the terrains, rulers, and indigenous peoples. In wives' letters, journals, and memoirs, however, a more intimate portrait often emerges, that speaks to a certain fearfulness, trepidation, and bewilderment. The writers share with family members a sense of dislocation, an overriding desire to stay connected with "home," along with a catalogue of day-to-day difficulties and discomforts. These domestic insights, nonetheless, are combined with acceptance and adaption, proposing new approaches and practices that provide a real sense of identity, purpose, and belonging. Unsurprisingly, then, the published accounts reveal an embroidered portrayal of new landscapes and peoples, and a new female identity, a woman who contributed to imperial ambitions. Similarly, within the journals and letters, whose content focused on the everyday dramas of family life, lay an implied and understood obligation of duty as an imperial agent.

The British and American officers' wives' narratives reveal voyages and immediate arrivals as spaces within which they designed their roles as imperialists. To consider the nineteenth-century British and American army officers' wives operating transnationally however, the term itself needs clarification, and an explanation given that speaks to its relationship with these women. Transnationalism implies the crossing of borders, physical and abstract, of actors, societies, and institutions that remain linked and connected in complex and multiple forms.

In considering the two distinct officer wife populations, both groups of women viewed their new surroundings as away from home. The realization of locations as alien terrains peopled by what appeared, in their view, the uncivilized, prompted the creation of a distinct identity. Through female performances, officers' wives represented an inflated model of core middle-class values. They chose to view places through comparisons of "home," attempting to make connections and see similarities. This defensive lens provided a level of security to allow new vistas to appear familiar and nonthreatening. The women saw the indigenous peoples, Anglo-Indians, and white settlers, however, as lesser-beings. The military wives, then, created a network that stretched from the core to the peripheries, and in journeying to join officer husbands they became links in a chain, reflecting and prescribing understandings, to form a collective, and elevated, imperial identity.[11]

This process of connection is explained by Pierre-Yves Saunier who posits that "travelers create or join a discussion about the relative characteristics, positions, and roles of the places they visit . . . the linkage is also about comparing 'home' and 'abroad.' This makes travel a propitious site for transnational historians," and "provides a thread through which the history of connections comes alive, unveiling the actors' agency." He further adds that "transnational history is an approach that emphasizes what works between and through the units that humans have set up to organize their collective life," that focuses on the relationship of such connections and circulations "between, across and through these units."[12]

In addition to travel as a space of connection, Saunier refers to Richard White's "middle ground," Mary Louise Pratt's "contact zones," and Homi Bhabha's "interstitial spaces" to suggest that these sites, "controlled and labelled according to national origins" should be considered as "the locus where connections were refused, made, and unmade between polities and societies." Yet "the establishment of national states did not ruin the business of connections across polities and societies." Acting then as brokers, journeyers took advantage of the opportunities to "adopt specific roles and develop specific mediations between communities, societies and polities." Peggy Levitt and Sanjeev Khagram agree that scholars should "uncover, analyze, and conceptualize similarities, differences, and interactions among trans-societal and trans-organizational realities. . . . [to include] the transnationally-constituted experiences of people who migrate internally within a country . . . [or] move across close or contiguous borders." Military wives operated within a national circuit of transmission, carrying values, ideas, and goods both outwardly from the core locations to the peripheries, and relaying information and material culture from the peripheries back to the core. Saunier suggests: "It is the dissection of these circuits that makes it possible to restore the agency of those who lived in-between and through polities."[13]

As they travelled west, the American wives crossed nation-states and territories, holding agency as intermediaries. As Saunier recognizes, "they enter or create situations where they can act as go-betweens," and "reconstruct the circuits in which they operated." He further clarifies circulation as more than transportation, to include the alteration of people, ideas, and objects in movement. He continues: "Circulations define spaces of their own. . . . These spaces are the middle grounds and contact zones. . . . They are sites for the production of attitudes, roles, situations, objects, and institutions." Circulations, then, provide spaces that cut across a national framework by allowing the mapping of journeys and sojourns to create a transnational "catchment area" to fully research military wives as intermediaries. In traversing the continental United States, American wives created connections and held agency in constructing circulations, thus adding to the collective identity as agents of imperialism.[14]

Scholars have identified patterns and practices, utilizing comparative strategies, to identify differences, similarities, and transmission processes, to reveal social transformation. To create boundaries and signal imperial status in the U.S. West and in British India, military wives fashioned a new type of consciousness, became arbiters of cultural reproduction, and generated a distinct, reconstructed model of "home" that reflected yet embellished cultural norms. By intensifying nostalgia as a collective memory, and through the exaggeration of national prejudices, the military wives, within a transnational circuit, created a distinct social reality that influenced the crafting and maintenance of imperial ambitions.[15]

To examine the intimate, imperial space within which the officers' wives operated, it is helpful to acknowledge the nature of female and male power bargaining. Scholarly studies have sought to explain the impact of transnationalism on gender relationships. To offer a working interpretation of gender, Sarah Mahler and Patricia Pessar usefully define this construct as a flexible human invention "using practices and discourses to negotiate relationships, notions of 'masculinity' and 'femininity,' and conflicting interests." They conclude that "conceptualizing gender as a process, as one of several ways humans create and perpetuate social difference, helps to deconstruct the myth that gender is a product of nature while underscoring its power dimension." In the transnational processes and imperial spaces, traditional gendered roles weakened. Officers' wives reconstructed their identities and relationships with the nation by reassembling social and gender hierarchies. The unfamiliar terrain, both geographical and cultural, of postings to imperial outposts afforded disorientation. Women and men reacted differently to such dislocation. Men, in losing a sense of identity, displayed greater commitment to maintaining ties with public institutions. Women, on the other hand, gained greater status via "social citizenship" in the receiving countries, through creating transnational social connections and communities.[16]

The creation of a new social reality implies the clustering of a consensus group of officers' wives who advocated an adaptive values system. In identifying the transnational interplay of power, class, and culture, Roger Rouse considers the roles of settlers and sojourners. The experiences of the officers' wives, whose long-term stay in British India and the U.S. West does not comfortably fall into either category, can be usefully examined by referencing Rouse's model. Many officers' wives experienced lengthy tours of duty, some for multiple decades, thus constituted a "military settler" group, who participated in a "transnational migrant circuit." A settler group, according to Rouse, possessed a cultural "bifocality. This worldview consists of a hybrid of embedded (original location) and adopted (new location) practices and understandings, whose claims are contested during the initial stages of settlement. Although bifocalism is traditionally understood as a period of time spent adjusting to new surroundings, Rouse firmly asserts that settler "bifocalism stemmed not from transitional adjustments to a new locale, but from a chronic, contradictory transnationalism." In British India, certainly this "chronic" transnational condition would have existed after two centuries of colonization. In the U.S. West, however, Anglo settlement was less established, although westward expansion, arguably, had been under way since the initial establishment of European colonies.[17]

The need to establish stability begins with the journey to environs new. Angelika Bammer analyzes travel to argue that a journey consists of separation, repair, loss and restoration, and a reconstitution of the family unit. She holds that objects, rituals, and stories carried in movement link the old and new communities. In this transnational space decisions are made to determine what is culturally sacrosanct, what can be abandoned, and what can be translated for survival purposes. In adapting to new environments, "masks" are created that disguise "cultural identity by which we are defined and as which we, in turn, define ourselves." When "home and country" fades as a working social reality, cultural identity destabilizes, and the nation mythologized. In employing such mythology, officers' wives made initial sense of their imperial roles through donning masks of aggrandized nationalism and extreme racial prejudice. In so doing, they sought to protect the increasing fragility of self-identity by close association with the nation, and distancing of the indigenous other.[18]

This shift to voice an aggrandized patriotic allegiance began with the outward journey. In making the decision to travel east and west, the military wives of the British and American armies generally offered emotional reasons to join their spouses. Many accounts speak of their duty as wives to ease the hardships and loneliness of their respective husbands. One such woman, Margaret, the fiancée of Medical Officer Taylor D. Murison, attached to the Twenty-Ninth Punjabis Regiment, set sail for India complete with a "modest trousseau." She commented in her unpublished memoirs, "I think that partings, though in life inevitable, are bitter, miserable, unhappy things, and the eagerness and pleasure of looking forward to my marriage was dimmed by an acute homesickness." The couple's long-term plan, she explained, "had always been that I would go out and marry him as soon as he was attached to a regiment." Likewise, Eveline, the wife of Col. Andrew J. Alexander of the Third U.S. Cavalry, received a telegram from her husband on 28 April 1866, asking her to join him at Little Rock, Arkansas. She reluctantly agreed, noting in her private diary: "I almost wish I was not going. And yet Andrew is so lonely."[19]

Yet a trip to the West to help cure a persistent cough encouraged Katherine Fougera (who would shortly meet and marry Lt. Frank Gibson of the Seventh Cavalry) to join relatives. When the day of her "great adventure" to "a totally different world" arrived, Fougera's family accompanied her to the railway station. Here, the women offered parting advice. "Remember your cod-liver oil . . . and your gentle breeding," counseled her mother. Her sister Sally instructed that she must "permit no license of speech or touch from strangers," and "black Nanny Lindy" tearfully added, "An' Honey Chile, don' you get tangled up with no Injun chief." All her female well-wishers contributed to the creation of a façade of gentility. Her mother reinforced her claim to gentility, Sally, the need to retire from strangers, and Nanny Lindy, a warning to avoid romantic entanglement with a Native American chief.[20]

Once en route to join their military husbands, however, apprehension and homesickness appears to have been replaced by cautious excitement. For example, in 1833, Harriette, the wife of Lieutenant Colonel William Ashmore of the Six-teenth Foot Regiment, left Gravesend and sailed on board the merchant ship *Protector* to Calcutta. Every Sunday, cadets from Addiscombe, the crew, and the women assembled on deck for a short religious service. In remarking that duty required the men to attend, she described the scene with: "The captain became the chaplain, and took his station at the capstan, over which was thrown that flag so dear to every British sailor, the Union Jack. To me, this was always an imposing sight." Her description of a "*Mussulmaun* [Muslim] *Ayah*" employed to attend to the female passengers, of whom "two were young ladies bent upon the somewhat hazardous expedient of seeking friends and fortune in India," further intensified nationalistic ties. She commented, "[W]e were not a little amused by her [Mona, the *ayah*] appearance and manners; for as yet our eyes had not become accustomed to the thin muslin garments and gaudy ornaments of the East." In the transnational space of the journey, Ashmore held firm to her embedded middle-class viewpoint. She described Indian dress and behavior as entirely inappropriate, adding, "Mona's ears were laden with rings . . . her black neck was encircled with innumerable silver chains. . . . her toes were covered with a kind of coat of mail, which passed for silver." After many sightings of the *ayah* "basking" on deck, the officer's wife concluded, "not infrequently was she [Mona] enjoying the luxurious hubble-bubble, or substitute for the hookah, used by the poorer classes of the natives of India."[21]

In 1835, sailing on the *Jupiter*, Emily Eden accompanied her brother George, 1st Earl of Auckland, to take up residence as the governor-general in British India. In private letters written to her sister, she complained of incapacitating seasick-ness during the early stages of the voyage, and of her prejudicial view toward an Indian maid. Miss Eden found her *ayah* indispensable during her bouts of illness. Indeed, "Rosina . . . a good merry old black thing," became "the happiness of . . . [her] life, and is a great favourite with everybody." Yet, despite this "happiness," she remarked, "the *ayah* took advantage of my weak and defenseless condition to establish herself for the night in my cabin . . . there she was wrapped up in a heap of Indian shawls, flat on the ground, with her black arms (covered with bracelets) crossed over her head—very picturesque, but rather shocking." Although these sleeping arrangements initially discomfited Eden, by the end of the journey she admitted, "I am used to it now."[22]

In 1833, Marianne, newly married to Lt. Thomas Postans of the Bombay Native Infantry, sailed to Cutch, India. Although finding the lengthy voyage to Bombay tedious, she nevertheless remarked, "The perfect accommodation provided by

the English merchantmen relieves the Eastern passenger from many of its hor-
rors, providing him with resources and comforts of no common order; but on
arriving in India, he finds his miseries commence." In describing the onward leg,
via a cotton-boat from Bombay to the "up-station," she revealed her prejudiced
worldview. She disdainfully described the craft as "of the rudest construction,
half decked, and totally deficient in privacy, accommodation, and cleanliness...
. From the ridiculous lowness of both its compartments, [it] seems to have been
intended only for . . . monkeys . . . [and the craft is] infested . . . with rats, and
every other description of the most uncompanionable vermin." She continued,
"The crew of these boats are usually half Hindu, and half Mahomedan; they
are a satisfied and slothful race, who lie scattered about the poop . . . alternately
sleeping and smoking." With greater viciousness she concluded, "I have never on
any occasion observed the crew use water for the purposes of ablution; neither
have I seen any attempt made to cleanse a boat, or to put it into any sort of order.
The whole scene is one of filth and confusion . . . surrounded by every ill savour
that bilge-water and native cookery can produce." Thus, during the transnational
space of voyage Ashmore reinforced understandings of identity by capturing the
images of imperial men offering obeisance under the flag, and revealed her race
and class viewpoint by highlighting the cheap adornments of the "poorer" society
of India. Mrs. Postans confirmed her sea voyage on board a British merchant
ship as "perfectly" representing imperial authority and influence. In contrast, her
scathing commentary on the Indian people as a "slothful race, who lie scattered
about the poop . . . alternately sleeping and smoking," and the whole scene as
"one of filth and confusion," reflected the worst of British racial assumptions,
exposing the insecurity of newly arrived settlers.[23]

The officers' wives traveling to join their spouses in the U.S. West likewise
crafted a transnational "mask." In so doing, these women renegotiated their
female role and cultural worldview by strengthening national attachment with
its attendant prejudices. Alice Baldwin remarked on her arrival at Fort Harker
in 1867, "I could see no buildings nor any sign of a 'fort' until it was pointed out
to me . . . I could see nothing but a spot elevated slightly above the rest of the
landscape . . . but God be praised! There floating in the storm was Old Glory." Just
as Harriette Ashmore found the Union Jack a comforting symbol of authority
within the empire, the Stars and Stripes "floating in the storm" reassured Mrs.
Baldwin that she had reached a place of imperial safety.[24]

Other wives echoed this pattern of identifying the West as a different place
than the East. For example, in 1862, a wartime romance developed between

volunteer nurse Elizabeth Reynolds and the wounded Capt. Andrew Burt of the
Eighteenth U.S. Infantry. A hasty wedding led to a fifty-three-year marriage, with
the couple spending forty years in the West. Determined to share his military life
and to privately record her experiences, Mrs. Burt set out from Piqua, Ohio, to
join her husband at Jefferson Barracks, Missouri. She recorded, "Pictures of the
trials of soldier life were given us from all quarters—principally of wild Indians,
tent life, in the snow and again in the burning sands." Shortly after her arrival she
underscored the primitive nature of the West by agreeing with Katherine Fougera
that "it seemed to me that I was going out of the world." Travelling by railway to
join her husband's regiment at Fort Smith, Arkansas, Eveline Alexander alighted
at Odin, Illinois. She negatively remarked, "I am spending Sunday in one of
these mushroom western towns . . . this is rather a heathenish place; none of the
servants at the tavern knew where a church was." Here, she boarded the steamer
Magenta to travel onward via the Mississippi River. The following day's entry
clearly indicated her fears of, and preparations for, life in the West. She remarked,
"I was very much amused this morning to discover that on retiring last night,
while I took the extraordinary precaution of loading my little pistol and putting
it under my pillow, I had neglected the very ordinary precaution of locking my
door." Both Mesdames Burt and Alexander identified the West as a primitive,
unworldly place, the latter woman masking her female role of dependency by
resorting to the "extraordinary" measure of carrying arms.[25]

Officers' wives often made the trip west unaccompanied, via covered wagon,
railroad, boat, steamer, stagecoach, or army ambulance. Katherine Fougera's
journey commenced with a train ride to Dakota. Her compartment, a "theatre-
box," illuminated the world for its occupant. In leaving Chicago, she announced,
despite her homesickness, that she had truly begun "a voyage of make-believe."
As the train hurtled forward it increased her sense of dislocation, and she "saw
everything through wide, astonished eyes, and the further west we penetrated the
more I pictured myself as being in an alien world." Her fellow passengers "were a
cosmopolitan lot," consisting of a softly spoken Southern conductor who insisted
on quoting Shakespeare, a pair of "gimlet-eyed engineers," and "impassive-faced
men with cold, appraising eyes, wearing imported English clothes." Fearful of
the strong winds buffeting the carriage, she accepted an alcoholic drink proffered by a fellow male passenger sporting a "row of gold teeth worth a ransom."
Feeling "oddly reckless," she began to "titter inanely" and fell asleep. On waking,
she realized she had had a "skinful," and chastised herself with: "Shades of my

conservative ancestors! First I picked up with sundry strange men on trains, and now I had imbibed too freely of the grain."[26]

After negatively comparing the railway passengers and her behavior with the standards of the East, she met with her sister Mollie in Columbia, and the pair set off by stagecoach for Fort Abraham Lincoln. On arrival at Bismarck, she described the town as "a far cry from Washington, D.C." She decided, "The picture was not alluring," adding, "it was unpaved . . . the low frame houses, weather stained, consisted of fodder stores, saloons, and laundries where moon-faced Celestials plied their trade." Legendary figures came alive: "Cowboys, resplendent in chaps," intermingled with "stony-faced Indians . . . wrapped in multicolored blankets," and she concluded, "I had heard of such scenes, but only stark reality could depict their primitive, picturesque, settings."[27]

The journeys, then, provided a transnational space for both sets of officers' wives to renegotiate and network their worldviews. Most women expressed a sense of homesickness and reluctance in leaving familiar surroundings. During the voyages to India, the British women clung to national symbols such as the Union Jack, and comfort given by "perfect accommodations" of English vessels. They negatively described the Indians with whom they came into initial contact with prejudicial assumptions, thus bolstering transported understandings of white supremacy. Both these strategies provided a method to allay uncertainty. An American wife, similarly, found security in catching a glimpse of the "Old Glory" flag, and other women sought protection by carrying firearms. The view of the American Indian carried westward was typically the negative mainstream stereotyping of "wildness," and "primitive." Hence, both groups of military wives faced alien terrain with preconceived views, the British women used national emblems to find reassurance, the Americans—loaded weapons.

Mrs. Monkland's fictional Elizabeth, the wife of Captain Bently, provides an illuminating starting point for understanding the attitudes of British women arriving at stations in India. "Barrackpore, though a large station, presents an air of quiet and retirement like a country village; which joined to its military neatness and propriety, make it one of the sweetest places in India," declares the novel's protagonist. She noticed, "The bungalows in four lines stand each separated from the others, every one surrounded by its own corn-ground, flower-garden and neatly trimmed hedge; while the whole cantonment is at right angles intersected by well-kept roads as smooth as bowling-greens." Emily Eden, in her private letters, agreed, declaring, "Barrackpore is a charming place, like a beautiful English villa on the banks of the Thames—so green and fresh." Both Mesdames Monkland and Eden overlaid English rural virtues upon an alien landscape, and by adding the security gained by structured military housing, Barrackpore (city of barracks) became the "sweetest place in India."[28]

Mrs. Major Clemons found the "garden-houses" built for the officers stationed in Fort St. George, Madras, equally delightful. The "commoner kind of house," nonetheless, "resemble[d] English barns." All was not lost, however, as Clemons pronounced, "unsightliness is occasionally remedied by the ingenuity of the ladies." On arrival in Madras, the major's wife revealed her strong connection to home by stating that she "fancied that the bazaars in London were but a humble imitation of those in the East." Heartily disappointed in her palanquin trip to the Triplecane market, she grumbled, "[M]y ideas of Oriental magnificence were much lowered." The streets she described as dirty and narrow, but she reserved the most vehemence for the Indian vendors. "Black people," she observed, "more than half naked, of the lowest description, served at each stall." Instead of smelling the exotic perfumes of "otto [attar] of roses, or millefleurs," she complained of the unpleasant odors of "lamp-oil, garlic, and other nauseous articles. So much for an Oriental bazaar!"[29]

Mary Sherwood arrived in Calcutta in 1815 and marveled at her new accommodations. She noted in her autobiography, "Fort William is regularly built with its drawbridges, its ditches, its magnificent gateways . . . all kept in the most elegant order. . . . I saw sentries standing at their posts and was aware that I was surrounded with all the circumstances of military life . . . such as denoted pomp, and riches, and past victories . . . [the] handsome buildings [were] appropriated to the use of the officers." Thus, by portraying the garrison as an extension of England, Mesdames Monkland and Eden transferred the familiar virtues of rural life, Mrs. Clemons highlighted the civilizing female role, and Mrs. Sherwood glossily described the reified military culture. Echoing the vitriolic racism of the British Mrs. Postans, however, the American Teresa Vielé found Brownsville, Texas completely unpalatable. On arrival she promptly labeled it a "curious, half-breed town. . . . It was what they call in Texas 'quite a settlement.' A mixed population of Americans and Mexicans formed a contrast at once striking and amusing." She compared the buildings of the States with the indigenous constructions to note, "On the one hand the red brick stores, and the white frame shops and buildings of every description, bore the marks of the inevitable progress, or go-aheadativeness, otherwise called 'manifest destiny;' of the expansionists." In contrast, the Mexican presence she remarked consisted of, "rudely constructed huts, or hackals, composed of rustic straw work, or mud bricks called adobes, in which there is generally but one apartment, where frequently they are found living together, eking out an indolent existence." Indeed, she announced, "vermin are the scourge of this country and cleanliness certainly not one of its virtues. This portion of the world may be set down as the birthplace of the flea; those found in other parts are merely occasional wanderers from this, their native land." The initial views of both the British and American military wife describe a transportation and exaggeration of national race and class markers.[30]

To further illustrate this imperial posturing, Isabella Fane, the daughter of the Indian Army's Commander-in-Chief, travelled with her father on an inspection tour. On reaching Mainpuri, she singled out a Native regiment to comment, "The poor dear blackies acquitted themselves beautifully. . . . I dare say you are surprised and disappointed that I never mention the face of the country to you, but you must understand there is nothing to mention." She disdainfully concluded, "You cannot conceive anything so flat and hideous . . . the villages even are not worthy of mention, but consist of the most wretched-looking mud huts, worse even, they say, than an Irish cabin, all huddled together and most unpicturesque." Miss Fane assumed a credible knowledge of life in India; this provided her with a sense of superiority and status, as an agent of empire whose opinion mattered. This supercilious sense of worth and authority, however, existed only in British India. She understood that her grandiose airs and graces held transient value, as she would resume "utter insignificance" on return to her "native land."[31]

Arrival at an American fort brought a sense of relief for the army wives but imposed a new set of difficulties in the condition, availability, and location of suitable accommodation. The construction of housing depended on several factors: how long the fort had existed, locally available building materials, and the proximity of railroad and supply routes. Army regulations specified that rooms be assigned to officers according to rank. A colonel could claim four rooms, a captain two, and a lieutenant one. The standard "room" required 225 square feet if located north of the 38° line of latitude, and 270 square feet south of that parallel—all to measure at least 15 feet wide. The quality and size of the accommodation, however, did not present the largest obstacle for the officer and his spouse. The newly arrived wives needed to confront the military tradition of allocating quarters according to rank. This privilege created a domino effect when a high-ranking officer joined the garrison. The new officer holding seniority selected suitable quarters as he wished, forcing the existing occupants to move. In turn, they ousted a junior officer from his home, and so the effect trickled down through the military tiers. Although a similar system operated in the Queen's Army for single officers, the British wives did not mention this issue.[32]

Home for the British officers and their families, both in the cantonments and as temporary quarters when travelling to new posts—a sort of travel lodge, was a single-story dwelling with a verandah. This "bungalow" derives from *banggolo*, a village hut in Bengal, and as a hybrid form of Indian and British culture was ideally suited to life in tropical areas, quickly mass-produced, and constructed from local materials. The uniform construction acted as a social leveler, but the addition of structural elaborations provided a method to display status. Mrs. Fanny Parkes travelled from one *dak* bungalow to the next on her journey to Allahabad, commenting "they are built by government, and are all on the same plan." Emma Roberts added that she found the bungalows in Barrackpore "built and fitted up in a superior style." Thus, the bungalow became more than pedestrian housing; it became a site to re-affirm imperial status.[33]

As we have seen, the American military accommodation was not a network of "superior" government built housing. Frances Roe, whose husband was Second Lt. Fayette W. Roe of the Third Infantry, commented on the system when she found herself ranked out by the arrival of a captain at Camp Supply, Indian Territory. "Call it what one chooses, the experience was not pleasant," complained Roe. "Being turned out was bad enough in itself, but the manner in which it was done was humiliating in the extreme. We had only been in that house three weeks and had worked so hard . . . to make it at all comfortable." On vacating a garrison home, the responsibility for cleaning fell to the exiting inhabitants. Following Lt. Col. George Custer's court-martial in 1867, Capt. Albert Barnitz of the Seventh Cavalry and his wife took up occupancy of the old Custer quarters in Fort Leavenworth. Jennie Barnitz spitefully wrote to her mother, "I had two Negroes here one day cleaning. Mrs. Custer did not leave the house as clean as she might." This process of ranking out for married officers was uniquely American. Frequent changes in British and U.S. military orders, nevertheless, required constant moves for both groups of officers' wives.[34]

The difficulties of such relentless transfers can be viewed through the correspondence of the Barnitzes. Albert encouragingly remarked in a letter to his wife, Jennie, on 23 March 1867, from Fort Harker: "The officers' quarters are progressing finely, and they will be handsome indeed." Henry M. Stanley, the intrepid *New York Times* journalist, however, visited the military installation in April 1867 and remarked, "when I mention a fort, you need not imagine one of those formidable affairs as built in ancient times . . . but a simple square, surrounded by some wooden shanties . . . the fort appears . . . like a great wart on the surface of the plain." Mrs. Barnitz visited the post in June and due to flooding was forced to stay at the less than comfortable garrison. Invited to lodge with "Mrs. Dr. Sternberg [the wife of the Assistant Surgeon George M. Sternberg]," she wrote to her husband that the surgeon's spouse found herself "delightfully situated in new quarters—five spacious rooms—very handsomely furnished, silver and china for her table, excellent servants." Unfortunately, the other less well-connected officers' wives slept in army ambulances and took meals in the officers' mess. The Captain's expectations of "handsomeness," however, found fulfillment within six months. After a return visit to Fort Harker in November 1867 he informed his wife of the completion of ornamental buildings, fenced gardens, and a "tall white flag staff . . . and from its top floats the broad garrison flag." Within seven months Fort Harker had transformed from an embarrassing blot on the landscape, at least to this officer, to a magnificent imperial fortress.[35]

Dislocated from home, these women felt strongly attached to, and identified by, their association with the United States and British armies. Honoria Lawrence published an article in the 1845 *Calcutta Review* that aimed to help newly arrived British officers' wives adapt to their new imperial role. She detailed "the inconveniences which the wife of a Regimental Officer, when she first 'buckles on the knapsack,' must calculate on, and the hopeless, endless evils that beset women in the Barracks." Having gained her military audience, she advised, "A woman when she marries a soldier, ought to recollect that his profession entails on her a definite and often a very arduous duty. Not that she is to become that most offensive hybrid, a soldierly woman. She may easily lay aside all that is becoming and delicate in her own sex, but she cannot in exchange assume any masculine qualities higher than those of slang and indifference." Mrs. Lawrence continued, "Her highest glory and best praise are of another kind. She has to bear as best she may, the privations peculiar to her lot, and to watch against its natural fruits, irritability, frivolity, slovenliness, and procrastination."[36]

Similarly, recent arrival American Katherine Fougera announced her distinct role as an officer's wife and imperial ambassador. Immediately after Lieutenant Gibson made a proposal of marriage, conducted "beyond the outskirts of civilization . . . in a desert wilderness . . . surrounded, though at a distance, by hostiles of various tribes," Miss Fougera realized she "had signed up for a permanent enlistment with the Seventh Cavalry." Her arrival, speedy marriage, and cooption to imperial status caused her some concern. Unable to sleep that evening, she was joined by Elizabeth Custer, who "spoke seriously . . . of associating with uncongenial people. . . . [She] stressed . . . the lack of comforts . . . [and] dangers, real and imaginary." Custer continued, "'[W]e army women feel that we are privileged, because we are making history. . . . Yes, my dear, we are the pioneer army women, and we're proud of it.'" Fougera's marriage to Lt. Frank Gibson of the Seventh Cavalry followed shortly, and the new Mrs. Gibson gushed contentedly, "I gloried in the fact that now I was really one with the other army women, and our joys and sorrows would be mutual." Correspondingly, Martha Summerhayes immediately "fell in love with the army, with its brilliancy and its glitter, with its struggles and its romance." In her military marriage and travels in the U.S. West this outlook continued. She recalled, "A feeling of regimental prestige held officers and men together. I began to share that feeling." Despite the sentimentality, these writings clearly underscore an awareness of belonging to, and active membership in, the British and American armies. Thus, illustrating an identification with, and sharing of, the obligations of their husbands' imperial role.[37]

As we have seen, nineteenth-century British and American officers' wives under-took long, tedious, and occasionally perilous journeys to join their husbands on the outposts of empire. In comparing the Oriental and Occidental journeys of the two groups of women, it becomes apparent that they shared similar transnational experiences. They often traveled unescorted, and the wives' journals, letters, and memoirs spoke to a real sense of "going out of the world." Most offered intimate reasons for uniting with their husbands, coupled with a reluctance to leave the familiarity of all things "home." Whether traveling by ship or stagecoach, most attempted to ameliorate a sense of dislocation by declaring an overstated attachment to, and pride of, symbols of nationalism, such as Harriette Ashmore underscoring the "imposing sight" of the British Union Jack. The Americans Mesdames Fougera and Alexander, however, illustrated the journey as a space to reconfigure gender norms. They tested new, imperial liberties—the former imbibed a "skinful," while the latter resorted to carrying a pistol. On arrival, the British women sought environmental familiarity by overlaying memories of home. Both groups defined themselves against the indigenous other, by reinforc-ing perceived Anglo superiority in malicious racial censure. Descriptions such as "shocking," "slothful," and "spooky," applied to western places and peoples, pepper the narratives. To ameliorate a sense of dislocation and isolation, these women created a new social reality by crafting a superior identity forged through military commitment, loyalty, and imperial duty—as agents of empire.[38]

The transnational spaces of the journey and arrival at the destination of the British and American officers' wives hold notable similarities. Both sets of women transported an aggrandized collective memory that increased a sense of national belonging, while exaggerating prejudicial attitudes toward the indigenous other. After arrival, however, the nascent beginnings of a new social reality crystallized into a distinct representation of empire, through feminizing the military world of imperial men.

4

Imperial Women

Military Adjuncts, Station Sisterhoods, and Senior Ladies

> If there is a woman whom one might delight to honor above all others it is the 'Army woman.' Her name could well be written on brass, high among the few exalted. For her position is unique among the sisters of men . . . [yet] she is part and parcel of an organization that officially ignores her.
>
> —*Army and Navy Journal, 1893*

After the weeks and months of travelling to join their military men on the outposts of empire, the officers' wives realized that they too, held a pivotal role in furthering imperial ambitions. Indeed, "It seemed very strange to me," puzzled Elizabeth Custer, "that with all the value that is set on the presence of the women of an officer's family at the frontier posts, the book of army regulations makes no provision for them, but in fact ignores them entirely!" She bemoaned, "It enters into such minute detail in its instructions, even giving the number of hours that bean soup should boil, that it would be natural to suppose that a paragraph or two might be wasted on an officer's wife!" Indeed, the nineteenth-century American army regulations afforded no provision whatsoever for the well-being of its officers' wives. Mrs. Custer further complained that "the servants and the company laundresses are mentioned as being entitled to quarters and rations." That "[t]he officers used sportively to look up the rules in the army regulations for camp followers, and read them out to us as they would the riot act!" only added insult to injury. She woefully continued, "In the event of any question being raised regarding our privileges. . . . If we put down an emphatic foot, declaring that we were going to take some decisive step . . . we would be at once reminded, in a laughingly exultant manner, of the provision of the law. . . . Nevertheless, though army women have no visible thrones or sceptres, nor any acknowledged rights according to military law, I never knew such queens as they, or saw more willing subjects than they govern."[1]

With no claim to official military status, the women who joined their husbands nonetheless played a central role in designing and maintaining imperial formations. In responding to their tenuous positions held at outposts, officers' wives manipulated formal and informal military practices to construct an elite and empowered female identity. In so doing, they disregarded accepted gender boundaries to occupy influential spaces in the male world of their officer husbands. By connecting to British and American army practices, they created a new social and class reality that sustained imperialism. Some adopted military titles, language, and dress, but more significantly, they identified themselves in terms of their husbands' ranks. By feminizing military markers, they generated a female hierarchy that also served as an imperial sisterhood, duty-bound to serve, and controlled by an influential and authoritative senior wife.

Female imperial empowerment developed from what appears to be an extremely weak position. Even before uttering the marriage vows, potential brides were subjected to an informal evaluation process conducted both by military bridegrooms-elect and their peers. The officers' views of a suitable partner indicate that as members of the army they selected wives with an eye to reflecting military rank, enhancing reputation, and transmitting imperial prestige. In British India, as John Morris, an early twentieth-century Indian Army officer, recalled, his colonel vetted all prospective regimental wives. Additionally, as Morris explained, "It was desirable that anybody coming into it [the regiment] should fit in." Echoing this idea, Kenneth Warren recalled that "an unfortunate senior subaltern was greeted . . . about twenty times a day, 'Sam, you're not going to marry that girl'—and Sam didn't marry that girl. The regiment was just making it quite clear that *that* girl was not going to come into the circle." Indeed, in Lansdowne station, the colonel's wife controlled the harmony and prestige of the company by acting as a one-woman marriage bureau. As Morris reported, "We had the most superb example of a memsahib you could find anywhere in India . . . [a] sort of super-colonel of the regiment. Nothing was done without reference to her and she provided . . . many wives for various officers . . . nobody would have been so bold as to get married without asking Mrs Fizzer's permission or advice about the suitability of the proposed bride."[2]

Once selected, approved, and married, some new wives revealed that they had committed themselves to a military man out of a sense of duty rather than on more romantic grounds. In 1902, Christian Stirling travelled to India with her uncle (General Alfred Craigie) and Aunt Alice. Within seven months, she met and married Major Herbert Showers. "Though not in the least 'in love' with him," she "thought it was . . . [her] duty to marry him." Her personal memoir written in 1960 reminisced, "To this day, I don't know if I did right or wrong." Similarly, Ellen Drummond's letters pitifully sought her sister's approval of her marriage partner, the Honourable James Drummond, Tenth Viscount of Strathallan and commander of the Seventh Hussars. Her groom she described as "neither dark nor fair, with brown whiskers and a lighter moustache, blue eyes and rather tall, thin, not good looking by any means." Although she did not indicate a duty to marry, she later revealed, "I am glad to see Papa getting fond of Jim because I certainly did not like him when we were first engaged."[3]

This less than loving relationship in British India would have been approved by Emma Roberts, who noted, "It is an amusing thing for a spectator to observe the straight-forward, business-like manner in which marriages in India are brought about . . . the expediency of short courtships, seems to prevail . . . and if there should be nothing very objectionable in the suitor, the marriage takes place." The self-appointed relationship counselor instructed the bride-to-be "that it is safest to begin with a little aversion . . . gratitude and esteem are admirable substitutes for love." She concluded, "It is rarely that a wife leaves the protection of her husband, and in the instances that have occurred, it is generally observed that the lady had made a love-match." Despite an emphasis on the ideals of romantic love during the Victorian era in England and America, it appears that "business" may have trumped love in establishing imperial partnerships, and that "aversion" constituted a positive sign of future success. Indeed, Miss Roberts's final flourish encouraged such "marriages of convenience," as "in nine cases out of ten, [they] turn out very happily."[4]

The British army set imperial standards, albeit informally among the officers, for prospective wives, and enforced these requirements with vigor. *The Queen's Regulations*, however, regulated the marriages of enlisted men, who needed their commanding officer's permission before entering into wedded bliss. This ruling advised, "It is incumbent on the Commanding Officers of Regiments, who have ample experience of the very great inconvenience arising to the Service, and to the Public, from the improvident and injudicious Marriage of Soldiers, to discountenance such connexions [*sic*]." The order continued that said officer should "explain to the Men that their comforts, as Soldiers, are in a very small degree increased by their Marriage, while the inconvenience and distress naturally accruing to them from such connexion are serious and unavoidable, particularly when Regiments are ordered to embark for Foreign Service." The young officers, while officially not prohibited from marrying, were generally discouraged from so doing. Regiments, apparently, had their own unwritten codes of conduct to which each man strictly adhered. At least one such unit, according to Byron Farwell, insisted upon a new ensign signing a legal contract that promised, should he marry before reaching a certain rank, a large sum of money would be forfeited to the mess. This practice endorsed the military adage—"subalterns must not marry; captains may marry; majors should marry; and colonels must marry." Yet, in restricting marriage of the lower ranks it clearly implied the importance attached to the role of a high-ranking officer's partner.[5]

Indeed, in the nineteenth century marriage below the rank of major was unusual, and marriage allowances were not provided until an officer reached the age of thirty. Should an ensign fail to abide by the informal yet ironclad practice and marry without his superior's consent, social consequences would be enforced against the newlyweds. One military spouse reported that the "commanding officer of the man's regiment would detail his wife to advise the regimental wives not to show any signs of friendliness to the bride who was considered to have caused her husband to disgrace his regiment." The severe ostracizing, in some cases, pressured the disobedient officer to apply for a transfer or resign. The importance of making a suitable choice of a wife who could further the aims of empire was articulated by the narrator in Rudyard Kipling's *Kidnapped*, who claimed, "We are a high-caste and enlightened race . . . [but] the Hindu notion . . . of arranging marriages . . . is sound. . . . [The] Government should establish a Matrimonial Department, efficiently officered, with a Jury of Matrons, a Judge of the Chief Court, a Senior Chaplain, and an Awful Warning, in the shape of a love-match that has gone wrong, chained to trees in the courtyard." He concluded that "marriage in India does not concern the individual but the Government he serves."[6]

Despite the sentimentality of mainstream ideals of love, at least two military wives admitted that they had married out of a sense of duty. Some wives undoubtedly ignored their husbands' professional commitments, yet many officers' wives, as Mary Procida argues, "took an active and intelligent interest in the work of the empire and served as their husbands' primary advisors and assistants." They held roles that required them to participate in imperial business by "touring the countryside, meeting the Indian people, and contributing to imperial decision making.... The professional partnership between husband and wife often blurred visible distinctions between the imperial official and his spouse, effectively erasing the line between private femininity and a public masculinity.... The subtle message conveyed to the Indians, however, was that husband and wife were equal partners in the business of empire." Within these carefully selected and accepted partnerships the gender negotiations revolved, not exclusively around home and family, but around a couple's duty to the empire.[7]

In the U.S. West, senior officers, like the British commanders, guided the amorous affairs of their juniors. In 1855, Lt. Col. Robert E. Lee cautioned the young Lt. John B. Hood, "Never marry unless you can do so into a family which will enable your children to feel proud of both sides of the house." This paternal advice was sensible. A wrong choice could wreak havoc in a young officer's life, as demonstrated by the flurry of correspondence in 1875 between the commander-in-chief of the Army, William T. Sherman, and Maj. Gen. Edward O. C. Ord. The subject of concern was a Lt. William Tiffany of the Tenth Cavalry, who, while conducting new recruits to Texas, quickly "became enamoured of" and married an army widow, a Mrs. Wallingford. All, however, was not what it seemed. Tiffany's father, a Methodist pastor, wrote to Sherman pleading for him to intervene and effect a prompt divorce. The commander's subsequent letter to Ord revealed that the new bride "was no widow at all—but a bold presumptuous woman . . . [who] had roped in this youngster." The reverend further requested that his son be placed where the new Mrs. Tiffany "cannot reach him in person or by letter." Sherman supported the father's plea, as according to Col. Samuel Sturgis, this very same woman was responsible for the court-martial of her previous husband, the still living (but dismissed from service) Lt. David Wallingford. The official proceedings described Mrs. Wallingford as "a notorious prostitute and lewd woman." Adding further interest, Sherman admitted to Ord that he had seen Mrs. Wallingford/Tiffany "once" in his "office," and she held his card and a personal letter from him. He, however, vehemently denied imputations of intimacy with "how she got them [card and letter] I do not know for I know her not." He ends his missive in full support of ending the marriage to "save" Tiffany "from the horrible and inevitable fate that must result." The official correspondence, unfortunately, does not make further reference to this tawdry affair. The very fact that it reached the highest echelons, nonetheless, confirms that the class and character of an officer's wife held great importance in upholding the prestige of the imperial service.[8]

Adding to the debate, Assistant Surgeon Rodney Glisan further elaborated on the importance of avoiding the charms of such bold and presumptuous women. "Officers . . . do not commonly seek to mate with mere ball-room belles," he opined, "but select women for their social, intellectual, and moral accomplishments." The surgeon lamented, however, that, "After one has been for a long time thus deprived of ladies' society, he [an officer] loses all power of just comparison of the relative charms of women, and, in some cases, falls in love with females altogether beneath him in social position." He continued, "when an officer thus circumstanced becomes married to an inferior person, as is sometimes the case, he commits an offence toward army society that is rarely forgiven; for the social code of ethics in garrison life is, that, as all commissioned officers and their families are really but one military brotherhood, no member of the coterie has any right to thrust upon them any uncongenial companion." Glisan then supported his claim by noting, "A highly accomplished young Lieutenant of my acquaintance . . . fell in love with and married an unpolished beauty against the protests of his most intimate friends. When he found that it was impossible for his bride to maintain her position in the society of the garrison . . . he finally concluded to send her east to receive an education and social polish." Clearly the uneducated western beauty did not meet the imperial class requirement for "social, intellectual, and moral accomplishments."[9]

Despite the military requirement for "social polish," an officer's wife was expected to exhibit a certain intrepid spirit that belied the traditional feminine role. Frances Roe offered several telling examples of how she viewed her imperial duty. Writing from Camp Supply, Indian Territory, in January 1873, she understood her female role in the West as greater than that in the East. She complained of the primitive conditions of the housing and noted her dislike of the "country itself." Her discomfort, however, reminded her that "at dreadful places like this is where the plucky army wife is most needed. Her very presence has often a refining and restraining influence over the entire garrison, from the commanding officer down to the last recruit." Leisure activities, such as regular horseback-riding, provided occasions for a woman's mettle to be tested. She recalled, "My ride with Lieutenant Golden . . . this morning was very exciting for a time. We started directly after stable call, which is at six o'clock. . . . I rode a troop horse that had never been ridden by a woman before." The ride proved to be a fearful experience, and after returning to the stables Golden suggested that she choose a less headstrong mount. Horrified at the thought of exhibiting such weakness, Mrs. Roe exclaimed, "Dismount before Lieutenant Golden, a cavalry officer and Faye's classmate, and all those staring troopers—I, the wife of an infantry officer? Never!" Gentility and background, tempered with a bold pluckiness that defied the traditional delicacy of nineteenth-century womanhood, were the requirements for an ideal imperial attaché.[10]

This oxymoronic ideal of rugged femininity may have provided a basic prerequisite for an officer's bride, but great care was also exercised to select a spouse who would uphold the respectability, honor, and prestige of the regiment. Generally, British officers' wives, as Lady Elizabeth Vere, the wife of Lord Birdwood, a lieutenant colonel of King Edward VII's Own Lancers (Probyn's Horse), pointed out, were from the "upper middle class. . . . It was very homogenous in the sense that nearly everyone in official India sprang from precisely the same educational and cultural background." Despite Lady Birdwood's assertion of a uniform imperial class, Florence Marryat resolved that "snobbism" provided an intolerable "evil" in British India. She warmed to her subject with the following vignette: "One day two officers and their wives were dining with my husband and myself. The husband most advanced in years and highest in rank had the youngest wife; the other lady being a much older woman. . . . My husband thought it best to waive the subject of their relative position in the army, and took the senior lady in to dinner." This social faux pas resulted in the arrival of "a long epistle from the affronted husband of the lady who *ought* to have gone in first, reminding him of the oversight of which he had been guilty, and begging that it might not happen again. Will people in England believe that intimate friends could find a subject of quarrel in such trivial nonsense?" Yet, while women such as Mrs. Marryat might grumble, rank, cemented by a rigid order of precedence, scaffolded the social hierarchy in British India.[11]

This "trivial nonsense" was not evident in the U.S. West. Yet a social uniformity existed that mirrored the British model, as most American wives hailed from middle-class Eastern families. Historians offer various explanations of women's roles in military communities. All confirm that women found substance and direction through their husbands' occupations, thus sharing nationalistic aims and ambitions. Elizabeth Custer underlined this sense of duty. She maintained, "As I look back upon our life, I do not believe there ever was any path so difficult as those men on the frontier trod. Their failures, their fights, their vacillations, all were before us. . . . You could not separate yourself from the interests of one another. It was a network of friendships that became more and more interwoven by common hardships, deprivations, dangers, by isolation and the daily sharing of joys and troubles."[12]

Marriage, duty, and class provided the foundations upon which officers' wives understood themselves to be qualified as imperial agents. Further female commitment to national objectives included the feminization of military titles, language, and uniforms. Addressing a wife by her husband's military rank became a common practice amongst both the British and American army communities. In India, Frances Parkes referred to her companion as "Mrs. Colonel W," and Emily Eden identified a fellow diner as "Mrs. Colonel ——," while Mary Sherwood titled all army wives with military honorifics such as "Mrs. Colonel Carr" and "Mrs. Sergeant Strachan." The adoption of such practices also occurred in the U.S. West. Marion Brown, the daughter of Maj. John H. Brown, regularly sent letters to her parents from Fort Sill. She referred to the commanding officer's wife as Mrs. Colonel Pearson and addressed other wives as Mrs. Captain Custer and Mrs. Captain Johnston. Similarly, in Alice Baldwin's published account, a caption accompanied a photograph of "General U. S. Grant and Party" taken at Fort Sanders in 1867, which identified the officers' wives as "Mrs. Gen. Potter . . . [and] Mrs. Gen. John Gibbon." Additionally, letters received by Elizabeth Custer were addressed to "Mrs. General Custer," and the soldiers of the Seventh Cavalry frequently called her "Mrs. Major-General George Armstrong Custer," her husband's brevet rank. These women, stationed in British India and the U.S. West, clearly determined their identity and status as concomitant with their husbands' rank.[13]

Living within the confines of the military world, officers' wives clearly understood themselves as belonging to, as well as representing, the nation. This new social reality reflected society at home, yet became adapted to the imperial environment. In identifying the difference Helen MacKenzie declared, "The average amount of talent appears to me decidedly above that of English society at home. . . . A military man [in India] . . . has often acted as quartermaster . . . been sole magistrate of a large cantonment . . . acted as postmaster, paymaster, brigade-major, and commissariat-officer, or has commanded a regiment in action . . . [and] acted as political assistant, made treaties with hostile tribes, settled questions of revenue or tribute." Unfortunately, she did not proffer such a glamorous review of their wives. Mrs. MacKenzie ruminated, "But if the gentlemen in India are above the home average, the ladies are certainly below it." The young wives, often marrying in their teens, missed the "best part of a girl's training—the advantage of intercourse with really good society." Thus, Mrs. Mackenzie concluded, they lacked "manners or taste" by adopting "the strangest phraseology from their husbands and their husbands' friends. It is common to hear ladies speaking not only of their husbands by their surnames (a thing unpardonable, except of a peer), but of other gentlemen in the same manner; talking of 'our kit,' and using such terms as 'jolly,' 'pluck,' 'a cool thing,' 'lots,' 'rows,' and 'no end of things!'" The construction of an imperial lexicon, although indicative of a distinct reality, shaped by wives, failed to impress this colonel's wife.[14]

The American officers' spouses understood their circumstances to be equally changed and, in accord with the British women, feminized imperial terms. On 30 April 1866, the day of her marriage to 1st Lt. Andrew Canfield of the Fifth Iowa Infantry, Sarah Canfield "opened a new chapter" in her personal diary to "begin a new life." She quickly adapted by embracing military obligations. While travelling by steamboat to join her husband stationed at Fort Berthold, she dined at the captain's table along with other officers' wives. After a stop in Sioux City, where the ladies purchased gingham for sunbonnets, she mentioned, "the ladies having previously held a *council of war* (we belong to the Army now and use military terms) and decided if we wanted to stay out on deck much we must have them." Protection from the sun obviously gave cause for concern, yet a graver reason for a ladies' meeting occurred twelve months later. While stationed at Camp Cooke, Montana Territory, Mrs. Canfield noted that "we have great excitement to-day . . . [as] Indians in great numbers . . . painted and mounted for war" approached the fort. She continued, "When we ladies saw what might happen we held a 'council of war' and decided that if the fort could not be held that we preferred to be shot by our own officers rather than to be taken captive. The officers promised to do so before surrendering." The feminization of military terms indicates a clear sense of belonging to the army. These women created committees that not only decided on protective headgear, but also on matters of life and death.[15]

In addition to employing military nomenclature and jargon, some of the American officers' wives identified with their roles in an extreme manner. Using their bodies as imperial symbols, Frances Roe, Mollie McIntosh, and Elizabeth Custer all donned military uniforms, complete with gold buttons, forage caps, gloves, and riding crops. Their dark dresses appeared to be tailor-made from worsted serge, the white leather gloves custom fitted for a smaller hand, and the caps bearing the crossed sword insignia of the Cavalry, perhaps purchased from the commissary store. Admittedly, dressing as representatives of empire may have been undertaken for a single photographic sitting. These women, nonetheless, ordered and paid for faux uniforms, modified from a trouser to a skirt suit to celebrate their roles as imperial attachés. British officers' wives did not adapt their husbands' uniforms for female wear. They did, however, express a clear sense of belonging to the military world. Margaret, the wife of Captain Simon F. Hannay of the Fortieth Bengal Native Infantry Regiment, provided an example of a sentiment that appeared repeatedly in the women's private and published writings. In a journal written for her mother, describing the regimental march from Mysopoorie to Mhow in 1829, Mrs. Hannay remarked, "I enjoy a march so much that I must have been cut out for an officer's wife." All women, whether they donned forage caps, or simply marched with the regiment, feminized the masculine world of their military husbands, to design an inclusive imperial reality.[16]

Textual symbols of language and attire signaled an imperial attachment, yet central to an officer's wife's identification was her husband's rank. To retain this status, women refashioned a transnational gender model. The terms "lady" and "woman" in both British and American circles indicated social distance between an upper-class or upper-middle-class female and the lower social levels. In the militarized community, however, the titles became adapted for use in the imperial community. A lady signified a wife of an officer, while a "woman" indicated the partner of a soldier, a laundress, or a domestic servant. Indeed, a female from the lower classes who married an officer received only partial acceptance as a "half-way" lady. During the British retreat from Kabul, Afghanistan, to Jalalabad in 1841–42, Lady Florentia, the wife of Major-General Sir Robert H. Sale, kept a daily journal with a view to publication. Here, the rigid divide between the commissioned and enlisted men's wives becomes clear. While imprisoned by Mohammed Shah Khan, she recalled, "We number nine ladies, twenty gentlemen, and fourteen children. . . . seventeen European soldiers, two European women, and one child (Mrs. Wade, Mrs. Burnes [both sergeant's wives], and little Stoker)." Assistant Surgeon Glisan illustrated this divide in America by advising that a "Mrs. Captain Gardiner" was the "only officer's lady" posted at Fort Wood, and Mrs. Captain Marcy, stationed at Camp Arbuckle, Indian Territory, gained much admiration as a "jewel of a lady." Yet, he warned, "There is a sharp line of demarcation drawn between all commissioned and non-commissioned officers. The latter may associate with the men or private soldiers, but never with the former.

The wives of the private soldiers and non-commissioned officers are denominated camp-women. There is a limited number of them allowed to each company."[17]

The application of the terms "lady" or "woman" to differentiate between wives of officers and wives of noncommissioned men occurred in both British India and the U.S. West. Madeleine Churcher gave an additional example of this rigid class divide in the British Empire. Recording daily events in a handwritten scrapbook, she described life with her husband, Captain Douglas W. Churcher, of the Eighty-Seventh Royal Irish Fusiliers. In underscoring the officers' wives' perception of their imperial class standing, an entry concerning a train journey to her husband's station at Bareilly, India, provided a telling vignette. Churcher sat in the "ladies compartment which I had to myself . . . till some second class woman tried her utmost . . . to get in, but 'D' got the guard to prevent her." In the U.S. West Elizabeth Custer similarly delineated the differences between the officers' ladies and soldiers' women. She described an enlisted men's ball, to which the commissioned men and wives received a special invitation. She unkindly recorded, "[T]he general [George Custer] was on nettles for fear we would be wanting in tact, and show our amusement by laughing at the costumes of the women . . . the toilets of these women were something marvelous in construction . . . in low neck and short sleeves their . . . well developed figures wheeled around the barracks all night long." Often complaining of loneliness, the officers' spouses could have extended friendship to all women at the isolated garrisons. Yet the class-conscious need to identify themselves as respectable, socially elevated wives overruled any such inclinations. By feminizing the military ranking system, these women found a perfect foil in the soldiers' wives, against whom they could construct an imperial hierarchy, positioning themselves at its apex.[18]

Acceptance in this upper social echelon of "ladies" required the British officer's wife to display and maintain a genteel decorum. In a letter written to her father in 1855, Frances, the wife of Captain Walter Wells of the Irregular Sikh Corps, stationed in Barrackpore, delineated the positive and negative attributes of an ideal officer's wife. She posited, "The letters we received at Shergotty brought us intelligence of Ellen Wells's engagement to Captain Shewell an officer of the Bombay Army. . . . I hear Captain S. is a very nice young man. . . . [A]t present [he] has merely his Captain's pay but she will make an excellent wife as I believe her to be not only a well principled girl but a capital manager." Not all officers' wives, however, received approval in such fulsome terms. Prior to a regimental march in 1854, Mrs. Wells received Mr. Dashwood (an ensign), who had recently married, though she had yet to meet his wife. She told her father that the groom was "such a coarse vulgar sort of man, smelling so dreadfully of smoke! I am sure if his wife is in his style she will be no addition to our society." Captain S. and his well-principled bride found acceptance into the imperial circle, but the habits of the vulgar smoker marked the Dashwood couple unsuitable.[19]

Florence Marryat, whose husband belonged to the Madras Army, revealed the class division between the Queen's and Native Armies. She recounted that "[o] ne of these newly-made ladies was asked at Bangalore whether she knew Mrs. So-and-So, whose husband belonged to the (supposed) inferior army. 'Oh, dear, no,' was the emphatic reply. 'I never call upon *Hen Hi Hofficers* wives.' And I am sure the Hen Hi Hofficers' wives ought to have been greatly obliged to her for the omission." Mrs. Marryat concluded her diatribe with: "There is an immense deal of party spirit in India . . . but there is also a great amount of tuft-hunting, which is less excusable, and far more vulgar, and which takes the form in so military a country, of worship of rank. . . . I have met with more than one instance where women have been so thoroughly imbued with this lowest of ideas, that they thought the standing of their husbands in the service entitled them to interfere in the private affairs of people not only better born and bred than themselves, but infinitely more capable of knowing what was the right thing to do." Thus, the imperial social reality constructed in British India by the officers' wives differed from the class system in England. Background and behavior played a pivotal role in determining inclusion, but even those "better born and bred' were usurped by the "worship of [military] rank."[20]

Rivalry may have provided an inter-army divide, but even within the supposed elite British Army, wives categorized one another. For example, Mary Sherwood described her female social companions as "on the whole respectable, but exceed- ingly different one from another, and with the exception of the Colonel's lady, by no means the kind of people with whom I could be intimate." She continued, "Mrs. C. was of a good family in Ireland, and could be extremely pleasing, but she could also be as vulgar. . . . What Mrs. E. had been I know not, but I suppose something very low. . . . Of Mrs. M., the assistant surgeon's wife, who was from Glasgow . . . her character was singular, and sometimes, I fancy, slightly deranged."[21]

The American Eveline, the wife of Bvt. Col. Andrew J. Alexander, echoed Sherwood's social evaluations. In illustrating the arrogant class division existing at Fort Smith in 1866, she decided, "The 'womankind' in this regiment are rather a queer set. Mrs. C. was a company washerwoman before her husband was promoted from the ranks. Mrs. K. and her daughter are very common. Mrs. H. and "Patrita" are Mexicans. . . . Mrs. Sutoris . . . not highly educated, but well behaved, and I like her." Both women alluded to military rank in determining a wife's acceptability, the colonel's wife being deemed eminently suitable for an intimate friendship, while Mrs. C, whose husband received promotion through the ranks, was not. Additionally, both inappropriate behavior and background could disqualify a woman from the imperial circle. The "deranged" Scottish assistant surgeon's wife clearly failed to meet the admission criteria, while one can only hope that the "well-behaved" Mrs. Sutoris, despite her husband's noncommissioned rank, received some acceptance in the Fort Smith officers' imperial cohort.[22]

As exemplified in Mrs. Alexander's "Mrs. C," the wife of a soldier who gained a commissioned promotion in the field received, at best, tolerance rather than acceptance by the officers' spouses. Annegret Ogden concluded that a military wife most clearly illustrated the dependency of a woman on her husband for definition of her own role. The class divisions between officers' wives and enlisted men's partners appeared inflexible. The spouse of a commander "presided over her frontier court" while the humble soldier's partner was relegated to the washtub on "Suds Row." Indeed, Assistant Surgeon Rodney Glisan confirmed this social divide in his personal reminiscences. "The black sheep in military society," he declared, "are the officers and their families who have been promoted from the ranks. Their generally unrefined, uncultivated and uncongenial manners make them unwelcome members of the army circle." In short, wives lived highly regulated lives observing codes of conduct appropriate to their partner's rank. Social custom prevented fraternization across the uncompromising system that separated the officers and soldiers' wives. Thus, even within the new social reality redesigned class divisions held firm.[23]

With the class structure generally enforced at the officer level, Elizabeth Custer recorded a bottom-up example. She gossiped, "One of the Irish laundresses at a Western post was evidently infatuated with army life, as she was the widow of a volunteer officer—doubtless some old soldier . . . who held a commission in one of the regiments during the war—and the woman drew the pension of a major's widow." Custer continued, "Money, therefore, could not have been the inducement that brought her back to a frontier post. At one time, she left her fascinating clothesline and sought domestic employment." She succeeded in finding a position with an officer's family stationed at Fort Riley. All did not go smoothly, as Mrs. Custer pointed out: "It seems that this officer's wife also had been a laundress at one time, and the woman applying for work squared herself off in an independent manner, placed her arms akimbo, and announced her platform: 'I ken work for a leddy [sic], but I can't go there; there was a time when Mrs. and I had our toobs [sic] side by side." Even though excluded from the officer's social clique, the widowed brevet major's wife supported the dictates of the class hierarchy. Her insistence on working for a lady demonstrates an understanding of, and adherence to, the rigid class divisions of the western community.[24]

The unladylike behavior of the American enlisted men's wives assured their exclusion from the imperial coterie, and relegation to the lower echelon of the manufactured class structure. The childhood memories of Mary Leefe Laurence offer insights into the coarse character of the laundresses at Ringgold Barracks, Texas. She recalled a "famous fight" between two soldiers' wives that took place over the fence in "Laundress Row." The quarrel between Mrs. Mary Gazelle and Mrs. Norah Truan "terminated in a fight with brooms and mud swept up from puddles . . . to the accompaniment of encouraging shouts from bystanders to 'Go it, Mary!' and 'Give it to her, Norah!'" To end the dispute, a couple of soldiers dragged the pugnacious Mrs. Gazelle from her mud-splattered opponent, Mrs. Truan. Regular outbreaks of such unladylike behavior also occurred at Fort Abraham Lincoln. In 1873 Elizabeth Custer noted, "They [washerwomen] had many pugilists among them, and the least infringement of their rights provoked a battle in which wood and other missiles filled the air. Bandaged and bruised, they brought their wrongs to our house, where both sides had a hearing. The general has occasionally to listen and arbitrate between husband and wife, when the laundress and her soldier husband could not agree." Lack of decorum and the frequent resort to public bickering and belligerence further legitimized the exclusion of such women from the imperial circle of ladies.[25]

To maintain an imperial class in British India, wives of sergeants could similarly be excluded on the grounds of unladylike behavior. Emma, who married William Wonnacott, a teacher assigned to the Eighth King's Regiment stationed in Nusserabad, India, wrote often to her parents. Although not an officer's wife, her personal letters described military life in a way that offers insights from an outsider's point of view. Particularly telling is her description of the station females: "There are a few, and only a few nice women in the regiment. Not one I would like to make a friend of. They are very illiterate and illbred [sic] and very fond of fighting and drinking which leads to worse." A letter received from her friend Mrs. E. Swain, stationed in Mhow, helpfully delineates the divide between "women" and "ladies." Swain wrote, "We are all quite well and very comfortable. . . . I met a great deal of kindness from the ladies here . . . and have found many good friends among them." While Mrs. Wonnacott found the soldiers' wives in Nusserabad unacceptable company, Mrs. Swain confidently enjoyed the company of like females at the Mhow station.[26]

Officers' wives who met the imperial class criteria in British India and the U.S. West faced new and challenging worlds. As a coping mechanism, and reflecting an understanding of a real commitment to imperial aims, these women created a distinct military sisterhood. In examining nineteenth-century female relationships, historian Nancy Cott argues that such discrete female groups developed, but the "bonds of womanhood" held a double meaning, the forging of all-women kin groups, and as a mechanism to sustain service and obedience to men. "The canon of domesticity made motherhood a social and political role that also defined women as a class," observes Cott, "and became the prism through which all expectations of, and prescriptions for, women were refracted." Women gained vital "identity and purpose" in unifying peer friendships. The female-female friendships among officers' wives fully support Cott's model. With no established civil institutions these women connected through exclusive all-female networks. Collective activities offered an avenue to forge bonds of friendship, encouraged the formation of support mechanisms, and promulgated a sense of duty to the nation.[27]

Mrs. Clemons's published memoirs offer an insight into the operation of this female coterie in British India. She explained that "there are seldom more than four or five officers in a regiment who are married. Your only society while in a single station will be entirely at their houses. The ladies in India, for the most part, are not of a domestic turn, so that visitors are always acceptable, and constant callers expected . . . you will be sure to meet with numerous kindnesses from them . . . and . . . feel as if among your sisters." The scarcity of companionship, as well as disorientation and loneliness, contributed to the fashioning of a military sisterhood. Indeed, Clemons further advocated establishing intra-regimental friendships and to abandon the need for chaperoned visiting. With regard to establishing friendships with European civilians, she warned, "officers do not visit any of the tradespeople [sic], however respectable or rich they may be; and . . . are not allowed to be intimate with [them], I mean in the way of receiving and paying them visits in a friendly manner." In forming kin networks within individual regiments, officers' wives created a discrete sisterhood that supported their husbands' profession, and shared the tensions of imperial duties.[28]

In recognizing the stress of living at isolated outposts, with petty jealousies and altercations, military spouses understood their responsibility to maintain a respectable and serene imperial façade. Helen MacKenzie proudly described a cooperative atmosphere within the First Native Infantry stationed at Lahore. She recorded, "I and the other ladies of the Sikh ka Pultan (Sikh Regiment) have been flattered at the surprise we have excited by never quarrelling. Colonel H., who commands the station, periodically exclaims, 'five ladies and four gentlemen, and no quarrels yet!!'" Bessie Fenton, however, found the society at the "gay station" of Dinapore her "greatest grief," as she was duty bound to "go out and visit among these censorious people." After being informed that she "could not remain incognito to the ladies," she reluctantly decided to accept visitors. To her surprise, she received approval from the regimental sisterhood stationed at Dinapore. Her husband, Captain Neil Fenton, reported that "it had been rumoured that you were a blue stocking of deep tinge; by others, that you were very reserved and eccentric; but the whole party voted you a pretty little person, and very ladylike and agreeable." Despite the bickering and gossip that occurs within all social clusters, the sisterhood in British India functioned to present, at least, a united and tranquil public imperial face.[29]

The female coterie, however, did not operate simply to create serene kin networks. These women held a duty to act as ambassadors of empire. In 1855 Florence Marryat recorded a *levée* thrown by a "Mrs. A" to honor a visit to Bangalore by the commander-in-chief of Madras. Mrs. Marryat, unwell at the time, informed another officer's wife that she did not intend to be present at the celebration. Apparently, her friend retorted, "Not going to attend the *levée!* Why, it is your *duty* to go." Responding to the outraged woman, Mrs. Marryat "told her that I could not view the matter exactly in that light, considering it was only the invitation of one lady to another, and that I was not under the orders of Mrs. A, as my husband was under those of the Commander-in-Chief." The conversation continued, "'No,' she [the friend] replied . . . although evidently shocked at my audacity in coupling the names of Mrs. A and myself together; 'of course not, but you will allow that she is the *rankest* lady in Madras and therefore I think we are all bound to show her respect.'" This vignette demonstrates a real understanding of the duty these women sensed, and the female policing of behaviors. Mrs. Marryat's defiant refusal to attend the event hosted by the "rankest lady" would have exposed the couple to social and professional reprisals. Perhaps, as she claims, her husband's obligations lay with the commander-in-chief. Thus, the couple could politely refuse and allow the rigid code of imperial sociability to remain undisturbed.[30]

Suitable employment for these imperial ladies included the all-female sewing bee. Few British wives, however, embroidered together but simply engaged *dirzees* to create gowns from patterns advertised in English magazines. Indeed, Emma Roberts observed, "It has been before remarked, that there is little scope for feminine industry in our eastern possessions. Charity bazaars, which put so many fair fingers into motion in Europe, are almost unknown out of Calcutta. . . . The climate in India is unfortunately adverse to needle-work, or any work whose beauty may be endangered by hands which cannot be kept at a proper temperature." She concluded, "Thus, it appears that there are many temptations to idleness and few incitements to industry; and in nine cases out of ten, where the ladies of a station only meet upon ceremonious occasions, all the work, both useful and ornamental, will devolve upon the native tailor employed in the household."[31]

This popular female ritual in the U.S. West, however, provided an opportunity for more than just needlework. Katherine Fougera, and other officers' wives, marched with the Seventh Cavalry from Fort Abraham Lincoln to Fort Rice in the spring of 1875. Fougera, Elizabeth Custer, Maggie Calhoun, and Charlotte Moylan met each morning to indulge "in an orgy of military gossip." Fougera devoted a whole chapter of her published memoir to this women-only gathering to reveal female viewpoints of imperial matters. The ladies deliberated over the battle prowess of individual officers during the Battle of Washita, the difficulties of policing the "restless South," and the "activities of the Ku Klux Klan." Miss Fougera, as the soon-to-be wife of Lt. Frank Gibson, enthused "how we enjoyed these impromptu sewing bees. . . . I would sit at the feet of these new friends and drink in thirstily their tales of the unfolding West." At the isolated posts, these women feminized military rank to construct an exclusive female cohort of "sisters."[32]

Both regimental sisterhoods enjoyed leisure activities, but they also held imperial responsibilities. Ellen Biddle provided an example of this cooperative female duty. She wrote, "During the reconstruction, General [Horace] Porter and General [Orville] Babcock, two distinguished officers of General Grant's staff, came on a visit of inspection to Jackson. . . . [W]e arranged a dinner for them by borrowing from the ladies in the garrison enough silver, glass and china. . . . Most of the officers on duty there were invited. . . . I was the only lady present as the scarcity of china would not permit of the others being asked; but they came and helped me arrange the table and to do many other necessary things, and joined us afterwards."[33]

Another example of the unity and cooperation of the imperial sisterhood concerned a ball given in honor of Giovanni, the Fifth Infantry Regiment's new conductor. Alice Baldwin underscored the excitement as the ladies "agreed to make the occasion as elegant and finished an affair as the supplies of the sutler's store would allow." After a flurry of preparations, the day of the ball arrived, and the women, "all arrayed in their best bibs and tuckers . . . arrived in the re-furnished and decorated barracks. Flags, guidons, and draperies transformed" the utilitarian building, and exhibits of "guns, bayonets, and crossed sabers" stood "glittering and grim" in the corners of the room. Thankfully, Giovanni exceeded all musical expectations, and the imperial soirée, designed by the women, was deemed a complete success. The sisterhood, as demonstrated through sewing bees, receptions, and formal dances, provided a central element in maintaining the cohesion of the imperial class. By keeping updated on military and political affairs, and through collaboratively celebrating and displaying nationalistic paraphernalia, officers' wives clearly understood, designed, and showcased symbols of imperial authority.[34]

Although most officers' wives declared close friendships with one another, Beatrice, the wife of Gen. George S. Patton, found her stay at Fort Riley, Kansas, in 1913 unbearable. Her daughter's published account of the couple's military life stated, "Ma didn't speak the same language that was spoken by other Army wives." Her "life of a cultivated Eastern heiress," married to a second lieutenant, made it difficult for her to "understand the gossip. . . . In those days the 'Old Army' was a club, with an inner circle of people who were the sons and grandsons and daughters and granddaughters of Army officers." Other officers' wives "made her feel shy . . . many of them had strong Southern accents, which she associated with the servant class." Thus, she began "to feel she was a terrible failure as an Army wife." She forged, however, a close friendship with Mrs. Hoyle, the wife of a senior captain and a member of the "inner circle." This charming female, as "wide as she was high," invited her to social events, thus enabling Patton's admittance to the military sisterhood.[35]

In creating a female coterie, the officers' wives stationed in British India and the U.S. West used background, behavior, and notions of gentility to admit members to the imperial clique. Yet all was not equal among this sisterhood. Military rank played an immutable part. Indeed, in feminizing the military chain of command a female hierarchy developed that paralleled their husbands' positions. At the apex of this imperial class pyramid stood the wife of the garrison senior officer. In commenting on this gendered social ladder, Lieutenant Colonel Lewis Le Marchand of the Fifth Royal Gurkha Rifles determined, "wives tended to acquire the rank of their husbands. The colonel's lady regarded herself as a sort of colonel and certainly commanded all the other wives of the regiment." Many British officers' spouses commented, both candidly and guardedly, on the character, influence, and authority of this alpha female, the *Burra Mem*. Minnie Blane wrote to her mother from Murree in October 1858 and described this paragon of greatness. She commented, "The Muters are living here now, quite nice, but Mrs is very prim, wears awfully shabby, old-fashioned clothes, and her back looks as if she had a poker down it. She never pronounces her 'r's' and talks of 'Webels' and "Wifles,' which nearly kills me with laughter." This unkind gossip, which utilized appearance, deportment, and enunciation to ridicule Mrs. Muter's reputation and status, underscored Mrs. Blane's envy and powerlessness. The captain's wife concluded, nonetheless, that the *Burra Mem* was "a kind-hearted body."[36]

Equally candidly, Isabella Fane, while on a tour of the interior with her father, recorded the onerous duties that befell her as the daughter of the commander-in-chief. She talked of difficulties of the march, the unpleasantness of the local peoples and terrain, and the boring social events. During a three-day stopover at Fategarh Station, Miss Fane had the opportunity to comment on the military society. She gossiped, "We have got into a horrible scrape about the wife of the colonel commanding here, about whom we were told all sorts of improper tales, *viz* that she was as black as my shoe and that she had lived for five years with this man before he married her. We were informed she meant to call, and were told we ought not to receive her. She did call, and we acted as above." Yet she faced the consequences of believing in the malicious gossip utilized by the ladies of the station. By suggesting an improper relationship, and that the commanding officer's wife was Indian, they hoped to diminish her status thus gain a sense of power. The ladies, apparently, used Miss Fane as a marionette to vent their malice, as her letter continued, "It afterwards came out that she was received by all the ladies of the station, although the tongue of slander did talk of her. Upon finding out all this, I took the most ladylike and proper manner of retrieving my error, *viz* by writing her a civil note. . . . Our not seeing her was put upon fatigue." The *Burra Mem*, apparently, was not impressed with the attempt to correct this social gaffe, as Miss Fane concluded, "they [the couple in command] have behaved like vulgarians [*sic*] and have taken no notice of either note or civil message." Perhaps she learned a worthwhile lesson, as her report of an official visit to the station of Mainpuri five days later appears to be couched in a more guarded tone. Miss Fane's brief entry read, "The head lady of the station called upon us, and we found her ladylike and talkative."[37]

Honoria Lawrence provided a personal account of the *Burra Mem*'s influence and power. As the wife of the commanding officer, she clearly understood herself to be an imperial authority, with full military and legal responsibilities. Lawrence recorded, "While on this frontier we travel with quite a little army. Most of my share I hope to dismiss tomorrow at Hussan Abdal. You would be amused to hear me, when we move, marshalling my troops. 'Let ten horsemen and ten footmen keep close to the young lady's *palkee* . . . let two horsemen accompany the elephant with the *ayahs*. The remaining troops divide in three, one party with the advance guard, another with the rear, and the third to keep by my *dhoolie*." Indeed, at Dummuk, she revealed her imperial authority in recording, "I must be quartermaster for the camp, and you would be amused at the arrangements I have to make and the complaints that come before me." She told of settling a caste dispute over the defilement of water between the washerman and water carrier. She also acted as an administrator by settling a local complaint. It was reported to her that the regimental elephant had "got loose" and destroyed crops, so she sagely decided to "let the villagers be paid for their loss, and the elephant's keeper be fined." Clearly, Mrs. Lawrence took her role and duties seriously, and carried them out with aplomb, with the full acquiescence of her husband and his men.[38]

Margaret Hannay, a captain's wife, also competently acted in her husband's stead. Her private journal described the day-to-day affairs of a regimental march with the Fortieth Regiment Bengal Native Infantry from Mysopoorie to Mhow. An entry for 21 February 1829indicates the complete effectiveness and confidence she held as an imperial agent. She advised that the colonel had ordered the march to begin at three o'clock in the morning. Her husband, the adjutant, was absent, supposedly fishing. Fishing or not, the captain's disappearance provided an opportunity for Mrs. Hannay to assert her authority. She wrote, "For the first time *I acted as Adjutant* the Colonel was *cross* as an old Bear—and I was afraid in his ill humour he might say something about Hannay's being out so long—I therefore took it upon me to give the parole and countersign and then sent about the orders." In issuing military orders, and adjudicating on imperial matters, the *Burra Mem* stood at the apex of the imperial sisterhood. This woman, who gained her status through feminizing the ranking system, did not simply grace her husband's arm at society events. She clearly wielded social, military, and legal authority, fully acknowledged by the institution of the army.[39]

"At the top [of the American military clique] sat the commanding officer's wife—known to the Army as the K.O.W., because the literal abbreviation would not do," Oliver Knight noted. This "female grenadier," a military figure equivalent to the British *Burra Mem*, likewise brandished authority in the nineteenth-century West. Elizabeth Custer mused, "When I first entered army life I used to wonder what it meant when I heard officers say, in a perfectly serious voice, 'Mrs. ——

commands her husband's company.' It was my good fortune not to encounter any such female grenadiers." This negative opinion of the commanding officer's wife seems rather unkind in view of Marion Brown's interaction with one such woman. While visiting Fort Sill, on 18 November 1867, Miss Brown wrote respectfully of Col. Edward P. Pearson's wife. Within a few days of her arrival at the garrison, and after calling, she concluded "Mrs. P is an elegant and lovely woman." With Christmas just weeks away, the newcomer reported that Mrs. Pearson had invited all the ladies to attend a meeting at her home to "discuss the ways and means for getting up a Christmas tree and entertainment." The women dutifully attended several meetings during which they made candle decorations, sewed banners, and filled candy bags to be distributed to "all the children, white, black, and Indian," on Christmas morning. Fort Sill, and its attendant children, certainly benefited from the gracious benevolence of such an influential senior lady.[40]

American Lydia Lane mirrored not a festive kindness but the imperial authority of the British *Burra Mems*, Mesdames Lawrence and Hannay. In February 1861 she recorded in her published narrative that, having traversed the four-day "Jornado del Muerto [Journey of Death]" from Fort Craig to Fort Fillmore with the U.S. Mounted Rifles, she "was the only lady at the post. . . . Lieutenant Lane was in command. . . . We were scarcely settled . . . when an order came for all the troops to go on an Indian scout to Dog Cañon. . . . A sergeant and ten men . . . were left behind to guard the post. . . . *I* was left in command of Fort Fillmore." She described her duties with: "All public funds were turned over to me, and the sergeant reported to me every day. He slept in our house at night, heavily armed. . . . The public money in my hands gave me considerable uneasiness. . . . I was determined no one should have that money while I was alive to defend it . . . if I lost my life in protecting it, I would have done my whole duty." When the soldiers returned from the scouting mission, she "relinquished the command of Fort Fillmore," and announced, "It was my first and last appearance in the role of commanding officer of a military post." Her husband delegated full responsibility to Mrs. Lane, which she accepted and dispensed efficiently and effectively. She undertook full responsibility for fiscal affairs, permitted an enlisted man to sleep in her home, and officially received daily post reports. The garrison, albeit for a short period, fell under female command.[41]

An incident at Fort Davis similarly illustrates a female grenadier's confidence in her imperial role. Clara, the wife of Col. John W. Davidson of the Tenth Cavalry, demonstrated the authority vested in a senior wife. On hearing of her son's arrest for walking on the grass of the parade ground in Fort Sill (breaking one of her husband's direct orders), she dashed to the guardhouse to affect her son's release. The arresting officer, Lt. Henry O. Flipper, narrated the heated verbal exchange between the couple, which ended in the teenager's release: "The general said to her 'Madam, I'll have you know I'm the Commanding Officer of this Post.' And she replied, 'I'll have you to understand I'm your commanding officer.'" Mrs. Davidson confidently demonstrated her authority over her son, husband, and implicitly, the garrison. The assurance of the British and American senior ladies clearly illustrates the women's adoption of their husbands' rank, and their confidence in its concomitant authority. Whether dealing with rampaging elephants or a family member walking on forbidden grass, these alpha females unabashedly brandished imperial authority.[42]

Whether a senior lady, or the new bride of an ensign, when arriving at the military stations of British India and the U.S. West, the officers' wives found themselves stranded from mainstream society. In the isolated outposts of empire their bodies and actions became appropriated to broadcast imperial prestige and power. Yet in feminizing military titles, attire, and jargon, they constructed an imperial reality that provided an elite identity and a sense of purpose. In transnationally replicating traditional female activities at the garrisons, they utilized sewing bees and organized social entertainments to sustain imperial prestige. Indeed, an active sisterhood developed that dutifully promulgated ambitions of empire. More importantly, in feminizing the ranking structure, these women created spaces of empowerment, most strongly demonstrated by the authority and influence of the *Burra Mem* and female grenadier. The men of the British and American armies officially and unofficially sanctioned and reinforced this female appropriation of male imperial power.

In addition to performing as military adjuncts and constructing an imperial sisterhood, however, officers' wives acted as imperial ambassadors. These women held a duty to design, and officiate at, social occasions and formally attend ceremonial performances to symbolize and maintain the authority and prestige of empire.

"After Our Wedding in Karachi, 1910." Margaret and Medical Officer Taylor D.
Murison, Twenty-Ninth Punjabis Regiment, Indian Army.
Murison Papers, Small Collections Box 17, Margaret Murison,
"Memoir: For Lucinda and Susanna by their Great Grandmother."
Courtesy of the Centre of South Asian Studies, Cambridge, UK.

"D.C. [Captain Douglas Churcher, British Army] in Shikar Kit."
Churcher Papers, Madeleine A. Churcher, "Indian Impressions
or A Diary of Our Indian Trip."
Courtesy of the Centre of South Asian Studies, Cambridge, UK.

"In the Jungle. M.A.C. [Madeleine Churcher] in the Howdah." Churcher Papers, Madeleine A. Churcher, "Indian Impressions or A Diary of Our Indian Trip."
Courtesy of the Centre of South Asian Studies, Cambridge, UK.

(opposite top)
"The Bungalow at Basti." Churcher Papers, Madeleine A. Churcher, "Indian Impressions or A Diary of Our Indian Trip."
Courtesy of the Centre of South Asian Studies, Cambridge, UK.

(opposite bottom)
Madeleine Churcher "Decorated with Marigolds." Churcher Papers, Madeleine A. Churcher, "Indian Impressions or A Diary of Our Indian Trip."
Courtesy of the Centre of South Asian Studies, Cambridge, UK.

"Natives with their *dallis*." Churcher Papers, Madeleine A. Churcher,
"Indian Impressions or A Diary of Our Indian Trip."
Courtesy of the Centre of South Asian Studies, Cambridge, UK.

(opposite top)
"Lt. Ralph Henry Hammersley-Smith" and "Magda after her wedding at St. Mary's
Abbots, Kensington." Hammersley-Smith Papers, Magda Hammersley-Smith,
"A Great Grandmother Remembers."
Courtesy of the Centre of South Asian Studies, Cambridge, UK.

(opposite bottom)
"Frances M. A. Roe and her dog, Hal."
General Collections, Print and Photographs Division, Library of Congress, LC-USZ62–108401.

"Group Listening to the Piano, Living Room of the Custer Home," 1875.
Photograph by Orlando S. Goff.
Courtesy of the National Park Service, Little Bighorn Battlefield National Monument, LIBI 00019 00215.

(opposite top)
"Interior of Parlor, Fort Apache, 1889." Lt. Leighton Finley, 10th U.S. Cavalry,
Leighton Finley Papers, 1879–1892, AZ005, Series II, Box 1, Folder 5.
Courtesy of University of Arizona Libraries, Special Collections.

(opposite bottom)
"Residence Interior of Capt. Emmet (Jack) Crawford, Fort Craig, New Mexico."
3rd U.S. Cavalry.
Courtesy Palace of the Governors Photo Archives (NMHM/DCA), 014512.

Imperial Pageantry

Officers' Wives as Public Actors and Ceremonial Performers

> The Nizam sat imperturbable at my side, while I went through
> the alphabet with subjects, in my attempts to talk to him:
> A—Arab horses; B—Colonel Barr; C—Calcutta and Curries;
> D—Diamonds; E—Elephants. . . . You would have thought that
> this magnificent variety would have lasted through dinner,
> but each topic died at birth and produced only a gentle 'Yes'
> or 'Exactly' from His Highness.
>
> —*Mary Curzon, Vicereine of India, 1902*

Although not a viceregal consort, a military wife constructed an imperial role
that mirrored the vicereine's efforts and understandings of duty. Indeed, in
prescribing female responsibility, the April 1883 edition of the *Army and Navy
Journal* honored American females who joined their military men by announcing,
"The mothers, the wives, the sisters of this country's sons have invariably kept step
with them to the west." The correspondent continued, "[P]osts wisely built will
elevate the character of the service . . . for it will render it both easy and proper
for them to take their families . . . thus securing to them the restraining, refining
influence of society, . . . a feeling of contentment . . . [and] the colonizing tendency
to strengthen the Territory where the post is situated."[1]

Officers' wives in British India, however, were not simply glorified by the press,
but *ordered* to represent the empire. In 1877 the viceroy, Edward Robert Bulwer,
1st Earl of Lytton, politicized women by incorporating their appearance as a

vehicle of imperial propaganda. Captain Lionel J. Trotter detailed the viceroy's official diktat by remarking on "a noteworthy reform in the fashions of feminine dress." In issuing "a decree that all ladies who wished to attend the State receptions at Government House should wear long trains, after the manner of European Courts. . . . It pleased Lord Lytton to invest his office with all the ceremonial splendour that beseemed the vicegerent of so great a sovereign as the Empress of Hindustan." Thus, Lytton instituted an official dress code that employed women's bodies to provide a textual representation of imperial power.[2]

With regard to this unusual command Charles Buckland further observed that "an attempt has been made to induce all the ladies of Calcutta to appear at the drawing-room with trains and feathers, but it has usually been left optional to them, the result being that the trains and feathers which do appear sometimes afford a sort of clue to the character and social position of the lady who wears them." Thus, public feminine attire became commandeered as both external and internal symbols of empire. Dress, together with behavior and participation in social rituals, outwardly displayed the affluence and civility of the British Empire to the Indian people. Within the imperial community itself, these markers reaffirmed the supremacy of its members. Additionally, officers' wives and other females received at the viceregal court held instructions to position themselves "on either side of the Viceroy's throne, in a sort of sacred semi-circle, in support of the Queen's representative." Thus, these rituals of pomp and pageantry officially incorporated the female body to demonstrate British authority.[3]

In the nineteenth-century American and British imperial formations, although not fully appreciated in the scholarship, officers' wives held prescribed roles as agents of imperialism. Indeed, the *Army and Navy Journal* indicated a female stoical enthusiasm to share the American mission of expansion, while Buckland underscored the women's official participation in creating a social reality that signaled imperial authority. Prescription, however, is not a total reality. In examining the public lives of the military spouses stationed on the outposts of empire, it becomes clear that these women understood themselves to be duty bound to the nation by presiding over public social rituals and actively participating in ceremonial performances. The British were enmeshed within strictly codified representations of power. The American experience, however, not bound by such rigid dictates, produced more informal displays of authority. All women, nonetheless, utilized dress and performance to legitimize internal class status, and constructed a divide between the military and civilian communities.

These women embellished the traditional nineteenth-century female role and generated social power to manufacture and control a distinct imperial class. In so doing, they played a central role in designing and maintaining national representations of British and American authority and prestige. By performing as adjuncts they shared their husbands' mission, and negotiated power within formal and informal spaces. In organizing and attending numerous social events, such as balls, formal dinners, operas, and concerts, these women socialized with statesmen and civilians. The exciting, or sometimes unpleasant, role as witnesses and documenters of military ceremonial performances suggests they shared their husbands' duty to sustain imperial prestige.

To understand the human contribution to "imperial prestige," René Maunier posits that "the legal sources of imperialism are to be sought in the . . . ideal of the gentleman . . . the polite and polished man . . . who knows how to command; the imperial man in a certain sense, who, having powers, makes it his duty and his right to use them for the common welfare. The ideas of authority-as-power and authority-as-duty are the heritage of an aristocratic tradition." Allen Greenberger argues that the British in India needed to maintain a prestigious appearance to affirm internal confidence in national purpose. In order to generate legitimacy, the male needed to appear "brave, forceful, daring, honest, active, and masculine . . . in short he is . . . in Victorian terms, 'manly.'" Greenberger further asserts that belief in national superiority, the strict maintenance of cultural exclusivity, and an overriding commitment to work hard to discharge one's duty confirmed and communicated an external image of prestige to the indigenous people.[4]

Having established an imperial reliance on the "manly" qualities of male representatives, Mary Procida helpfully studies their female counterparts—the wives of civil servants and army officers posted in British India. She attests that "femininity and masculinity . . . acquired different meanings in the Anglo-Indian community of the British Raj." She describes the female imperial archetype as "outdoorsy, sports-orientated . . . self-sufficient," frugal, with "a flair for music." In a role as "her husband's partner," she was not subordinated, but had "avenues of power and knowledge unavailable to most British women." Thus, an officer's spouse held authority in the administration and representation of empire by accompanying her husband on tour, interacting with the Indian people, and "contributing to imperial decision-making."[5]

A "husband and wife as a unit," according to Procida's analysis, "embodied status and authority." Unlike the landed gentry at home, the imperial couple did not hold responsibility in gendered spheres, but the "imperial marital partnership centered on governing the Raj." Ellwyn Stoddard and Claude Cabanillas, however, examine military gender relationships to offer a further ideal for consideration. They assert that as "an adjunct to her officer husband's quasi-formal responsibilities," the military spouse can be "best illustrated by the ambassador's wife. . . . She, in her quasi-legal capacity must share and supplement the official duties of her husband . . . by communicating symbolically the correct relationships between their government and others, mainly by engaging in the subtleties of diplomatic life and reciprocal entertaining." In examining the officers' wives' experiences, Stoddard's definition of "adjunct" most accurately conveys the roles of these imperial women, who were expected to be active, symbolic diplomats, who shared and supplemented formal and informal duties by facilitating "correct relationships." Although clearly not delegates to round-table negotiations of state affairs, or commanders of military men in the field, these females nonetheless wielded power in the nexus points between formal and informal avenues of imperial authority. In so doing, they participated in the creation of an inclusive imperial reality, complete with a distinct military community, rigid class hierarchy, and rules of social interaction.[6]

Officers' spouses, as adjuncts, held an obligation to manage both formal and informal relationships. In evaluating the sociability of the British Raj, Procida advises British women built and sustained an imperial community in India by attempting to replicate British cultural traditions to clearly demarcate the "racial, legal, cultural, and personal" borders between the rulers and the ruled. Similarly, Sandra Myres surveys the social behavior and background of officers' wives stationed in the U.S. West to argue that these women transported mainstream ideas of gentility that mirrored British practices. In holding "conservative [and] traditional . . . ideas and values," they created an exclusive group that "lived more public lives" and judged western neighbors as "unsuitable" acquaintances. In "gratefully . . . return[ing] home to a more civilized society in the East," however, Myres argues they made little cultural impact. Yet, in approaching the experiences of these "conservative and traditional" women who "lived more public lives" through an imperialist lens, a different picture emerges. These adjuncts skillfully constructed an exclusive coterie, understood themselves to be active ambassadors, and held responsibility and social authority to promulgate imperial prestige.[7]

Reputation and status depend, in part, on how one presents oneself. Both dress and public behavior contribute to the creation of a specific identity, and dining etiquette provided a central component in the nineteenth-century image-making portfolio. This ritualized gathering symbolized upper- and middle-class status throughout the British and American empires. Yet a difference appears in the level of formality exercised by the two groups of women. In India, this transnational practice became aggrandized to act as a diplomatic text symbolizing authority, affluence, civility, and orderliness. Margaret MacMillan describes the government-issued *Warrant of Precedence* that codified sociability in British India. In conferring social status according to official rank, the women religiously followed the ordering of the list. Whether dining at the mess, playing badminton, or merely sitting on the ladies' sofas in one of the "clubs," the most senior *memsahib* expected to be treated with deference. At official balls, it was considered "improper for single ladies to dance" unless led by a higher-ranking wedded woman. Additionally, at the end of the evening one had to wait for the *Burra Mem* to depart before even the most tired of guests could bid farewell. Indeed, "A Lady Resident" provided an instruction manual for newly arrived wives commanding, "At solemn dinners the lady of highest rank goes away first, and it is not considered etiquette for anyone else to make the first move, whether there may be a baby at home, or a long drive, or any other reason why she is anxious not to be detained late."[8]

Isabella Fane recorded the effects of this social practice while attending a dinner at Government House. She reported: "In the morning we had been studying the book of precedence appertaining to rank and quality. . . . I was nobody at all and need not trouble myself as to when and where I was to be in any grand march or . . . great dinner . . . it is little matter to me whether I am first or twentieth. Conceive my horror and amazement when Lord Auckland stepped forward . . . and walked me out . . . before *three* other *married* ladies. It was totally wrong . . . but I hope and trust my character may be spared." The requirement of an official mandate to dictate dining protocol reveals the efforts to ameliorate the insecurities of the British power holders in India. By standardizing etiquette, a collective and cohesive display of respectability reassured the superiority of the imperial class.[9]

The women in India recreated a social life that reflected, yet militarized British middle-class rituals and social ordering. Their efforts to exhibit genteel status became commandeered by the empire to boost confidence and present a public façade of affluence and superiority—not just for a social class, but for an entire nation. While visiting the Hill Station of Simla in 1902, Mary, the American wife of George, Lord Curzon of Kedleston, Viceroy of India, realized the overwhelming obligation of her imperial role as vicereine. She wrote to her father that "George never does any social functions of any sort and they all devolve on me. . . . Duty is a wonderful incentive. . . . I go out to races, parties, concerts, weddings, prize-givings, polo matches, and the Lord knows what. It is all work and very little pleasure." Correspondence by another American woman stationed in India with her British officer husband provides us with a glimpse of what "all work" encompassed. Lieutenant Colonel Offley Shore, Eighteenth Tiwana Lancers, Indian Army, married Caroline Sinnickson in Philadelphia in 1908. Shore accepted a position as assistant quartermaster-general of training in the Indian Army in 1909, and the couple took up the appointment immediately. Caroline's letters excitedly record details of her new social role, interspersed with frequent requests for new dresses and hats from Wanamaker Department Store as "we are gay, dining, dancing, picnics, luncheons, polo, cricket, and a Horse Show, the day is spent for me changing from one costume to another." Despite this apparent frivolous social diary, Lt.Lieutenant Colonel Shore, in writing to Caroline's father, revealed the hidden agency and social power of military wives. He detailed a court ball to advise, "The little lady [Caroline], having got into touch with the Mintos [Viceroy and Vicereine of India] and conquered them with ridiculous ease, attached a few 'members of Council (equals Ministers)' to her train and a handful of Generals with scarcely an elevation of the Supercilious Eyebrow, still looked around for the most difficult Tiger in the Jungle, to wit Lord Kitchener. . . . Well, last night we *were* at the Maneater's Den, at *last*! And despite the fact of our being very little people who had just permission to breathe in a retired corner, this daughter of yours sidled up to the Man of Cross Green Eyes . . . and lispingly plastered him with flattery. I being kept hard at in the dancing room . . . to trot out all his young lady guests. . . . You will see what the game was! The little lady played it so well, that Tiger-ji capitulated . . . and finally, contrary to all prognostication, consented to be fed, one day soon, in our humble abode." In her letter home, Caroline simply wrote that Kitchener agreed to dine with the Shores, although she had to lunch with his aide de camp "to arrange the date and take my small list of guests for his Excellency to approve or change." She concluded that General Sir George Duff told her "the honour is a very personal one and we hear the Viceroy has said 'why am I not invited to dine with Mrs. Offley!' Very flattering of course."[10]

It is impossible to provide evidence of the content and purpose of these social conversations without being able to access them. This recorded episode, provided by both marriage partners, however, indicates the gendered roles of sociability. The husband would cultivate the women and the wife exercise power over men. Caroline was certainly successful in her mission. Obtaining an acceptance to dine from Lord Kitchener, the commander-in-chief of India, was a fabulous coup for the Shore couple. As Offley excitedly reported to his father-in-law, "Up went the winning No. to the top of the telegraph Board. . . . Lord Kitchener, who only consorts with acting Kings and Deputy Assistant Duchesses, over whom all Simla trips over its own feet to get near and catch a cat green glance of approbation, that he should have been lassoed and brought to heel is, you must admit, quite an achievement!!" Implied within these social occasions, then, was exercise of the officer's wife's power, to cultivate and manipulate high-level officers and statesmen. Hence, a classic case of not what you know, but who you know. These women accessed knowledge and influenced decision-making, especially with regard to their own position. A woman's social standing, determined by her husband's rank, could be elevated through networking and the control of information. Caroline reported that as "Chatelaine or hostess . . . [she must] always have a luncheon or dinner table ready to receive any of the Great and Big of this empire." Indeed, the couple hoped to take leave "on the condition" that her husband was offered promotion to "a much higher General Staff appointment" on their return. With total confidence in her social power she concluded her letter with "I shall do my part well in Calcutta this winter—as you can imagine."[11]

Mirroring the vicereine's and Shore's laundry lists of duties, Miss Fane recorded countless "boring" social engagements. She somewhat disdainfully noted "a station ball, which proved a nuisance to us all . . . [the next day] a dinner party no more amusing than the ball." Similarly, Mrs. Sherwood wrote at length about a ball thrown by the *nawab* of Bengal. Dressed in "splendid dresses" the women accompanied their gallantly uniformed men to the palace. Yet the elaborate entertainment of dancing, theatricals, and fireworks failed to impress this officer's wife. Somewhat disdainfully, she considered the music as nothing more than a "fearful screeching." Seated for dinner with the nawab's sons, Mrs. Sherwood begrudgingly admitted that they held a "princely" air, yet "they looked melancholy. It is impossible that they should witness the prosperity of the English without pain." Finding her duty to showcase English "prosperity" tiresome, she hoped to be able to give "up going into public in order to do good." Clearly, the Mesdames Curzon, Fane, and Sherwood considered their appearance at, and participation in, formal social functions as a tedious, yet necessary imperial obligation. Curzon and Fane's status placed them at the apex of the social hierarchy in India, thus their negative view somewhat makes sense. The need for either woman to manipulate male power players was simply redundant, yet their appearance an imperial necessity.[12]

Echoing such sentiments, the requirement to perpetuate British superiority, wealth, orderliness, and authority likewise irked Georgiana Paget. Again, her attitude can be somewhat explained by her connections with the royal family and England's aristocracy. In recording a regimental New Year soirée to celebrate the arrival of 1858 at Kirkee (Western Ghats), she remarked, "Last night we indulged in the unwonted dissipations of a dinner-party and dance. The latter was rather a solemn affair, and at twelve o'clock every one shook hands and wished each other the compliments of the season." She underscored the rules of cordiality by mentioning, "Then *we* sat down to a supper which nobody ate, and then we, in defiance of Indian manners (which forbid the departure of any guest till he lady of highest rank has taken leave), went home to bed." Mrs. Paget's description of the "unwonted dissipations" of a regimental dance indicate a reluctant acquiescence to participate in the affairs of empire. Her haughty departure before the *Burra Mem* represented a social insult and a daring dereliction of duty. Hailing from such a prestigious background she undoubtedly found the requirement to defer to a rank-based senior wife an outrage. Yet such was her imperial obligation.[13]

The officers' wives' recollections of social engagements may appear to some as descriptions of unnecessarily frivolous and formalized entertainments. Yet in viewing their participation in formal receptions as an imperial obligation a different picture emerges. Dressed in their "splendid" outfits, these women held a shared responsibility to project an image of gracious civility and affluence to authoritatively maintain "correct relationships"—clearly a female imperial duty. Recollections, notwithstanding the exasperation of the imperial elite, include countless examples of eagerness to participate in, and enjoyment of, imperial sociability. Magda, the wife of Lieutenant Colonel Ralph Hammersley-Smith, recorded her experiences in British India for her great-grandchildren. She filled the pages of her memoir with stories of tiger hunts, jungle walks, and social gatherings. Arriving in 1906, she made the acquaintance of Hammersley-Smith at a garden party. As the aide-de-camp he approached Magda, and proffered an invitation for her to meet an "Indian Princess," which she excitedly accepted. Eight months later she attended the "XIV Murray's Jat Lancers" regimental ball. Magda described her surroundings as a veritable "fairyland . . . [populated by] fair women and brave men," and reencountered the charming aide-de-camp. By the end of the evening they were engaged to be married. Despite such romantic accounts, some members of the imperial class voiced irritation with such public duties. The *nawab*'s ball with its melancholic princes, however, and the unwonted indulgences of a mess dinner-dance, played out on a fantasized landscape. This indicates the imperial locations as otherworldly, a place apart from familiar home locations, hence masking insecurities through the construction and showcasing of British prestige.[14]

The American officers' wives who traveled west also held a duty to allay internal class and imperial anxieties by creating and enacting social rituals that showcased national confidence. Historians assert that officers' wives accompanied their husbands from a sense of love and marital duty, attempting to replicate Eastern roles as wives, civilizers, and homemakers. Yet Anni Baker's analysis of American army officers' wives argues that women played a central role in maintaining the embedded traditions and values of the army. She suggests that army wives generated a distinct female identity differing from the nineteenth-century models of eastern "delicacy" and western "roughness." Michele Nacy supports Baker to contend that neither "True" nor "Southern Womanhood" adequately describes the lives of these nineteenth-century military spouses, and introduces an empowered female role as a "Member of the Regiment." By further examination of military spouses as architects and arbiters of social rituals and ceremonial performances, it becomes clear that they were not confined by the tenets of "True" or "Southern Womanhood"—nor were they simply "Members of the Regiment." These women enjoyed a unique identity and status as imperial agents who understood themselves to hold a duty to design and display imperial symbols, orchestrate social rituals, and police behaviors.[15]

Such enterprises undertaken by the American officers' wives mirror the endeavors of their British counterparts, albeit through far less grandiose and formal practices. Both groups, by participating in public functions, assisted the construction of an imperial reality that sustained notions of national prestige. In the West, Margaret Carrington offered a veritable catalogue of entertainments enjoyed en route to Absaraka, Dakota Territory, in 1866. She remarked, "It is an old army fashion to enliven the monotony of frontier life by extemporized opera, charades, readings, and the miniature drama." In recording the "last reunion" of the Eighteenth Infantry Regiment, she described the use of hospital tents to furnish a "grand pavilion," where a concert, complete with "iron-clad Minstrels," and a string orchestra provided the farewell amusements. Indeed, she explained, army life was "bound closely in social intimacies, separated from the affinities of active life in the States . . . full of fraternal endearments . . . when gentlemen *are* gentlemen and ladies *are* ladies."[16]

During "the days of the Empire," and far from the "active life of the States," Ellen Biddle confirmed the frequency of social functions in the U.S. West. In identifying the benefits of the transnational imperial model of sociability, she remarked, "There was, and is, a 'hop' or informal dance every Friday evening in most army garrisons. . . . [T]hese gatherings bring the officers' families together and are generally delightful." Indeed, she promoted the benefits of such events with, "An army woman usually keeps her youth because she dances so much . . . and aside from the pleasure it is a most healthful exercise." Apart from keeping one's youth, she also enjoyed the freedom to interact with bachelor officers. "Colonel [Joseph G.] Crane had been a great favorite," she confided, "I remember meeting him one morning and asking if he were going to the 'hop' that night. 'Oh, yes,' he said, 'I am going to see you dance, for I know if the floor were covered with eggs and you danced over them, not one would be broken.'" She further indicated an embellished Eastern gentility with: "I recall walking with Colonel Crane one morning across the garrison, when we were joined by General [Adelbert] Ames and Major [Thomas H.] Norton. We came to a wide puddle of water . . . as quick as thought Colonel Crane seized the military cape from Major Norton's shoulders and threw it across the puddle, and taking my hand led me across, saying as we went, 'Sir Walter Raleigh outdone.'" Colonel Crane undoubtedly enjoyed the social freedom to interact with a married woman, and Biddle took pleasure in accepting his mild flirtatiousness. The conditions of living in an isolated military community, then, forged an alteration to mainstream social mores. By connecting with the masculine ethos of an officer and gentleman, the women constructed a hybrid society that dismissed traditional gender roles. Far from the "active life of the States," officers' wives understood themselves to belong to the army, ergo the empire, dispensing with certain elements of public etiquette and confidently relying on the code of honor that claimed "gentlemen *are* gentlemen and ladies *are* ladies."[17]

Lydia Lane provides a further example of such latent social empowerment within imperial protocol. In 1860 the Third Cavalry transferred from Fort Leavenworth to New Mexico and the officers' families made the long trek in army ambulances. Each vehicle "was given its position in line according to the rank of the officer whose family occupied it." This demonstration of internal imperial status was nonnegotiable. Despite the dust cloud encountered by the second lieutenants' families relegated to the rear, however, Mrs. Lane considered, "The truth is, all army women, from the wife of the commanding general down to the wife of a second lieutenant, are treated with so much courtesy and politeness by army officers that they do not like anything that has the least appearance of a slight or an infringement of their rights." Additionally, she echoed Mrs. Biddle's sentiments regarding the almost eternal youth of an officer's wife with, "They never grow old in a garrison, and always receive attentions to which no woman in citizen life is accustomed when no longer young." She also reiterated the development of a distinct esprit de corps by confirming that "[t]he hops are more like a family reunion than a gathering of strangers." Indeed, she glowingly confirmed that she "was in the army and part of it." Yet this image of an idyllic imperial family was just that, a halcyon ideal. Alice Baldwin revealed the rigid divide between officers' and soldiers' families that existed in the U.S. West. Commissioned men and their wives were not permitted to participate in lower-ranked social events. The garrison commander and his wife, however, held a duty, not a familial commitment to attend. For the opening dance, the most senior officer was responsible for partnering the "ranking non-commissioned officer's wife," while "his wife . . . danced with the ranking non-commissioned officer." The restriction of this ritual, then, endorsed and signaled the inflexible, internal divide between the officer and ranked imperial men. The ceremonial dance duty was shared by the commander and his wife, an imperial invitation neither could refuse.[18]

In comparing the American and British rituals of sociability, then, the official Indian *Warrant of Precedence* contrasts starkly with the unwritten practices of public sociability in the U.S. West. Yet an undercurrent of class insecurity, just as in the British experience, lay beneath the less formalized customs. The portrayal of an affable family community masked the operation of a rigid class hierarchy. Women were expected, at all times, to adhere to military codes of behavior and respectability. In juxtaposing Ellen Biddle's record of a garrison dance with Frances Roe's experience in Fort Lyon in 1871, however, internal tensions regarding the uncertainty and instability of imperial male identity become clearer. Mrs. Roe, in accompanying her husband to the regimental mess dinner, delighted in the "bright buttons" of the uniformed men. Being unaware of honorary or brevet ranks among the officers, she committed an unforgivable social faux pas. She confessed, "It seems that in the Army, lieutenants are called 'Mister' always, but all other officers must be addressed by their rank. . . . But in Faye's company, the captain is called general, and the first lieutenant is called major, and as this is most confusing. . . . I called

General Phillips 'Mister!'" Unfortunately for Mrs. Roe, "everyone heard the blunder. General Phillips straightened back in his chair . . . [and a] soldier, who had been so dignified and stiff, put his hand over his mouth and fairly rushed from the room so he could laugh outright. And how I longed to run some place, too—but not to laugh, oh, no!" She further compounded her mistake by "smiling" at a soldier who had acknowledged her with a "Yes, sorr [sic]!" After informing her husband of the incident, she recorded that "he looked vexed and said I must never laugh at an enlisted man—that it was not dignified in the wife of an officer to do so." Although a formalized order of precedence did not exist in the U.S. West, an adherence to rank was strictly enforced by practice. Frances Roe, in failing to acknowledge Civil War brevets and behave publicly in the fashion dictated for an officer's wife, faced a reprimand delivered by her concerned husband. She resolved the problem by designing a cunning strategy to act dutifully. As she explained, "the safest thing to do is to call everyone general . . . if I make a mistake, at least it will be on the right side." As an officer's wife she held an obligation to explicitly uphold and reaffirm the military masculine identity—and by extension—imperial prestige.[19]

The need to behave appropriately as recognizable national representatives applied equally to both sexes. Some British and American officers' wives, however, found themselves ostracized, and even removed from the garrisons for failing to meet female standards of imperial behavior. Joan Mickelson attests that the outward appearance of "female respectability became linked with . . . patriotic pride. Thus when a woman's behavior did not meet with the standards of the ideal she violated more than social codes. She also jeopardized the empire." Marriage, rank, background, and social accomplishments all featured in determining acceptability. For example, Minnie Blane described the vetting procedure in India. She wrote to her mother of Lady Montgomery's musical party held at Murree (Punjab) and proudly recounted, "Two ladies sang as well as any I have heard in an Opera. . . . It is quite delightful to meet with really nice gentlefolk." Some guests, nonetheless, did not receive such warm plaudits, as Minnie recalled, "Among the 'ladies' here two have been *actresses*, and one, the wife of a Captain, a bar maid from a small inn near Plymouth! Really, society is very *recherché* [unusual]!" Clearly, the suitability of the accomplished vocalists was not in doubt. Mrs. Blane's use of quotation marks and italics, however, emphasize this officer's wife's refusal to accept actresses and a barmaid as qualified ambassadors of empire.[20]

An officer's wife needed to symbolize, and enact rituals of, imperial prestige. Frances Wells, however, found the obligation to attend social events troubling. She complained, "Allahabad [United Provinces] is to be very gay this next week with two large balls . . . I have never danced since my marriage and never intend to do so: I am universally laughed at but I do not think it consistent with the quietness and sobriety which are enjoined on married women." In her next letter home, nonetheless, she shared her understanding that imperial duty *required* her to appear publicly. She informed her father, "I fear I must go to a ball on the first Thursday in June, as Walter has been accused of shutting me up and not letting me go out and he is so excessively indignant about it that he is determined to go." Along with her reservations regarding dancing, Mrs. Wells underscored her obligation to participate in military social functions. The station accusation that her husband "shut her up" suggested perhaps that her public presence would be detrimental to their social standing. That Captain Wells insisted that she appear in public to dispel such rumors evidences the embedded value of his wife as holding a responsibility for his, and by implication the empire's, reputation and prestige.[21]

In American military society, an episode that occurred in the U.S. West illustrates that failure to conform to socially accepted codes of public conduct resulted in much greater sanctions than just harmful speculation. For example, Charlotta, the wife of Lt. Martin P. Buffum of the Fifteenth Infantry, threatened the code of female respectability that existed in Fort Craig. In 1870, despite suffering from an "internal disease" that prevented sexual intercourse with her husband, she allegedly participated in extramarital relations with a Capt. George Shorkley at Fort Wingate. This indiscretion, apparently, provided no cause for alarm until 1876, when the lieutenant's wife supposedly engaged in an illicit affair with the household striker (an enlisted man who acted as a paid servant for officers and their families), Pvt. William F. Vanstan. "Mrs. Lieut. M. P. Buffum," declared Vanstan in a sworn deposition, fully consented to "criminal carnal intercourse" with him and the pair had regularly exchanged love letters. This "decidedly disagreeable subject" became the object of countless urgent missives between the post commander, Capt. Charles Steelhammer, and the acting assistant adjutant general's office in Sante Fe, New Mexico.[22]

Steelhammer initially reported to Lt. Col. Peter T. Swaine, regimental commander of the Fifteenth Infantry at Fort Wingate, "with no ordinary degree of reluctance," that Mrs. Buffum "had had improper relations . . . of the most disgusting character" with "an enlisted man under his command." After informing the cuckolded husband of his wife's behavior, Steelhammer insisted that the lieutenant remove her, forthwith, from the fort. Failure to do so would be "at the risk of his commission." Buffum immediately agreed to "send her to the States." Despite Buffum's acquiescence, Swaine then insisted that "for the sake of the regiment . . . Mrs B. [should] be legally investigated," and Buffum forced to "resign to save the regiment publicity from the scandal." On hearing of the latter orders, Buffum refused to remove his spouse or surrender his commission, "emphatically and indignantly" dismissing the charges "preferred against his wife." The drama continued to unfold as Swaine, unsatisfied with the situation, charged Steelhammer to "legally present his testimony."[23]

The couple moved to Fort Wingate, and their response to Steelhammer's deposition consisted of a fifteen-page rebuttal written by Buffum, and a sworn affidavit drafted by his wife. The missives deny any adulterous behavior, and Mrs. Buffum provided a solemn oath that "no unusual familiarity or intercourse criminal or otherwise . . . took place." Steelhammer remained convinced that Vanstan's testimony was a true record, and produced a letter written by the striker addressed to "My darling Lottie" to support his opinion. He further informed Swaine that he had arrested Buffum for public intoxication, and purported that the lieutenant's denial was made whilst when he "was intoxicated or insane." Indeed, the strength of Steelhammer's conviction led him to declare that he wished to "prevent [future] . . . social intercourse with people [the Buffums] I know to be morally diseased." The documented affair halts abruptly with a missive from the acting assistant adjutant general's office. 1st Lt. Thomas Blair asked Steelhammer to provide further evidence of Buffum's "drunkenness on duty or other acts prejudicial to good order," and insisted that "in order to avoid giving more publicity to this scandal than necessary it is desired that the official recording of these from here be omitted." Thus ended the paper trail of this episode. Yet it becomes patently obvious that Charlotta threatened the reputation and orderliness of the imperial presence in the West. *Her* supposed adultery with a mere soldier placed her *husband's* career in jeopardy, and the couple was removed from the garrison. A brief addendum dated 11 January 1877 indicated how Swaine safeguarded military prestige—it simply stated "Buffum resigned." Charlotta's conduct prompted official action and she was found guilty of inappropriate female behavior. This, in turn, caused her husband to lose his appointment; thus, her social actions appropriated economic male space. Swaine responded quickly and decisively to a feminine threat—a threat that would imperil the regiment's reputation and legitimacy.[24]

While dealing with the tawdry affairs at Fort Craig, Swaine faced a larger problem brewing at another western garrison under his command. The alleged erstwhile lover in the Buffum drama, Captain Shorkley, now the commanding officer at Fort Garland, was once again enmeshed in scandal. Problems initially arose when an officer's spouse failed to act as imperial protocol demanded. Rumors circulated that Lt. John Conline's wife regularly frequented the laundresses' quarters to gossip, thus crossing the class divide. On another occasion she had acted indecorously by chasing Annie Lee, the hospital matron, "around the yard with a pistol in her hand." 2nd Lt. Basil N. Waters of the Fifteenth Infantry added further weight to the accusations of unladylike behavior by reporting that "Mrs. Conline came into his room without knocking when he was only partially dressed, and instead of retiring she took a chair and sat down." An additional charge remarkably read that "Mrs. John Conline willfully and indecently expose[d] her person in a state of partial and entire nudity to officers and enlisted men of the garrison." The ultimate offense, however, was her accusation that the post's commanding officer, none other than the alleged lover of Charlotta Buffum—Capt. George Shorkley, had fathered Mrs. Rogers's (a soldier's wife's) child. For such violations against the code of respectability, and for disturbing the "order and quiet of the garrison," Shorkley ordered an official investigation into Mrs. Conline's character, reporting that he believed her to be insane and requesting urgently that the matter be dealt with to "relieve the garrison of this disturbing presence." Indeed, his memoranda of charges included eight individual specifications of unacceptable conduct for which her husband assumed "official and personal" responsibility.[25]

Following an examination, Assistant Surgeon Justus Morris Brown declared Mrs. Conline "insane," and her husband received orders to remove her from the post. Conline refused, thus facing a court-martial, and the affair spiraled out of control. Scandalous accusations and counterclaims reached soap opera proportions, including the refusal to allow the supposedly insane woman use of an army ambulance because she "had used it to convey her to the houses of citizens where . . . her conversation was not to the credit of the army." The final outcome, nonetheless, resulted in Mrs. Conline's removal from the post, with the lieutenant barely escaping court martial—through, ironically, an insanity plea. This officer's spouse, then, held a responsibility to conduct herself publicly as a national representative. In fraternizing with women of a lower class, visiting with a lightly clad officer in his room, exposing herself indecently, and making public accusations against the fort commander, she threatened both her and her husband's social and economic positions. Capt. Edward Whittemore (the investigating officer) judged that "whether insane or not," the officer's wife had "disturbed the peace and quiet of the post." Her behavior, he declared, had "not been such as is to be expected from a Lady." The failure in controlling officers' wives' behavior, then, signaled the importance of the army authorities' efforts to sustain the respectability, prestige, and legitimacy of its imperial presence.

Mrs. Buffum and Mrs. Conline, then, did not meet the expectations of female national ambassadors, and their public performances threatened prestige. The appearance of Shorkley in both episodes, however, casts doubt on the guilt of these women. His reputation was called into question in both cases, and at least in the latter episode, he was forced to go on the offensive. In attacking the character of a lower ranked officer's spouse, he neatly shifted the focus of the investigation away from his actions (Shorkley was not reprimanded and retired at the end of his service on 23 September 1885). Additionally, both Lieutenants Buffum and Conline were well-known heavy drinkers. So, calling their wives' reputations into question provided an easier route to force the resignations of military liabilities—ungentlemanly officers. Regardless of the true intent behind the removal of these women, the high-level interventions confirm that officers' wives had responsibility for policing both male and female sexuality and integrity of speech, and maintaining military class boundaries.

Most officers' spouses in America and India, nonetheless, did not furiously chase soldiers' wives around the garden brandishing a weapon. They conformed to expected behaviors, to act, at all times, as genteel ambassadors. In addition to enacting the social rituals of entertaining, these women dutifully participated in an array of ceremonial performances. David Cannadine argues that power gains visibility through formal observances. What kind of authority is displayed, however, depends on the individual society and the particular public ritual. In delineating the connection between pomp and power, he considers anthropological methodology that interprets, amongst other artifacts, flags, costumes, and festivities as historical texts. In considering both the British and American imperial formations, the public rituals that display military strength and authority cannot be omitted from the record. As Cannadine attests, "no approach that ignores spectacle and pageantry can possibly claim to be comprehensive. . . . Ritual . . . is itself a type of power." In legitimizing an empire, extravagant state performances would strengthen a relatively weak position. In witnessing, participating in, and glorifying national pageantry the officers' wives actively validated and sustained nineteenth-century imperial power. In so doing, they bolstered the Anglo military minorities' confidence in their status and roles, and assisted the display of perceived superiority and authority to civilians and indigenous peoples.[26]

In India, male and female bodies provided physical sites to display imperial texts, simultaneously placating internal insecurities while demonstrating a façade of confidence to the indigenous peoples. The responsibility to uphold the exhibition of civility and authority rested with officers and their wives. Kenneth Mason, a member of the Survey Department in nineteenth-century India, offered a perfect summary: "We had to rule by prestige; there's no question about it. It wasn't conceit. . . . We were there to rule, and we did our best." Indeed, outward appearances and behavior during public celebrations played a central role in legitimizing British authority, both for the rulers and the ruled. Frances Wells, while travelling with the regiment from Barrackpore to Allahabad in 1854–55, described such portrayals of strength. She excitedly told her father, "the Regt . . . march in and out [of Camp Burdwan, West Bengal] with the band playing and all their bayonets flashing in the sun: a dozen elephants follow carrying the sepoys' tents." This ceremonial march, prior to the Sepoy uprising, clearly utilized pomp and pageantry to confirm the virility and stability—the imperial manliness—of the British Empire to the rulers and ruled alike.[27]

Stationed on the Black Plain with her husband's regiment during the Sepoy Mutiny, Georgiana Paget offered additional instances of British public attempts to legitimize and reaffirm authority. On 24 May 1857, she noted, "A Royal salute was fired at daybreak in honour of Her Majesty's birthday. No parade took place, as the troops have no full dress." With no mess uniforms available to demonstrate a physically striking, disciplined, and confident face of empire, the celebration was restricted to an artillery salute. On 31 May, however, she recorded, "A little demonstration was got up here this afternoon, to show the natives we still had some English soldiers left. The few remaining Highlanders, accompanied by the one miserable gun, sallied forth . . . and marched in . . . I think it was questionable whether the whole affair was not rather a display of our weakness." In the midst of the military confusion and uncertainty of the mutiny, the British needed to boost morale through a visible show of strength. In proffering her opinion, Mrs. Paget clearly indicates an understanding of her duty. First, by including the words "our weakness," she understood that she was an integral member of the empire. Second, in acknowledging that the demonstration sought to "show the natives" British prowess, she understood the imperial agenda behind ceremonial performances. Third, in questioning the parade of the "few Highlanders," she revealed her role as an informed attaché, by doubting the wisdom of such an order. Finally, in noting the restriction of the Queen's birthday celebration to a salute, as the men did not have their most prestigious uniforms, she confirms that the costuming of such rituals held a central role in broadcasting the health and wealth of the British Empire.[28]

Madeleine Churcher further confirms the exploitation of the body as elemental in upholding the imperial image by underscoring the prime importance of appropriate dress for public appearances. She recorded a state visit to Bareilly by the Viceroy and Lady Ampthill on 16 November 1904. Not satisfied with simply describing the pomp and ceremony of the salutes, cavalcade, and troop review, she took two rolls of still photographs with her new Kodak camera. The soldiers, she noted, paraded in their finest military regalia, and Lady Ampthill dressed in a pale gray outfit, sheltered from the sun under a gold and scarlet umbrella. The keen photographer, unfortunately, had to remain at a polite distance. Her husband "had no full mess uniform" with him, so the couple failed to receive permission to attend the formal state banquet. Thus, the soldiers and the vicereine clearly promoted the prestige of the empire through dress and performance. Churcher and his wife, however, could not publicly represent the empire as the captain had failed to pack his mess kit.[29]

At the zenith of the ceremonial performance pyramid in India sat the resplendent durbars. Traditionally, a durbar in India welcomed visiting heads of state to royal receptions. This adoption and adaptation of an Indian ceremonial ritual provides an example of the British imperial strategy of sustaining indigenous cooperation by fusing Anglo-Indian customs. Christian Showers-Stirling participated in "Lord Curzon's Great Durbar" held on 1 January 1903. She recorded, "I shall never forget Lady Curzon in her wonderful peacock dress. . . . It was all light and colour. . . . Then there was the State Ball . . . [and a] review of the whole army." She delighted in the "prancing horses, elephants, and camels," but "the armies of Native State troops," provided the "cream" of the day for this military wife. The expense incurred for this lavish spectacle, however, caused concern at the highest levels, fueling the longstanding antagonism between the prime minister, Arthur Balfour, and the viceroy, George Curzon—with Balfour privately ridiculing Curzon as "the purple emperor." The landmark event, despite the lack of accord between the statesmen over tax reductions, took place as proposed. In an addendum to her report Showers-Stirling clarified the role of pageantry as integral to the more mundane operations of empire. She added, "A few explanations on the Durbar, etc.—It was Lord Curzon's idea to glorify himself and to gather all India together in a vast concourse of every nation, tribe, Native States, etc., their chiefs to meet and discuss their problems in a Durbar. . . . Many were at enmity with each other and the rivalry for Government favour was tremendous—each State vieing [*sic*] with a display of their wealth and grandeur." Mrs. Showers-Stirling's description highlights that ceremonial exhibitions functioned as a central element of imperialism. The durbar, with its prancing horses, troop review, and state ball, provided a space for political, diplomatic, and economic negotiations at the highest level. Displayed in their most lavish outfits, officers' wives were required to attend state functions to symbolize and legitimize, through their bodies and demeanor, imperial authority, affluence, and prestige.[30]

Both dining at the local military stations and the more formal state occasions underscored the inclusivity of an imperial coterie. Acting as representatives at official functions of the empire provided a means not only to participate in displays of national strength, but also to police and protect the borders of the imperial set. Indeed, Frances Duberly outlined the perils of such authority. She declared, "The *great* mistake in this world is making hasty or promiscuous acquaintances." She considered herself among the lower ranks of the imperial community as the wife of a mere major, and continued that she could not afford "to know any but the best people of those among I am thrown. For the rest there is no mercy and no appeal." Lady Curzon, as vicereine of India, provided insightful observations of female social authority in action at the highest level. Her letters regularly describe the pageantry of the constant round of curtsies, bows, and handshakes, accompanied by the ubiquitous rendering of "God Save the Queen." Writing from Barrackpore in 1900 she candidly described dining at the residence of the commander-in-chief (General Sir William Lockhart), where she "had to make the move to leave the table [other guests were forbidden under the *Warrant of Precedence* to leave the dining table until she retired] and for all the fuss and ceremony we might as well be monarchs."[31]

One telling vignette, nonetheless, related a process to exclude undesirables from the vicereine's social, hence the imperial, circle. Lady Curzon confided, "Some *awful* people *insisted* on being asked to the ball at Government House . . . a Mr and Mrs Jack *Latta* of Chicago. They got the American Consul to write and say they expected to be asked just as though I were the wife of an American Minister abroad upon whom they looked as a creature paid to entertain them. They appeared, Mrs Latta wearing an immense Scotch plaid *day* dress *turned* in at the neck, I had seen her at polo with the same dress in the afternoon." To prevent admission of such unsuitable interlopers she decided, "If I am overrun with such people I shall have to tell the Consul that only those who bring letters to me or are known to me or whom he recommends *can* be asked to Government House." A fellow American officer's wife, Caroline Shore wrote home in equally unpleasant terms following a visit to the Taj Mahal. She stated, "While we were there some *horrible* Americans came in—and I was very shocked at the pushing way they looked at everything." She continued, "we have seen some dreadful examples of the globe trotter from the U.S.A. and where and how *this* class of my fellow countrymen can afford to travel I cannot imagine," Thus, the exasperated American wives of British officers understood themselves as belonging to an elevated class, and the vicereine clearly exercised social power by determining who could be admitted to the imperial set, and the official conditions of such an entrance.[32]

Some British officers' wives similarly expressed frustration with the requirement to perform as imperial representatives. Jeanette, following her marriage to Field Marshal William Riddell Birdwood of the Eleventh Bengal Lancers (knighted in 1916 and raised to the peerage as 1st Baron of Anzac and Totnes), objected to her "confined and totally male-oriented" life in India. After marrying into the regiment she complained, "The army wife was not expected to do anything or be anything except a decorative chattel or appendage of her husband . . . she was not expected to be clever. It didn't matter if she wasn't beautiful, so long as she looked reasonable and dressed reasonably and didn't let her husband down by making outrageous remarks at the dinner table." This requirement, although belittled by the irritated Lady Birdwood, who clearly had no reason to elevate her already lofty position, revealed the space in the imperial male world in which a military wife both represented British prestige and wielded social power. Ruby Gray similarly expressed annoyance in performing as an imperial representative. She attended a ceremonial review of the native troops in the early 1900s, "in honour of some Maharajah," and admitted, "in due course Charles and I appeared at the Commander-in-Chief's [General Philip Chetwode, 7th Baronet of Oakley], here I disgraced myself." The officer's wife confessed her moment of shame with: "[W]e entered a long rectangular hall, as I remember its walls of polished marble, stairs going straight up. . . . Ladies on the right, Gents on the left." In turning to face her husband she "said, '[T]his place reminds me of a London Underground lavatory,' saw an awful look on Charles face, turned and found myself facing the Commander in Chief at the top of the stairs . . . surrounded by his entourage, and then [heard] 'Captain Gray and his wife [announced]' in a loud voice." After committing such a faux pas, Mrs. Gray wisely avoided her host for the remainder of the reception. The next morning, unfortunately, she compounded her lack of graciousness. While riding to the railway station in a horse-drawn carriage, she was spotted by General Chetwode, who watched her "progress down the mall," as she sat amongst an assortment of "pots and pans." She clearly understood that she had not presented the most impressive of sights, as she concluded, "This trip to Delhi was the only time I took part in the pomp and pageantry of the British Empire."[33]

Most officers' wives, nonetheless, maintained imperialism by performing their roles with éclat and élan. Despite recognizing attendance as a duty, many American wives found military ceremonial performances both thrilling and delightful. The British utilized display as a vehicle to legitimize the vitality and supremacy of the empire. The American military, however, showcased imperial authority on a much smaller scale than the fantastical durbars. In most instances, parades and celebrations were designed for themselves, their families, and the local civilian population. For example, Frances Grummond recorded a Flag Day ceremony at Fort Phil Kearny that she likened to "a veritable Thanksgiving in the States." With the men on full-dress parade (the entire garrison were issued with new uniforms), the celebrations began with a keynote address given by the garrison commander, Henry Carrington. After reminding all of the "glory and power" they symbolized as representatives of the "land of the free and the home of the brave," he proclaimed, "The Indian dead numbers [sic] yours, fourfold, while your acquired experience and better cause afford you constant success in every encounter. This is not all. . . . The steam whistle and the rattle of the mower have followed your steps in this westward march of empire. You have built a central post that will bear comparison with any for security, completeness and adaptation to the end in view."[34]

The officers' wives witnessed the parade congregated on a purpose-built plat-form, with the commander's wife positioned in the center. "Then," Mrs. Grum-mond recalled, "in quick succession, rang out the orders, Attention! Present arms! Play! Hoist! Fire! With the simultaneous *snap* of presented arms in salute, the long roll of the combined drum corps was followed by the full band playing 'The Star Spangled Banner,' the guns opened fire, and the magnificent flag . . . slowly rose to masthead and was broken out in one glorious flame of red, white, and blue!" The officer's wife then admitted, "The thrill of contending emotions was almost overpowering for the moment. . . . The epaulets and decorations of the officers and the freshly burnished brass shoulder scales of the troops added intense brilliancy." To conclude the day's festivities, "the customary *levee* at headquarters . . . under

Margaret Carrington's genial administration" provided "dancing, singing, and general merrymaking" until midnight. For this officer's wife, the men in their newly issued dress uniforms, the "brilliancy" of the performance, and the "genial administration" of the female grenadier reaffirmed and showcased the strength, competence, and prestige of the American Empire.[35]

Ellen Biddle further illustrated the officers' wives' pleasure in witnessing the pageantry of a military review. Soldiers demonstrated the "principal drill movements required in battle, advancing and firing both mounted and dismounted as skirmishers, and . . . the field-guns . . . shelling the hills. I could well understand their enthusiasm, for, notwithstanding the hundreds of times I have seen it, I am yet, always thrilled with excitement." Writing in the same enthusiastic vein, novelist Mrs. M. A. Cochran's protagonist, Captain Prescott's wife, echoed Mrs. Grummond's exhilaration regarding the Fourth of July celebrations. This distinctly American festivity, although totally devoid of prancing horses and elephants, echoed the resplendent descriptions of the British state visit and durbar described by Madeleine Churcher and Christian Showers-Stirling. Cochran listed the athletic events, fireworks display, "and lemonade by the barrel for the whole command." With the arrival of the "grand moguls [senior military officials and state political leaders] . . . the band would play, and the cannon roar, the troops turn out in force, and the ladies, dressed in their best, would assemble at the commanding officer's quarters to receive them." Officers' wives "dressed in their best" recorded their excitement as participants in the formal displays of power. Acting as adjuncts, they held a duty to meet and greet the "grand moguls," thus underscoring female roles as imperial representatives.[36]

As in the British experience, the duty to display imperial prestige included participation in civilian social events. Located near Silver City, New Mexico, the military community at Fort Bayard interacted regularly with the townspeople in the 1870s. Mrs. Boyd, somewhat disdainfully, described the town's efforts at polite entertaining as "comical." She related a typical evening: "Imagine a ball at which every element is represented, from the most refined to the most uncultivated, from the transplanted branches of excellent Eastern families . . . to the rudest specimens of frontier life, who . . . were devoid of all education, yet, like true Americans, regarded themselves as the very quintessence of knowledge and good breeding." Mrs. Boyd, nonetheless, enjoyed the entertainments and talked of the officers' wives' "pretty dresses . . . shawls and head-gear." With regard to the military events, however, she described the officers' wives' efforts to decorate the garrison ballroom with "beautiful flags, cannon, stacked bayonets and swords," concluding that the military soirées "contrasted favorably" with the civic events. In juxtaposing these social events, Mrs. Boyd delineated the military community as distinct from the civilian. She clearly enjoyed her identity as an attaché, and took great pride in her efforts to display ceremonial artifacts to reaffirm a superior class status, and her confidence in the imperial mission.[37]

A different audience, however, was recorded in Albert Barnitz's letters to his wife Jennie. He described the Seventh U.S. Cavalry's preparations for a reception and escort duty for the United States Peace Commission in October 1867. He reported, "I am getting everything in perfect readiness for the reception of the commissioners, and for the march to the big 'Medicine Lodge!' Have had all the horses shod, and new shoes made, and nails pointed. . . . Have drawn new tents, and clothing, and plenty of ammunition." He continued, "(but you want to hear about the ladies who are going with Genl. Sherman! And about the preparations that Mrs. Genl. Gibbs is making for the grand reception and everything don't you darling?) Yes, and I have had the Gatling Guns put in the nicest order . . . [and] the recruits drilled. . . . Mrs. Genl. Gibbs appears to be having all her best silver ware put in the very best possible order. . . . [A]nd a big tall 'liberty pole' with a golden globe on top, is to be erected on the parade . . . and an immense new garrison flag will be flung out, amid the volleys of artillery." He failed to describe the actual reception, but mentions that the soldiers, during the fourteen-day council at Medicine Lodge, performed a daily drill. He told Jennie, "Well, there are a great many Indians here now—probably 7,000 in all. . . . We are drilling daily, and the camp is daily thronged with Indian spectators, of all ages, sexes and tribes." This unique reference to a daily drill during the government's peace negotiations, witnessed by many indigenous groups, suggests the soldiers demonstrated a show of proficiency, perhaps to gain an advantage for the commissioners. Clearly this echoes the British ceremonial practices recorded by Wells and Paget.[38]

Not all performances, however, consisted of merrymaking, fireworks, and lemonade. Pomp and ceremony played a central disciplinary role within the empires. Although the British officers' wives studied here failed to record an internal punitive ceremony, three American women did. In analyzing two of these accounts, it becomes clear that officers' wives played a passive, but nonetheless important role in observing, recording, and justifying the measures to maintain imperial obedience. Elizabeth Custer provides the first example. Following the Confederate surrender at the Appomattox Courthouse in April 1865, the Custers led the Third Cavalry to Texas. In reaching Alexandria, Louisiana, the military spouse recorded that a "spirit of reckless disregard of authority" pervaded amongst the soldierly ranks. A mutiny of sorts threatened when a petition called for the resignation of a much "hated" officer. George Custer, wishing to maintain order, court-martialed a sergeant (a petitioner who failed to withdraw his complaint) for insubordination and sentenced him to death. This somewhat excessive order prompted the officer's wife to justify her husband's decision. She explained, "Pomp and circumstance are not alone for 'glorious war,' but in army life must also be observed in times of peace. . . . The more form and solemnity, the deeper the impression; and as this day was to be a crucial one, in proving to the insubordinate that order must eventually prevail, nothing was hurried, none of the usual customs were omitted." Five thousand soldiers apparently mustered for the ceremonial execution of the aforementioned sergeant and a deserter. Elizabeth Custer recorded, "The wagon . . . bearing the criminals sitting on their coffins, was driven at a slow pace around the square, escorted by the guard and the firing-party, with reversed arms." She continued, "The coffins were placed in the centre of the square, and the [convicted] men seated upon them at the foot of their open graves." The firing squad took aim and shot the deserter. Remarkably, the recalcitrant mutineer, who had unknowingly received a last-minute reprieve, was spared. George Custer deliberately delayed announcing the sergeant's pardon to fully utilize the power of pomp and pageantry for internal deterrent purposes.[39]

This example of regimental discipline illustrates that Elizabeth Custer, as an officer's wife, witnessed, reported, and validated her husband's decision-making process. Although she played no active role in this episode, she clearly understood the differences in active and peacetime soldiering, and the tensions of maintaining unquestioned military obedience. Despite expressing sympathy for the condemned sergeant and his family, her overriding fear concerned the safety of her husband. Scholars agree that her memoirs, published after Custer's death, promoted and reified the military hero, thus must be interpreted through this purposeful bias. In her writings, she portrays her husband as a fair and effective commander of men, and the incident as one effected for its preventative value. Additionally, in witnessing the ceremonial execution Mrs. Custer understood that in recording such "pomp and circumstance" to ensure "that order must eventually prevail," she assisted in legitimizing such actions.[40]

Alice Baldwin also included an account of pageantry utilized as an internal mechanism to maintain the façade of military strength. In 1867, while stationed at "one of the most remote military posts on the frontier," she penned the following vignette: "Desertions from this post were frequent. I witnessed my first spectacle of this sort at [Fort] Wingate." An American and an English soldier had been captured following deserting and "were sentenced to one side of their heads shaved and to be drummed out of camp." Watched by the entire garrison, the deserters walked ahead of a drummer and fifer who played "The Rogue's March." On reaching the camp perimeter, the Englishman turned "the shaved side of his head to toward the spectators" and proffered "a mocking salute and a bow." The American soldier simply "went his way." Not quite the harsh punishment meted out by Custer, or the branding inflicted by the British Army. Yet, the removal of hair and the symbolic march of shame clearly functioned to diminish masculinity in the disgraced men. Mrs. Baldwin recorded the event in a factual style, under the chapter title "Monotony of Garrison Life." Perhaps the frequency of desertions and punishments reduced these ceremonial performances to simply normal affairs, and the brazen insolence of the Englishman rendered this parade noteworthy. Mesdames Custer and Baldwin, nevertheless, acted as witnesses, alongside the soldiers, to the power play of disciplinary pageantry. Tasked by William T. Sherman to act as imperial observers, these adjuncts held power through their writing to justify rituals of obedience, thus sustaining the internal authority of the army.[41]

In the U.S. West we do not see magnificent durbars or state receptions staged for the American Indian elite—spectacles performed to facilitate diplomatic overtures and legitimize authority. Yet external episodes occurred, albeit on a far less ostentatious scale. Martha Summerhayes described a unique attempt to engage, on an official social footing, with the tribal peoples. She attributed this "project" to the monotony of military life during the winter months. Whilst stationed at Camp Apache, Arizona, the commander, Bvt. Maj. William Worth, decided to stage a social event for the indigenous elite. Worth "decided to give a dance in his quarters, and invite the chiefs. I think the other officers did not wholly approve of it, although they felt friendly enough towards them, as long as they were not causing disturbances." Summerhayes, however, exclaimed, "But to meet the savage Apache on the basis of social equality, in an officer's quarters, and to dance the quadrille with him! Well, the limit of all things had been reached." Despite this reluctance, Worth was "determined to carry out his project." So, the commander set about decorating his quarters with "evergreen boughs," and secured banjo and guitar players from amongst his men. Summerhayes noted that all officers and wives attended, "and the chiefs with their harems, came to this novel fete." The festivities she described as follows: "A quadrille was formed, in which the chiefs danced opposite the officers. The squaws sat around, as they were too shy to dance. These chiefs were painted, and wore only their necklaces and the customary loincloth, throwing their blankets about their shoulders when they had finished dancing.... Conversation was carried on principally by signs and nods, and through the interpreter." She concluded that "[t]he party passed off pleasantly enough and was not especially subversive to discipline, although I believe it was not repeated."[42]

This single recorded social event to entertain, on equal social footing, the Native American elite bears similarities to the British imperial sociability. The local Apache tribal bands, according to Summerhayes, assisted the garrison with scouting duties. Perhaps Major Worth was a progressive commander who understood the value of elevating affinity between the American and Apache communities. Or, perhaps as Summerhayes stated, he simply suffered from ennui. In a later meeting with Major Worth she advised, "He was no longer a bachelor, but a dignified married man." So, a third interpretation suggests that Summerhayes brokered the information to excuse this highly unusual episode as the excesses of a single man. The officers, nonetheless, despite their disapproval, all dutifully attended the dance. Summerhayes recorded her understanding of the "White Mountain Apache [as] a fierce and cruel tribe, whose depredations and atrocities had been carried on for years." Yet hostilities had been somewhat controlled by the "surveillance of the Government, and guarded by a strong garrison of cavalry and infantry at Camp Apache." Indeed, on several occasions she described Diablo, one of the Apache chiefs, not as hostile and forbidding, but as "a handsome fellow" with "extraordinary good looks."[43]

Other social interactions with the American Indians occurred in the U.S. West, but in a far less formal manner. Angelina, wife of Lt. Charles Johnson of the Fourteenth U.S. Infantry, recorded life at Camp Robinson, Nebraska. She described in letters to her sister the events surrounding the death of Crazy Horse in 1877, and of the Cheyenne escape attempt in 1879. But she also wrote of daily life in camp and mentioned an incident when "Mrs Brown, Mrs Yates (both fellow officer wives) and I 'called' on Mrs. Red Cloud. . . . It was the first time I had been in a tepee. It was just like the one at the [Philadelphia] Centennial." Johnson also recorded that one morning after Crazy Horse's death, his "father was out walking across the parade [ground] and crying and mourning greatly. I felt sorry for the old fellow and Charlie went out and brought him in and gave him his breakfast." Another social occasion, detailed by Frances Roe, concerned entertaining Powder-Face, an Arapaho chief, and his partner Wauk for a luncheon. She found, despite her initial reservations, that she enjoyed the event, describing Wauk as a "remarkable squaw" who appeared to be "a princess by birth."[44]

Similarly, Elizabeth Burt described a "festive event" when "Mrs. Iron Bull" conducted a formal visit to see the "Big White Chief's squaw." As the partner of

Chief Iron Bull and ambassador of the Crow tribe, she wore what Burt describes as her "best attire" consisting of "a buckskin dress . . . adorned with elk teeth and embroidery of porcupine quills. . . . A black leather belt . . . [that] had embedded brass tacks spelling the name 'Iron Bull' . . . was fastened with an army buckle. Round her neck were strung rows of bright beads. . . . Every squaw seemed to possess a handsome suit for festive occasions of which this was one." Although somewhat reluctant to allow her infant daughter to be held by Mrs. Iron Bull and her entourage of Crow women, Burt decided to acquiesce. She remarked, "This was certainly a puzzling request as their reputation for cleanliness was not of unquestionable nature; but they were all in gala attire and looked as if their skins had been well scrubbed with soap and water." Additionally, Burt recorded her visit to Chief Iron Bull's home inside the stockade. "As a mail carrier for the garrison in winter and so employed by Uncle Sam he was given this great privilege. His wife kept their two rooms in presentable condition and seemed anxious to acquire something of the ways of white people. Of her merits as a cook I had no means of judging, and possessed no desire to test her culinary progress." Burt chose not to accept the Crow women with social grace despite their great care to dress with respect, and Mrs. Iron Bull's home and capabilities as a homemaker were disparaged. The informal "festive event," then, provided the Anglo woman with an opportunity to display and record her assumed notions of superiority, thus alleviating her own anxiety with regard to her identity and status.[45]

As a final example, Elizabeth Custer reported her role as an observer, and the observed, when visiting the Cheyenne prisoner stockade near Fort Hays. George Custer acted as the ambassador between the U.S. Army and the imprisoned Cheyenne, and his wife accompanied him to a traditionally all-male council meeting. This unusual episode required her to interact with the captured tribal peoples as a national representative. Elizabeth's report of the episode provided an opportunity for her to articulate a claim to superior identity and status. In undertaking her duty, she constructed differences through appearance and behavior. She wished, contrary to custom, that the young, attractive Cheyenne women had formed a reception committee, and totally lambasted the female elders who traditionally held Cheyenne societal roles as diplomats. Her description of these women includes "withered and wizened. . . . [R]epulsive. . . . Hideous old frights. . . . Cunning and crafty . . . [and] bent old witches." Despite Custer's clear distaste, however, she apparently "forced a smile of feigned pleasure." She described the Cheyenne female attire as fashioned in a primitive way, the children as naked apart from loincloths, yelling, gesticulating, and scuffling. She considered their keen bowmanship, like "embryo chiefs," demonstrated "how truly the child is the father to the man." Additionally, she noted that when the hunting parties returned with buffalo meat, "the tiny sons of braves cut strips from the raw meat and ate it, turning with wide-eyed wonder when we exclaimed at this evidence of barbaric tastes." Even in taking her place beside her husband at the diplomatic meeting, she noted that the couple sat on the floor, and she experienced discomfort due to the "the peculiar Indian odor, but etiquette forbade my going into the open air." In recording the official visit Custer elevated her status and role, and, as Leckie points out, in her published narratives indigenous lifeways were compared negatively against Anglo norms, thus providing an ideological rationalization for subjugation.[46]

Despite the informality of social performances in the U.S. West, all officers and wives at Camp Apache dutifully attended Major Worth's social event, Roe entertained an Arapaho chief and his wife over luncheon, Burt participated in Crow festive events, and Custer inspected, and was inspected by, the Cheyenne women, and attended a diplomatic gathering. Unfortunately, we are not told of the social role undertaken by Summerhayes at the dance project, but Roe, to her own surprise, enjoyed meeting and greeting Chief Powder-Face and Wauk. Burt, however, describes her meeting at Fort C. F. Smith with Mrs. Iron Bull in negative terms. The episodes, although far less formal than in the British experience, indicate the requirement for the American officers' wives' to be fully immersed and involved with the operation of imperialism. They were required to attend functions as national representatives, and to legitimize the superiority of the American armed forces operating in the western reaches.

British and American officers' wives stationed with their husbands in India and the U.S. West fully participated in furthering imperialist ambitions. They were expected to participate in public events as adjuncts who shared and supplemented their husbands' duties. In the evolvement of an imperial masculinity and femininity, it becomes clear that certain ideals, values, and characteristics determined who could be accepted as representatives of national prestige. The bodies and behaviors of the dutiful "manly" officer and his genteel "self-sufficient" wife became appropriated to symbolize affluence, civility, and authority. Female complicity in acting as dutiful ambassadors generated avenues of social power unavailable to women from the mainstream "home" societies. These military spouses constructed exaggerated military versions of transnationally carried Victorian practices of dining-out and ceremonial performances. They dutifully participated in social rituals, determined admission criteria, and personified class status. In presenting a veneer of superior sociability these women reinforced an aura of civility and confidence within the imperial communities, broadcast images of authority to civilians, and, in the British experience, to the external indigenous population.

Both sets of military wives, however, understood their imperial status as temporary—existing only on the peripheries. Indeed, the redoubtable Isabella Fane illustrated her understanding of her role as transitory. She wrote to her aunt, "[A]nother great military dinner [at Cawnpore] . . . and grand station ball. . . . [Y]ou talk of my grandeur, and the airs I shall give myself when I return. I thought of you on this occasion much, I was *so* great." She confirmed her status as the senior lady at a regimental mess dinner by explaining, "I was met at the door by the two greatest men at the station and marched into the room supported by them. . . . Well, it was supper time and no one could go [in to dine] till I did." In recognizing the distinctness of her privileged position in India, she mused, "I don't dislike my position, but I shall feel my utter insignificance again on my return to my native land, and act as before." American Lydia Lane similarly observed, "After Colonel Lane was retired, and we lived in the East and North, it took me some time to understand that I need not look for the numerous courtesies to which I had always been accustomed at an army frontier post, and that if I went out at all, I must join the army of 'wall flowers,' and expect nothing." Nineteenth-century military women such as Fane and Lane recognized that their social power and imperial status would be unavailable to them in mainstream societies. By performing as adjuncts they negotiated within the spaces between formal and informal authority. Pomp and ceremony, therefore, functioned as a source, not just a reflection, of status and authority. In constructing this avenue of power, the officers' wives shared their husbands' remit to promote and preserve internal and external imperial images of prestige.[47]

In examining the public duties of the officers' wives in "the days of Empire," it becomes clear that they identified with their military husbands' sense of mission and responsibility. These women enacted public sociability, yet the home itself played a central role in determining how they manufactured and exercised power. In referring specifically to this intimate site, Elizabeth Custer announced that, in "keeping the home fires burning," officers' wives shared the responsibility to overcome "insurmountable obstacles" to open "up the country to civilization." Indeed, she realized that the obligation to support the imperial mission existed not only in the public realm, but also dominated the domestic landscape.[48]

6

Imperial Gender Crossings

*Officers' and Wives' Dress and Homemaking
on the Edges of Empire*

> Common dangers, common hopes, common interests: these
> three go far to make India the friendly land she is: and it is to
> her Englishwomen that she looks for her social wellbeing. Every
> Anglo-Indian wife is by necessity a hostess. . . . Whatever her
> natural inclination, she must needs accept the fact that her house,
> and all that therein is, belongs, in a large measure, to her neighbour
> also.
>
> —*Maud Diver*

In addition to acting as public imperial functionaries, officers' wives modified core ideals of the middle-class home to articulate the authority and prestige of the nation. E. M. Forster's novel *A Passage to India* offered a social commentary of life in nineteenth-century India that demonstrates the centrality of the domestic space. One of the characters, Ronny Heaslop, a minor civil servant, frustratingly announced, "[I]t's not like home—one's always facing the footlights." His mother, "accustomed to the privacy of London . . . could not realize that India . . . contains none, and that consequently the [social] conventions have greater force." In clarifying his understanding of the imperial mission Ronny concluded, "[W]e're out here to do justice and keep the peace. . . . India isn't a drawing-room." Yet military homes were appropriated as imperial sites. In holding control of this domestic space, officers' wives generated female power within the intimate spaces of the cantonment and garrison accommodations to produce and reproduce national status and prestige.[1]

The armed forces in both nations regulated appearance through uniforms to distinguish the men as imperial representatives. Wives, however, utilized transported middle-class dress codes to signal identity. In British India the female body became regulated as an imperial text to ensure a cohesive front in providing a visual distance between the rulers and the ruled. Kevin Adams asserts that consumer consumption in the U.S. western garrisons, however, was "a class imperative" and officers "used consumption to define themselves as the socio-cultural elite," to "reif[y] their upper-class standing in the fluid social world of the western frontier . . . [and] to illustrate prosperity and gentility." So, in the American western experience, although far less formalized than the British model, dress and décor became a tool to create a domestic design that would socially distance the officer class from the enlisted and civilian populations. Within both military settler communities, for different purposes, women and men designed and self-regulated image to construct and maintain an elevated status.[2]

By making personal choices in dress and home décor, two visual texts that bridged public and private spaces, it is clear that officers' wives crossed the Victorian borders of gendered authority. Utilizing transported ornamentation they had at their disposal, these women generated an imperial identity that reflected yet transformed upper- and middle-class gender models. They created and enforced a dress code of respectability for women and men, and adapted middle-class markers of interior design. This female effort became appropriated to symbolize status and prestige. In gaining power, however, officers' wives also lost power, as the female appearance became controlled, more so in the British experience. The imperial strategy of "going native" (assimilation of indigenous elements into dress codes), within limits—although sanctioned for their male counterparts—was prohibited to the female. This strategy was utilized to a far greater degree in India, where the British Army adopted certain indigenous style elements into regulation uniform. This course of action attempted to facilitate and symbolize benevolent imperialism. The informal absorption of American Indian clothing by the U.S. Cavalry appears to have occurred due to the practicality of such dress. As incorporated imperial representatives, officers' wives contributed to regulating the image of the empire. This encroachment upon masculine territory, however, suffered a direct counterassault—forays by the men themselves into the feminine realm.[3]

Nineteenth-century officers' spouses stationed on liminal national territories utilized middle-class values and markers to demarcate an imperial class. But what identified the middle class? Victorian domesticity, a reaction to industrialization and urbanization in both England and America, viewed Queen Victoria—who ruled both as a mother and a sovereign—as a role model. A thriving business class had emerged in England that looked to the monarch for guidance on tasteful respectability. Her court became a "symbol for morality," and she governed successfully by manipulating male statesmen through personal influence, while projecting a public image of doting wife and mother. The model of royal aristocracy, which the middle class sought to emulate, pivoted around the principle of respectability. Having no ancestral legacies, the rising capitalist middle class engaged in conspicuous consumption, imitating emblems of taste, refinement, and virtue to furnish a middle-class identity. In short, the middle-class stratum commandeered markers of gentility, purchased and exhibited such tasteful artifacts, thus creating a reproducible and recognizable image. The woman became the artist, her body and home the canvas to display claims of social positioning.[4]

Scholars advise that homes, food, dress, and internal décor established reputation. Indeed, the social activity of conspicuous consumption gained the notice, approbation, and emulation of community members. Display, then, of specific tasteful commodities provided visual social knowledge that set definitive class boundaries. Women, as homemakers and purchasers, determined and maintained these public symbols of status. To promote, standardize, and stabilize these recognizable class markers generated social anxiety caused by rapid industrialization and changing patterns of urbanization. The arrival and popularity of Mrs. Beeton's *Book of Household Management* in 1861 both answered and exploited these tensions, yet, in reflecting and specifying a model middle-class female, Mrs. Beeton provided the nascent social group with a sustainable image. The concomitant rise of an equally insecure American capitalist class generated an ideology of sentimental sincerity to furnish markers of identity. Like Mrs. Beeton's manual, Catharine Beecher's *A Treatise on Domestic Economy* (1845) acted to provide a cultural reflection of claims to status and to inculcate a universal style of genteel female clothing. Differing from the British experience, the practical instructions advocated simple and sensible gowns, hoping to inspire adherence to a sincere mode of attire that would reflect a more practical and democratic people.[5]

The focus for Victorian, middle-class American woman, according to Glenna Matthews, appeared to be less materialistic and emphasized the practical, democratic, and ceremonial. This reflects, perhaps, the nation's political identity and ambition. Additionally, Karen Halttunen posits that the post–Revolutionary War society sought to establish a unique American identity based on republican values.

She argues that with the rise of a new capitalist class, and its concomitant need to forge an identity, a negative female stereotype of a "painted lady" became embedded in the collective consciousness. This figure of hypocrisy, who dressed in the latest fashion styles, arose from "a crisis of social identity" during the early nineteenth century. To counteract such a virago, the middle class invented cultural symbols of sincerity and a less ostentatious dress code that sought to establish claims to gentility. Indeed, Halttunen posits that the "sentimental ideal of sincerity . . . was central to the self-conscious self-definition of a unique middle-class culture."[6]

An important connection between British and American middle-class women during the late Victorian era, according to Maureen Montgomery, lay "in their [American] adoption of polite European conventions in order to press home their social claims." The "ideal" woman used dress to signal tasteful respectability. Indeed, the symbolism of fashion-forward dress lay in its role of creating social distance between the classes. Working-class women, now able to purchase mass-produced garments, had reduced the social void, so wearing the latest Paris and London fashions became essential. In comparing experiences, it becomes clear that dress and homemaking played a central part in forging identity. Scholarly interpretations proffer different national means to establish identity based on tasteful gentility. The English lady looked to royalty as a model for respectable behavior and decorum, and used elegant markers of conspicuous consumption to signal status. Her American counterpart looked across the Atlantic for guidance, and then adapted this model by creating sentimental sincerity, a supposedly less ostentatious representation of middle-class womanhood. In both cultures the home provided the central locus for cultural and social determination and transmission of class status. Claiming sole authority for cultural symbols of identity, women employed dress and domestic décor to establish, and broadcast, an image of middle-class respectability.[7]

Before the 1980s, scholars tended to regard dress choices as unimportant. This perception changed with the rise of feminist scholarship. Emma Tarlo, for example, insists that "clothes are badges of identity," and as historical artifacts play an active role in assembling, maintaining, and expressing individual and collective identities. Fashion wear provides an avenue to classify oneself, through the processes of identification and differentiation, as inside or outside a particular social group. Anthropologists agree that clothing should be interpreted as symbols of power and authority. Imperialism contains, in addition to the political and economic strands, this cultural element, and women's bodies and outfit selections functioned as authentic textual symbols.[8]

The British woman incorporated clothes to represent imperial vigor and the superiority of the empire. Dress, according to one anonymous nineteenth-century commentator, functioned to distinguish the individual by projecting an image. Indeed, this social observer advised, "there should be harmony between your dress and your circumstances. It should accord with your means, your house, your furniture, the place in which you reside, and the society in which you move." With regard to daywear for the mistress of the house, the author warned, "A Lady, while performing the morning duties of the house may wear a plain loose dress, made high in the neck, and with long sleeves fastened at the wrist. It must not look slatternly." This routine of wearing different dress styles, according to the time of day, was transported empire wide. Regarding the central significance of imperial costume, Sylvia Leith-Ross, an imperial officer's wife, while traveling by canoe on the Benue River, Nigeria, recalled, "We had always dressed for dinner. This was the rule that could not be broken, either at home or abroad, at sea or on shore, in the Arctic Circle or on the Equator." In obeying this call of duty, no matter where she found herself, this officer's wife changed her clothes to uphold "our own and our country's dignity." Indeed, Mrs. Leith-Ross continued, "when you are . . . dazed by unaccustomed sights and sounds, bemused by strange ways of life and thought, you need to remember who you are, where you come from, and what your standards are." As Helen Callaway asserts, "dressing for dinner" emphasizes race and rank to symbolize British "innate superiority." She analyzes the gender division signaled by attire by adding, "the prescribed dress of colonial officers was characterized by pomp and plumage enhancing masculinity; that of their wives was marked by propriety and femininity." The purpose of this binary opposition, Callaway determines, was to heighten the masculinity of the British imperial male by utilizing his wife's body as a foil. She concludes that "the uniforms and prescribed clothing brilliantly enhanced the imperial spectacle and the dominant power this represented."[9]

Military wives of both nations attempted to maintain upper- and middle-class styles in the imperial holdings. The utilization of personal dress to symbolize identity and status clearly transported itself to India, literally within the ladies' portmanteaus. A survival guide for the British in India dictated that female, male, and military dress must replicate the current British trends. With regard to evening dress the author suggested, "silk, moiré, even velvet is worn; in fact, exactly what is worn at home; but light blue always spots and turns yellow, and every shade of lilac and mauve looks dreadful in the light of the oil lamps. A white and a black lace dress are a *sine qua non* [an indispensable element] . . . as well as some dresses unmade, as the tailors make beautifully from a pattern. But it is necessary to be very particular in taking every requisite in the way of trimming, fringe, lace, buttons, blonde, sewing silk, &c., . . . [as it] is certain to be very far dearer than at home."[10]

Similarly, Flora Steel and Grace Gardiner published an Indian housekeeping manual, providing instructions on fabrics, styles, and necessary items. The need to exercise moderation in packing British outer, inner, and under wear provided a constant theme. The authors recommended, however, "A *few*, and for small stations, *very few*, good evening dresses should be brought out . . . [as] you naturally want to appear well and fashionably dressed. This you cannot hope to do, unless you are a millionaire . . . since they will go hopelessly out of fashion. . . . On the other hand, there is a vast amount of friendly entertainment in India. . . . [O]*ne* should always be ready for an occasion." Social life in India, the authors cautioned, can seldom be anticipated, yet, they warned, "dress becomingly . . . and never, even in the wilds, exist without one civilized evening and morning dress. That important envelope with the big red seal may come any day and you may find yourself in the paradise of a big station unable to appear for the want of clothes!"[11]

An officer's wife fulfilled a duty to promote prestige through dress. Indeed, the knowledgeable Steel and Gardiner warned, "We do not advocate any sloppiness in dress; on the contrary, we would inveigh against any yielding to . . . lassitude and indifference." Aware of being continually under the imperial gaze, officers' wives anxiously attempted to stay in vogue. They copied dress patterns from magazines and wrote letters home and to each other for details of the latest styles. For example, in a letter from "a lady in camp to a lady in cantonments," Honoria Lawrence wrote, "The *durzee* you sent me works neatly enough, but cannot cut out. Will you send me a good *dobee*? Ours is a very bad one. When the *boccas-wallah* comes, will you get me some European buttons and a thimble? I should be obliged if you will let me have the pattern of your collar, and desire the *chiccau-wallah* to work one like it. . . . I am really ashamed of giving you so much trouble. . . . I want something to make a warm dress . . . and I shall be much obliged by your sending me some cloth for the purpose." Not only do we read of a female anxiety to keep up appearances in camp, but another point worth making is the level of adoption of the indigenous culture. Illustrated within five lines of a letter written to another officer's wife, the vocabulary used included a very natural, everyday use of Indian terms, which the recipient undoubtedly understood and utilized. This level of absorption is not evident in the American narratives, yet most of the British officer's wives' accounts regularly include a wide array of such indigenous words.[12]

Another example, recorded by the British Madeline Wallace-Dunlap, demonstrates the requirement to don a complete ensemble—at all times. Madeline reported of her unwell sister, "Her hair had all been cut off during her fever . . . it was very inconvenient for her to wear a hat, and I saw not the slightest impropriety in her going without one, particularly as we rarely met anyone in our quiet neighbourhood. But the good people around thought differently, and after two or three hints on the singularity of our proceedings, poor Nora was obliged, in deference to public opinion, always to have a hat at hand, ready to pop on if any English person approached us." Such a level of anxiety—about a mere hat—speaks to the extent of British insecurity of identity, and the very real need to project a collective image of imperial authority.[13]

In describing her trousseau, newlywed Ellen Drummond appeared totally prepared to represent the nation—and in readiness perhaps for the coveted red-sealed envelope. She listed the muslin, silk, and satin dresses and jackets, and ordered new outfits, petticoats, silk stockings, and colored ribbons to be sent to her in India. She instructed her mother to "get fashionable ones [dresses], they [women] all seem to wear them short now," along with matching hats and a blue satin ball gown. Additionally, she demanded, "[G]et Mrs Croxton to make them and not Mrs Mason for the latter does not fit half as well and she makes [them] in an old-fashioned way." Eliza, the wife of Calcutta solicitor Anthony Fay, confirmed Drummond's anxiety: "The ladies here are very fashionable I assure you. I found several novelties in dress since I quitted England which a good deal surprised me, as I had no idea that fashion travelled so fast." Outfits, then, perhaps styled by the fashion-forward Mrs. Croxton, proved to be not simply a feminine frippery but an obligation for the imperial ladies stationed at the remote settlements of empire.[14]

On the perplexing problem of maintaining an *exclusive* dress code, essential to the display of status in an age of mass consumerism, Mrs. Beeton offered the following observation: "[D]omestics no longer know their place . . . the introduction of cheap silks and cottons, and still more recently, those ambiguous 'materials' and tweeds, have removed the landmarks between the mistress and her maid." This identification of lower-class mimicry spoke to the anxiety of losing textual claims to social ranking. This problem found a resolution in upper- and middle-class fidelity to seasonal and designer trends. This social and cultural commitment voiced itself with unnerving regularity throughout the journals and memoirs of the officers' wives. Isabella Fane, in her gossipy and condescending style, spoke to this imitation by writing, "I wish you could have seen a specimen of the Calcutta gentry in the shape of a lady who called upon us this morning. . . . This woman was once a cook. Upon this occasion she was drest [sic] Oh! So fine, with little plaistered [sic] oval curls. . . . Her bonnet was put well back on her head to . . . display two gold combs. She was rouged to the eyes. . . . Her person was enveloped in white and blue, and in her hand she carried a feather fan. . . . Before she had well left the room I burst into a roar of laughter." Miss Fane's unkind response reveals the fragility of the reliance on tasteful attire to demonstrate status. A more gracious vignette found inclusion in a journal written by Emily Eden. In attending a regimental ball, she noted a shortage of single women for dance partners. She noted "the only other unmarried woman also appeared for the first time as a lady. Her father has just been raised from the ranks for good conduct. The poor girl was very awkward and ill-dressed, but looked very amiable." The reliance on dress codes compelled the more insecure Fane to deliver a character assassination of a former cook. The refined Miss Eden, even while excluding the enlisted man's daughter from pretensions to imperial status, had the good grace to describe the ill-dressed young lady in a kindly manner.[15]

The obligation to remain fashionably dressed in British India, to mark one's membership in the imperial class, appears, however, to have an unexpected reverse effect. Harriette Ashmore identified this process by declaring, "Persons [in India] seem to have established a kind of right to ask impertinent questions, which, in good society at home, would stagger the most self-possessed. . . . I have frequently heard a lady newly arrived from England questioned as to the price of her bonnet, the name and residence of her milliner, and her particular charges." Furthermore, the participation in the local economic culture encouraged such bad form, and "may in some measure be accounted for by the deceit and cunning which is practiced by every native tradesman." Indeed, the vulgar inquiry into wardrobe costs outraged Florence Marryat, who complained, "Some of the European women in India have a horrid custom, when they are leaving a place, or tired of their wardrobes, of sending round a native with a box to the various houses, with their old things for sale, and faded ball-dresses, crushed wreaths of flowers, and other articles of female gear." She continued, "They thought I held my head 'very high' the first time I expressed my unmitigated disgust at the bare notion of wearing an evening robe which had already been worn by another, and affirmed that I would rather go without a dress." Mrs. Marryat made no attempt to hide her revulsion at the idea of wearing a secondhand garment, or of discussing costs. In aping the aristocracy, she reflected the notion that to mention wealth, in any situation, constituted a severe breach of polite manners.[16]

Women's clothing, as a cultural statement of status, traditionally belongs in the female gendered space. Yet the sources indicate that this duty to dress impeccably—not only in a British style—but fashion-forward, was an obligation equally imposed by an interloper, the imperial *male*. Emma Roberts recalled, "Nor do these gallant cavaliers [army officers] disdain to attend to trifles which are generally deemed to belong exclusively to the feminine department; they condescend to report upon flounces and furbelows, descending to all the minutiae of plaits and puckering, and criticizing the whole paraphernalia, from the crowning comb to the shoe-tie." She admitted that the men preached to a female choir, yet this intrusion into the female arena evidences a power shift. Not only did the women generate a standard code of dress, but military men acted as the imperial fashion police.[17]

"In all this the gentlemen are the ringleaders," disclosed Roberts, and confessed, "[I]t is the dread of their ridicule which influences the weaker sex." She, however, modified this claim with, "It may be said that their sarcasms are encouraged by their female friends, and their gossiping tales well received; but as they are clearly the majority, it must be in their power to introduce a better system." No doubt appears in Miss Roberts's mind that military men held substantial power in this feminine arena. Another, rather impudent, masculine incursion into traditional feminine affairs occurred in Simla. Apparently a change in hairstyle fashion caused the junior officers on leave at the hill station to stage a protest. Sir Edward Buck recalled, "It was in the early [eighteen] sixties that the feminine chignon attained such a size that it sorely troubled the masculine mind, and a few subalterns in 1863 decided to signify their disapproval of the fashion. They accordingly appeared one evening at the band stand with their ponies' tails tied up in chignon form." In causing such a sensation, Buck concluded, "Not only were they sent to 'Coventry' by the fair sex, but they received a plain hint from a high military authority that the plains were more suitable for such jokes than the hills. And down they went." This male incursion into the feminine world of fashion acted to prescribe and police the imperial dress standards. Although the young officers were banished to the plains, these "ringleaders" clearly enforced the imperial dress and ornamentation norm, compelling—through ridicule—wives to self-regulate their style choices.[18]

The flexing of male muscle across traditional gender boundaries was not a one-way process. Imperial women set and policed male standards of dress and behavior, with far greater impact. Their sanctions threatened not simply ridicule but the real loss of reputation, and even ostracism. Reflecting the female consensus, in 1841 Mrs. Clemons published a behavioral code for the newly arrived young officer. Dress, she advised, should combine "good sense with good taste," and warned of the dangers of slovenly appearance. Indeed, the following cameo stressed the importance of a wife's responsibility for her husband's habits. She instructed, "I once knew a gentleman who had practiced, during the years he was an ensign and lieutenant, this unbecoming attire [disgraceful undress], though he never appeared either in company or on parade without being suitably dressed. But when he married," she continued, "he found himself incapable, in the house, of keeping on his shoes, stockings, or jacket. . . . Frequently ladies have called upon Mrs.—, and been ushered into her hall, before the bare feet of her husband could make their escape at an opposite door, which caused the blush of shame to mount her cheek, from the slovenliness and dirty appearance of her husband." The potency of rumor-mongering becomes apparent as she concluded, "[A]nd a lady once remarked to her, that she knew many ladies did not call so frequently as they otherwise would do, as they always found Captain — undressed. The habit, however, was so strong . . . he was less respected in society . . . and his amiable wife partially neglected on this account."[19]

Similarly, Isabella Fane frequently carried out her visiting duties, as befitted the female representative of the commander-in-chief. On one such occasion a pregnant "nice lady" received Miss Fane, her sister-in-law, and a Captain Campbell "*en robe de chambre*," an inappropriate dress code that Fane determined "a very disgraceful sight." Here then, are examples of the married female, within her home, holding accountability for imperial representations. The lack of control over a husband's slovenly appearance impacted social acceptability, reducing a couple's reputation. Even a heavily pregnant woman, resting in her own drawing room, could not escape censure by the critical imperial eye.[20]

As an "enlisted" American ambassador, Teresa Vielé described herself as a "tough, weather-proof, India-rubber woman," by whom "the allurements of dress, petty artifices, tears, or any other little feminine failures" were "scorned contemptu-ously." In arriving at Galveston, Texas, in the early 1850s, her contempt for the white populace became clear. Whilst at dinner in a local hotel she "noticed several of these honored [Texan] ladies at the table. . . . Their toilets reminded me very strongly of the baboon's sister in nursery tales, described as wearing 'a dark black frock, and green glass breastpin.' None of them, however, excited my spontaneous admiration." Mrs. Vielé's scornful regard of the wrong kind of feminine frippery, shows that officers' wives, just like the British women, fulfilled their fashion duty. By reporting negatively of the pioneer women in Texas, this officer's wife reassured herself that she, in dressing according to the dictates of fashion, embodied the superiority of a national representative.[21]

The officers' wives' exertions to present—through silk ball gowns, uncrushed flower wreaths, and hats—a face of imperial strength and cohesion required solidarity of the communities in British India and the U.S. West. Scholars frequently identify a sense of class uncertainty in the need to standardize and control the image of empire, and women played a pivotal role in allaying such fears by designing and maintaining a harmonious façade of prestige. The British officers' wives attempted to replicate social and cultural standards in a different geographical and cultural location, yet they eagerly adopted local customs. Tiger hunting, *zenana* visiting, and elephant riding became accepted genteel pastimes—a far cry from the pastoral female world in England, yet perfectly acceptable in India. A passive imperial process, designed to create an affinity between the rulers and the ruled, lay in cultural exchange, although, the levels of assimilation had to be kept in close check—the British needed to remain identifiably British at all times. High-level East India Company men, whose ideas of protocol filtered down the ranks of civil and military officers, dictated an aristocratic Anglo-Indian society norm. William Huggins, an independent commenter, observed of the company officials, "They are deeply imbued with its [Indian] manners, and acquire something like the pride of nabobs, in their notions of self-importance. Accustomed to a luxurious style of living, which equals that of noblemen in England; to authority over a numerous population; to flattery and submission from underlings." The nabob, as a hybrid male figure of Indian and British culture, blurred imperial boundaries. His aspirations to grandeur threatened the domestic upper class, who censured the arriviste as an arrogant parvenu. To define and project a British identity in India then, one needed to retain Victorian ideals of respectability, somewhat adapting, yet limiting, the process of transculturation. Thus, while having to adjust to changes, such as climate, diet, and terrain, the "well-entrenched horror of going native" provided a self-regulating force that standardized and controlled the cultural integrity of the imperial community—and attire functioned as a major determinant.[22]

The rigidity of a dress code, imposed by both sexes, signaled the authority, civility, and superiority of the British community. "The necessity which tyrant custom—perhaps policy, has imposed on us, of continuing to appear in European dress—particularly *uniform*, on almost all public occasions, and in all formal parties" made it one of life's miseries, exclaimed Royal Navy surgeon James Johnson. He conceded, however, "that this ceremony is often waved [*sic*] in the more social circles." Yet, he observed, even in the Indian heat, "It too often happens . . . that a spice of ceremony attaches to the kind host—or perhaps hostess, in which case . . . no encouragement will be given to derobe." This social ritual, nonetheless, served a far more important function than simply "a spice of ceremony." An Englishwoman who adopted Indian styles might signal to European men sexual availability comparable to the Indian mistress. As the consummate symbol of Western civilization, morality, and refinement, most wives dutifully conformed to Victorian dress and behavior codes. To fall prey to the delights of Indian styles and ornamentation would render them ineffective representatives, and irreparably ruin their reputation—and that of the empire.[23]

The analysis of female bodies, as sites and texts for imperial symbolism, allows the centrality played by officers' wives in imperial affairs to become visible. An observation made by Captain Thomas Williamson of the Bengal Army in 1790 presents an additional facet to the fear of a British woman "going native." He commented, "The ladies of Hindostan smoke their *goorgoories* in very high stile [*sic*]; as do those of inferior rank their *nereauls*, or cocoa-nuts, with no less glee. . . . After a while, we become reconciled to seeing [Indian] females smoking; though I must confess, that . . . a certain idea, not very conformable to feminine propriety, creeps into our minds, when we see an European lady thus employed." He continued, "We revolt at a habit not authorized by what we have been accustomed to . . . and consider it an intrusion upon masculine characteristics." An Englishwoman smoking in public not only failed to represent imperial and accepted social values, but also threatened male identity by its appropriation of masculine space. Williamson's rhetorical use of "revolt," "not authorized," and "intrusion" indicates an aggressive response to such a foray across established gender boundaries.[24]

Observing an even greater hazard to imperial identity, Captain Williamson protested, "Several ladies have gone yet further, by adopting the entire costume of the natives; a circumstance which, however gratifying it may have been to themselves, by no means raised them in the estimation of those whom they imitated; while, at the same time, it gave birth to opinions, and occasionally to *experiments*, by no means favorable to their reputation." Unfortunately he gave no further details of these occasional experiments. Not satisfied with criticizing the women, the captain further complained, "[T]he same kind of ridicule attaches equally to gentlemen, who at times allow their whiskers to grow, and who wear turbans, &c., in imitation of the Mussulmans of distinction. . . . [T]he Mussulmans regard these renegadoes [sic] in costume much the same as we do such of the natives, as, being smitten with our general character . . . to the utter degradation of their persons, and reputation, in the eyes both of their new, and of their old, companions." Adopting Indian cultural customs and clothing beyond limits necessary to establish affinity and account for climate difference posed a threat to standards and social rules. "Going native" presented a real risk to both male and female identity, thus posing a liability in the projection of imperial authority and prestige.[25]

Unlike the men and women of the East India Company, officers' wives, understanding their roles as ambassadors, recognized the perils of embracing the indigenous styles of dress and ornamentation. Emma Roberts announced, "Silver and gold lace, of every kind and pattern, fringes, scalloped trimmings, edgings, and borders of all widths, are to be purchased at Benares exceedingly cheap, when compared to the prices demanded for such articles in Europe; but the Anglo-Indian ladies rarely avail themselves of these glittering bargains, excepting when fancy balls are on the *tapis*, as there is a prejudice against the adoption of decorations worn by native women." In 1827 Bessie Fenton voiced another example of the "prejudice" identified by Roberts. In attending a ball in Dinapore Mrs. Fenton remarked, "[A]ll the company are European and all the dresses English or French; for it is, I must tell you, the extremity of bad taste to appear in anything of Indian manufacture—neither muslin, silk, flowers, or even ornaments, however beautiful." Wishing to purchase "Dacca muslin," Mrs. Fenton was flabbergasted to realize that she "must not be seen in it as none but half castes *ever* wore them. These dresses sell in London as high as £7 and £10. I do remember thinking myself as fine as the Queen of Sheba in one given me by dear Aunt Angel. So much for the variations in taste." Taste, however, was not the issue—remaining identifiably British was. Although the London fashion houses incorporated "Dacca muslins" as the latest vogue, to uphold the seamless authority of empire in India officers' wives could not appear in any costume akin to an Arabian queen.[26]

Unlike the British women, who remained formally attired, several American wives adopted, as Lydia Lane posited, "the primitive customs of my neighbors." Lane purposely challenged her obligation to don the prevailing national fashions. In 1866, her husband received orders to New Mexico. She declared, "It was amusing to an old campaigner like myself to see the brides start off from Fort Leavenworth for an ambulance expedition of six hundred miles. Their dainty costumes were far more suitable for Fifth Avenue [in New York City] than camp. . . . Hoops were fashionable then, and . . . [s]ome of the ladies wore little turbans with mask veils and delicate kid gloves." Mrs. Lane, like Teresa Vielé, showed little concern with ornamentation and fashionable attire. She announced, "I started out as I intended to dress throughout the march—a calico frock, plainly made, no hoops, and a sun-bonnet, and indeed I must have looked outlandish to my young friends just from New York." This relaxation of dress codes, quite different from the British formality, perhaps illustrates an unwritten easement of duty when marching with the units. Relatively few accounts, however, corroborate this staunch stand against the dictates of required dress, and most women retained Eastern attire to reaffirm their class status.[27]

Another fashion rebel, Martha Summerhayes, decided she wished to relax her outfit choices. Writing from Arizona in 1875, she repeated both Vielé's and Lane's nonconformist challenge. She admired the female Mexican dress and enviously described the benefits of wearing white linen *camisas*, calico skirts, and stockings. She cried, "[I]f I could only dress as the Mexicans do! Their necks and arms do look so cool and clean." Although hoping to "adopt their fashion of house apparel," she disappointedly confessed, "I yielded to the prejudices of my conservative partner, and sweltered during the day in high-necked and long-sleeved white dresses, kept up the table in American fashion, ate American food in so far as we could get it." Despite her yearning to adopt "the primitive customs of my neighbors," Mrs. Summerhayes dutifully remained a symbol of imperial America.[28]

In comparing the costumes worn within both nineteenth-century military communities, it becomes clear that these wives and husbands shared an obligation to represent the nation. Almost without question, these military couples actively created and policed an imperial dress code to legitimize status. It comes as no surprise that the prescribed male dress, as Callaway notes, "was characterized by pomp and plumage enhancing masculinity." Yet male military garments worn in British India and the U.S. West allowed limited acculturation to the locales. The Indian Army recruited indigenous soldiers who retained their cultural identity, partly through incorporation of traditional clothing elements into uniform dress. Adoptions of the Irregular Regimental uniform by the British, made post-Mutiny, included incorporation of the turban, knee-length tunics, and brightly colored cummerbunds. The turban, made of over thirty feet of cloth, afforded greater protection of the head against sabre blows than a peaked cap or cork pith helmet. In addition to this utilitarian purpose, Bernard Cohn suggests that imperialists sought to prevent further insurrections by enacting a "strong hand capable of smashing any . . . disloyalty, combined with an acceptance of Indians." By the end of the nineteenth century, this acceptance included the "orientalization" of British uniforms in India. Officers officially clothed in "Mughal grandee" costumes expected to establish cultural affinity to gain immediate and unfaltering obedience. Hence, the adoption of elements of Indian military dress served a practical defensive, and imperial cognitive, purpose.[29]

Although dress was codified in official uniform regulations, this rationale appeared equally expedient in the U.S. West. The more flamboyant officers, such as the Custer brothers, unofficially adopted outfits made of buckskin. Despite a weak case that argues this outfit facilitated an affinity with American Indian scouts, co-option of elements of indigenous dress and military tactics were not primarily established to create ruler-ruled affinity as in the British model. The most convincing explanation, however, is that the American army in the West adopted the indigenous military wear to facilitate comfort and expediency on long winter missions. Both the British and American officers, nevertheless, despite differing justifications, adapted indigenous garments for imperial purposes. The British controlled the Indian population through such cultural hybridity; Americans used the same mechanism to subdue. Officers' wives, however, did not enjoy the same privilege. In both locations, these women made extreme efforts to transport and display fashion styles of the core locations. Feminine flounces and furbelows were all carefully assembled to represent the nations. Their attempts to "go native" often resulted in strong male responses of contempt and prohibition. This male reaction, perhaps not unexpected, represents a male incursion into the intimate feminine world—and a clear indication of the officers' wives' responsibility to act as standard bearers of the empire.[30]

When scrutinizing dress as a cultural emblem, a surprising but clearly apparent crossing of gender boundaries by both sexes is visible. To ensure the cohesion and stability of the imperial holdings, male and female cultural spaces operated in constant flux. In British India and the U.S. West gendered roles and responsibilities within sexually determined geographical sites held less importance, less functionality, and less relevance than in the core regions. The imperial forts housed military regiments: if attacked, no allowances would be made for noncombatants. The parade ground, battlefield, and campaign operated as male territory. Female authority, however, shattered domestic boundaries to encompass entire garrisons and cantonments. The imperial husband embodied the character of a warrior-protector, steadfast in his promise to, and obligations of, the empire. The British officer officially adopted limited items of indigenous clothing styles to develop an affinity with the Indian people. His American counterpart utilized certain elements of the Native American culture to gain expertise in missions of removal. The military wife held a greater responsibility to protect and exhibit the symbols of power. She was not allowed to go native, as this served no imperial purpose. Both women and men negotiated across the gender divides to ensure a cohesive display of power. Turbans, buckskins, and high-necked blouses then, were not an officer's, or his wife's, fashion choice, but textual symbols that communicated status and power.

Another element of visual imperial power, homemaking in British India and the U.S. West, again demonstrates, albeit in different processes, the fluidity of gender roles. A nineteenth-century commentator, Mrs. L. C. Ricketts, published an article in the 1912 edition of the *Contemporary Review* in which she perceptively captured the inability of the British to relinquish the trappings of their culture. She explained that this occurred as "Anglo-Indians" remained constantly aware of their exile from all things "Home," and to compensate for this disorientation "they all, quite unconsciously . . . [m]ake their houses as little oriental and as much like an English home as possible." Coupling this observation with Maud Diver's disclosure that one's home and chattels also belonged to one's neighbor suggests that officers' wives living in India held a responsibility to design and display the intimate space as an imperial site. Mary Procida argues that "British domesticity was reconstructed in India in a manner that reinforced the practice and ideology of imperialism. The most private and intimate spaces . . . were colonized by the demands of empire." In so doing, both the housewife and the physical home were commandeered as imperial symbols. Procida claims that as "social gatekeepers," and hostesses for frequent all-male gatherings, wives created an environment conducive to discussions of the "imperial business of the day," as their homes functioned "as branch offices in the business of empire." Despite the impossibility of faithfully recreating a British home, these women, Procida concludes, nonetheless incorporated "elements of European and Indian cultures . . . that could uphold the imperial ethos and facilitate the business of empire in a physical and ideological environment vastly different from that of Great Britain." To this end, military spouses held a duty to construct an environment unlike anything they had previously encountered, one that showcased imperial prestige and emphasized the superiority of British rule.[31]

The cantonment bungalow provided standard housing, and appeared very different to newcomers accustomed to the Victorian multistoried house. The open-plan design with numerous doorways, windows, and ceiling fans maximized the effect of cooling breezes. This clean and open construction, it was hoped, advertised that the imperial home would not degenerate into moral or unhealthy practices. The internal aesthetic created by furnishings and décor in India was the polar opposite to that of Victorian England. Due to transportation problems and inflated costs, the heavily carpeted, furnished, and curtained British middle-class home, burgeoning with dark furnishings and ornaments, could not be replicated in India. Instead, wives reconciled themselves to the idea that clean but spartan homes represented, as Procida suggests, "seriousness of purpose and singular devotion to the empire." These female proto-minimalists perhaps understood the financial, logistical, and imperial rationale. The choice of function over form provided a vital solution to reducing unwanted "invaders"—scorpions, centipedes, ants, and fleas. Additionally, frequent changes of station and the inherent transport challenges created perennial difficulties. A realistic solution lay in purchasing or renting secondhand furnishings and fittings. This practice, however, startled upper-middle-class newcomers, as to purchase secondhand furniture signaled a lack of class consciousness. For example, in 1902, when Christian Stirling arrived in Karachi, India, her uncle, General Alfred Craigie, purchased a "dreadfully shabby" carriage complete with "a pair of rather old and shabby walers." Miss Stirling also expressed her astonishment at the practice of the British "incomer" having to purchase tattered household goods and transportation from an "outgoer."[32]

Another new arrival in India, Ruby Gray, expressed the difficulties of military housekeeping with its constant and often immediate orders to a new posting. She recorded from her new home in Almora, "I had just finished making the curtains for the house when I learnt my first lesson as a soldier's wife. Charles walked in one day and said he had orders to go to Bareilly on a temporary job and would then be rejoining the battalion when they moved down for winter manoeuvers, it was decided I go with him. That was the end of my first home exactly two months after landing in India." She concluded, "I was now beginning to realize what being married to the Indian Army would mean to me in the future . . . that for the rest of my days spent out in India we were to have no permanent home of any kind, always in temporary accommodation, bungalows, boarding houses, lisson [sic] huts, tents, on the move all ones [sic] serving days." This officer's wife understood she held a duty, by naturally including herself as a "serving" member of the imperial force, subject to the inconveniences of orders.[33]

A march through the Himalayan mountain range took Lucy, the wife of Second Officer Harry L. Grant of the Royal Artillery (attached to the Kashmir State Mountain Battery), to her new quarters. After traversing the Komri Pass to reach their temporary home in Ruttu, situated at ten thousand feet, this intrepid wife and mother portrayed her quarters, four rooms and a bathroom, in a positive light. She recorded two of the older rooms "had only beaten mud floors and walls but the newer portion had boarded floors and the walls . . . were plastered, with a dull greenish clay which made quite a good background. The sitting-room, which when decked with cretonne covers and cushions, muslin curtains, jars of wildflowers, etc., looked quite civilized." The dining-room in the older section, however, "had table and chairs, some *numdahs* on the floor, and an improvised sideboard made of boxes with a cloth over it." Mrs. Grant packed and transported "some heavy linen curtains with a bold white stencil design which were invaluable as bedspreads, portieres and so on—one set green and one set rosepink." She concluded, "I was thankful to get in and settle down for a month." Grant could not recreate the grandeur of a middle-class home, but one can understand that simply adding her linens, carried across miles of formidable terrain, provided a comforting ambience that could surely pass imperial muster amid the glacial scree.[34]

Another officer's wife received orders to a new (and much less extreme) posting to Madras. Honoria Lawrence found her new home charming in many ways. Arriving in 1837 she explained, "On entering the house, my first feeling was strange familiarity, surprise at how true had been my notions of Indian arrangements." The home provided "perfect tranquility," and the simplicity of the white *chunum* walls and matted floors seemed "delightful." The window treatments consisted of venetian blinds of green painted bamboo, and *tattie* "made of the fragrant kuss-kuss grass." The canvas and white-painted wood "frilled" *punkah*, whose cooling "current of air" proved "indispensable to the Europeans during the hot weather," claimed the title as the "most important article of furniture." Viewing the "ceiling with naked beams" juxtaposed against the "damask couches and rosewood tables," however, she found the "unfinished comfortless appearance" disturbing. Mrs. Lawrence's observations of what a culturally hybrid Indian imperial home should look like seemed to match her expectations. She used such words as "tranquil [and] delightful" to convey her impressions. Yet she voiced uneasiness and an incompleteness of not being quite respectably British.[35]

With regard to the American officers' wives' attempts at homemaking, examples of officers' housing will assist in understanding that a standardized bungalow was not the housing norm in the West. The surgeon general's health survey of 1870 included his view on the adequacy of accommodations at all posts. The reported conditions of married quarters ran the gamut from Fort Macon's "harmful" to Fort McKavett's wholesome constructions. John S. Billings, assistant surgeon to the U.S. Army, condemned the conditions of quarters at Macon as "the most wretched description . . . they all leak, and afford but little protection from the weather. . . . [D]ifferent families are crowded together in a manner that almost violates decency. . . . The rooms are . . . inconveniently ventilated by the cracks in the doors, windows, and floors. The quarters are supplied with water by the prisoners, who bring it from the wells and place it in barrels at the back doors. There are no water-closets or bath rooms." At the other end of the spectrum, McKavett thrived under the attentive leadership of Brig. Gen. R. S. Mackenzie of the Forty-First U.S. Infantry. On his watch, renovations to barracks, kitchens, and storehouses commenced. Additionally, he ordered the officers' quarters to be completely overhauled. The excellent condition of the garrison received an official commendation. Billings announced, "I have served at no post since . . . 1865, where more attention is paid to cleanliness of quarters, and where all sanitary and hygienic rules are more thoroughly enforced." Praise indeed for the imperial conditions showcased by Mackenzie and the men and women of the Forty-First.[36]

Although differences existed between the British bungalow and American accommodations in the U.S. West, officers' wives who joined their husbands hoped to replicate the domestic décor of East coast homes. Core American middle-class status was demonstrated by projecting a genteel identity through fashionable domestic ornamentation, tempered with contempt for showy ostentation. In attempting to delineate identity as a combination of sincerity and moderation, these women utilized parlor décor to present an environment of softness and harmony, reflecting accepted styles. Homes acted as the standardization and communication centers of middle-class values. Wives, as administrators and guardians, created and maintained this cultural space as a psychological refuge from the intrigues and exhaustions of a brusque business world. Women, by holding responsibility for the shaping of personal character, played an important role in constructing the national persona. Thus, the home relayed the domestic to the public, the personal to the state. Fashionable manufactured furnishings, textiles, and objects all signified the sentimentality, gentility, and cultivation of the Victorian American.[37]

The western officer's wife who arrived at her new imperial post with an enchanted vision of creating a "psychological refuge"—a brass button home— repeatedly experienced disillusionment at the condition of the married quarters. For example, Ellen Biddle arrived to join her husband in post–Civil War Macon, Georgia, only to find no officer's quarters available at the garrison. Fortunately, "the Colonel had secured a small cabin (that had been used as negro quarters before the war) which was near the garrison. After it had been thoroughly cleaned with several coats of good sweet whitewash, it was made habitable, and when we got the little furniture we owned into it (for the Government allowed an officer but a few hundred pounds of freight), a few household gods that I always had about me, and a great big fire on the hearth, we had our first Army Home." High haulage costs made transportation of more than the most essential furniture impossible, adding to the general discomfort. In 1870 a lieutenant's salary decreased to the pre–Civil War level of $1,400 per annum, and the frequent orders to new posts proved transportation of more than a few cherished items financially impossible. As a lady with a duty to perform, Mrs. Biddle nevertheless maintained a positive attitude, opining, "The life was entirely new to me, but I soon discovered that I had adaptability, which made things easier. I was entirely without luxuries and comforts, and had many privations, but all of the army ladies had the same discomforts, though there were few complaints, and never by a thoroughbred." Ellen Biddle's reference to maintaining genteel status in facing severe adversity, similar to Lucy Grant's attitude towards her Himalayan home, prevented the disclosure of actual disappointment or distress suffered by an imperial officer's wife.[38]

Conditions at Fort Bayard, however, garnered a less than discreet response to the living arrangements. Mrs. Orsemus Boyd described the hardships of living in "so-called by courtesy" houses with mud floors. Frequent storms rendered many industrious attempts at creating a comfortable home completely ineffective. Mrs. Boyd recounted an enlightening case study of an eastern woman, married to a recent graduate from the Military Academy. This "little bride" arrived at Bayard with "at least a dozen large trunks" of "pretty contents," and with expectations, much the same as those Mrs. Boyd had held, that life in all military stations would be similar to that at West Point. Indeed, she "had brought from New York the most luxurious outfit ever seen on the frontier. Magnificent carpets and curtains from Sloan's [sic], fit for a New York palace." The first storm, however, destroyed all attempts at creating a respectable home, and Mrs. Boyd revealed that "her fairy bower had been transformed into a mud-bank; the pretty white curtains were streaked and discolored . . . the carpets covered in mud, while the pictures and ornaments were unrecognizable." She continued, "That lady was like many I have met . . . she expected ordinary modes of life to prevail at the frontier . . . her experience was pitiable. Having an abundance of money, she naturally supposed it would purchase some comfort; but money was of no use to her." This cameo clearly juxtaposes middle-class expectations against the harsh realities of imperial service.[39]

"A general depression" and a desire to escape gripped Frances Grummond on arrival at Fort Laramie. She observed, "The adobe houses of gray appearance imparted their somber hue to the whole surroundings." Quickly recovering her sense of duty, she brightly added, "The attempt to adjust myself to the surroundings began at once, although I knew perfectly well that our stay would be transient. I was learning the army habit, and this was but another step in the process of development into a full-fledged army woman." Mrs. Grummond reported that she "with alacrity, if not delight . . . took possession of . . . [her] first adobe" quarters. Not one to procrastinate, she decided that "[t]he first duty after a survey of the rooms was to unpack trunks. . . . Gray army blankets were tacked upon the floors to the extent of their capacity. Hospital cots were utilized for beds, and we began, as the children say, 'to keep house.' And now for my nick-nacks [sic] and such belongings to reproduce home environment." Despite Mrs. Grummond's initial despair, this enterprising officer's wife quickly created, not a Victorian show-home of middle-class status, but an agreeable adaptation. This ability to adjust to less than perfect conditions suggests that the military wife transported notions of respectability, rapidly modified military issue furnishings as functional items, and incorporated knick-knacks to create an imperial home.[40]

Although many American officers' wives expressed depression and frustration, most related satisfaction in their efforts to construct respectable civilized homes. The replication of a Victorian showcase home appeared to be an unobtainable objective in the West—an evanescent "fairy bower." Yet a collection of photographs of military quarters, spanning the period 1860–1900, suggests the polar opposite. As the editor, William Brown, points out, undoubtedly the officers' wives purposefully arranged their quarters for the photographer. Yet, he contends, the physical furniture and ornamentations reveal remarkable connections with nineteenth-century civilian homes of the same class. The collection included ten identifiable married officers' quarters and six assigned to bachelors. The photographs of the couples' rooms mirrored the décor of a Victorian middle-class parlor or drawing room in England. An analysis indicates that 80 percent held musical instruments (pianos, harps, organs, and violins), and 100 percent had floor coverings of Brussels or ingrain carpeting, and/or area rugs. All had heavy curtains, complimented with netting or venetian blinds, wall prints, and wicker furniture. Ninety percent displayed wall prints, and drapery-accented mantels whose surfaces burgeoned with photographs and all manner of ornamentation. Thirty percent of the parlors appeared wallpapered, and 60 percent beautified with fresh flowers, pot plants, and/or embellished with oriental fans, parasols, and screens. Although 80 percent of the photographs revealed heavy hardwood furniture, all had at least one piece of lightweight wicker work, a practical solution to the high-priced transportation costs. Photographed married quarters, then, greatly support the argument that military wives reproduced domestic symbols of middle-class gentility and taste in their imperial homes. The images, mostly from well-established forts, when considered against the rustic postings, and the officers' wives' written accounts of army-trouser rugs, warped doors, and *Army and Navy Journal* wallpaper, represents a very different reality. Undoubtedly some quarters provided comforts on a par with eastern homes, but most boasted minimal middle-class symbolic paraphernalia. The photograph collection, then, unsurprisingly, provides a slanted, prestigious view of the nineteenth-century imperial space. The officers' wives, when approached by a photojournalist, undoubtedly wished to portray themselves as accomplished ambassadors, by incorporating identifiable styles and symbols of middle-class status.[41]

A survey of the six bachelor officers' quarters' proves valuable, though this low number can hardly be representative of all lone officers stationed in the West. The photographs reveal a further reconfiguration of traditional gender boundaries within the imperial garrisons. For the unmarried men, lower pay and the limited social obligations of the junior ranks discouraged and negated the requirement of a wife. Two photographs, with one taken of the quarters assigned to 2nd Lt. Philip Reade of the Third Cavalry, stationed at Fort Dodge, reveals what one would expect from an unmarried soldier. Reade sits on the only chair in his billet; a field desk stands behind him littered with writing accoutrements and books—the stark walls enlivened by a solitary display of military paraphernalia and a small framed print. These images of bachelor officers, to whom domestic comforts appear unimportant, epitomize the imperial warrior at moments of repose. The four remaining photographs of lone officers' quarters, however, reveal a very different military man.[42]

Lt. Leighton Finley of the Tenth Cavalry and Capt. Emmet Crawford of the Third Cavalry exhibited a considerable panache for the homemaking process. The parlor space, in both examples, appears unmistakably feminized. The window treatments included heavy, festooned drapes and net curtains; the floors boasted area rugs, and both rooms featured wicker furniture. Accent drapery included antimacassars, floral tablecloths, tasseled and bowed mantel coverings, and prints, portraiture, and military paraphernalia adorn the walls. Fresh or dry flowers provided decorative flair, and Finley's least masculine items included several fanciful arrangements of peacock and ostrich feathers. Crawford's ultra-feminine touches included three dolls and an elaborately tasseled table centerpiece. Such attempts to domesticate masculine spaces in a Victorian style, by two bachelor officers at remote posts (Fort Craig and Fort Davis), signals a feminization of their role, an apparent breach of traditional gendered boundaries.[43]

The domesticity of the military man stationed in the West—arguably the quintessential rugged and courageous American male—presents an anomaly in traditional interpretations of gendered space. The close attention paid by the two bachelor officers to the placement of objects, drapery accents, and feather and flower arrangements appears incongruous in the western forts. So, what conclusions can be reached from these instances of male encroachment into female territory? The editor of the photographic collection suggests that these men attempted to remain in fashion and perhaps used the latest homemaking magazines to so do. Taking this explanation a step further might indicate that in conforming to the Victorian design trend bachelors wished to project a middle-class status. Alternatively, perhaps these officers expressed effeminacy in their décor choices. A third possibility suggests that each had illicit live-in female companions or visitors who transformed the quarters into a home. Or could the wives or relatives of brother officers have genuinely inspired and encouraged their lone male friends to such creative heights? In considering these four options, the latter reasoning carries the greatest weight. Lieutenant Finley, although characterized as fussy and supercilious, had numerous female acquaintances and finally married Ida, the niece of Capt. William Davis Jr., in 1889. Crawford never married, but Lt. Britton Davis of the Fifth Cavalry described him akin to "an ideal knight of King Arthur. . . . His respect for women amounted to veneration." Whatever the true explanation of these model Victorian rooms, markers of masculinity and femininity and the gendered boundaries of authority were blurred, renegotiated, and accepted to present the imperial face of the U.S. West.[44]

To consider the internal décor of the bachelors' billets, and the fluidity of gender boundaries in the U.S. West, Adele Perry, in studying the imperial experience in British Columbia from 1849 to 1871, analyzes the intersection of race and gender and class within a developing colonial hub. She argues that despite the expectation of a successful colonization, the dominance of Anglo men who acted as homemakers failed to produce 'a model of bourgeois, metropolitan manhood.'" The arrival of women as an oft used "imperial panacea" nonetheless did not produce the "stable, respectable, white society" envisioned. In analyzing the gender fluidity in the U.S. West, it appears that the presence of women in the isolated garrisons prompted a female incursion into male private space. In this situation her purpose was not to cultivate an imperial man, but to craft a national, class-based space. Thus, the officer's wife held, perhaps, voluntary responsibility for ensuring class representations within the homes of unattached officers.[45]

Returning to the photograph collections, military interiors of the British quarters in India, unfortunately, seem to have been a much less popular subject to record for posterity. Two photographs, however, offer vivid sketches of nineteenth-century imperial life. An image titled "Our Drawing Room in Lahore, India," taken between 1883 and 1887 by Royal Artillery Assistant Apothecary John Burke, provides a rare glimpse of an Indian Victorian interior. The cluttered room held wicker furniture, elaborate drapery, pot plants, bookcases, prints and photographs, oriental fans, and tasseled tablecloths—all in accord with the furnishings displayed in the American officers' quarters. Differences, however, appear in the incorporation of numerous indigenous design features. The walls are wainscoted with an elaborate and tasseled Indian print fabric, the side tables feature arched fretwork, and the ornamentation includes beautiful lotas jars and slim-necked brass urns. An Anglo-Indian ivory and sandalwood watch-stand proudly occupies the front and center of the mantelpiece. This imperial drawing room, then, exhibits a more hybrid interior design than its American counterparts. Draped loops and bows gracefully complement the finely painted lotas jars, exotically patterned wainscoting enhances the oriental theme, and the Anglo-Indian watch-stand completes the hybrid gentility of a British army officer's home.[46]

A single image of what appears to be a British officer's Indian quarters illustrates an excess of masculinity that beggars belief. In 1870, amateur photographer Captain Willoughby W. Hooper of the Seventh Madras Light Cavalry captured the image "Englishman Being Served Coffee in Bed." The casual disarray of the room centers on an officer reclining under a tartan coverlet, attended by a young male servant who proffers a drink served in a cup and saucer. Two tiger skulls, family photographs, and a gun rack holding three rifles further masculinize a dingy wall. A saber rests against a makeshift sideboard, and a small table holds the minimum of dining crockery and cutlery, complete with an empty wine bottle. Clothing is strewn across a wicker chair, and his knee-high leather boots lie where they supposedly fell, completing the display of casual virility. This meticulously arranged cameo, clearly arranged by the captain-turned-photographer, presumably represents what he imagined to be an idealized masculinity.[47]

So much for the single image of imperial super-masculinity, but what did officers in British India say, if anything, about their living situations? The answer to that question is very little. The bachelor officers shared cantonment bungalows to make the best use of housing allowances, thus reducing furniture rental, food bills, and servants' wages. Called a "chummery," the conditions could be at best termed basic. Captain Francis Bellew provided a humorous glimpse of life in his multi-occupancy bungalow at Barrackpore. He advised, "The ceilings . . . are composed of coarse cotton cloth tied . . . to a framework of bamboo . . . between this and the rafters is a dark void, the airy hall of the rats and bandicoots." He added, "My friend's bungalow was a regular Indian sub's abode, and fell woefully below my standard of comfort. . . . the grand *salon*, or *salle à manger*, contained one square camp-table, two chairs and a half, a footstool of basket work . . . and hard by hung suspended his library; not quite so large as the Bodleian, to be sure." A fellow officer's room he described as "scantily furnished." Captain Bellew's lighthearted description of bachelor quarters again emphasized a utilitarian imperial masculinity. The adoption of Indian furnishings combined with military issue basics confirmed the limited assimilation permissible to imperial officers.[48]

Both the written narratives and photographic sources indicate the efforts of British and American officers and their wives to transport symbols of class-appropriate domesticity to their imperial postings. Finding this an impossible task due to transportation difficulties and prohibitive costs, both groups innovatively introduced alternatives. In India, the minimalistic interior of the Indian cantonment bungalow reflected the serious problems of insect and reptile infestations. The incorporation of indigenous elements such as *punkahs, tatties*, and *numdahs*, signaling assimilation, proved essential for survival in a completely different climatic zone. The one photograph of a British-Indian drawing room displays the Victorian middle-class cluttered style, and integrates Indian and Anglo design features and artifacts. This cultural hybridity, as in the male dress codes, sought to generate affinity between the governing and governed peoples. In the U.S. West, with perhaps less change in environmental conditions, and with less imperial necessity to commandeer the home as an imperial site, minimal assimilation, whether practical or aesthetic, of indigenous artifacts occurred. Indeed, a loyalty to American manufactures was voiced by Capt. John Bourke whilst stationed in Prescott, Arizona, the post–Civil War home of the Military Department of Arizona. He stated such devotion "preserved the distinction of being thoroughly American. . . . Its inhabitants were Americans; American men had brought American wives out with them from their old homes in the Far East, and these American wives had not forgotten the lessons of elegance and thrift learned in childhood." He continued, "The houses were built in American style; the doors were American doors and fastened with American bolts and locks, opened by American knobs. . . . There were carpets, mirrors, rocking chairs, tables, lamps, and all other appurtenances. . . . There were American books, American newspapers, American magazines—the last intelligently read. The language was American, and nothing else. . . . The stores were American stores, selling nothing but American goods." A few photographs of bachelor quarters, however, depict Native American blankets covering trunks, and wall decorations of tribal weaponry and regalia. Officers' wives, nonetheless, rarely utilized or incorporated local methods or artifacts in their domestic affairs.[49]

Homes in the U.S. West, as evidenced by the Surgeon General's Report of 1870, ranged from abysmal to healthy. Military spouses, no matter what the shabbiness or inadequacy of their quarters, attempted to assert their middle-class status through domestic design. The photographs of the American married residences present showcase homes. The cluttered rooms expressed ultra-femininity complete with the latest fad in statuary, musical instruments, and designs copied from homemaking journals. Wherever stationed these officers' wives, utilized ornamentation and décor to convey class status. One can sympathize with the British Lucy Grant, who transformed a Himalayan shack into a home with two lengths of fabric, or the American Katherine Fougera, who laid a rug made of army-issue trousers in her drafty Dakota Territory quarters. With few genuine articles of Victoriana transported across the miles, they innovatively constructed makeshift versions of home, to proudly and respectfully represent middle-class status.[50]

In transforming rudimentary conditions, and functional items, both groups of women directed much energy to reconstruct nineteenth-century middle-class norms and create imperial homes. This does not hold any element of surprise. In both the written and photographic records the responsibility and authority for this endeavor was placed squarely in the feminine realm. Yet in the American photographs the male incursion into the domestic space demonstrates the fluidity of gender roles. Lieutenant Finley's and Captain Crawford's official apartments reveal an astonishingly feminine decorative flair. The inclusion of flower arrangements, drapery accents, feathers, and dolls strongly suggests the influence of officers' wives in these bachelor apartments. This evidence, then, extends female authority beyond the walls of individual homes, to influence the mindset and masculine spaces of the lone officers. Female influence in British India failed to penetrate the super-masculinity of the army officers, yet it appears that U.S. officers' wives literally generated the blueprint for the domestic design in the U.S. West.

American Eveline Alexander's diary provides a perfect opportunity to examine the reworking of middle-class dress and homemaking markers to represent the nineteenth-century imperial class. She described her changing views toward attire while marching with the Third Cavalry in 1866, from Fort Smith to Fort Stevens. On leaving the civilized environment of the garrison she wore a "black and white traveling dress and black and white flat [hat] with blue veil . . . to give me a warlike appearance, I wore a miniature pistol belt with . . . a little pistol in a holster . . . and a silver-hilted dagger. . . . This is to be my costume for crossing the plains." Clearly Mrs. Alexander represented, in her own view, an adversary not to be trifled with. Within five days, however, her veiled hat had been crushed by the couple's pet dog, and she now donned a poncho around her waist to keep dry. Within six weeks the formal traveling outfit was replaced by her husband's military rubber cloak. In August, however, due to her "proximity to civilization [Fort Union]" she resumed wearing her "proper riding habit and a small cap." Thus, she understood that her appearance held importance. Due to conditions of the march, and the unlikelihood of encountering fellow Americans, she temporarily relaxed her responsibilities and adopted a practical dress code.[51]

Upon reaching her destination of Fort Stevens, accordingly, Mrs. Alexander quickly re-assumed her formal role. Dressed in her "best bib and tucker," she awaited her husband's return from a visit with the august William T. Sherman, commanding general of the Army. She ordered a table to be built that accommodated eight, had it placed in her tent, served General Sherman his saddle of mutton on a tin plate, and conducted postprandial conversation with him seated on a trunk. Despite these substitute furnishings, which would clearly not pass muster in the East, Eveline confidently undertook her imperial role. Spending time in a "tête-à-tête" with his genial hostess, General Sherman endorsed her suitability as an imperial ambassador. He shared details of departmental authorities, boundaries, and remits, and listened attentively to Eveline's observations of the West. Greatly impressed, Sherman remarked, "I declare Alexander, your wife knows more about the country than you do"—an assertion that her husband "stoutly denied!"[52]

Mrs. Alexander's experiences represent the British and American military wife's acceptance and execution of duty. Living within isolated and institutionalized enclaves, these women forged a distinctive imperial identity that reflected, yet deviated from, civilian norms. In intimate spaces, utilizing dress and homemaking, women drafted and projected an imperial class identity that adopted and adapted mainstream gender models. Officers' wives in both locations rigidly displayed, as a duty, respectable core fashions. Any and all attempts at adopting the muslins or *camisas* of the indigenous women were immediately and unmistakably forbidden. Their officer husbands, however, adapted limited indigenous clothing styles and fabrics for different imperial purposes. The British soldiers sought to subjugate the Indian people through affinity gained by incorporating elements of the male military dress. The Americans unofficially utilized elements of tribal attire and military tactics, not to subordinate but to fulfill their remit to remove the Native Americans from western lands. In considering female and male dress choices as dutiful performance, then, the imperial role of such cultural artifacts becomes visible.

The second strand of inquiry, internal décor, an imitation of the class-appropriate models of British gentility and American sincerity, traditionally fell under the female purview. In India, the gendered spaces mirrored the British status quo. This model, however, extended female authority to enable and assist the imperial ambition of control of the indigenous peoples through affinity. Indian artifacts and decorating styles were incorporated to provide a visual cultural correspondence, thus assisting goals of subordination. In the U.S. West, the cult of sentiment and its concomitant female authority expanded to encompass Anglo male spaces—greatly increasing female power in designing cultural imperialism. The lack of any real integration of Native American cultural artifacts, although opposite to the British experience, supported imperial ambitions, not of domination *in situ*, but of removal of the indigenous peoples.

The almost unfettered movement across gender borders by both sexes, and in both locales, reveals the fluidity of feminine and masculine authority in the imperial formations. Officers clearly exhibited power in controlling female choices in dress, and in India, the women responded with greater social authority to police male dress and behavior. It was the American wives, nonetheless, who made the greatest advance into male space. By instructing and influencing homemaking in the West, these women feminized military environments. Officers' wives dismantled national gender boundaries and class models to wield power and influence.

Dress and interior design reveals the silent yet latent power of imagery as a central element of imperialism. Dutiful efforts, made by British and American officers and their wives, to utilize bodies and domestic spaces to construct, maintain, and project imperial authority indicate the construction of distinct nineteenth-century gender models in the military communities. In order to fulfill their duties these men and women effortlessly crossed, and re-crossed, gender borders to regulate a cohesive and unified front. To provide a more textured interpretation of the officer's wife as an imperial ambassador, however, the discussion must shift from inanimate artifacts to active roles. An analysis of the social ritual of calling and assessment of class attitudes within the domestic sphere will reveal female design, manipulation, and protection of imperial sociability, not as caretakers—but as imperial gatekeepers.[53]

7

Imperial Gatekeepers

Officers' Wives as Social Arbiters of Empire

> Our next subject of consideration is influence, and here
> we come at once to the great secret of woman's power in
> her social and domestic character.
>
> —*Mrs. Sarah Ellis*

> Social distinctions . . . are perhaps more rigidly observed
> here [India] than at home. . . . Each man depends on his
> position in the public service. . . . Wealth can do nothing
> for man or woman in securing them honour or precedence
> in their march to dinner . . . or in the dance.
>
> —*Edward Buck*

Fanny Parkes observed that military men in Allahabad spent much of the hot
daytime hours indoors, pursuing language skills, painting, and enjoying
musical activities. This, she claimed, they preferred to do "in the society of ladies,"
and drew the conclusion that "women have more influence over men in India
than in any other country." Indeed, this "influence" can plainly be seen through
an episode recorded by Jean Hamilton, daughter of Sir John Muir. Jean met and
married Major Ian Hamilton who served with the Ninety-Second Highlanders,
stationed in India. Utilizing her privileged status, she accessed and influenced
high-ranking military officers and statesmen to advance her husband's career.
She noted that after a stint at the War Office in London, her husband hoped to
take up a position as an official observer with the Japanese army. With several

political intrigues muddying the waters, Ian (away on a tour of duty) wrote to Jean asking for her help to secure his position. With no hesitation, Jean commenced a public relations campaign to support her husband's cause.[1]

Her journal entries read, "I did not speak to [Secretary of State for War] [Hugh] Arnold-Foster about getting Ian attached officially to the Headquarters in Japan, I felt it was better not. I consulted little [Leo] Amery [a leading journalist with the *Times* newspaper] after dinner . . . he thinks he [Ian] might be made to represent India . . . so I will talk to Lord Roberts about this." Jean hosted several luncheon and dinner parties, inviting influential couples, and attended "an evening party at the [Sir Henry and Lady Victoria Beaufort] Somersets, where [she] wanted to catch Lady Bobs [Nora, wife of Lord Frederick Roberts, 1st Earl of Kandahar]" to clarify certain foreign appointments. The flurry of letters exchanged between the Hamiltons delineate Jean's battle plan. Ian wrote, "[Y]ou are sure to be questioned a good deal," so she should present his views to various statesmen, and, "If you see Mrs Leo [Maria de Rothschild, wife of a millionaire banker] you might tell her." Although her husband was not posted to Japan, Jean's manipulations still proved highly successful. She recorded: "I wired to Ian . . . that it is arranged that he represents India [official observer of the Indian Army]. Lord Roberts told me this was arranged at Mrs. Beaufort's dinner." This episode makes visible the usually hidden element of female social power. Indeed, Mrs. Hamilton illustrates the very real information and communication networks embedded, yet obscured, within vehicles of sociability. Beneath the polite entertaining and amusing small talk, officers' wives could not only commandeer one another's support and share knowledge, but also network with, and direct outcomes through influencing, male power players. Officers' wives operating within domestic space generated authority that clearly influenced the British Empire.[2]

A comparable episode, recorded by an American officer's wife, demonstrates an astonishing exercise of social power at the highest political level. Martha Summerhayes had the opportunity to visit with President Grover Cleveland during a visit to Washington, D.C., in 1889. With promotions in the army apparently at a standstill (her husband had remained at the rank of lieutenant for twenty-two years), she broached this subject with the president himself. "He listened with the greatest interest and seemed pleased with my frankness," she recalled, but initially noted that he could not interfere in such military affairs. However, his later comment advised, "[I]f anything turns up for those fine men you have told me about, they will hear from me." Shortly after this conversation, Summerhayes noted, "A vacancy occurred . . . in the Quartermaster's Department, and the appointment was eagerly sought for by many Lieutenants of the army. President Cleveland saw fit to give the appointment to Lieutenant Summerhayes, making him a Captain and Quartermaster."[3]

Although not operating at the national level, Alice's letters to her husband, Col. Benjamin Grierson of the Tenth U.S. Cavalry, contain many incidences of her authority within the marriage, home, and garrison. An example that highlights her social power is perfectly stated in a letter from Rachel Beck, whose husband, Lt. William H. Beck of the Tenth U.S. Cavalry, had just been dismissed from duty, without pay, for a period of twelve months. Mrs. Beck wrote, "I beg that you will pardon me for bringing my troubles to you but I know that your request, to the Gen. on our behalf, will guarantee his endorsement in our favor." Lieutenant Beck had been found guilty of "drunkenness and ill treatment of his men," a shortcoming Mrs. Grierson did not tolerate. Alice duly wrote to her husband discouraging any clemency to be shown to the discredited officer.[4]

Articulating the British officers' wives' imperial attitude, homemaking expert Flora Steel announced: "We do not wish to advocate an unholy haughtiness, but an Indian household can no more be governed peacefully, without dignity and prestige, than an Indian Empire." Similarly, Glenda Riley posits that "women provided the real glue of [American] empire, from attitudes and folkways to domestic consumerism." This female role held such influence, according to Nancy Shea, that when an American married military couple received a posting "the government gets the full-time service of two people for the pay of one . . . a wife plays an integral part in representing the government." Female social skills became appropriated, gratis, to further (or retard) a husband's career, and acted as a central element of performing and projecting imperial prestige. Furthermore, wives held an obligation to police the military community, through designing and controlling the social processes of calling and dining rituals. These obligations, led to the construction of a reflective yet flexible model of female behavior that shattered the boundaries of traditional social conventions. This authority, however, prompted an institutional and national backlash of criticism that specifically targeted the military wife. In creating a less restrained and empowered model of mainstream sociability, these women became vulnerable to a vicious response, more so in the British experience, that tarnished their reputations—a woman's most valuable social currency.[5]

In creating a distinct imperial class, the British and American women transported social rituals of calling and dining, yet differences in the level of formality existed. In British India, the *Warrant of Precedence* regulated dining etiquette, and calling operated via an unwritten yet equally rigid system of calling cards and visitor books to legitimize status. In the U.S. West, according to Kevin Adams, social rituals provided a "formalized 'off-duty' leisure culture. . . . To assert . . . membership in and commonality with elite society." This "reflected a fair amount of insecurity concerning" their class status as military officers. Indeed, such activities as calling and dining out served to define the officers and wives living in the western reaches as the elite, providing a class boundary between themselves and the enlisted men. Despite less formalization than the British model, Adams posits that "calling was an institutionalized ritual" that "virtually had the force of law: those who spurned its dictates could expect to be shunned."[6]

The reconstruction of national middle-class values in remote postings, by British and American officers' wives, then, became pivotal to the construction of identity and status. So, what nineteenth-century class ideals did these women transport to India? Leonore Davidoff argues that a "[s]ociety is a self-defined status group based on communal lifestyles." She further explains that a fully-fledged member of the upper- and middle-class social echelon enjoyed the benefits of a substantial information network, career opportunities, and access to restricted political news. "At the *same time*," Davidoff notes, "participation in the group is a reward and a badge of arrival into these positions, a public seal of acceptance into elite status." Introductions, calls, and entertaining provided a mechanism to construct, populate, and maintain an exclusive class. A newcomer seeking admission to this exclusive set sought entrance by forming an acquaintance with an established family—the pathway zealously guarded by the lady of the house. This "English rule," according to an American etiquette manual, operated on both sides of the Atlantic. Hostess approval sanctioned pan-acceptability. Indeed, an introduction contained a considerable amount of embedded social power. An etiquette manual published in Great Britain usefully instructed, "It is neither necessary nor desirable to introduce everybody to everybody. . . . You confer no favour on us . . . by making us acquainted with one whom we do not desire to know; you may inflict a positive injury. You also put yourself in an unpleasant position; for 'an introduction is a social endorsement,' and you become, to a certain extent, responsible for the person you introduce. If he disgraces himself in any way, you share, in a greater or less degree, in his disgrace." Thus, a middle-class woman, whether British or American, held substantial social power. It was she who vetted callers, determined eligibility, and proffered introductions.[7]

Calling in upper-middle class America, just as in British society, functioned as an assessment of acceptability. This "ceremonial act" of an "urban custom," Catherine Allgor notes, determined the suitability of newcomers as members of a reciprocal "social world where [social, political, and economic] claims could be made on any member." Karen Halttunen adds that the American middle class sought to advertise their social identity through notions of gentility, a sentimental politeness, and by behaving with "true courtesy." The design, operation, and sustainability of this model of sociability pivoted around the practice of formal visiting.[8]

Because of the social, economic, and political power conferred by acceptance of a newcomer, etiquette manuals codified this process. According to Mrs. Beeton's homemaking manual, formal calling was conducted under the following auspices. "After luncheon, morning calls and visits may be made and received. These are divided under three heads: those of ceremony, friendship, and congratulation or condolence." She further instructed an optimum length of encounter, and dictated a dress code. Mrs. Beeton systemized, then, a sociability that signified membership in the British middle class. In the Americas, Catharine Beecher's household manual mirrored her British counterpart's codification of domestic rituals. Mrs. Beecher delineated the American "duties of hospitality," and insisted that "[p]oliteness requires us to welcome visiters [sic] with cordiality; to offer them the best accommodations; to address conversation to them; and to express, by tone and manner, kindness and respect." Halttunen asserts that in proffering such hospitality, American elite women formalized and maintained "the fabric of Society, as semi-official leaders . . . [and as] arbiters of social acceptance or rejection." The requirement to call, then, functioned as a central element of sociability. A social endorsement provided access to economic and political power holders; a rejection—ostracization from the privileged elite.[9]

Calling provided a mechanism for an outsider to obtain admittance to, and enjoy the benefits of, middle-class status. The requirement to present a calling card provided a liminal social space to scrutinize, classify and accept suitable persons, and according to Allgor, reject "vulgar peoples, social parvenus, and imposters." Women, in both England and America, policed this social portal to guard class boundaries and restrict access to privileges. In the outer regions of the nations, however, this reproduced social ritual provided the officers' wives with substantial responsibility. They not only determined markers of suitability and controlled membership, but also held responsibility for establishing and maintaining imperial representations.[10]

Pat Barr briefly describes calling in India as a practice that convention demanded, and scholars who have in large part studied the Indian Civil Service community extend this argument to highlight this social act as a duty, a portal to gain entrance into the imperial set, and a social mechanism for inclusion and integration. Indeed, a female host had no option but to accept a bona fide civil servant. Proffering a card that confirmed a caller's employment removed the need for a wife to assess the credentials of a caller. Thus, the Indian Civil Service reduced female social power, as the simple production of a card affirmed imperial worthiness. Within the military world, however, a calling card embossed with a rank and regimental crest did not automatically guarantee entry to the imperial coterie. Officers' wives, particularly the *Burra Mem*, used the practice of calling to personally screen each officer. Incorporating this transported custom in British India, with its highly mobile military population, provided the officers' wives with a very real duty to identify and exclude social pariahs and parvenus from accessing social, political, and economic networks. By this flexing of female domestic power, these women dictated and reinforced internal coherence, confidence and authority, and consolidated an external public image of a unified empire.[11]

Delivering a calling card on arrival in a station provided a device for the immediate assessment of suitability based on a person's background, appearance, and behavior. Originally an aristocratic custom, with a card placed on a silver salver and passed to her ladyship by a servant, it became mimicked—minus the salver and solemn-faced butler—by simply dropping a card into letter boxes. Agreement, post card scrutiny, to welcome newcomers acted as a public endorsement of a couple's social acceptability. Ruby Gray described this female agency in action. Shortly after arrival at a new station she grumbled, "Charles told me that there was to be a dance at the Club given by a senior wife, she let it be known that as we had not called on her we could not be asked to it. I had somehow not connected life in Almora [United Provinces] with visiting cards, we had some hurriedly printed in the bazaar, the results were quite unique, then with a sketch map I wandered around the footpaths dropping my cards into letter boxes." The discombobulated Mrs. Gray neglected to post the senior lady's card, so she hastily retraced her steps, whereupon she "was shown into the room where a lady was having tea, she looked rather startled, I had apparently broken another custom, you never called in person." In failing twice to act according to the demands of social protocol, Mrs. Gray found herself in jeopardy of exclusion from the imperial set. Her memoir, unfortunately, does not report on whether the couple gained approval and a subsequent invitation to the aforementioned Club dance.[12]

Advice on calling etiquette from "A Lady Resident" in India provided clear and nonnegotiable social forms to follow. All newcomers, she instructed, "will have to commence a series of visits in the following absurd Indian fashion. If Captain and Mrs. A arrive in a station, the captain is expected to call upon all the ladies, who then return the visits with their husbands. . . . Bachelors call on ladies, whether old inhabitants or not. Up country, in the hot weather especially, people pay friendly visits early in the morning, at the 'chota hazree,' or 'little breakfast' hour, when tea, coffee, fruit, biscuits, &c., are offered to the guests. Large parties are often asked at this hour, instead of to dinner." Indeed, Captain Jones-Parry, on arrival at Vellore recorded, "My first duty was to call and report myself to the Brigadier, to the Colonel commanding, and then on all who were on my sister's visiting list."[13]

Georgiana Paget agreed with Mrs. Gray to confirm that the social convention of calling in British India operated as an imperial obligation. She explained, "It is the custom in India for all the gentlemen in a station to call on newly arrived ladies, and I was considerably amused and surprised at first, at my morning *levées* of officers in full uniform, with their swords on." A time difference appears to be the only change from the traditional British ritual that created cause for concern. Both Ellen Drummond and Georgiana Paget found that calling in India occurred earlier in the day, and the latter noted, "I am not yet reconciled to the hours for visits being so early—between eleven and two; but the plan of sending in your card, that no mistake is made in your name, is an excellent one." The ladies in India adhered to the station protocol that dictated that cards should be delivered, or credentials entered in a dedicated "visitors book," prior to an actual meeting. Corroborating this practice, Christian Showers-Stirling recorded that "life was full of 'people' coming and going—mostly wives, as the soldiers were on manoevres [*sic*] . . . and we had to return all the 'calls' written in the 'book.'" This method of introduction not only allowed officers' wives to filter out social undesirables, but also required a corresponding return call. This process, then, provided an essential function in a military world of constantly changing orders. The transient nature of the station population afforded even greater social power than in the core location, as the officer's wife's remit required her to protect—through vetting—the privileges of an exclusive and homogenous imperial coterie.[14]

Calling as an institutionalized duty operated throughout British India. Although Mrs. Paget attested that the bachelor officers held an obligation to call on the newly arrived wives, Madeleine Churcher agreed with Mrs. Gray by asserting that as a newcomer, she held the responsibility to call on fellow officers and their wives. On arrival with her husband at the Bareilly station, Upper Provinces, they made eight such calls on their first day. Reaching the commander's home, they intended simply to enter their names in the senior wife's visitor book. Mrs. Gray commented, however, that "Mrs. Henry" recognized her husband so invited the couple in for "a little chat." Although breaking with protocol, the *Burra Mem* had prior knowledge of the officer and thus deemed the couple appropriate for immediate inclusion in the station's social set. Margaret Hannay also demonstrated the obligation to call, even in tented accommodations. She mentioned whole afternoons dedicated to visitors during the regimental march from Mysopoorie to Mhow. Mrs. Showers-Stirling similarly confirmed the pervasiveness of this imperial duty. She complained that visiting and entertaining occupied most of her time from "October to March" of each year. She found the constant "curtsies and handshaking" both tiresome and irritating. Yet her account substantiates that in British India, calling functioned as a duty, a mechanism to create and sustain a social network whose privileged members legitimized and broadcast prestige.[15]

Similarly, American military wives stationed in the West adapted transported social rituals to create a distinct imperial community. Patricia Stallard describes garrison sociability as "an exchange of social courtesies," with officers dressed in "full-dress uniforms" celebrating "the glitter of the good life." Army surgeon R. H. McKay described the informal, yet institutional rituals that facilitated the creation of an imperial class. He advised, "There were no social relations outside of the post, and no effort or disposition to form acquaintances. . . . At Fort Garland . . . there were about the full complement of officers, several of whom were married, and it proved to be an unusually pleasant place socially. There was no formality, and so far as I know, this was true at all the military posts on the frontier. . . . [T]he officers' wives would make informal visits with each other and maybe spend an hour or so, very much as if they were sisters." Lt. John Bigelow also commented on the low-level formality. Whilst stationed in San Antonio, Texas, he described a constant whirl of social events. He recorded a dinner party during which "with the freedom of manners peculiar to army officers . . . [the men] spent most of the evening outside on the porch. . . . I had heard and seen a good deal of the informality of army society but had never before seen anything like this. It opened my eyes to a cause . . . of the general disinclination of army officers to establish social relations with civilians; they know that the latter would not allow them the same liberties that they enjoy in their own circle." Yet despite this social informality, he understood that within the army rank outmatched class. Bigelow, nonetheless, complained that whilst staying at the Menger Hotel, "I observe a disposition on the part of Mr Menger to show preference to superior rank in his attention to his military guests. While I appreciate the respect and deference due to my superiors and elders generally and to those wearing the Army uniform especially I do not like to have a sense of my inferiority of rank forced upon me three times a day by the hotel keeper and his waiters, for whose attendance I pay as much as any Capt, Major, or Colonel in the house." Bigelow further objected when an officer's wife pulled rank at a civilian ball. He complained, "When a set was being formed for a quadrille . . . I placed myself with Miss [Harriet] MacKenzie opposite to Col [George Lippett] and Mrs [Emily] Andrews. . . . Mrs Andrews swelled up and pointed to the Col. . . . then to herself and said, 'This is the head couple.' She should not have . . . presumed to take the lead on the ground of her husband's military rank." These examples suggest the formation of an American discrete officer class and community, regulated quite differently than civilian sociability. This imperial class, then, facilitated social distancing from the enlisted men, and afforded more relaxed dining protocol, but imposed stricter rules of deference determined by an officer's rank.[16]

An American etiquette manual written by Mary Sherwood provided instructions to correct "[t]he vulgar worship of wealth, the imitating of foreign vices and follies. . . . [T]he manners of our people must proceed from their morals; and, as we have no queen, no court, no nobility, to set our fashions, we must set them ourselves." In a complete chapter dedicated to the correct etiquette of visiting, Mrs. Sherwood considered the calling card as the "Alpha and Omega of all social intercourse." She instructed that the correct protocol of calling required visits to be scheduled between two and six in the afternoon, and returning a card as "sent by mistake" inferred a refusal to receive an introduction—a social snub. The social currency contained in this ritual could not be ignored or bypassed. Furthermore, the etiquette coach cautioned, "Indeed, a fashionable woman . . . reads the cards on her hall table as a merchant reads his day-book or ledger. It is her debit and credit account [as all visits must be returned]. It is a record of her social bankruptcy or her soundness. . . . For all, the little white messenger, engraved with a name, is the ready-money of society." The American officers' wives, however, did not simply trade welcomes and indulge in glittering festivities. These women, like their British counterparts, reworked the mainstream model of sociability to generate female power that designed, controlled, and maintained imperial authority.[17]

In reconfiguring this "debit and credit" accounting in the U.S. West, Alice Paulding (before her marriage) illustrated not only the social "ready-money," but also female authority attached to the "white messenger." In 1894 she accepted a cordial invitation to spend a winter at Fort Sill. In joining Geraldine and her father, Maj. Henry Wessells of the Third Cavalry, Mrs. Paulding hoped to find glamour and adventure in the "wild west." On her second day at the remote garrison, she recorded that she "was introduced to the good old army custom where everyone called on a visitor, beginning with the Commanding Officer and his wife and on down to the newest Second-Lieutenant." Eleven years later, and as the wife of the lieutenant colonel of the Tenth Cavalry, she managed a greater and more elaborate duty of entertaining as the female grenadier. As a new post commander's wife, she appreciated that "the women in our own regiment gave me loyal support," and dismissed criticism with "if a few outsiders were rather disagreeable, I don't think it worried me or cramped my style unduly." Thus, "the good old army custom" of visiting dutifully undertaken in a strict rank order functioned as a screening process. Mrs. Paulding clearly understood her imperial obligation to lead junior wives, control access to social currency, and to simply treat complaints from the rejected "outsiders" as a hazard of her authoritative position.[18]

Jennie and Albert Barnitz arrived at Fort Riley in 1867, and Jennie reported, "We were at once invited to Gen. Custer's . . . and were his guests until yesterday. Mrs Custer [senior lady] is a charming woman, very gay. We were constantly receiving calls from officers, sometimes a half dozen at a time. They are splendid—I should think all of them are from the best class of society." Indeed, a sense of duty prompted Martha Summerhayes to extend immediate overtures of welcome to newcomers. She recorded that "the boat arrived one day bringing a large number of staff officers and their wives . . . [bound] for Fort Whipple. . . . [I] went to the boat to call on them. . . . [I] asked them to come to our quarters for supper." In these instances, the ritual of card-leaving appears abandoned. Mrs. Summerhayes mirrored the Indian Civil Service practice by relinquishing her social power to the inherent endorsement of the military institution. She, without hesitation, accepted the imperial credibility of Fort Whipple's latest arrivals based on their army commissions alone.[19]

Reflecting the experiences of Margaret Hannay and Christian Showers-Stirling in British India, Marion Brown, who arrived at Fort Sill on 18 November 1867, confirmed the pervasiveness of calling in the U.S. West. After entertaining thirteen guests during her first evening at the garrison, she informed her parents "one is expected to receive callers until 11 P.M." Over the next eight days she and her cousin Carrie attended numerous hops and dinner parties, and reported that they had successfully returned "all of our calls." Echoing Miss Brown's comments, Ellen Biddle, on the day after her arrival at Fort Robinson recalled, "We were just finishing dinner, when two officers called and their cards were brought to me." Both Miss Brown and Mrs. Biddle found calling enjoyable. Yet beneath the veneer of social pleasantries this social ritual functioned to distinguish the imperial class, protect social, economic, and political currency, and police behaviors and practices.[20]

Adding a viewpoint of sociability from the upper echelons of the military institution, Elizabeth Custer confirmed how she, as an officer's wife, held authority to regulate behavior. She described the expectations of Maj. Gen. Alfred Gibbs, who commanded the Seventh Cavalry at Fort Riley in 1866, to explain that her "husband, absorbed in the drilling, discipline, and organization of the regiment, sometimes overlooked the necessity for social obligations, and immediately came under the General's witty criticisms. If a strange officer visited our post, and any one neglected to call, as is considered obligatory, it was remarked upon by our etiquettical [sic] mentor." In penning the following vignette, Mrs. Custer demonstrated her considerable power. A military man who drank alcohol but stayed "sober enough for duty" was acceptable. She wrote, however, of her experience with a "hopeless case" of an inebriated officer. "A new appointee," she advised, "made his entrance into our parlor, when paying the visit that military etiquette requires, by falling in at the door, and after recovering an upright position, proceeded to entangle himself in his sword again, and tumble into a chair. I happened to be alone, and was, of course, very much frightened." Determining that the new officer's behavior was inappropriate, she immediately reported her concern to her husband. Later that same afternoon, "the officers met in one of their quarters, and drew up resolutions that gave the new arrival the choice of a court-martial or his resignation before night; and by evening he had written out the papers resigning his commission." In determining the unsuitability of this officer as an imperial representative, Mrs. Custer not only rejected him from the social circle, but also stripped him of his commission. Officers' wives' social authority, then, encompassed far more than simply managing polite hospitality. They designed an imperial model of sociability, policed its boundaries, and instigated social, political and economic sanctions.[21]

Calling in British India and the U.S. West operated as a duty with its own weighty currency. This informal yet rigidly controlled process, transported from the home nations, functioned to sift out unsuitable pretenders to the imperial class. Officers' wives held roles as designers, managers, and gatekeepers of this social practice. In comparing the British and American female experiences, it becomes clear that similarities existed. Mary Sherwood aptly identified calling as ready-money, a means to vet and determine the suitability of newcomers, and this process operated in both locations. In British India, nonetheless, calling protocol appears more formal and disciplined with the use of a dedicated visitors' book. Both communities, however, adhered to set times, specific dress codes, and the use of a personal cards of introduction.

The pervasiveness of calling as a central element of duty occupied much of a woman's time. This ritual, as Christian Showers-Stirling complained, invaded her private time and intimate space, with its endless curtsies and handshaking. Yet behind the cordiality lay a mechanism to create and sustain a privileged network whose members accessed, legitimized, and displayed power and prestige. Indeed, the forced resignation of an American officer following Mrs. Custer's interview plainly illustrates the level of authority wielded by an officer's wife. These military women, then, shared similar experiences in garnering a substantial amount of power in the imperial holdings. They exclusively regulated the process of calling, determined markers of suitability, awarded entrance to those whom they deemed fit, and rejected, sometimes damagingly, unsuitable applicants.

The ritual of social calling, adapted from mainstream social mores, provided a central stratagem to impose standards of respectability, sift applications for admissions to the imperial circle, contain privileges, and promote imperial prestige. The *Times* of London reporter William Russell clearly understood the centrality of such performances in maintaining imperial legitimacy. He recorded, "Our position would be improved, and our national character would be exalted by the repression of [unprincipled] acts. . . . [W]e must provide some means of correcting the evils of the low standard which Indian life has forced upon us. I think that every Englishman in India ought to look upon himself as a sort of unrecognized unpaid servant of the State, on whose conduct and demeanour towards the natives may depend some of the political prestige of our rule in the whole empire." Additionally, an editorial published in the *Calcutta Review* titled "Woman in India: Her Influence and Position" charged each female to understand the expectations placed upon her and to realize "the influence she herself is having on the destinies of that great Empire."[22]

Once one gained admission, invitations to formal dances, balls, and regimental dinners swiftly followed. Dining etiquette, just as visiting, became formalized to demonstrate status, civility, and authority throughout the British and American imperial holdings. To enable readers to understand values, the indomitable Mrs. Beeton delineated the correct ordering of entrance and seating in England. She advised, "Dinner being announced, the host offers his arm to, and places on his right hand at the dinner-table, the lady to whom he desires to pay most respect, either on account of her age, position, or from being the greatest stranger in the party. If this lady be married and her husband present, the latter takes the hostess to her place at the table, and seats himself at her right hand." She added, "The rest of the company follows in couples, as specified by the master and mistress of the house, arranging the party according to their rank and other circumstances which may be known to the host and hostess."[23]

The British communities in India adapted these social rituals, and women held responsibility for supporting a distinct and inflated imperial model. Indeed, the procession and seating of guests became so important to the orderliness and stability of the empire it became officially regulated. Mimicking royal protocol, the nineteenth-century Indian *Warrant of Precedence* became the hostess's bible. In denoting prestige to all personages according to title and official rank, British women followed the dictates of the list religiously. Indeed, after visiting India, George O. Trevelyan commented on the "strong official element in the composition of Society. Nowhere are the rules of precedence so rigorously observed as in Calcutta. I have heard a Member of Council complain that for a whole fortnight he always took the same lady in to dinner; and, inasmuch as I am a very minor Sahib, I have never had the pleasure of descending the stairs in other company than that of male personages of my own calibre." This ordering rippled outwards to encompass all social encounters. Whether dining, playing badminton, or even sitting on the designated ladies' sofa in one of the "clubs," the most senior *memsahibs* demanded and received deference. These women clearly reconfigured middle-class conventions by intensifying ritualized domestic practices to legitimize status and power. In so doing, they forged an imperial class that relied upon strict obedience to a rank-determined order of social positioning.[24]

Once one was accepted into the privileged circle, one's attendance at dinner parties, another central element of imperial sociability, was obligatory. Located in the home, a domestic site, these spaces became appropriated to conduct the business of the empire. Officers' wives, then, operating as event planners, directors, and entertainers gained access to male knowledge and became instrumental in the assembly of power and privilege. Building professional relationships as informal confidants and advisors, these imperial wives obeyed, and enforced, the ranking conventions. To fail to do so would immediately result in expulsion from the imperial set, thus disconnection from the source of power. . Such adherence, however, required compliance with an exact system of social ordering. Additionally, at the end of the evening one had to wait for the *Burra Mem* to depart before even the most tired of guests could bid farewell to the host. The requirement of an official mandate to dictate dining protocol reveals the insecurities of the British power holders in India. In enforcing a precise official and unofficial etiquette, a collective symbol of respectability would reinforce the class hierarchy, orderliness, and stability within the military settler community.[25]

Such rigorous obedience caused many officers' wives to find their social obligations tiresome, as Emma Roberts atmospherically described: "At the hour prescribed by a goddess . . . [the] votaries of fashion began to arrive; carriage after carriage drove up to the door . . . the ladies dressed in ball attire, and the gentlemen uncomfortable in the prospect of being obliged to sit with their feet *under* instead of *on* the table." Roberts then complained, "The dinner of course was dull, the conversation confined to those common-place topics . . . which offer lenten [meager] entertainment to a formal circle. After a few hours, wasted in vain attempts to amuse people who belong to the most difficult class in the world, a sort of universal joy takes place at the separation; the guests are glad to go, the hosts are glad to see them depart . . . they rejoice that a disagreeable duty has been performed, and that a considerable period will elapse before they shall think themselves called upon to perform it again." Clearly then, some officers' wives' viewed entertaining at home an eminently dreary imperial obligation.[26]

With regard to the imperial currency of an invitation to dine, Miss Roberts provided an unambiguous example of the social significance and ramifications inherent within domestic hospitality. She explained, "With a regiment passing through, the family were anxious to invite all the strangers as well as the individuals composing their own circle, but it could not be accomplished" due to sheer numbers. The *Burra Mem* of the station decided to offer two functions, but "not a soul would condescend to come to tea; it was therefore necessary to make a selection: the married people were asked, and the young men were left to their tents. There was no use in giving them the option of coming in the evening, they would have been offended by so great a mark of disrespect as the supposition that they could be induced to act in a manner so derogatory to their dignity." Thus, the rigid social protocol could not be short-circuited, even by a well-intentioned senior wife. The insistence on exact performance reveals the uncertainty of these imperial representatives, who needed standardization of all rituals to ensure that their privileged identity remained stable and intact.[27]

On the prevalence of such formalities, Miss Roberts continued, "This spirit pervades every part of India; in Calcutta, the seats at a dinner party, vacated by any unforeseen contingence, cannot be filled up; intimate acquaintances, who would readily come in a friendly way at a day's notice, will not submit to stop a gap after invitations to others have been sent out." Thus, even close friends would not deign to make up numbers for fear that their reputations would be blemished. She further explained that if more than a couple of invitees declined, "the evil becomes very serious . . . illnesses or deaths assume the character of affronts, for the guests who fulfill their engagements are, in nine cases out of ten, annoyed at having so few persons to meet them, and receive the apologies of the master and mistress of the house with ill-concealed resentment." The hostess, therefore, held a responsibility to ensure a good number of visitors attended to provide a networking event. The difference from dining in England, apparently, lay in the hospitality afforded to "young men, who in England would feel honoured by being invited to attend the ladies in the drawing-room, must in India be treated with all the respect and consideration due to age and rank; they are offended by any distinction, and the ensign, if invited at all, must be invited with the same form and ceremony observed towards his colonel." Thus, the officers' wife held a duty to invite all appropriate guests, schedule the event at an appropriate time, guarantee a high attendance, and ensure that all imperial men receive the correct level of social courtesy.[28]

A failure to appear at a required social ritual could spell disaster for an imperial couple. In December 1856, surgeon Walter Wells became ill and was unable to attend the many regimental domestic functions. His wife, however, expressed relief that illness provided a *bona fide* excuse for non-attendance. She revealed a lack of interest in imperial sociability, and her general antipathy toward military wives, by noting that she did "not care" about attending regimental balls, as she found it "quite disgusting to see how some married ladies dance and go on in this country." Yet she proceeded to criticize the behavior of the Forty-Eighth's newest bride, a Mrs. Lewin. This subaltern's wife had apparently committed a fatal social *faux pas*, as the captain's wife grumbled: "They are the only people here who have not called upon us as they are neither of them worth knowing." Despite her lack of interest in attending social functions, Mrs. Wells clearly considered the failure to call a breach of the imperial class protocol.[29]

Two further recorded episodes illustrate the rigid code of British sociability; both concern ignored social solicitations. In 1875, Alice, the wife of Lieutenant Colonel Charles Massey, Indian Army, invited two military men to dine at the couple's home in Rawalpindi. She "was very much astonished at not getting an answer to either of . . . [her] notes of invitation and they did not turn up at dinner time," a clear infringement of imperial duty. Frances Duberly, however, penned a far more rancorous account. On 28 July 1855 (stationed at this time with the Light Cavalry in the Crimea), her letter to her sister advised, "you will be delighted to hear that there is a Mrs [Annie] Forrest out here, wife of a man in the Heavies. . . . A very dowdy sort of woman. . . . Her immaculate virtue has not allowed her to return my call!!! Very possibly . . . she sees all sorts of swell people in my tent . . . and thinks I keep too good company for my station." On 30 July she advised "I have seen Mrs Forrest, she is a stupid little ass." The very next day a simple line in her letter announced, "Oh—Mrs Forrest *has* returned my call." It appears that any delay in responding to a social invitation was not acceptable, even in camp during the last days of the siege of Sebastopol. The members of the imperial class were required to undertake social duties promptly, failure to do so negatively impacted reputation, hence membership of the elite set.[30]

Similarly, the ladies in the U.S. West standardized behaviors within the garrison, albeit with less formality, by creating a distinct model of imperial sociability. The military spouses transported and applied exaggerated social rituals that upheld pretensions of class status. In so doing, they did not directly challenge traditional roles, but extended their sphere of influence. Thus, templates of female-governed sociability, transported to the outer reaches of the American empire, became enhanced and enforced by the officers' wives to ensure the stability of their class identity.[31]

Frank Leslie's Popular Monthly, published in 1888, included an article titled "A Lady's Account of Life in the Far West." The author posited, "The ladies, besides overseeing the domestic affairs of their households, entertain largely and elegantly. One of their dinner parties presents a scene pleasant to look upon, as well as to participate in. The table, with its snowy linen, rich china, cut glass, silver, and epergne of fruit in the centre; the ladies in evening toilets of various hues, but all blending so perfectly that the most fastidious could find no fault." The article suggested that "the gentlemen in evening-dress or full-dress uniforms: the bright lights, gay laughter and good cheer, make it also a thoroughly enjoyable occasion." In commendation of the military spouse, the contributor claimed, "The hostess deserves the praise bestowed upon her, for it is not an easy matter to provide for such a dinner party." This published accolade found confirmation in Ellen Biddle's memoirs with, "I soon found that the life here was much more formal. . . . Invitations to dinners were sent out a week in advance, and when seated at the table you would not have known you were not in Washington, or some large city, the silver, glass, and china were so beautiful." Plainly, the officer's wife stationed at the remote western garrison transported and embellished the eastern middle-class dining model and accoutrements with snowy linen and an epergne of fruit. Although not operating within the rigid confines of the British *Warrant of Precedence*, the increased formality similarly spoke to the need for stability and the showcasing of an American imperial class.[32]

These military women also strengthened their version of ambassadorial authority and status by participating in male activities. In expanding the sphere of female occupations, they participated in buffalo hunts, observed bullfights, and attended American Indian councils. Such activities provided an avenue to discard traditional gender boundaries and experience multicultural rituals. Within the domestic space, however, the American officer's wife demonstrated an imperial sociability that reflected class conventions. Officers' wives stationed at the western garrisons extended hospitality to complete strangers based on the social currency of rank. Providing lodgings and meals for new arrivals became an accepted practice. Mrs. Boyd confirmed this duty by recording that in 1870, newly arrived at Camp Bowie, she and her husband "received a hearty welcome, and were feasted and fêted in true army fashion." This exclusive welcome to fellow officers and their families, within the domestic space, produced a cohesive class identity. This social ritual, however, was not simply a matter of exchanging pleasantries. As a host, Lydia Lane complained, "we had guests to entertain—people passing from one post to another,—and we had more than our fair share of them. . . . We became very weary with entertaining people of whom we knew nothing." The British Harriet Tytler illustrated the same practice of welcome in India. She considered, "I have learnt long since that English houses are not built so elastically as our own Indian homes, where we make room somehow for any amount of visitors, not only for friends but even for utter strangers." She concluded, nevertheless, that these unknown men could be completely trusted as they were "officers in the army or covenanted civilians [who formed] . . . a brotherhood of gentlemen." Hence, this obligation to offer hospitality to socially equal visitors, for both groups of women, was often seen as an onerous duty.[33]

In returning to the "great Western Empire" in 1908, as a guest rather than a host, Frances Grummond revealed her view as an imperial agent. With regard to her posting to Fort Phil Kearny in 1866, she commented, "The ladies of Sheridan [Wyoming Territory] were charming hostesses in their well-appointed homes. To one born and reared in the East, suddenly transported to the environment of our Western cities, she would observe that the people generally are refined, her equals—if unprejudiced—perhaps *crude* in some things." Thus, as an officer's wife she regarded western civilian society not quite of imperial caliber. The female American military host, then, held an obligation to provide and control imperial hospitality. It appears that in addition to demonstrating cultural and social graces, officers' wives needed to conform to a genteel type. In private letters to her family, Helen, the wife of Capt. William Chapman of the Second Artillery stationed at Fort Brown, described a remarkable, yet in her view ungainly, military lady. Maria, the wife of Maj. David Hunter, an army paymaster, stationed in Matamoros in 1848, failed to fit Mrs. Chapman's ideal of a female imperial representative. Apparently, Mrs. Hunter had "too much spirit to be exactly a fine lady." The spirited woman, nonetheless, became likeable despite being "rather dictatorial, and fond of power." With regard to the Hunter marriage Mrs. Chapman ventured that the major "has the feminine, she the masculine qualities and she controls [him], not always delicately. . . . However, his chains hang very lightly, for she never annoys him with trifles, adapts herself perfectly to every situation, never frets at inconvenience, makes him perfectly comfortable, entertains company handsomely, and makes a delightful home for him." This case study offers an example of an almost complete transfer of gendered authority as, according to Mrs. Chapman, an excess of spirit allowed Mrs. Hunter to have masculine control over her husband.[34]

In taking an authoritative role in the remote settlements of the empires, officers' wives gained visibility, but this visibility had its cost—a concomitant vulnerability to criticism. In considering the British women in India, Jane Haggis argues that "[c]olonialism and empire have both been seen as a boys' own frontier by participants and historical researchers alike." In this setting, *memsahibs* gained notice as "indolent, pampered socialites." In focusing on the Anglo community, and the reconfiguration made to middle-class social rituals to craft a template of imperial sociability, it becomes apparent why officers' wives acquired such bad press.[35]

Mrs. Ricketts contemplated the underlying causes for such a rise to notoriety. She insisted, "In India it is one of the conspicuous facts of life that everybody knows everybody else's affairs. Nothing that could affect the reputation of any member of the community ever passes unnoticed. No skeleton is ever permitted to rest in its cupboard." Paralleling this social control, however, ran a "live and let live" standpoint, "inscribed above the portals of Anglo-Indian society." This "dangerously elastic" situation occurred, posited the author, because of the lack of "sobering influences" provided by children, retirees (most returned to Britain), and English servants. Fortunately, according to Mrs. Ricketts, this unrestrained type of person only populated the minority. Most members of the Anglo-Indian society, she proclaimed, "are the pillars which are at once the support and its ornament, and it is in their clean, strong hands that the fame of the great Indian Empire rests."[36]

In considering women in India, Thomas Tausky claims, "For all that she played no part in the administration of British India, the *memsahib* . . . has figured prominently in the complex mythology of that society. . . . [She] has been portrayed as heroine, martyr, and villainess." Various commentators interpreted the attitudes, actions, and representations of British women in India as detrimental to imperial harmony. For example, John Morris, a retiree from the Gurkha Rifles, succinctly expressed the male disdain with: "Most of them started out as perfectly reasonable, decent English girls, and many of them in the course of time developed into what I can only describe as the most awful old harridans." Additionally, nineteenth-century novelist Sarah Duncan, the Canadian wife of a civil servant working in Calcutta, described the English *memsahib* in a very unflattering light.[37]

Why did these claims become generated and more importantly, what purpose did they serve? A female observer in British India argued that cultural rituals undertaken at the clubs encouraged such accusations. Found in every station, this social establishment, with its "green lawns, cooling drinks, a multitude of English papers, a library, tennis, racquet and badminton courts, bridge tables, and billiard rooms," fueled the claims of frivolity and scandal—a charge this female author vehemently denied. Similarly, Valentine Prinsep blamed the holiday atmosphere of a hill station for the allegations of indiscretion. He opined, "At length I have left Simla and its civilized gaieties and scandals, and can resume my journal with some chance of recording therein something more than the flirtation of Captain A. with Mrs. B., or the quarrels and jealousies of C. and his wife." He considered the society at Simla "a curious study . . . like an English watering-place gone mad. Real sociability does not exist. People pair off directly they arrive at a party . . . [and] do not trouble themselves about the general hilarity. Indeed, the *muffin* system, like that in Canada, is the order of the day." Hence, these two commentators regarded imperial society in India as far less reserved and straight-laced than that at home—a curious study indeed.[38]

This derogatory image of the imperial community made good copy, and women became targeted as the culprits. An 1891 critique of Rudyard Kipling's work, published in the *Fortnightly Review*, included a review of *Plain Tales of the Hills*. "Here, then," reported contributor Francis Adams, "we have at last the Anglo-Indian 'society' life of to-day, and we see it from every side. Duty and red-tape tempered by picnics and adultery—it is a singular spectacle." Sir Edward Buck, however, described the refining influence of Ladies Lansdowne, Elgin, and Curzon to counter such indictments, "Surely," he asked, "it is women such as these who have done, and who continue to do, more to raise the tone of Simla society, its morals, and its general influence than a dozen carping detractors of ordinary innocent amusements." Buck concluded, "The Anglo-Indian lives 'en evidence' from morning till night and night till morning, and many a peccadillo is enlarged into a scandal in consequence, in which a Londoner might indulge and go scot-free. Society at home is not, as many suppose, more irreproachable than it is at Calcutta and Simla." In comparing the major urban centers of England and India, Buck underscored a central element of imperial life—public visibility. Representatives held an obligation to act, both in private and public, as an unquestionable model of British civility and respectability.[39]

Officer's wife Florence Marryat supported Buck's rebuttal to declare, "I believe the charge of extra levity against ladies in India to be unfounded, and to have taken its rise simply in the reason that there are, comparatively speaking, so few of them, and those few have so much leisure, that liaisons and flirtations, that we should at home have no time to talk about, are considered sufficient to form matter of discussion for a whole cantonment abroad." This excess time fueled intrigue and rumor-mongering. "Questions such as Who Mrs. So-and-so is flirting with now, and why Captain Dash is to be seen constantly at Sucha-one's house, are untiring themes for inquiry and decision." Indeed, she concluded, "The women who were fondest of relating such stories, I generally found to be those most open to suspicion themselves." Hence, the consensus among detractors, apologists, commentators, and imperial women alike was that females enjoyed greater social autonomy to interact with males than they did at home. Despite Kipling's condemnation of life as "duty and red-tape tempered by picnics and adultery," most accounts understood that the British in India, whose behavior mirrored the urban centers in England, lived under extreme public scrutiny. As imperial representatives, officers' wives, however, held a responsibility to model an impossible ideal. Inappropriate behavior and any hint of sexual indiscretion quickly became not just local or regional, but national knowledge that rippled throughout the entire empire.[40]

In considering and comparing the nineteenth-century military protocol in the United States, Darlis Miller suggests that the army, like American society at large, observed a double sexual standard that tolerated "male indiscretions," but punished "outward promiscuity" exhibited by a wife. Here, then, is an explanation as to why females bore the brunt of criticism in both India and the West. The gendered construction of behavior implicitly included acceptance of a certain level of masculine excesses. As Miller observes, the female role met with no such tolerance. For example, Duane Greene, former lieutenant of the Sixth Cavalry, penned a vicious exposé of the American army wife. Published in 1880, the prose read like the very worst kind of sensational reporting. The disgruntled officer opined, "[T]he presence of ladies in the Army is prejudicial to good order and military discipline," and blamed these wives for forcing men to neglect duties and disobey orders. He continued his rant with: "A lady of fine social qualities, whose husband may be an irredeemable drunkard, a disgrace to the Army . . . insures his commission by the adroit manipulation of her admirers. If he stands condemned before a court-martial, she may be the means of his salvation. Her artfully planned supplicants . . . restore her lord to all the dignity of his former rank and position. Thus the nation, as well as the Army, feels her power."[41]

The former officer continued his diatribe with, "There is more caste distinction among the ladies of the Army than among its officers," and continued, "[W]hen *Mrs.* General A meets *Mrs.* Captain B, she assumes an air of superiority which is incompatible with her intellectual accomplishments. Mrs. Captain B realizes that Mrs. General A is her inferior in everything that distinguishes a lady, but is too polite to show that she notices her pomposity, and charitably covers it with the veil of submission." Additionally, Greene warned, "jealousy and imaginary slights produce much of the unpleasantness," and many wives "are inflated with aristocratic ideas . . . [with no] desire for anything but 'brass buttons,' costly dresses, fine dinners, and flirtations with bachelors." Recognizing more than just a penchant for frocks, food, and flirtations, he announced, "The ladies do not only manipulate the social affairs of the Army, but they are the power behind the throne which directs the administration of much of the official business." The commanding officer's wife, Greene complained, "chooses the garrison of the Headquarters Posts . . . designates the companies . . . most agreeable to her. . . . He [the commander] is simply her executive, and through him she persecutes with an excess of onerous and unpleasant duties all officers who are unwilling to 'bow and sue for grace.'" While attacking the officers' spouses, Lieutenant Greene, inadvertently, revealed their exercise of social, political, and economic power.

A wife who could gather male supporters to defend a drunken husband at a court-martial, and successfully pleaded his case, plainly commanded considerable influence. As the "power behind the throne" and her husband merely the "executive," there was no doubt, in this officer's opinion, who held the ultimate imperial authority.[42]

The requirement for officers to proffer obeisance to military wives was not a one-way ritual. The ladies also held an obligation, albeit potentially a pleasant one, to provide company and conversation for the commissioned bachelors. In 1868, Annie, the daughter of Col. George Getty of the Thirty-Seventh Infantry, and fiancée of Capt. Charles McClure of the Subsistence Department, Fort Union, recorded a dinner party held at the home of Mrs. Casey. Miss Getty remarked, "There were nothing but married men there so we did not have as nice a time as at the other posts." To an eastern onlooker, just as the British at home viewed the imperial wives in India, this agreeable element of sociability appeared incongruent with the ideals of female gentility. These friendly, and perhaps flirtatious, interpersonal relationships between the married women and single men, however, constituted a duty at the isolated posts. As Elizabeth Custer explained, "Officers all watch and guard the women who share their hardships. Even the . . . bachelor officers . . . soon fall into a sort of fatherly fashion of looking out for the comfort and safety of the women. . . . It often happens that a comrade, going on a scout, gives his wife into their charge. . . . [And] I have known of acts so delicate that I can hardly refer to them with sufficient tact." She continued, "In the instance of some very young women . . . I have known a little word of caution to be spoken regarding some exuberance of conduct. . . . [S]ometimes, when we went into the States . . . it would not occur to us . . . [that] the freedom and absolute naturalness of manner that arose from our long and intimate relationship in isolated posts ought perhaps to give way to more formal conduct . . . [so] that we might satisfy the exactions of that censorious group of elderly women who sat in hotel parlors." Custer concluded her fawning dialogue to justify, even further, this unusual custom of married women dancing, walking, and visiting—unchaperoned—with young officers. She also mentioned that lone officers would police male candidates for imperial class membership, by sending word that "they did not want us to continue to cultivate someone of whom we knew nothing, save that he was agreeable. How my husband thanked them . . . and said his say about what he owed to men who would not let a woman they valued be even associated with anyone who might reflect on them." She delineated the difference between civilian and military life with, "A man is supposed to be the custodian of his own household in civil life;

but it must be remembered that in our life a husband had often to leave a young and inexperienced bride to the care of his comrades, while he went off for months of field duty. The grateful tears rise now in my eyes at the recollection of men who guarded us from the very semblance of evil as if we had been their sisters." Mrs. Custer clearly explained the facts to justify mixed-sex relationships as purely natural, kindly, and familial.[43]

Despite Elizabeth's "grateful tears," Lieutenant Greene disputed such innocence, claiming that a patent sexuality existed within these "intimate relationship[s]." He commented, "It is a recognized privilege of an Army lady to call upon any officer for a favor in the absence of her husband." To support this assertion, he provided an example of the independence and authority of an indisposed woman who invited male guests to her home—in predictably derogatory prose. He recounted, "Here she [the officer's wife] held her little court, all the bachelors and some of the married gentlemen nightly gathering at her bedside, smoking and drinking, and entertaining her with songs. Madame de Staël surrounded by the most distinguished men of her time, discussing literature, politics, and philosophy, was not happier than this woman, who exclaimed on one of these occasions, 'I'm in my glory now!' Her husband, hearing of her 'indisposition,' came and took her back to his station." Undeniably, this officer's wife shattered Victorian gender boundaries by entertaining bachelors in her bedroom. Additionally, she enjoyed the freedom to actively participate in cultural and political discourse. In so doing, this American "Madame de Staël" blatantly ignored the confines of the traditional middle-class female space and role to take full advantage of her autonomy as an imperial host.[44]

Officers' wives in both British India and the U.S. West, then, garnered substantial freedoms, and an influential and visible role. This very power, nevertheless, triggered a female vulnerability to public notice. Dinner parties, although located within the domestic domain, became an integral imperial ritual element, providing a space for military women to gain access to heretofore male knowledge, and to generate power. Military spouses, as social arbiters of empire, designed the events and ensured compliance with all requirements of etiquette. As confidantes, wives shared many military, economic, and political conversations. As consultants, they cultivated male members of the imperial coterie, and negotiated, not military tactics, nor political treaties, but a shift into the masculine world of information. In so doing, they proceeded to access and influence the male decision-making processes. As in British India, the unconventional model of sociability constructed by officers' wives in the U.S. West created a backlash of scorn and contempt. The censorship did not reach the heights of the British response, but clearly caused comment. Despite this, officers' wives in both imperial peripheries acted as national hosts and ambassadors, holding a duty to offer hospitality—a welcome that intrinsically permitted or refused access to power.

※

In comparing the experiences of the British and American spouses, formal calling, in both India and the U.S. West, operated as a national duty. This social practice transported from the home nations provided a process to vet and sift pretenders, who hoped to access the privileges of the imperial class. Officers' wives held roles as designers, managers, and gatekeepers of the imperial communities, gaining substantially greater power than their counterparts at home. In British India, regulated visiting protocol utilized both cards and visitors' books, and the pervasiveness of calling as a central imperial duty occupied much of a woman's time. This ritual, as Christian Showers-Stirling complained, invaded her time and privacy, with its seemingly unending round of "curtsies and handshaking." In the U.S. West, the calling etiquette appears to have been equally prevalent, but less formalized. Behind the veil of obligatory cordiality in both imperial sites lay a mechanism to create and sustain an imperial class, and to facilitate a privileged network whose members accessed, legitimized, and exercised power. Indeed, the forced resignation of an American officer following Mrs. Custer's interview plainly illustrates the level of authority wielded by an officer's wife. These military women, then, shared similar experiences in garnering a substantial amount of female power in the imperial holdings, unavailable to women in the core territories. They exclusively regulated the calling process, determined markers of suitability, awarded entrance to those whom they deemed fit, and rejected, sometimes ruinously, unsuitable applicants.[45]

Dining, as an attendant imperial duty, required officers' wives to perform as unpaid event planners. Both sets of women held high-profile roles as social architects, logisticians, administrators, directors, food and beverage managers, and gracious entertainers. The British women operated under the stifling strictures of the *Warrant of Precedence*. The Americans, although less regulated, also held obligations to offer hospitality to all commissioned visitors, even when doing so became, as Lydia Lane confessed, a duty both tedious and tiresome. Thus, the officers' wives in both locales generated female power through their positions as imperial hosts. In vetting membership, and through influencing high-ranking military and political statesmen, these women gained access to knowledge and considerable authority and, as Lieutenant Greene revealed, became the power behind the throne.

This female empowerment, nevertheless, held a downside. Visibility of efforts in India to construct a reflective yet adapted model of middle-class sociability became the subject of national censorship and disparagement. The *memsahib*'s reputation deteriorated empire-wide into one of laziness, frivolity, and disrepute, generating claims that women caused the ruin of the empire. In the U.S. West, the reputations of the military spouses received less public attention. All women, however, generated greater autonomy to visit, dance, and dine with the bachelor officers stationed at the isolated stations and forts. Acting as gatekeepers of the imperial set, these women manipulated gender boundaries and practices to substantially increase female access to power and privilege. Consideration of the dynamics of sociability, however, only tells half the story. To understand more fully the authority and impact made by nineteenth-century officers' wives, in India and America, the dialogue must shift to examine attitudes and behaviors toward servants employed in the home. In considering race, ethnic, and class prejudices, a more complete picture emerges that identifies the erstwhile overlooked authority and empowerment of imperial women.[46]

8

Imperial Intimacy

Race, Ethnicity, and Class Relationships within the Home

> I always felt the keenest sympathy with the action of an officer . . .
> who, aggravated at the slow and solemn manner in which a young
> Mussulman in his employ was carrying a pile of plates . . . jumped
> up, and . . . gave the tardy domestic such an energetic kick that
> he sent him flying. . . . Their [Indian] characters may be summed
> up in a word: the men are cruel, crafty, and indolent; the women
> notoriously vicious.
>
> —*Florence Marryat*

With less hostility than that articulated by Mrs. Marryat, but in like vein, Honoria Lawrence scolded her husband for his verbal abuse when communicating with the household servants. She admonished, "I do not think you are aware, darling, of the way in which you habitually speak to the natives around you. Their provokingness [*sic*] I fully feel; and acknowledge how often I lose patience. But you, dearest, scarcely ever address a native without an abusive epithet—even when you are not angry. So I think it is very much a habit." In addition to such abuse, both physical and verbal, a British journalist traveling through post-Mutiny India added a far more telling layer of Anglo prejudice and notions of superiority. On arrival at Allahabad he noted, "At the gateway of the bridge . . . Sikh sentries are on duty, who examine all natives, and force them to produce their passes; but on seeing my white face they present arms. My skin is the passport—it is a guarantee of my rank. In India I am at once one of the governing class—an aristocrat in virtue of birth—a peer of the realm; a being specially privileged and exempted from the ordinary laws of the State." Indeed, a gentleman's advice manual advised on the internal role of an imperial male: "[W]e occupy in India a double social position; that which belongs to us among our friends, and that which belongs to us in the market, in the hotel, or at the dinner table, by virtue of our servants. Please yourself . . . in the choice of your personal friends and companions, but as regards your servants keep up your standards." Maria Graham remarked not upon a white complexion, or on the prestige afforded by one's domestic workers, but specifically on being British. She observed, "Calcutta, like London, is . . . peopled by inhabitants from every country in the world. Chinese and Frenchmen, Persians and Germans, Arabs and Spaniards, Armenians and Portuguese, Jews and Dutchmen, are seen mixing with the Hindoos and English, the original inhabitants and the actual possessors of the country. This mixture of nations ought, I think, to weaken national prejudices; but, among the English at least, the effect seems diametrically opposite. Every Briton appears to pride himself on being outrageously a John Bull."[1]

In the U.S. West, although not likening herself to Uncle Sam, Frances Roe accompanied her husband to his new position in the Department of the Platte Headquarters in Omaha, Nebraska. She complained of missing army life at Fort Shaw, and felt restricted and uncomfortable in the city, being "not of the Army— neither are we citizens." Mixing with female civilians she reported, "All the women here have such white skins, and by comparison I must look like a Mexican, my face is so brown from years of exposure to dry, burning winds." Used to the exclusive attention afforded to her as a military wife, she added, "It is the feeling of loneliness I mind here—of being lost and no one to search for me. . . . I shall never forget how queer I felt when I heard myself discussed by perfect strangers in my very presence—not one of whom knew in the least who I was. It made me think that perhaps I was shadowy—invisible." Complaining of her tanned skin, then, she used a biological reference to indicate a lack of imperial whiteness, a central indicator of nationality. In addition, the citizens of Omaha failed to acknowledge her status or assign value to her as an American ambassador. The awareness of her presence as "shadowy" and "invisible" plainly caused her discomfort and fostered a desire to return to her "cheery garrison."[2]

Within the British and American imperial landscapes, then, a white skin provided the foundation of identity and authority. Race is described by today's scholars as an elastic social construction, yet in the nineteenth century a person's physiognomy, in particular skin color, provided the central defining marker. In British India and the U.S. West military wives viewed their new neighbors through the prism of Anglo prejudice. They utilized complexion and cultural difference as vehicles of subordination, constructing a binary opposite to reify the white imperialists. Focusing solely on the home, it becomes clear that the relationships these women developed with their servants mirrored the larger ideologies of the empire. The home in India, scholars argue, operated as a microsite of imperial governance. The white occupying minority insisted on discipline and respect to subdue and control indigenous peoples. An officer's wife not only utilized these principles within her home, but concomitantly personified and thus legitimized Anglo superiority. Thus, in the remote military stations private and public spaces collapsed, leading Steven Patterson to contend that homes and households "represent the ground zero of empire in India."[3]

In testing this assertion by comparing the British and American imperial practices, it becomes clear that officers' wives held critical roles in the maintenance of imperialism. The British women were required to present a standardized and formalized domestic performance, to supervise the appearance, yet respect the personal lives, of Native servants, and learn (to a degree) the indigenous languages. Procida maintains, "Like the empire, the Anglo-Indian home must be ruled by example, not physical compulsion. As her husband was expected to embody certain tenets of Western civilization, applying European logic rather than despotic force to govern . . . his regiment, so the wife should rule her household by presenting to the servants a stellar example of European womanhood." To both prescribe and reflect benevolent imperialism, Procida concludes, "A wife must rule her servants with a firm hand. She must not hesitate to point out errors. . . . [T]o instil household discipline." Officers' wives in the U.S. West, however, had a substantially different—less codified and less intimate—relationship with the indigenous peoples. Yet, like the British women, the American wives inscribed racial norms that insisted on white superiority. Although less directly a colonial relationship, it did embody similar imperial attitudes. Within the domestic space, then, these women both racially censured Indian, American Indian, Mexican American, African American, and Chinese staff, and feminized the male other. Additionally, they subordinated—through class—their Anglo servants. In so doing, they constructed an empowered female identity that reinforced imperial superiority and authority at the most intimate point of contact.[4]

The nineteenth-century domestic role in India cannot be directly aligned with that of the core British model. An officer's wife experienced greater leisure time, made possible by a retinue of servants under her employ, and this was dedicated, according to Mary Procida, "to the work of the Empire." Wives having no recognizable role as working, philanthropic, or domestic women, they understood their occupation and identity as that of their husbands, and even entered this employment on the 1881 *Census of India* returns. Despite this awareness of imperial work, officials altered the record to classify women employed in the home as "unoccupied." This move officially removed any claim to an imperial appointment and buttressed the assumption that all wives generated identity and purpose through housekeeping chores. Yet, argues Procida, "the central paradox of the Anglo-Indian domestic life, as indeed of the Raj itself, was that the crucial mechanism for running the home and empire were entrusted to Indians, with the British relegated to the role of symbolic, if authoritative, presence."[5]

An officer's wife then needed to manage her imperial household through confidence, power, and command. With no real experience of how to project such an image, household manuals attempted to coach women on how to perform this unofficial service of empire. Steel and Gardiner counseled, "In India, the attention of the mistress is infinitely more needed," and if she failed to supervise her staff rigorously "she will find the servants fall into their old habits. . . . This must be faced as a necessary condition of life until a few generations of training shall have started the Indian servant on a new inheritance of habit." According to the domestic experts learning the language ranked as the first duty in imperial supervision. Indeed, army officers commissioned to serve in India had to pass the Lower Standard Urdu Examination within one year of taking up duty. This requirement to communicate in the *lingua franca* was essential to gain respect, maintain relationships, and enforce order in the ranks. Although the government sponsored three-month courses in Urdu for the British women, only one officer's wife mentioned attending such a course. In their recollections most incorporated individual terms, but communicated little more than the most rudimentary knowledge of the language. Indeed, E. M. Forster considered that a *memsahib* "learned the lingo . . . only to speak to her servants, so she knew none of the politer forms and of the verbs only the imperative mood."[6]

The officers' wives' resistance to learning Urdu, despite the sage advice from Mesdames Steel and Gardiner, appears curious. An explanation offered by the wife of a civil servant (Madras Woods and Forest Department) indicated that Englishwomen understood more of the language than they revealed. In so doing they could issue orders effectively, and eavesdrop on servants' conversation. This strategy she considered "a good plan on the whole though we did not relish all we caught." Florence Marryat, however, revealed a perhaps more accurate justification. She recounted "a lady going out to India nowadays has no more need to speak the language than she would have to speak French on going to Paris. . . . I was rather desirous at first of studying Hindustani with my husband, but he would not permit me to do so." Mrs. Marryat apparently overcame her disappointment as she advised, "Afterwards I saw the sense of his decision; for as he was either quartermaster or adjutant of his regiment . . . the sepoys, who were constantly coming up to his office [sited within the home] with various complaints, are not very choice in their language, and what is said in one part of an Indian house is heard all over it, it was better I should not understand them. I have been told that the conversation of the natives, as a rule, is too filthy to be imagined." This episode clearly indicates that imperial business was regularly conducted in the home, and officers' wives, as ideal representatives of imperial values and superiority, could not be allowed to establish cordial relationships with the Indian people. The continuance of imperial control relied upon a distinct and nonnegotiable separation of rulers and ruled. If language barriers were broken, the *memsahib* would have access to power that would enable her to bridge and reduce Anglo and Indian social divides. A second duty, the manual insisted, was that orders given to servants were to be carried out without question. "The secret lies," Mrs. Steel stipulated, "in making rules, and *keeping to them*. The Indian servant is a child in everything save age, and should be treated as a child; that is to say, kindly, but with the greatest firmness." A reward system offered the most effective way to gain obedience. With the docking of wages prohibited by law, wives were encouraged to introduce a bonus system of "*bakshish*, conditional on good service." With obedience thus firmly entrenched, the new mistress should quickly gain respect as the voice of authority.[7]

Such manuals contained, along with recipes, gardening tips, and dress suggestions, detailed information on what duties are performed by each servant—from the *khansamah* (head servant) to the *ga'ola* (cowman)—and the individual wages to be paid. The picture becomes even more complicated in India as caste determined a servant's occupation and limits of social interactions. The intricacies inherent in this stratified social system created a veritable supervisory minefield for a new officer's wife. Without exception, page after page of household arrangements filled the officers' spouses' letters and journals. A military household generally employed a minimum of six employees; a commander-in-chief employed sixty-eight, while a vicereine supervised a number in excess of nine hundred! As Mary Sherwood noted, servants not only provided manual service, but also indicated status. Thus, she found the home of a newly arrived gentleman acceptable to visit as it contained "the usual complement of servants found in and about the houses of persons of certain rank in India." Construction of imperial identity rested, in part, on the employment of servants, and the number engaged reflected status within the imperial hierarchy. If one expected to read of the general delight in the availability of such domestic assistance, one might be disappointed. The officers' wives frequently expressed exasperation with, and hostility toward, their Indian servants.[8]

For example, in 1827 Mrs. Fenton explained, "The retinue of servants you are forced to keep is absurd, but one of the tyrannies of custom that cannot be remedied." This captain's wife usefully described her household staff, mirroring many other officers' wives' lengthy descriptions. She advised, "A set of servants have been transferred to me by an officer going home, at least those connected with the table, and they are eight in number—a cook, a *mussolgee*, who is a sort of cook's attendant and holds a lanthorn [lantern], which none of the bearers will do, as perchance it might have been made of a cow; a *khaunsamah*, or principal attendant at table, who receives your orders and purchases all things for food." She continued, "There are two *kitmutgars* who stand by your chair and all but cut your food. The *khaunsamah* is only supposed to carry in the last dish, the soup, and, standing behind his lady's chair, to superintend. . . . [N]o other person's servant will wait on you. . . . Next," she listed, "there is a *bheestie*, whose sole employment is to carry water. . . . A sweeper, who is to sweep your mats twice in the day; then a *dobee* or washerman. I am told we still require about eight or ten others: four bearers, two of whom are to attend Neil, the sirdar bearer holding the same place in a gentleman's retinue that the *ayah* does in a lady's." Given the sheer number of servants, the *memsahib*'s confusion seems perfectly understandable. Fanny Parkes summed up the general opinion of Indian servants. She ventured, "Some of the natives are remarkably handsome, but appear far from being strong men. It is *impossible* to do with a few servants, you *must* have many; their customs and prejudices are inviolable; a servant will do such and such things, and nothing more. They are great plagues; much more troublesome than English servants." With this statement Mrs. Parkes captured the majority of women's attitudes regarding their indigenous staff. The observation of male attractiveness supports scholarly interpretations that debunk the Victorian female stereotype of sexual reticence.

Yet, by modifying her admiration with weakness, she reaffirmed the virility of British masculinity. Finally, Mrs. Parkes chose to interpret caste limitations, not as socio-religious structure, but as a sign of idleness.[9]

Some officers' wives attempted to work with the caste system's occupational limits. In 1815 Eliza Fay mentioned, "Since I wrote last, we have had a good deal of trouble with our Mahomedan servants on account of an old custom. Not one of them would touch a plate in which pork had been laid. So that, whenever we had any at our table, our plates remained till the cook or his mate came up to change them. This being represented as a religious prejudice, I felt it right to give way, however ridiculous it might appear. In fact it was an inconvenience we felt in common with the whole settlement, except the gentlemen of the Army." Losing patience with such inconveniences, however, the European community dismissed the offending servants. After four days of unemployment, the *khitmatghars* returned to work with the agreement that after touching "the very vessels which contained this abhorred food, they were allowed to bathe and cleanse themselves." She, nonetheless, summed up the situation with, "From this you may judge of their excessive idleness." The military wives were well aware of the caste-determined dogma but chose to ignore and explain the occupational restrictions as ridiculous and inconvenient.[10]

Ladies' maids, similarly, came under fire. Many officers' wives' transparent prejudice regularly appeared in descriptions of their *ayahs*. As Mrs. Guthrie unkindly noted, "Our *ayah* . . . so stiff and shrivelled . . . was very small, and very black . . . she looked exactly like a monkey wrapped up in white muslin." Mrs. Fenton disclosed an abhorrence of the *ayah*'s services, "Observe," she instructed, "I had declined the service of Mrs. C.'s *ayah* . . . [who] is always supposed to stand at your side to *put on* and *take off your* clothes—a ceremony which nothing could ever induce me to comply with. I could not endure their hands about me; the oil which forms a part of their toilet, the pawn [shrimp] they eat, renders them so offensive that I could not bear them in my room." Yet, she admitted, "To every lady I have met, but myself, these women are necessary. I am satisfied it is in many cases from ostentation. . . . I looked into the next room where an *ayah* lay on the floor, on which was strewn many articles of a lady's dress; she seemed so like a dog keeping watch on them." Like the majority of officers' wives, Mesdames Guthrie and Parkes viewed their ladies' maids through an imperial lens of class and race. The employment of Indian domestics consolidated internal class status, and provided a foil upon which the identity of the officer's wife could be constructed. Their disdain and extreme racism clearly subordinated the Indian women.[11]

In concluding this summary of the British military spouses' views of their indigenous servants, two final elements add layering to the discussion. Emma Roberts captured both factors: "In India, we may almost invariably read the character of the master in the countenances and deportment of his servants." Indeed, "If they be handsomely, but not gaudily dressed, respectful but not servile in their demeanour, quiet, orderly, and contented, they bear evidence of the good qualities of their superiors," observed Miss Roberts, "but where servants exhibit any signs of terror or of absurd obsequiousness . . . where they are dirty, ragged, noisy . . . the head of the house may safely be pronounced tyrannical, unreasonable, or a bad paymaster." This comment reveals that not only did the number of the servants reflect status, but also that their appearance and behavior symbolized the respectability of the imperial household.[12]

In some households, particularly those of high-ranking officials, personalized liveries added yet another cultural vehicle to signal imperial status. Harriette Ashmore and Harriot Georgina Hamilton-Temple-Blackwood, Marchioness of Dufferin and Ava, commented on these handsome outfits. The marchioness, who accompanied her husband to his appointment as viceroy of India in 1884, recorded, "The principal servants in the house wear scarlet and gold . . . The 'khidmatgars' or men who wait at table, have long red cloth tunics, white trousers, bare feet, white or red gold sashes . . . and white turbans. The smarter ones have gold embroidered breastplates, and the lower ones have a D. and coronet embroidered on their chests. . . . [T]he housemaids (and they are legion) are men with long red tunics, turbans, and gold braid—oh, so smart!—while every now and then . . . a creature very lightly clad in a dingy white cotton rag makes an appearance." She concluded, "The consequence is that, instead of one neat housemaid at work, when you go to 'my lady's chamber' you find seven or eight men in various stages of dress, each putting a hand to some little thing that has to be done." The number and dress of Indian servants, however, provided status symbols to define Anglo status and gentility. Such was the British reliance on the display of prestige to command legitimacy that even a servant's body—through livery embroidered with golden coronets and the letter D—displayed imperial prestige and status. The marchioness, like Fanny Parkes, repeatedly feminized the male servants by referring to them as "housemaids," thus accentuating British imperial masculinity. The service clothing embroidered with a "D" suggests a darker interpretation that categorized servants as possessions, uncomfortably resonating with the portrayal of the domestic lower ranks as creatures, by Katherine Guthrie and Bessie Fenton.[13]

Echoing these disparaging remarks, officers' wives in the U.S. West similarly incorporated animal references to describe their domestic servants. For example, on reaching Fort Abraham Lincoln, Katherine Fougera revealed her prejudice toward African American servants. She observed, "Cuff was a small negro waif to whom someone had once fed a decent meal.... [T]he little darkey promptly adhered to the regiment in true barnacle fashion . . . he concentrated a slavish devotion upon Lieutenant Gibson . . . and even began to dog *my* footsteps like a black poodle." After asking Cuff about the origins of his nickname, the child replied, "'I'se de general handy man 'bout here . . . and,' he added proudly, 'I'se de regimental masculot.'" Additionally, when her sister Mollie introduced the McIntosh cook with, "Iwilla . . . this is my sister," the newcomer responded, "I had heard many odd names given to the dusky race, but this one capped them all." The servant obligingly explained, "Yas'um. Dey calls me Iwilla for short, but I was christened 'I Will Arise,'" and Miss Fougera heartlessly admitted, "I controlled my impulse to laugh." These prejudicial attitudes provided a way for an officers' wife to subordinate African American servants by unkindly belittling both Cuff and Iwilla.[14]

Despite evidence of such prejudicial attitudes, some scholars attest that the isolated garrison environment encouraged more tolerant and integrated communities. In examining the military home in the West, it is clear that, unlike the imperial household in British India, the American officer's wife did not manage six servants, let alone a viceregal complement of nine hundred. Thus, unlike the British experience in India that utilized domestic space as a site of imperialism, and servants as a symbol of social standing, the servant population in the U.S. West provided a utilitarian purpose only. A genteel household in the East, according to one scholar, required at a minimum a cook, a maid, and a nursery nurse. In the western garrisons, however, not a single officer's wife recorded employing more than two full-time staff members. The most popular (and necessary) imperial servant proved to be a cook, and in this role the officers' wives generally preferred an African American female. Despite this demand for culinary services, interactions with racial minorities who undertook domestic work for the army ladies reveal negligible change in transported prejudices. These women considered the African American, Mexican American, American Indian, and Chinese servants racially inferior, thus reaffirming and reinforcing notions of an elevated Anglo class status within the garrison homes.[15]

Yet officers' families often brought their African American servants to the West, and most women expressed fondness and gratefulness for their devotion.

"Army people like the Negroes, and find a quality of devotion in them that is most grateful when one is so dependent on servants, as everyone is in military life," declared Elizabeth Custer. The normally vituperative Teresa Vielé illustrated this gratitude when finding herself in "a new country and [surrounded by] new people." In losing her maid to marriage in Brownsville, and now stationed at Ringgold Barracks, South Texas, she recorded, "I was left to the tender mercies of an African valet de chambre, who took the place of *femme* de chambre, to which he had been drilled by some navy officers, whom he had accompanied on a cruise in the Mediterranean. . . . This faithful negro *shone* both literally and figuratively; he was at once chambermaid, waiter, and housekeeper and . . . prided himself on keeping up the *style* of the family!" She continued, "No matter how forlorn the fare, silver, glass, and china glistened in immaculate purity, and Joseph Williams always I may say, *presided* at our board with untiring grace and elegance of demeanor. A soldier officiated as cook, and with the occasional assistance of a drummer-boy as scullion, divided the labors of the household, with which I would never dream of interfering." There are several items of note in this vignette. Vielé uniquely identified her African American servant by providing both his first and last names, an act that reduced the social distance between mistress and servant. She described his assistance in multiple service roles—including that of a lady's maid, an intimate domestic position. In presiding over meals with grace and elegance, and in maintaining the family style, Williams held a level of authority. Yet implied within these positive statements Vielé reduces his status by inferring that his dignified and faithful behavior was instilled by navy officers, and his service supported—echoing the British model—the couple's claim to an elevated class status.[16]

Many officers' wives also hailed the African Americans as valuable domestic servants. Caroline Winne wrote home, "I have two or three [people] on the lookout for a servant and hope to have a colored woman." Seven months later she advised, "I have at last succeeded in getting a girl. She is very good—a colored woman." Fanny Corbusier similarly recorded a positive and familiar relationship with "a very large and very African American woman, Julia, who was a fine cook. I told her she might have one beau at a time and one she always had. . . . [After] I scolded her for neglecting her work on account of the attentions of men, she picked me up and carried me from the kitchen into the dining room." Julia plainly considered her relationship with Mrs. Corbusier as familial, and following her not unexpected marriage, the Corbusiers engaged Maria, again viewed as a "very excellent mulatto woman." Reflecting the attitudes of the British women, praise and gratefulness were tempered with character flaws—in Julia's case her familiarity and romantic liaisons served as a vehicle for subordination.[17]

Penning a less than kindly account of an African American male, Frances Boyd, while stationed at Fort Clark, wrote, "[T]he peculiarities of our colored servants would fill a volume." She recalled, "It took our first colored cook, a huge, strapping creature, who seemed a very giant in strength and stature, three days to scrub our tiny kitchen floor. . . . our last colored cook was so surly I was afraid of him, and rejoiced when he was replaced by a white man." The latter servant, Mrs. Boyd sensationally recounted, moved rapidly from surliness to murder and arson. Indeed, the death of an "innocent widow" led to the detachment of a full garrison of men to prevent the lynching of the aforementioned servant. Captain Boyd, however, diffused the situation and returned home to his wife, who gratefully concluded, "I was allowed to have a white cook; for although they sometimes indulged in dissipation . . . and there is no fear known on earth as that a woman experiences when confronted by a drunken negro." Her use of the terms "peculiarities, strapping creature," and "surly," and an unproved murder charge, reveals the concerns and prejudicial views that categorized the African American male as racially inferior, tragically echoing the British women's view of the Indian.[18]

Another illuminating account of African American domestic service is offered by Frances Grummond. She described a Native American "siege" of Fort Phil Kearny to report, "Everybody's senses seemed under fair control . . . with a single exception . . . Mrs. Carrington's colored servant Dennis, who seemed to be actually possessed by a demon. . . . [H]e would strike his head with all possible force against the boards of the partition. . . . [L]ike a veritable mad-man." Fortunately, with the arrival of Colonel Carrington touting a revolver, "equilibrium was restored and Dennis became contented to live a while longer and discharge the normal functions of his usual employment." The ladies, as a group, retained their composure and contained their fear in the face of what they imagined as imminent death. The "single exception . . . Dennis," however, allegedly exhibited insanity, uncontrolled emotional outpourings, and a need for protection—all feminine characteristics. The white women remained calm and collected, watching "the surrounding Indians . . . brandishing spears, yelling like very demons, desperate for our blood." This vignette provided a race and gender binary opposition. Dennis became a foil through which Mrs. Grummond could illustrate the dutiful stoicism of the imperial women.[19]

In the examples given, garrison life reinforced the women's prejudicial attitudes toward African Americans. Mesdames Fougera, Winne, and Boyd hailed from

Washington, D.C., and New York, and Mrs. Corbusier from Amite, Louisiana, and their accounts were written of time in the West between 1867 and 1908. Although servants generally received gratitude for their loyalty and culinary skills, such appreciation became overshadowed by negative character assessments. Three of these women traveled west from the northeast coast and one could expect their attitudes to be less vitriolic toward the African American servants. Yet they recorded the surliness of a cook, the "demonic madness" of Dennis, and likened the disarming Cuff to a poodle. Mrs. Corbusier, the lone Southerner, was actually the least caustic of the four women. This becomes even more intriguing as the officer's wife disclosed that "with the Tenth Cavalry came a crowd of women and children, we had no difficulty in procuring servants." Hence, both Julia and Maria were camp followers of an African American regiment. Patricia Stallard argues that Mrs. Corbusier stayed loyal to the Southern cause "in spirit," but deferred to her New York husband in most matters, and performed her "official duties with grace and style." Corbusier was certainly more graceful in her criticism of her African American servants than her Northern counterparts, Mesdames Fougera, Winne, and Boyd. This is not an unexpected pattern of racial prejudice as scholars have identified discrimination throughout the nineteenth-century United States. The small number of wives in this sample, however, would not be representative of a complete survey of officers' wives' attitudes toward African American soldiers, servants, and civilians. It does reveal that prejudice was one of the elements utilized by these women to ensure the continuing superiority of Anglo identity and authority.[20]

In considering another minority group encountered in the western reaches, the officers' wives' views of Mexican Americans reveal seemingly contradictory attitudes. Scholars note that some women reflected negative nineteenth-century class prejudices, yet others viewed their new neighbors as helpful and vibrant. In examining the officers' wives' accounts, it appears that the peons of the working class were considered amusing or unseemly, yet the *ricos* (land-owners), whom the army wives considered of equal social rank, became acceptable as suitable acquaintances. For example, Teresa Vielé viewed Mexican Americans as a whole as "an amiable, smiling, innocent race of people, utterly unconscious of the higher emotions of civilization." She created, however, "a new circle of friends and acquaintances" throughout her husband's assignment in the Southwest and befriended "a specimen of the high life," the "handsome and intelligent" Dolores. The women enjoyed intimate discussions and smoking *cigaritos* together. Despite Vielé's positive interaction, Mrs. Summerhayes described her maid as, "Quite young and very ignorant and stupid, and spoke nothing but a sort of Mexican 'lingo' . . . the girl did not know anything . . . sometimes I succeeded in getting an idea through her impervious brain, but more often she would stand dazed and immovable . . . we had to let the creature go." Her troubles with domestic help did not stop at the dazed and immovable girl. Following the birth of her first son at Fort Apache, in 1874, she revealed, "Mounted men scoured the country around, to find me a nurse. . . . Finally, the sutler sent word that a girl had been found in a Mexican wood-chopper's camp near by. . . . I borrowed a Spanish dictionary . . . and tried to teach the girl to be of some use to me, but she was very stupid." Maria, the wife of Col. James P. Kimball, deputy surgeon general, made a telling statement regarding relations between the Anglos and Mexican Americans by maintaining that "[i]n the garrison, lines were strictly drawn. Turks and Christians never hated each other worse than Northerners and Mexicans."[21]

Mexican Americans often worked as garrison laundresses and held responsibility for the officers' wives' clothing. The identity of the Seventh Cavalry's "superlaundress"—a Mrs. Nash, who upon her death was discovered to be a man—clearly illustrates the intersection of class, race, and gender within a domestic environment. Nash, who faultlessly washed and repaired clothing, cooked wonderfully, and supervised childbirths—all working-class female duties—was in fact a Mexican male who partnered several soldiers. Elizabeth Custer described Nash as "one of the camp women, who had long followed the regiment as a laundress, and had led a quiet, orderly life . . . she was our laundress, and when she brought the linen home, it was fluted and frilled so daintily that I considered her a treasure." Dispensing with the need for official divorces, as a third husband Mrs. Nash had "captured the handsomest soldier in the company . . . we often admired the admirably fitting uniform his wife had made over, and which displayed to advantage his well-proportioned figure. . . . The bride and groom returned from the ceremony performed by the Bismarck clergyman, and began housekeeping."[22]

Katherine Fougera continued the story as her wedding to Lt. Frank Gibson approached, and she required the assistance of "the superlaundress [sic] of the regiment. . . . Swarthy of countenance, black-eyed, with a mass of thick black hair, she nevertheless preserved the Latin coquetry of always wearing a veil." In addition, Fougera recorded, "No party was complete without her culinary assistance, and few births occurred without her expert help. . . . [T]hings jogged along uneventfully, until one day the garrison received a shock. Mrs. Nash suddenly died. . . . The regimental laundress, midwife, and cook was no more. . . . But the worst was yet to come," exclaimed Fougera, "[S]he had been a man! Rumors about Mrs. Nash filtered through the reservation as far as Bismarck, where her Mexican tamales were conceded to be of the best." The tale of the superlaundress, remarkably, does not stop here. According to Mrs. Custer, Nash's latest husband, Cpl. John Noonan, who served as Thomas Custer's "right hand man" and "trusted servant," committed suicide. This she ascribed to garrison derision and ridicule that targeted the widower, which made life "unbearable to the handsome soldier who had played the part of husband in order to gain possession of his wife's savings and vary the plain fare of the soldier with good suppers." Although Mrs. Custer initially offered a positive view of Mrs. Nash, she countered this by likening her to a "giraffe," and stating, "[L]ike the rest of that hairy tribe she had so coarse and stubborn a beard that her chin had a blue look after shaving, in marked contrast to her swarthy face. She was tall, angular, awkward, and seemingly coarse, but I knew her to be tender-hearted." Thus, she subordinated the "coarse woman" on grounds of race and class.[23]

With regard to the gender and sex issues raised, both Mesdames Custer and Fougera chose to disregard the fact that gender boundaries had been navigated and crossed by a male dressing as a woman. Both women contended that the relationship between Nash and Noonan "was certainly a *mariage de convenance.*" Elizabeth Custer made a considerable effort to convince the reader that Mrs. Nash "was undeniably homely, she could cook well . . . and . . . she was already that most desirable creature in all walks of life—'a woman of means.'" In applying a smokescreen that emphasized Nash's domestic and financial allure, the officers' wives attempted to broker, manipulate, and control the information (which had reached the national newspapers). In so doing, they feminized and racialized Mrs. Nash's body and identity, whilst normalizing Noonan as a masculine American soldier. As Peter Boag argues, "At best, Mrs. Nash has been seen as some misplaced figure in the grand narrative of western history, while at worst she has been depicted as a displaced and demasculinized Mexican border ruffian made subordinate to the penetrations of imperial white male heterosexuality." He asserts that "the male-to-female cross dresser, his gender, and his sexuality, all ran counter to cherished regional and nation-building myths." In recognizing this, the officers' wives utilized a domestic episode to, through publication, protect and preserve the masculine identity of the Seventh Cavalry, and by extension the U.S. Army, and the nation.[24]

This episode offers perhaps the most sensationalized account of the mistress-servant relationship, but it was the Native Americans who commanded the most attention, filling page after page of the officer's wives' narratives. Generally expressing nineteenth-century mainstream views that cast these indigenous people in ways combining good/bad and noble/ignoble, the officers' wives' attitudes ranged from outright fear and loathing to friendliness and admiration. For example, Lydia Lane (whose fearfulness of the American Indians remained with her throughout her fifteen years in the West) recorded a journey of a military party from Fort Bliss to San Antonio, Texas, which examples a belief in the "savage" stereotype. Her overwhelming trepidation found an outlet through her sensationalized writing. "Woe to the hapless party that fell into the devilish hands of a band of Indians!" she warned, "Men were generally put to death by slow torture, but they were allowed to live long enough to witness the atrocities practiced on their wives and children, such things as only fiends could devise. . . . Do you wonder at our dread of them?" The American Indian clearly remained to Mrs. Lane a heartless and savage enemy.[25]

Ellen Biddle, however, held the opposing view. She "was never afraid of the Indians . . . they always seemed so peaceful and quiet." She reiterated this lack of fear with, "As I have said, I was never afraid of these Indians. The Shoshones and Pah Utes often came into the house and brought skins . . . baskets and beadwork, for sale." Similarly, Mrs. Dyer reflected, "While it is impossible to make men equal, because God has put the stamp of inequality upon them [the Cheyenne and Arapahoe] it took but a glance to distinguish those of aristocratic tendencies. Inflexible, erect of carriage, broad of shoulder, deep of chest . . . combined dignity with the ease and grace of an earl." These positive accounts plainly support the noble warrior stereotype.[26]

Few American Indian servants were employed in the West, and the brief glance at the attitudes of Mesdames Lane, Burt, and Dyer illustrates the range of the officers' wives' prejudices. Mrs. Lane's outrage and terror, carefully listing the expected atrocities, follows the style elements of captivity narratives. This genre delineates the other as a negative foil through which Anglo societies, during times of anxiety, forged a positive, superior, and civilized identity. Mrs. Lane used this vehicle to reaffirm the notion of imperial legitimacy by reiterating images of devils, torturers, and fiends. Mrs. Burt, however, provides a more respectful view of Shoshones and Paiutes, with whom she shared, if not a friendship, then a mutually supportive trading relationship. The intrepid souvenir collector Mrs. Dyer, however, offered an admiring account of the Cheyenne warriors whom she likened to Anglo aristocracy, thus elevating their status. With this brief survey of the officers' wives' racial references, the four following accounts of American Indian domestic encounters can be more fully understood.

In 1866, Marion Russell, stationed at Fort Bascom, provided a rare account of a Native American child servant. She recounted, "[A]n old Spaniard gave a little Indian slave boy to Richard. . . . Our José Russ . . . was a problem child. Ambitious and willing, his little feet were forever running errands for me. Yet," she complained, he "was a liar. . . . [He was also] a thief. Nothing was safe from his pilfering fingers." Shortly after the arrival of the boy, her husband took a corn shipment to the Navajo reservation. Here, by coincidence, he met the child's father, to whom he returned his son—to the Navajo parent's "great . . . joy." Mrs. Russell heaved a sigh of relief and admitted, "I was glad to get rid of the first and only slave I ever had." Not quite the fiendish character penned by Mrs. Lane, José Russ, nevertheless, was depicted in prejudicial terms by this officer's wife.[27]

Martha Summerhayes provided an astonishing description of an American Indian male servant. In Ehrenberg, Arizona, she employed "Charley," a Cocopah Indian, as her "man about the place, my butler in fact . . . as he knew how to open a bottle of Cocomonga [sic] gracefully and to keep the glasses filled." He appealed to the officer's wife's "aesthetic sense in every way. Tall, and well-made, with clean cut limbs and features, fine smooth copper-colored skin, handsome face, heavy black hair done up in pompadour fashion . . . a small feather at the crown of his head, wide turquoise bracelets upon his upper arm, and a knife at his waist—this was my Charley, my half-tame Cocopah." On hosting friends from the "States," she astonished her guests when her servant "waited on them at the table, for he wore nothing but his gee-string, and although it was an every-day matter to us, it rather took their breath away." This practice, clearly different from eastern norms, confirms imperial female autonomy and authority. No longer operating within the social or sexual confines of the domestic United States, officers' wives designed behavioral privileges that clearly delighted Mrs. Summerhayes.[28]

Additionally, Assistant Surgeon McKay's memoir provides an insight into the positive relationship between his wife and an American Indian servant. He recalled, "We had . . . a Cherokee Indian woman [Charlotte] employed as a servant. . . . She was exceedingly neat and clean and a thorough housekeeper and an exceptionally good cook and a most devoted servant, but she would take orders from no one except my wife." Unfortunately, he continued, "she informed my wife that she was going to leave us, and this she did. . . . My wife was surprised and so expressed herself and also her sorrow at having her go. . . . It developed afterwards that she was offended at some orders given her by Mrs. Spencer." Robert McKay, however, added a further episode to "show the Indian blood: One of the colored sergeants took quite a fancy to her and would often stand in the door and talk to her, which was all well enough with Charlotte until she wanted him to go." On one such occasion McKay "overheard her say in a loud and angry tone, 'Now you go, I won't talk to you again. Go now!' I hurried to the kitchen and opened the door just in time to see the butcher knife sticking in the outside door jam [sic] and still vibrating from the force that sent it. The sergeant had jumped in time, but Charlotte was furious. When I asked, 'Why, Charlotte, what is the matter?' she simply replied, 'Next time I tell that nigger to go I guess he will go.'" Clearly Charlotte and Mrs. McKay had established a reciprocally positive and cordial and relationship. McKay appreciated the exceptional domestic service, yet underlined Anglo superiority in mentioning Charlotte's devotion. We can only surmise what offenses, committed by Mrs. Spencer and the Tenth Cavalry sergeant, caused Charlotte's infuriated reactions.[29]

An episode concerning a visit to Alice Baldwin's home by a medicine man usefully adds a final study of the attitudes of the officers' wives toward the American Indians. Openly penning her empathy for the "enemy [Lakota Sioux] . . . half dead with exposure" held at Fort Keogh, Mrs. Baldwin argued that the "harassed, cheated, lied to, and deceived" were "shorn of their very birthright by an already rich nation professing Christianity and humanity." Tempering this impassioned plea, however, she declared that despite the absence of "unfriendly demonstrations they were not always to be trusted." Largho, an elderly Navajo medicine man who walked unannounced into her home, nonetheless contradicts this doubt. The healer sat beside the cradle of her "fretful and crying" baby and "began to chant, meantime shaking the [rattlesnake] rattles ceaselessly, while I looked on in wonder and astonishment. Sure enough! The baby's cries grew fainter . . . and she fell asleep." Additionally, a group of Navajo women who admired Alice's curled hair paid frequent visits to her home to learn how to use hairpins. She concluded, "[S]uch an array of giggling, crimpheaded squaws had never before been seen in all the history of Fort Wingate. Feminine vanity and tastes are much the same the world over, no matter what the race or color. . . . [T]hereafter the Indian women were my firm friends, and rendered me various favors and kindnesses." So, this officer's wife who apparently distrusted Native Americans allowed a medicine man to minister to her teething child and played hairstylist to a group of giggling women, both encounters within her home. While this imperial ambassador espoused the racial line, in actuality, Mrs. Baldwin's domestic interactions with the Lakota Sioux and Navajo illustrates a political sympathy for, and genuine affinity with, the indigenous peoples.[30]

To present an analysis of attitudes toward the American Indians based on three brief servant examples would not adequately explain the women's complex views. Various scholars consider that women in the West initially expressed fear of the indigenous people, yet over time and with frequent contact changed their opinions regarding individual tribes and actors. Initial articulations of dread moderated to acceptance, even friendliness and empathy for the indigenous people's plight. Indeed, according to Sherry Smith, no single military mindset existed, and perceptions differed according to the reputation of a specific tribe, an officer or his wife's particular temperament, and the circumstances of the encounter. Gendered attitudes existed, according to Glenda Riley, who claims that men did not change their convictions of American Indian inferiority. The posturing of Anglo male military prowess fueled an indigenous militant response that further justified white encroachment. Women, she argues, due to the learning experience of life in the West, adjusted self-images and developed sympathetic and friendly relations with the Native Americans.[31]

In considering the officers' wives' views of their American Indian servants, Mrs. Russell acknowledged José Russ's willingness to run errands, but diminishes such praise by calling him a liar and a cheat. Although we are not given the time spent with the military family, which appears to have been fairly brief, Mrs. Russell shows no friendliness or sympathy in her attitude toward her "slave." Similarly, Mrs. Summerhayes had lived in the West for about a year when Charley became her servant. The handsome butler clearly did not cause her any fear or discomfort, in fact quite the opposite. Unfortunately, we are not privy to Lieutenant Summerhayes's opinion of this half-clad Cocopah. These relationships suggest that neither wife felt fearful of her American Indian servant. José Russ was at worst considered a nuisance. Charley was paraded in front of eastern visitors as living evidence of Mrs. Summerhayes's more liberal and authoritative lifestyle—as an imperial adjunct she proved she could employ and control an armed Native American.

Although this population was infrequently mentioned by the officers' wives, interactions with Chinese servants usefully illustrate the understandings and attitudes of the women. For example, Ellen Biddle, while stationed at Fort Whipple in 1878, threw a dinner party for an extremely important guest. "All of the officers and their wives, as well as all of the bachelor officers, were asked to meet him. When I was presented he took my hand [and]. . . . He had a chair placed beside him for me to sit down . . . I felt quite like a queen . . . it seemed to me a great thing to have this great man make much of me." The military dignitary in question was no other than William T. Sherman. Mrs. Biddle excitedly continued, "The evening came for our dinner to the General and it was very good. I had a most excellent Chinaman cook named 'Flang,' quite young, and he always dressed in very pretty Chinese coats, and, to match the costume, a hat that had a tassel on it, which he had a peculiar way of throwing to one side." The main course for twenty guests was a great success, yet this officer's wife exclaimed, "When the dessert was brought in I had a great fright. A large fish was presented to me. 'Oh! my,' I thought, 'has he [Flang] cooked another fish?' My heart was beating very fast, when someone said, 'Did you ever see anything so perfect?' It was a Charlotte Russe; the Chinaman had imitated the fish, and it was perfect, greatly to my relief." Mrs. Biddle's view towards Flang appears positive, she thought him an excellent cook, and praised the innovative mousse dessert. Yet by describing his "pretty" outfit, the tossing of his hat tassel, and the "perfect" quality of his baking, Mrs. Biddle feminized the "excellent Chinaman," thus aggrandizing the masculinity of the American male guests.[32]

Another officer's wife, who employed a total of four Chinese servants, adds another layer to the officers' wives' racial attitudes. Frances Roe revealed her initial prejudice while stationed in Fort Kit Carson in 1871. She admitted she preferred Cagey's (her African American cook) less than wonderful cooking to a "China-man's . . . judging from what [she] saw of them" in the garrisons. She supported this view with a tale of Mrs. Conrad's servant who was considered an "excellent servant in every way except . . . doing the laundry work." When informed of his failings, Mrs. Roe repeated, "The heathen . . . said to the lieutenant's wife, 'Allee light, you no like my washee, you washee yoursel'" and emptied a pan full of wet clothes onto the floor. Seven years later at Fort Shaw, however, Roe announced that "we are almost settled now, and Sam our Chinese cook, is doing splendidly. At first there was trouble, and I had some difficulty in convincing him that I was mistress of my own home and not at all afraid of him." The lieutenant's wife does not explain why she experienced fear in managing Sam. Perhaps the "heathen's" temper tantrum that ended in wet washing all over Mrs. Conrad's floor caused her anxiety.[33]

Sam, nonetheless, was quickly replaced by another Chinese servant, Charlie, whom Frances Roe considered "a treasure." Unfortunately for all concerned, it did not remain smooth sailing for long in the Roes' kitchen. The officer's spouse complained, "I made some Boston brown bread. . . . I went to the kitchen to put it in the oven. . . . When he saw what I was about to do he became very angry. . . . He said, 'You no put him in l'oven.' I said 'Yes, Charlie, I have to for one hour.' He said, 'you no care workman, you sploil my dee-nee [dignity], you get some other boy.' Now Charlie was an excellent servant and I did not care to lose him, but to take that bread out was not to be considered. I would no longer have been mistress of my own house, so I told him quietly, 'very well,' and closed the oven door with great deliberation." Charlie calmly departed, considerately informing Mrs. Roe that he would send "another boy." This assured servant threatened the officer's wife's sense of superiority. The closing of an oven door reestablished her authority, and denied her servant any claim to autonomy. The officer's wife's very next line in her memoir advised that "the 'other boy [confusingly also called Charlie]' came in time to give us a delicious breakfast, and everything went on just the same as when old Charlie was here." It appears that by the time the lieutenant's wife had employed three Chinese cooks, she had learned how to assert her imperial authority, even at the cost of losing a domestic "treasure."[34]

The second Charlie apparently adored the Roes' fowls and like his predecessor showed signs of self-confidence, becoming irritated if anyone interfered with his avian charges. After a move to Fort Shaw, Mrs. Roe encouragingly reported that "the Chinaman, squirrels, and chickens" had settled well into their new home. Mrs. Roe found this Charlie "splendid and most resourceful," but without warning he resigned. Despite the officer's wife's entreaties to stay, he left admitting he "feel vellee bad." Frances soon discovered that the "splendid" servant was in fact "a high-binder . . . the Chinamen in the garrison. . . . were afraid of him, yet he seemed so very trustworthy in every way. But a highbinder in one's own house!" Undeterred by such scandal, and now apparently a seasoned mistress, she hired a fourth Chinese servant, Hang. Indeed, in assisting at a dinner party given by a fellow officer's wife, this Chinese cook had "a glorious time. He evidently frightened the old colored cook into complete idiocy, and was ordering her about in a way that only a Chinaman knows." When Lieutenant Roe received a posting as quartermaster at Fort Ellis in 1884, necessitating another move, his wife provided the servant with the greatest of compliments, "I shall miss Hang! How am I to do without him I do not quite see."[35]

In recording domestic interactions with Flang, Sam, the Charlies, and Hang, the officers' wives observed and acknowledged a high level of domestic competence, yet overlaid such positive comments with race and class prejudices. The women used descriptors such as "pretty," and "treasure" to feminize and undermine their cooks' masculinity. All of them recorded dialogues that mimicked and belittled attempts at English pronunciation and, in calling the servants "boys," emasculated and subordinated the Chinese male.

In examining the attitudes and behaviors of imperial wives stationed in British India and the U.S. West, both groups clearly utilized prejudice and discrimination to subordinate domestic servants. In India, the number of servants symbolized status and one's position in the imperial hierarchy. Indian bodies became appropriated, through dress and behavior, as a marker of the employer's external and internal imperial identity. The British women generally viewed the Indian male servants, such as the *khansamah* dressed in his gold and scarlet finery, as handsome. This viewpoint expressed a certain level of admiration, a physical attractiveness in the indigenous male. Yet invariably, qualifying comments of weakness or over-obsequiousness reduced masculinity. In contrast, American spouses articulated no such admiration for the physical presence of African American, Mexican American, or Chinese male servants. The description of the supposed insanity of Dennis, and the surliness of Mrs. Boyd's "creature" cooks, removed any claim to gentility. Similarly, the commentary concerning Mrs. Nash highlights the complex issues of identity raised by a male-to-female cross-dresser. Thus, these minority groups, while praised for their domestic skills were feminized, utilized as foils to magnify American masculinity and prowess. The American Indian, uniquely, received sensual appreciation. Who could forget the Cheyenne warrior with the grace of an earl, or Charley, whose tall and handsome figure, bedecked with turquoise bracelets, delighted Mrs. Summerhayes? Yet, echoing the British wives' responses, the Cocopah servant was reduced to "a half-tame man about the home," and the Cheyenne combatant judged to be unequal. Thus, all male servants employed within imperial households were feminized and subordinated. This process allowed the British and American masculinity to be aggrandized, and legitimized the mission and supremacy of empire.

With regard to the female domestics, few military spouses on either side of the Pacific Ocean afforded positive portrayals of these service employees. The Indian *ayah* invariably was described as "idle, slatternly, and dissipated," with veiled references to promiscuity. Her domestic usefulness to the officer's spouse was both utilitarian and as an instrument through which imperial identity could be constructed. By contrasting and denigrating the body and behavior of this lady's maid/wet nurse/nanny, the mistress of the house rendered her own identity superior, genteel, and civilized. The American spouses, in comparison, employed female kitchen staff, but relatively few maids or nannies. They clearly thought highly of the African American cook, preferring "colored women" for their unfailing "devotion." Yet a rider to such appreciation, just as in the British case studies, subordinated the dedicated employees. The ridicule of Iwilla and the tale of promiscuous Julia substantiate this construction of race and class borders. The admiring accounts of the male "other," however, suggest that these imperial women safely observed, pondered, and commented on indigenous bodies. A nonwhite male could be admired as he did not represent a potential sexual partner. In most descriptions, officers' wives added negative codicils, however, reducing indigenous masculinity and removing respectable femininity. In so doing they created a foil on which imperial strength and superiority could be showcased.

Such was the prejudice expressed by the officers' wives in both British India and the U.S. West toward their Indian, African American, Mexican, Native American, and Chinese servants. If these domestic workers created such problems, why didn't the officers' wife simply employ Anglo servants? Many working-class women and men traveled eastward and westward to find employment and, perhaps, economic opportunities not available at the core centers. To help unravel the mystery, consider the terms in which the British imperial observer Emma Roberts in 1828 compared the Indian *ayah* with a European woman. She explained, "The difficulty regarding female domestics is certainly very great. It is generally considered essential for the *ayah* to be a Moosulman [Muslim] woman, as none but a low Hindoo [Hindu] would take the office; and it may safely be averred that not one respectable woman out of a hundred is to be found in this class." Adding insult to injury, these female servants apparently did not even take "the slightest pains to make themselves acquainted with the mysteries of the European toilette; they dress their ladies all awry. . . . Folding up dresses is an art wholly unknown, and Griselda herself would find it difficult to keep her temper in the midst of crushed flounces, broken feathers, and gauzes eaten through and through by cock-roaches." So, the Indian servant appeared completely unsuitable, yet, this officer's wife appended, "European women, if attainable, demand enormous wages; they soon learn to give themselves airs, and require the attendance of natives during the hot weather." Plainly, Emma Roberts considered the servant situation extremely problematic. She confirmed the disadvantages, at least in the imperial women's view, that employing Anglo staff would result in the working-class female's aspiration to middle-class status through appearances and behavior—thus reducing the social divide.[36]

The British and American Anglo servant remains, in the most part, a puzzling cipher. There are few diaries, letters, or memoirs that articulate this actor's life. Two memoirs of enlisted men's wives, although not servants, offer a brief glimpse of imperial life from the bottom up. Ellen Williams, wife of bugler Charles Williams, entered the army as a laundress with Company A of the Second Colorado Volunteer Cavalry, who were mustered into the U.S. Army in 1861. She recorded the regiment's answer to the orders to pursue "bushwhackers" throughout eastern Kansas and western Missouri. Here Mrs. Williams served as both laundress and nurse and chronicled the "trials and travels of the Second Colorados [sic]." In describing the regiment Ellen Williams characterized both the commissioned and noncommissioned men in honorable terms. When Company B saw action in the "fierce and desperate" Battle of Valverde, she recorded that each unit "grandly perform[ed] their duty.... In the battle General [Edward] Canby showed himself the brave, considerate commander and after it was over, as he went through the ranks of the wounded, he wept as only a comrade would who loved his fellow soldier; a truly noble man he was." Company A, meantime, reported at Santa Fe, and were immediately dispatched to Fort Union. The women were ordered to stay in situ and sadly watched the men march away. Almost immediately a rumor warned that the "rebels" were en route, and "in a few hours' stragglers began to arrive, and began to take all they could lay hands on from the soldiers' wives." The women dug hiding places for their provisions, and Mrs. Williams noted, "About the time we had finished we learned that the officer in command was Captain Battles, with whom our Captain's wife was acquainted, and at her request he put a stop to such doings." It is clear that Mrs. Williams held the general, as a leader on the battlefield, in high regard. The captain's wife, nonetheless, in staying behind with the women, demonstrated her class identity by utilizing social power to end the plunder and pilfering that unsettled the soldiers' wives.[37]

Another laundress, Mrs. Rachel [Lobach] Brown Matthews, married Pvt. Henry F. Brown of the Fourth Infantry in 1874 at Fort Sanders, Wyoming. Moving to the Red Cloud Agency, Nebraska, Rachel laundered for the men from the Browns' log cabin home. Her reminiscences included memories of the officers' wives dressed in bright bustles and basques, an American Indian warrior who attempted to trade multiple items for her infant son Henry, and claimed a friendship with Calamity Jane. In June 1876, following the news of Custer and his men's massacre, she traveled by train and stagecoach along with other military women to a "safe" location. She remarked, "The officers' wives were very kind in helping me with the baby. They saw that I was sick with fear and frequently offered to take care of him. I was relieved when they took him for I thought that they could protect him better than I." Despite the officers' wives' generally low opinion of the servant class, Mrs. Brown appeared to have established cordial relations with the elite females. This practical revelation nonetheless illuminated a very real social divide. Passing Henry to an officer's wife would command greater protection for her son. The military men would, without question or hesitation, safeguard a child in the arms of a member of the imperial class.[38]

These two lone accounts written by laundresses in the U.S. West do not represent the attitude of the servant class as a whole. Both hold interest as neither Mrs. Williams nor Mrs. Brown, appears to be the insolent, drunken, or coarse woman portrayed in the ladies' reminiscences. This indicates that the officers' wives used rank as a class marker to stereotype the privates' wives as the worst of characters. Thus, by measuring themselves against this ill-behaved female archetype, an imperial figure of opposition could be crafted—a genteel and refined lady. Characters such as Mesdames Williams and Brown provided a necessary service. Yet, as Miss Roberts noted, aspirations to middle-class status formed the central obstacles to satisfactory servitude. In both locations Anglo servants proved extremely difficult to hire and retain, hence the low numbers. In the instances when white domestics appear, however, the officers' wives, lacking a racial justification to determine inferiority, ridiculed hireling claims to status to reemphasize their own class suitability as imperial ambassadors.

In British India the officers' wives made mention—albeit brief—of Anglo governesses, cooks, maids, housekeepers, and handymen who shared their daily imperial life. Captain Williamson somewhat explained the invisibility of these individuals by venturing, "Regarding European servants, and English cattle. It might be said, in brief, that neither the one, nor the other, is found to answer in India." Validating Miss Roberts's opinion, he confirmed that "[a]n European servant must have nearly as many natives to attend him as an officer requires; he must have a house; and a million of indulgences. . . . [And] after saving a little money . . . they have set up in some business, and with very little warning, or ceremony, quitted their masters." In considering the Anglo woman Williamson postulated, "Whenever a lady has carried out an European female servant, whether old or young, ugly or beautiful, it has usually happened that a speedy separation has taken place: many, indeed, have deserted from their mistresses [once they arrived] at Madras." Alternatively, the captain suggested, working conditions in India did not offer a welcome prospect for even the most desperate of maids and governesses.[39]

Soldier-servants and their wives, nonetheless, did find employment with the imperial families, and became visible through the *memsahibs'* recollections. Mary Sherwood engaged her house-servants on board the *Devonshire* before the weighing of the anchor in Portsmouth. She wrote, "I could do no other than choose our man-servant's wife, Betty." She described "Mr Sherwood's servant" as "Luke Parker, a private soldier. . . . [He] had attended Mr Sherwood in every capacity of servant nearly as long as he had been in the regiment. . . . [He] was singularly hard-featured . . . most generally well-conducted, and invariably honest when not under the temptation of strong liquors." It appears that the captain's wife found her husband's batman acceptable; however, she recorded that "in arranging a table, a room, or whatever else it might be. . . . He was a perfect martinet . . . when he had set the dishes at meals, he would make a retreat . . . to judge correctly whether the lines of plates, dishes, spoons, and cruets were in perfect exactness." Few accounts mention the military servants in British India, but Mrs. Sherwood offered a view of the army system of the commissioned officers enjoying the privilege of a soldier-servant. Private Parker appeared to be the perfect batman, trustworthy, respectful, and honest. Yet, as this officer's wife pointed out—only when sober. His lack of control with regard to alcohol allowed her to place him firmly in the lower level of the imperial hierarchy.[40]

During the voyage to India Mrs. Sherwood called upon another Anglo servant, "Mrs. Sergeant Strachan . . . [who] was the first person of her kind with whom I had then ever had the honour of conversing. . . . She had the most decided and most fearful cast in one eye . . . and her person was broad and clumsy in the extreme . . . but, such as she was, we should have been lost without her." The officer's wife appreciated the ministrations of the Parkers and Mrs. Strachan, yet a clear class divide existed. In describing the sergeant's wife as a "person of her kind" and "broad and clumsy," Mrs. Sherwood identified her as a member of the servant class, who would be of great service to the *memsahib*.[41]

Another sergeant's wife, referred to simply as "poor thing" by Georgiana Paget, accompanied the Royal Horse Artillery to India in July 1857. The imperial mistress reported that the "poor thing, was obliged to leave me . . . [and] established with her husband in a little house near ours. . . . I have engaged a Portuguese *Ayah* for myself, but my greatest comfort in the house is in old James, our soldier servant, who is left to look after me." Mrs. Paget expressed her relief of having a British servant to attend to her needs, when on arrival in Bombay she exclaimed, "We . . . went straight to our hospitable friends . . . who had provided in every way for our comfort . . . even to *borrowing* an experienced English maid, who undertook the care of baby for some hours." It is unclear whether this purloined maid was a military spouse, but this random sentence uncovers a preference, and a status value, in employing an Anglo servant.[42]

Minnie Blane delightedly recorded hiring "a most excellent nurse for my approaching confinement. . . . She is the wife of our Quartermaster Sergeant Benaham, and bears an excellent character. Our great comfort is that she drinks neither wine, beer, nor spirits of any kind. So many of these women do so to excess." Mrs. Blane reassured her mother that the nurse had "good certificates, and the ladies of the regiment all recommend her as an industrious and hard-working little woman." Yet the imperial woman removed any threat to her identity and status by reference to the lower-class alcohol consumption and ability to work hard. Adding an example of Anglo upward mobility in India, Edith, the wife of Lieutenant Colonel Thomas G. Cuthell of the Thirty-Eighth Foot, spitefully remarked, "The convalescent detachment, as it is called, of white-faced invalid soldiers, young recruits, and whiter women and children, marched away down the Mall days ago *en route* for a hill sanatorium. The women are more or less a poor feckless folk, their English physique enfeebled by the climate, and their moral fibre enervated by the unwonted possession of a servant or two." Thus, evidence of class status, partially signaled by the employment of servants, was available to even the lowly soldiers' wives. No wonder Mrs. Cuthell thought it necessary to remove any claim to respectability by implying fecklessness and feebleness on the part of the Anglo working class.[43]

Harriette Ashmore provided another example of efforts made to portray servants as less than worthy to represent the nation. While preparing to march with her husband's regiment from Calcutta to Cawnpore, she listed the Indian servants and "a very active Irish woman as my own servant." During the leg from Bankipore to Dinapore, Mrs. Ashmore revealed her inferior view of the Irishwoman, Mrs. Carigg. The officer's wife recounted an episode of high drama as "thieves had attacked the . . . hackeries [transport wagons]. . . . [T]he loss fell the most heavily upon my Irish woman, who ran to meet me . . . wringing her hands, and, as usual with her, vociferating in a most violent manner. Some time elapsed before I could understand one word that she uttered. . . . Poor Mrs. Carigg exhibited all the violent grief so characteristic of her country people." The Irishwoman further compounded her mistress's dim view of her during an Indian festival. Ashmore reported, "During the Mohurrun [*sic*], little booths are erected on the road-sides . . . where the rich dispense sherbet [fruit and spice punch] to the poor. . . . I was once somewhat disturbed at seeing a remarkably well conducted female servant of my own sadly overpowered with its effects." Apparently Mrs. Carigg had added "ardent spirits" to the sherbet and "had been tempted to taste and taste again, the consequence of which . . . [s]he fell; again and again . . . sprawling on the floor." Such unladylike behavior clearly reinforced the officer's wife's view of her servant's subordinate place in the imperial hierarchy.[44]

Bessie Fenton, however, delightedly recorded the employment of a British maid whom she recognized as an old neighbor. She noted, "Anne . . . had been born beside my father's house and left an orphan. . . . She shared the fate of most pretty country girls and married a soldier. . . . Her gratitude to Neil and affection for me was unbounded, and though she had just been confined she brought baby and ayah and all, determined to stay while she could serve me." The satisfied officer's wife added, "[N]urses are privileged gossips. . . . [T]he ladies did not stand high in her estimation, and she boldly pronounced that there were no companions for *me* there [Calcutta]." Mrs. Fenton plainly appreciated her servant's considerate attention. The fact that Anne employed an *ayah* indicated upward social upward mobility. Hence, the officer's wife highlighted the impertinent gossip of the otherwise helpful nurse.[45]

Finding and retaining domestic servants such as Anne proved extremely difficult, not only in British India but also in the U.S. West. With no batman system operating in the American army, the officers' wives could not avail themselves of an orderly's wife as a servant, which created enormous difficulties. Col. Forrest R. Blackburn commented on the challenges of obtaining reliable Anglo help at the remote garrisons. Just as Williamson discerned in India, young girls, Blackburn argued, seemed "useless to import" as they quickly married one of the many eligible bachelors. Elizabeth Custer confirmed this critical state of affairs with, "The question of servants was a very serious one to those living on the borders of civilization as we did. . . . [S]ervants . . . were almost certain to marry. . . . It often happened that delicate ladies had to do all kinds of menial service for a time. Except for a kind-hearted soldier now and then, who was too devoted to the wife of his company officer to see her do everything, I hardly know how army ladies would have endured their occasional domestic trials."[46]

Most military spouses echoed Mrs. Custer's grievance. The engagement, let alone the retention, of female servants often proved impossible. Almost immediately after arrival young domestics were courted and wed by lonely soldiers. The officers' wives, finding such affairs of the heart frustrating, changed tactics and sought plain, middle-aged spinsters. This strategy unfortunately failed to solve the problem. Mrs. Boyd, for example, procured an Anglo nurse whom she described as "a grenadier in looks and manners; and although not absolutely hideous, was so far from pleasing that we were confident of retaining her services, so made a contract for a year." Within what appears to be less than a month, nonetheless, the "plain" nurse received a proposal, married an enlisted man, and left the household. Her ex-mistress recalled, "We had soon discovered the fallacy of our belief that her plainness would prevent the possibility of a lover. . . . The one who she finally married . . . engaged a carriage at Las Vegas for the wedding trip before ever having seen her . . . she had made my life harder in every way, and taught us the folly of taking a servant accustomed to eastern civilization into the Western wilds." It appears that no matter how unmarriageable domestics appeared to their imperial employer, enlisted men sometimes hastily proposed—sight unseen! Working-class females, then, who ventured west had no difficulties in finding a marriage partner, typically preferring to be a soldier's wife rather than a lady's maid.[47]

Officers' wives experienced great difficulty not only in retaining Anglo female servants, but also in controlling the behaviors of these women. In December 1867, Frances, the second wife of Col. Henry Carrington, stayed for a short time at Fort Casper. Events worth recording during her stay included the regimental band's passable rendition of the *William Tell* Overture and the "flailing" of Laura. Laura, a domestic servant, refused to obey orders from her mistress, Mrs. Wands, who whipped the girl "into subordination by the help of a 'trunk strap.'" In the absence of any official army regulation concerning the punishment of women, neither Carrington nor Wands felt any compunction in beating the allegedly "obstreper-ous and independent" female domestic to quell the "rebellion." By challenging the authority of the upper echelon of the imperial class structure, this servant threatened the flimsy threads by which it hung. Needing to sustain the illusion of class status, the elite females reacted violently. This incident reveals a structural weakness: the working-class Anglo, unfettered by mainstream conventions, could act with greater independence. The physical punishment administered on this occasion, nevertheless, appeared to shore up the cracks in imperial authority.[48]

Caroline Winne also mentioned her difficulties in hiring and retaining a reliable servant, writing, "I have had all sorts of trouble with servants . . . the green Irish girl . . . came as promised early Monday morning, and glad was I on Tuesday to send her off on Wednesday. She knew nothing, and I don't believe she ever will. She was worse than no one." She haughtily continued, "Servants ought to obey their masters in this primitive state of Nebraska—but servants don't. . . . I have heard of my good Fanny (and really if she wouldn't drink so, I never would ask for a better servant) in jail two or three times lately. I fear she is past redemption.

Poor girl. It is too bad. She is a nice cook and a most beautiful washer and ironer as I ever saw." After confiding in Mrs. Sumner (a fellow officer's wife), Mrs. Winne disclosed the depth of anxiety by admitting, "She [Sumner] said she did pity me so for she always felt trouble with servants was only next worse to a death in the house." Although one can understand the domestic difficulties presented to these women, the attitudes toward their female employees exposes the fragility of imperial class status. In the remote garrisons where traditional social divisions provided only a tentative hold, officers' wives sought to reinforce their superiority by utilizing beatings, verbalizing unmistakable class and ethnic prejudices, and underscoring troublesome behaviors.[49]

Not all female servants, however, caused problems. Maria, the wife of Col. James Kimball, experienced her own considerable dilemmas with domestic help. Her first cook, the "faithful Norah," soon married; Norah's replacement Lona managed to serve every dish undercooked, so was quickly exchanged for the "imposing and fanciful" corporal's wife, Signora Luca. After the Kimballs transferred to Fort Marcy, however, Marjorie, a Scottish cook, joined the family. This "intelligent and capable" Highlander stayed with the Kimballs for over a year. Marjorie diligently attended to her duties, yet Mrs. Kimball observed, "Her ideas of propriety were often amusing. To her a soldier must be viewed askance by a self-respecting girl, but a tradesman was another story. . . . [T]hough Marjorie was slow to recognize socially our infantrymen, she was friendly enough with the butcher and baker of the town." The capable servant unexpectedly inherited an ostrich farm in the Transvaal, married a Private Duncombe, and according to Mrs. Kimball "lived happily ever after." Whether a recalcitrant Laura, an imprisoned Fanny, a fanciful Mrs. Luca, or a redoubtable Marjorie, the Anglo female servants at best provided a relatively short-term but efficient service, and at worst threatened to reduce the social divide. Mrs. Kimball plainly held confidence in her imperial identity and took the loss stoically. Mrs. Carrington and Mrs. Wands, however, revealed their insecurity by taking a surprisingly harsh punitive line—resorting to flailing a young woman with a leather trunk strap to coerce obedience and respect.[50]

Relief, then, from domestic duties proved problematical to the ladies of the U.S. West who expected to delegate such mundane tasks. The services of an enlisted man, not exactly the equivalent of the British batman, nonetheless, presented a solution to their dilemma. Alice Grierson, during her husband's tour of duty at Fort Davis, found that the enlisted "striker" proved to be the most dependable source of domestic labor. Due to depletion in the army ranks, the use of a soldier for such purposes received no official sanction, and became explicitly forbidden in 1870 by General Order No. 92. In practice, however, the soldiers enjoyed the extra work that provided additional income, better living quarters and meals, and furnished release from military duties. In 1872 Nannie, the wife of Lt. Cyrus S. Roberts of the Seventeenth Infantry, stationed at the Cheyenne River Agency, Dakota Territory, stated that her "girl" was entirely unsatisfactory, and informed her in-laws, " 'Miss Mulligan' is to marry her lover tomorrow. . . . She is so dirty, and after she put pepper and salt in my pumpkin pies and sugar in the dressing for chicken I concluded I did not want her services anymore." However, she found the replacement soldier-cook "a real comfort as he is so clean and good-natured." Thus, the officers' wives came to depend upon the ministrations of their strikers—the loyal, indispensable, and trustworthy soldier-servants of the imperial ladies.[51]

Miss Forrestine Cooper provided many descriptions of her daily interactions with the men under her father's command. At Camp Supply she recalled that "all the enlisted men of the Tenth Cavalry were colored soldiers of the best type. Their wives became cooks, laundresses, and nursemaids to the children of the officers." She also observed, "The presence of a manservant was a feature of each home. . . . Soldiers who were not strikers, probably because such positions were limited in number, called them "dog-robbers," intimating that the family dog was deprived of tidbits by the presence of the striker." On a trip to meet with her father returning from Austin to Fort Concho, she described the noble actions of the family striker, Pvt. George Clark of A Troop. After lights out, loud voices woke the young girl's mother who noticed "white soldiers . . . looking toward Clark [who had stationed himself in front of the Coopers tent]. Then they started toward him." Forrestine then heard her mother "askin[g in] a low voice, 'Clark, do you think there is any danger?' 'Not so long as I'se [sic] alive, ma'am!' he answered. After that I heard him call out, 'I'll shoot the first man that comes near this tent. Keep back. I'll shoot to kill!' They knew he mean't it . . . Old George Clark sat all night long with his loaded carbine, protecting the wife and children of an officer." As a young bride, Alice Baldwin, on arrival at Fort Harker in 1867, similarly discovered the value of such a servant. In recording her horror when she discovered that her new quarters were nothing more than a squalid dug-out, her anxiety became lessened under the loyal administrations of her "family factotum," Joe Bowers, who may have held the rank of private. His contributions to her comfort allowed her to cope with the primitive circumstances and to declare she felt able to "make the best of everything."[52]

Several journals reflect the high value officers' wives placed on the domestic talents of these military attendants. Fanny Corbusier, while stationed at Camp

Sheridan in 1877, remarked on the benefits of having an enlisted man to help around the house. She recounted what appears to have been a regular domestic event: "Louie [the maid] was a fine cook and never tired of work but about once a month had paroxysms of rage, and then she would fling saucepans, flat irons, or anything else she had at hand at our soldier striker, Lewis. . . . He wished to return to his troop but was too good a man to lose." Similarly, Catherine, the wife of Col. William O. Collins of the Eleventh Ohio Cavalry, wrote to her daughter from Fort Laramie in May 1864. She admitted "boarding" with John, who was engaged by her husband to "keep the table" for her during the colonel's absence. This unusual living arrangement allowed Catherine to pursue her genteel hobby of sketching the local fauna and flora.[53]

Frances Boyd hailed the domestic talents of the family striker when she joined her husband at Fort Halleck in 1867. Calling her soldier-servant a "treasure," she recalled, "the delight with which an offer of help from a soldier in my first effort at housekeeping . . . his forethought when the floor was soaked with rain in always having a large adobe brick heated ready to be placed under my feet when dining, will never be forgotten." Mrs. Boyd continued, "The greatest proof of devotion I ever received was when that man, learning that the laundress declined employing her services on our behalf, saw me preparing to essay the task myself. To prevent that he rose sufficiently early to do the work, and continued the practice so long as we remained there, despite the fact that it subjected him to ridicule from other soldiers." Martha Summerhayes supported such complimentary views with, "In the long march across the Territory [in 1874], they [soldiers] had cared for my wants and performed uncomplainingly for me services usually rendered by women." Mrs. Summerhayes's soldier-cook, "Bowen the Immortal," with his "white apron . . . [and] his hair rolled back in his most fetching style," copied recipes such as "Aunt Hempsey's Muffins" and "Hatty's Lemon Tarts" from her cookery book into his ledger, "in large illiterate characters; and [wrote] on the fly leaf, 'Charles Bowen's Receipt Book.'" This caused the officer's wife to "burst into a good hearty laugh." Although Bowen proved indispensable to the survival of this officer's wife, her feminization and derision of him placed him securely in the lower class.[54]

Despite such positive accounts, Eveline Alexander displayed little patience with her domestic soldier. While encamped at Camp Creek in 1866, Rudolf the family cook visited with the Choctaw Indians and returned with two small polecats as "pets for Mrs. Alexander." He placed the gifts in his mistress's "lunchbox," which Eveline found unacceptable. For this crime, Colonel Alexander "reduced him to the ranks, and fetched me up another cook." She also found her husband's "body servant . . . most amusing," as "Sullivan is a great character; he has always been a 'striker' to the officer commanding the company and is consequently perfectly worthless." Francis Roe, however, was not amused by the profanity of her husband's striker Volmer. This officer's wife decided to immediately reprimand the foul-mouthed soldier. Her Chinese servant warned his mistress, "He vellee blad man—he killee man—he killee you, meb-be!" Despite her cook's concern, she decided to go ahead and manage her own affairs rather than call upon the company commander. She "delivered a lecture" to Volmer, who departed the home on her instructions, only to later return, "cap in hand," to apologize for the outburst. Mrs. Alexander and Mrs. Roe both clearly considered themselves entitled to respect and deference from the enlisted men. The former's complaint resulted in a reduction of rank. The latter, who immediately dealt with the insolence, confidently asserted her female authority.[55]

Scholars have holistically examined military communities in the U.S. West to conclude that the dynamics of military and civilian interactions were unique and fascinating, and agree that women played a crucial role in the structure of garrison life. All confirm that the wives of officers or enlisted men ameliorated an otherwise desolate life, and thus played a historic role by providing a clearer picture of the army's function in the West. Yet the role and impact of the domestic servants within the imperial communities has not been fully explored. Anglo female servants employed in the U.S. West proved problematical for the majority of officers' wives. Instant, sometimes sight unseen, marriages provided practical inconveniences, and claims to greater independence threatened the delicate social framework on which identity rested. These women resorted to corporal punishment and character defamation to preserve the class line. With regard to soldier-strikers, however, they sought helpful orderlies, whose troublesome language could be controlled by the threat of punishment. Thus, any peril to imperial identity attempted by lower-class men and women who provided domestic service in the U.S. West was quickly ameliorated.[56]

Such scholarly analysis of the nineteenth-century military communities in British India has not been made. A general study of white women emigrants during the late nineteenth century, however, argued that such females served demographic and ideological purposes, particularly in South Africa, Canada, and Australia. Due to high numbers of male settlers, working-class females became encouraged to relocate through such agencies as the British Ladies Female Emigrant Society, founded in 1849, and to reproduce the imperialist markers of civilization. Gendered roles of wife and mother existed throughout the empire, and single working-class women viewed marriage or domestic service as the only alternatives available. Marriage, as the discussion of the civilian servants demonstrates, proved the favored course as it held the opportunity to enter the privileged community. The latter course, domestic servitude within a *memsahib*'s home, provides a juncture of class, gender, race, and ethnicity. Officers' wives such as Mesdames Sherwood, Paget, Ashmore, and Blane demonstrated their claim to imperial authority by subordinating, through ridicule, both the "poor thing," and the "vociferous" Mrs. Carigg.[57]

In comparing the two imperial settings similarities appear. In attempting to procure Anglo civilian females as servants, both groups of officer's wives failed to retain reliable domestics, sometimes losing them immediately to a military marriage. In British India, the wife of a batman or sergeant proved beneficial to all parties involved. By employing a husband and wife team, such as Luke and Betty Parker, the officer's wife gained two servants and allowed the couple to stay together. The assigning of an orderly to a commissioned officer was not, however, an official practice in the U.S. West. A different system evolved of employing a striker who earned extra pay in exchange for domestic duties. The army ladies gratefully and glowingly recorded such characters as Joe Bowers, Lewis, and of course, "Bowen the Immortal." These soldiers, then, tended to all the domestic chores, some boarded overnight, and one placed hot bricks under his mistress's cold feet. In both the British and American experiences these rank-and-file defenders of the nation became feminized. Luke Parker with his meticulously arranged table, and Bowen's hair styling and recipe compilation, indicate a shift in gender roles that protected the officer's wife's imperial status. In some households domesticity became a male space, and the command of, and deference due from, a soldier became a female privilege.

In the nineteenth-century American imperial home, just as in the British bungalow, issues of class, gender, race, and ethnicity intersected. The striker belonged to the rank and file of the army; thus the officers' wives could reassure themselves of elevated class status through aligning his social position with the mainstream working class. The showdown between Mrs. Roe and the quick-tempered Volmer revealed this officer's wife's fearless assumption of military command. By inverting the traditional female-male roles, an empowered gendered authority evolved that feminized the soldier and masculinized the mistress. The officers' wives' recollections of Anglo servants and soldier-servants, then, provide not just a fleeting glimpse of the lives of these working-class actors, but also an important insight into the fragility of the imperialist identity. To sustain a sense of social superiority and imperial identity, the officers' wives manipulated Victorian gender traditions to reinforce existing military divisions. In so doing, they subordinated servants, batmen, and strikers, crossing gender divides to garner and wield imperial power.

An officer's wife who joined her husband on the outskirts of empire, whether she was British or American, brought with her notions of middle-class values, understandings, and status. In analyzing the British and American gender, race, class, and ethnic attitudes toward service staff, and how such standpoints influenced imperialism, the discussion has been restricted to relationships within the home. To be sure, the military spouses interacted with a much larger landscape of indigenous actors. They toured the villages of the Indian *mofussil*, entered curtained *zenanas*, and strolled within the Caddo and Arapahoe reservations. In India, the elementary level of empire, and certainly the most intimate of multicultural contact points, was the imperial home. Here, the public and private spaces fused, and military spouses donned the mantle of imperial command and maintenance over a retinue of indigenous servants; hence, they constructed, communicated, and reflected the larger principles of empire. The relationship between the indigenous peoples and American officers' wives, however, was considerably different. Due to the lower level of intimacy, with many servants transported from the East, the prescription and reflection of benevolent imperialism was not required. Yet within the domestic space, both groups of women racially censured Indian, American Indian, Mexican American, African American, and Chinese staff, and feminized the male other. Additionally, they subordinated—through class—their Anglo servants. In so doing, they constructed an empowered female identity that reinforced imperial superiority and authority.

9

Conclusion

Imperial Women

There is a freedom of manners among the ladies of the Army
that does not obtain in the best civilian society. This may be
attributed to their exclusive mode of life. . . . There is always an
Egeria to dictate, but, not being of celestial origin, her oracles are
not infallible.

—*Duane Greene, former U.S. Army lieutenant*

Writing from India in 1841, Emily Eden reflected Lieutenant Greene's statement on such female authority by repeating an observation uttered by a
head of state. She recorded, "Dost Mahomed [Emir of Afghanistan] was here again
on Tuesday at a very small party . . . when George [Eden, the governor general]
said something to him about our customs, which allowed of women coming into
society, &c, he said, 'You are quite right; you make a Paradise; now this [British
India] looks like one.'" His version of paradise, however, did not include a more
liberated role for women, as during a tour of the Upper Provinces Miss Eden
reported, "they [the Emir and his son] were very amusing about the liberty which
Englishwomen have. . . . [A]nd [that] it was the only foolish thing they had seen
in Englishmen. . . . 'In fact,' Hyder Khan [the emir's son] said, 'You are the slaves
of your women, and we are the masters of ours.'"[1]

It is very unlikely that the army wife considered herself a nineteenth-century
Egeria, or that the military officers imagined themselves enslaved. Yet the experiences of the British and American women add an important dimension to studies

of imperialism. By centralizing and comparing the female experiences, it becomes clear that, acting as informal imperial agents, officers' wives understood that they held a duty to design and promulgate imperial ambitions. Despite many similarities, in most social situations examined the comparison revealed more formalized British practices, indicating a difference in the imperial formations. In British India, benevolent imperialism sought to dominate and control the indigenous peoples through affinity. Thus, social practices presented an orderly, unified, and prestigious face of authority. This model, redundant in the U.S. West, is echoed, nonetheless, by the construction of an informal system to assert internal legitimacy of an imperial class. Both sets of women, however, transferred, adopted, and adapted core cultural values and rituals to construct a unique social reality that cut across and reconfigured gender, race, and class borders to influence the course of empire.[2]

In joining their spouses in India and the U.S. West, officers' wives sensed a dynamic military esprit de corps. The academies of Sandhurst, Addiscombe, and West Point installed a distinct imperial mindset and class, complete with codes of behaviors that reflected conventional values, to produce an officer and gentleman. The commissioned men carried this model of gentility to the remote stations and garrisons. American Martha Summerhayes captured the sense of noblesse oblige in recording, "I am glad . . . to have lived amongst men . . . who stood ready, at the call of their country." The evidence suggests that most wives who joined their spouses understood they shared this call to duty. In so doing, they connected into the military ethos and practices to generate an imperial femininity, and a distinct role as imperial agents.[3]

On the physical journeys to join their husbands, these women created trans-national connections and circuits to shape a new identity. Honoria Lawrence described this new distinctiveness when she first buckled her knapsack and married a soldier. During travel and arrivals, these women expressed patriotic rhetoric and draped mainstream class and race images across unfamiliar land-scapes and peoples. Describing the journey from Gravesend to Calcutta in 1833, Harriette Ashmore illustrated how these women allayed insecurity and forged an imperial identity. To her, the Union Jack symbolized that she belonged to a civilized and superior nation, while the disdainful description of the appearance, manners, and jewelry of her *ayah* clearly cast her as the "other." Within the space of the journey, officers' wives espoused prejudice to vilify and subordinate the indigenous peoples, thus crafting a distinct superior identity.[4]

Post arrival, the feminization of formal and informal military practices produced a new social reality, an empowered female identity, and a cohesive community that sustained imperialist ambitions. These women adopted military titles, language, and dress, and feminized military markers, to generate a female hierarchy—an imperial sisterhood—that appropriated masculine space and authority, commanded by a powerful senior wife. As Elizabeth Custer announced, "[T]hough army women have no visible thrones . . . I never knew such queens as they, or saw more willing subjects than they govern." The British *Burra Mem* and the American "female grenadier" often built extremely powerful and influential positions. Honoria Lawrence clearly illustrated this role of command. She adjudicated on caste disputes, and acted as an official administrator when a regimental elephant ran amok, damaging local crops. Amid "weeping and wailing for *insaf* and *dohai*," she confidently imposed a fine on the elephant keeper and awarded damages to the indigenous villagers. As *Burra Mem* she held full imperial license to preside confidently over such politically charged matters. Under the watchful gaze of these matriarchs, some wives donned tailor-made military riding habits, and others held all-female "councils of war." An active sisterhood evolved, each woman gaining status according to her husband's rank, and each contributing to the maintenance of an imperial sociability. Officers' spouses performed as self-appointed military adjuncts, observed a female hierarchy, and promoted the order and aims of the empire—these duties both encouraged and sanctioned by the men of the British and American armies.[5]

The female appropriation of military processes facilitated empowerment as social functionaries and ceremonial performers. Women held a duty to design and officiate in formal public occasions. High-level events, such as the magnificent durbar, signaled British authority to the Indian statesmen, but held no imperial currency in the U.S. West. Yet display utilized on a smaller, less formal scale by the Americans reaffirmed class status to both the internal military community and local Anglo urban centers. Traditional feminine and masculine values, bodies, and behaviors became appropriated to symbolize the vitality, civility, and prestige of the expanding nations. The traditional Victorian male archetype became adopted and adapted as an imperial model, and his genteel, outgoing, and gracious wife shared and supplemented official duties—a corresponding role of representation. Such tasks, specifically in the British experience, became viewed as both unwelcome and onerous. For example, Lady Curzon voiced a complaint that her "duty," of sociability, not shared by her husband, provided "very little pleasure." Military spouses, then, performed as adjuncts and dismissed limitations imposed by traditional gender roles, to generate power to arbitrate, promote, and police the actions of the imperial class. In this capacity they played a central role in reaffirming internal confidence within both communities, and legitimizing external representations of British power and prestige.[6]

The social element of imperialism, nevertheless, did not simply materialize in parades, prize-giving, and polo matches. Private domiciles acted as the design centers, production lines, and shop windows of status and prestige. Utilizing dress and home décor, officers' wives drafted and projected a distinct identity that reflected, yet transformed, middle-class gender models. Forbidden to wear the *saris* or *camisas* of the indigenous women, officers' spouses dutifully conformed to traditional dress codes. The defiant Martha Summerhayes, in dealing with the near one hundred degree summer temperatures in Ehrenburg, fervently wished to wear the loose-fitting Mexican garments, yet her husband forbade her adoption of such female dress. Military men, nonetheless, adapted limited indigenous clothing styles, the British to control the Indian peoples through association, and the Americans to effect American Indian relocation. Additionally, both sets of officers' wives utilized internal décor to signal British gentility or American sincerity. In British India, these intimate gendered spaces remained static, yet the incorporation of Indian designs and artifacts supported the empire's ambition of subordination through affinity. Female authority in the garrisons of the U.S. West, however, expanded to encompass private male space. The crossing of gender boundaries in both imperial formations, by both sexes, facilitated control over male and female dress and behavior to define and demonstrate the orderly, authoritative, and cohesive elite in India, and in the U.S. West, internal class status.[7]

The significance of the officers' wives' role in the social processes of calling and domestic rituals confirms the formation of a distinct and influential female identity. The reflected but exaggerated mainstream etiquette allowed military wives to design and sustain imperial sociability and class membership. In so doing, they gained access to, and manipulated, knowledge normally reserved to male power holders. Throughout the cantonments in British India, personalized cards of introduction and dedicated registers indicated a highly ritualized model of etiquette in operation. Similarly, an equally pervasive but less formal practice functioned within the western garrisons. A hidden agenda, however, lay concealed within this overly pedantic protocol. Should a newcomer pass muster, a network of privilege and power became immediately available. The duty of protecting the imperial gateway rested with an officer's spouse who vetted and approved suitable applicants—and convincingly rejected parvenus. Furthermore, as the host of dinner parties, recitals, and luncheons, a wife acted as a confidante, diplomat, and, in some instances, a public relations campaign manager. British women dutifully followed, to the letter, the official *Warrant of Precedence*. As we have seen, American wives, although less regulated, held a duty to host all commissioned visitors, no matter the situation or time of day. This visible female empowerment, however, became subject to criticism. Vicious public attacks smeared the *memsahib*'s reputation. The military wives in the U.S. West received less bad press, but weathered accusations of flirtatiousness and flamboyancy while continuing to undertake duties as guardians of the imperial class.

To gain a more complete picture of the impact made by officers' wives, an analysis of race, ethnic, and class attitudes toward domestic servants reveals much about the insecurities of imperialism. Although these women had a much greater landscape of contact, in focusing on the domestic sites in British India and the U.S. West it becomes clear that the mistress-servant relationship both formulated and reproduced imperial ideologies. Hence, in the remote cantonments and garrisons, private and public spaces disintegrated, leading one scholar to portray the British home in India as imperialism's point of origin. An officer's wife, whether British or American, transported a mainstream model of a middle-class household, with its complement of servants. Within the imperial holdings the home, the most intimate of contact zones, the physiological trait of a white skin, and the exhibition of cultural artifacts signaled identity, status, and authority. Women sought domestic assistance through employing Indians, American Indians, African Americans, Mexican Americans, Chinese, and Anglo servants. Holding command of the domestic site, officers' wives demanded obedience and respect through demarking, sometimes cruelly, race, ethnic, and class boundaries, to subordinate domestic workers. The American model sought to stabilize identity by creating social distance between the classes. This was also true of the British model, but it contained an additional operational layer. Within this female-controlled site, women both initiated and reproduced the larger ideologies of empire.[8]

Traditional imperial histories have focused on masculine actions that emphasized battlefield strategy and prowess, territorial expansion, and economic market, production, and distribution systems. The experiences of nineteenth-century American officers' wives have received insightful scholarly attention, unlike the corresponding British military female accounts that largely remain on the fringes of historical analysis. Perhaps this has been due to strictures such as the one offered as "Colonel Whistler's Rules for Wife Behavior":

1. You will see that all meals are served on time.
2. You will come to the table in a wrapper.
3. You will smile at breakfast.
4. If possible, you will serve meat at least four times a week.
5. You will not move the furniture without my permission.
6. You will present the household accounts to me by the fifth of each month.
7. You will examine my uniforms each Tuesday and if they need repair you will take the necessary action.
8. You will do no work in the evenings. You will entertain me.
9. You will not touch my desk.
10. You will remember you are not in command of anything except the cook.[9]

Despite this list of rules, shockingly sexist to the modern eye, officers' wives on both sides of the Pacific generated and wielded substantial power. Indeed, in holding pivotal positions to shape and sustain imperialism they exerted female power in a heretofore accepted masculine arena. Clothed in a wrapper and smiling at breakfast, the officer's wife appropriated male space, created a powerful role, and enjoyed a distinguished ambassadorial identity. Wives emanated such power, poise, and authority that it is no surprise that Hyder Khan recognized and confided to the governor general of India—"You are the slaves of your women."

Appendix A

Glossary of Nineteenth-Century Anglo-Indian Words

The following glossary represents a selection from five original glossaries published in the following sources: Mrs. Maria Graham (Lady Maria Callcott), *Journal of a Residence in India* (Edinburgh: Archibald Constable and Company, 1812), xi–xii; Helen MacKenzie, *Six Years in India. Delhi: The City of the Great Mogul* (London: Richard Bentley, 1857), xi–x; Lady Florentia Sale, *A Journal Of the Disasters in Affghanistan, 1841–1842* (London: John Murray, 1844), xi–xv; Honoria Lawrence, *The Journals of Honoria Lawrence*, edited by J. Lawrence and A. Woodiwiss (London: Hodder and Stoughton, 1980), 241–250, and Flora Steel and Grace Gardiner, *The Complete Indian Housekeeper and Cook* (1890; reprint, Cambridge, 2010), 31–32. Many of the same servant duties have multiple Indian titles. This can be explained by the three presidencies, Bombay, Bengal, and Madras, plus the women's spelling, which often appears to be a phonetic attempt.

For additional Anglo-Indian terms and pronunciations, see George C. Whitworth, *An Anglo-Indian Dictionary* (London, 1885). Whitworth was a civil servant in Bombay and a fellow of the University of Bombay.

ameer or **amir** commander, chief, a non-Hindu lord

ayah female attendant, nurse, lady's maid [and/or nanny]

bakshish reward

banggolo Bengal hut whose construction inspired the bungalow

bheestee or **bhisti** water-carrier

boccas-wallah or **boxwallah** peddler, small goods traveling salesman

Brahman or **Brahmin** the sacred and highest caste of Hindus

bungalo or **bungalow** garden-house, cottage, thatched house

Burra Mem senior wife of a military company

chiccau-wallah tailor

chota-hazree breakfast

chota-mem Anglo wife, not the **Burra Mem**

chunam lime, or the sort of stucco made in India of shell-lime mixed with curdled milk and sugar.

chupatties unleavened cakes, made of ottah

cummerbund or **kammerband** waist-band, girdle

dak letter post; also identified as a bungalow generally used by travelers

Dalits untouchable caste group

dallis baskets for fruits, panniers

dhobi or **dobee** washerman

dhooley or **dhoolie** palanquin for the sick

dohai mercy

durbar levee

durzee or **dirzi** tailor

ghat or **ghaut** a pass through hills, or a landing place

ga'ola cowman

goorgoorie hookah

Hindoo Hindu

insaf justice

jungle forest, waste land

khan nobleman, lord (In Cabul the title is assumed by everyone.)

khansamah or **khaunsamah** head servant, head-waiter, male housemaid, valet

khidmutgar or **khitmatghar, khidmat-gar** man-servant, table waiter

kshatriyas political caste group

maharajah Hindu king, literally "great prince"

massal or **massalgee, mashal** or **masai** the person who carries and takes care of the light, torch

mem sahib a lady

mofussil rural, frontier regions

mussolgee kitchen attendant

Mussulman or **Moosulman** Muslim

nans cakes of bread

nautch a dance or dancing girl

nawaub or **nawab** prince, nabob, a Muhammadan noble

nereuls coconut

nizam prime minister

numdas coarse felt carpets

ottah or **atiah** ground wheat, flour

palkee or **palki** palanquin

punka fan of any kind, chiefly used by Europeans to denote a very large fan suspended from the ceiling, and kept in motion by a cord pulled by a servant

raj government, province, kingdom

rajah prince, a Hindu prince

rupee silver coin; its value is about two shillings English

sari a traditional Indian female dress

shah or **padshah** king, not a Hindu

sherbet a drink little different from lemonade; it is often perfumed

shudras merchant/laboring caste group

tatti screen of thatch kept wetted for the hot winds to pass through

Varnas four main caste groups

zenana harem, the ladies' apartments

Appendix B

Nineteenth-Century Forts of the U.S. West

Fort Location	**Fort** Location	**Fort** Location
Abraham Lincoln North Dakota	**Gibson** Indian Territory	**Rice** North Dakota
Apache Arizona	**Graham** Texas	**Riley** Kansas
Bascom New Mexico	**Grant** Texas	**Ringgold Barracks** Texas
Bayard New Mexico	**Halleck** Nebraska	**Robinson** Nebraska
Berthold North Dakota	**Harker** Kansas	**Sanders** Wyoming
Bliss Texas	**Hays** Kansas	**Sedgwick** Colorado
Bowie Arizona	**Inge** Texas	**Shaw** Montana Territory
Bridger Wyoming	**Keogh** Montana	**Camp Sheridan** Wyoming
Brown Texas	**Kearny** Nebraska Territory	**Sill** Indian Territory/Oklahoma
Casper Wyoming	**Kit Carson** Colorado Territory	**Smith** Arkansas
Concho Texas	**Laramie** Wyoming	**Stevens** Colorado Territory
Craig New Mexico	**Leavenworth** Kansas	**Stockton** Texas
Camp Creek Texas	**Lyon** Colorado	**Union** New Mexico
Clark Texas	**Macon** North Carolina	**Vancouver** Alaska
Craig New Mexico	**McKavett** Texas	**Whipple** Arizona
Cummings New Mexico	**Marcy** New Mexico	**Wingate** New Mexico
Davis Texas	**Morgan** Colorado	**Wood** Bedloe's Island New York
Dodge Kansas	**Phil Kearny** Dakota Territory/Wyoming	
Ellis Montana	**Reno** Indian Territory/Oklahoma	
Fillmore Arizona		
Garland Colorado		

Notes

Colonel Whistler's Rules for Wife Behavior

1. Reeder, *Born at Reveille*, 15; Heitman, *Historical Register and Dictionary of the United States Army*, 1:1026; "Military Times Hall of Valor: Colonel Forrest E. Williford http://valor.militarytimes.com/recipient.php?recipientid=18367. Col. Joseph Whistler of the Fifteenth U.S. Infantry handed his new bride his personal regulations during their honeymoon in 1869. In 1909, Col. Red (Russell Potter) Reeder Jr., who later became a much decorated World War II hero, received a copy of the rules from his aunt, wife of Col. Forrest E. Williford, and included them in his autobiography.

Chapter 1. Introduction

Epigraph: Diver, *Englishwoman in India*, 87–88.
1. Diver, *Englishwoman in India*, 18, 21, 27–28, 59–60.
2. The term "British India" indicates a certain time period of British rule in India's history, 1765–1947. The historical actors understood themselves to be operating in British India, therefore for clarity the term has been retained throughout this study.
3. Buchan, *Lodge in the Wilderness*, 28.
4. Colley, "What Is Imperial History Now?," 132, 134, 144; Limerick, "Going West and Ending Up Global," 5, 14, 16–17.
5. Van Alstyne, *The Rising American Empire*, 1, 6; Immerman, *Empire for Liberty*, 4, 6. Please see pages 1–19 for a full discussion. Go, *Patterns of Empire*, 29–36; Colley, "The Difficulties of Empire: Present, Past and Future," 371–72.
6. Kramer, "Power and Connection: Imperial Histories of the United States in the World," 1348–50, 1352, 1354–57, 1381, 1371, 1391. Kramer identifies six problems in utilizing the imperial in U.S. historiography: exceptionalism, methodological nationalism, interpretive status of nation-states, distinguishing dichotomy of structure and agency, formal and informal empires, and periodicity. He fully responds to these issues and concludes that "foregrounding power, narrating connection, and engaging in comparison, efforts aided greatly by the concept of the imperial, are all necessary for making sense of the

United States' global history." For scholarship on comparative studies, see Limerick, *Legacy of Conquest*; Jacobs, *White Mother to a Dark Race*; Kakel, *U.S. West and the Nazi East*; White, *"It's Your Misfortune and None of My Own"*; Doyle, *Empires*.

7. Hixson, *American Settler Colonialism: A History*, 4–5, 11, 113, 198; Schueller and Watts, *Messy Beginnings*, 2; Rosier, *Serving Their Country*, 3. See also Smith-Rosenburg, *This Violent Empire*. For a description of the variations of colonialism, see Shoemaker, "A Typology of Colonialisms"; Go, *Patterns of Empire*, 29–36. For a discussion on American exceptionalism, see Go, *Patterns of Empire*, 14–27. Hixson advises that "under conventional colonialism the colonizer eventually departs, but under settler colonialism the colonizer means to occupy the land permanently." This violent conquest visualized "a powerful, modernizing continental empire" and removed the indigenous peoples from colonial space.

8. Kaplan, "Left Alone with America," 4, 16; Pease, "New Perspectives on U.S. Culture and Imperialism," 22–23; Guha, "Not at Home in Empire," 482; Mickelson, "British Women in India 1757–1857,", 162, 258; Joseph, *Reading the East India Company*, 93–95,122; Marcus, *Apartment Stories*, 5, 7; Burton, "The White Woman's Burden: British Feminists and the 'Indian Woman,' 1865–1915," 137–39. Emphasis in the original.

9. Fields, "Slavery, Race, and Ideology in the United States of America," 101, 110, 113; Myres, "Frontier Historians, Women, and the 'New' Military History," 36–37. For a full discussion of nineteenth-century female roles, see Welter, "Cult of True Womanhood," 151–74; and Kerber, "Separate Spheres, Female Worlds, Woman's Place," 9–39.

10. Coffman, *Old Army*, 254. For a discussion of American imperialism, see Van Alstyne, *The Rising American Empire*, 1, 6; Weeks, *Building the Continental Empire*, 13; Brauer, "The United States and British Imperial Expansion, 1815–1860," 32; Graebner, *Empire on the Pacific*, vi, 217–18, 228; Hietala, *Manifest Design*, x–xi, 257, 261; Eblen, *First and Second United States Empires*, 239, 318; LaFeber, *New Empire*, 24; Johnson, *Birth of the Modern World Society 1815–1830*, xvii, xix, 58, 285, 911–12, 923–24; Tate, *Frontier Army in the Settlement of the West*, 308; Smith, "West Point and the Indian Wars 1802–1891," 25, 28, 32–34, 43, 45, 55; Cunliffe, *Soldiers and Civilians*, 169; Anderson and Clayton, *Dominion of War*, xiv–xv, xxiii.

11. Kramer, "Power and Connection," 1381; Coker, *News from Brownsville*, 165–66; Heitman, *Historical Register*, 1:296. Emphasis is in the original.

12. Riley, *Female Frontier*, 13, 62, 93, 99, 176, 195–96; Baker, "Daughters of Mars," 22–23; Nacy, *Members of the Regiment*, 10, 12, 104–5,107; Venning, *Following the Drum*, 1, 11, 57, 290, 321.

13. Stallard, *Glittering Misery*, 64; MacMillan, *Women of the Raj*, 2, 56, 180–81; Coffman, *Old Army*, 289; Ogden, "Queen or Camp Follower", 11, 15; Miller, "Foragers, Army Women, and Prostitutes," 56, 148.

14. Pratt, *Imperial Eyes*, 4, 6–7. In colonial India the appellation "memsahib" was given to a white married woman. The honorific derived from ma'am (mem), added to the Urdu *sahib* that indicated respect to a male European.

15. Biddle, *Reminiscences of a Soldier's Wife*, 166–67; Carrington, *My Army Life and the Fort Phil Kearney Massacre*, 50, 223, 236, 239, 249; Heitman, *Historical Register*, 1:217, 286.

Ellen Biddle was married to Capt. James Biddle, Eleventh U.S. Infantry. Carrington quotes from George Berkley's 1792 poem *On the Prospect of Planting Arts and Learning in America.*

16. Custer, *Tenting on the Plains,* 447, 580, 675, 698, 331–2, 334 (page citations to the reprint edition); Heitman, *Historical Register,* 1: 348. Custer refers to Emanuel Leutze's *Westward the Course of Empire Takes Its Way,* 1861.

17. Anonymous, *Anglo India,* 1:24–5. Emphasis is in the original.

Chapter 2. Imperial Esprit de Corps

Epigraph: Kinevan, *Frontier Cavalryman,* 148; Heitman, *Historical Register,* 1:271, 284. Captain Carpenter was a member of the Tenth U.S. Cavalry and in command of Fort Davis, Texas, in 1879.

1. Hervey, *A Soldier of the Company,* vii, 3–4; Hodson, Biographical Index of Indian Army Officers, Box 22. Hervey received a posting to the British East India Military School at Barasat, Calcutta. Here a commander, adjutant, two lieutenants, and one drill sergeant attempted to emulate training offered at the Royal Military College. Founded in 1803, the school lived a short, unsuccessful life and was abandoned in 1811. See Mason, *A Matter of Honour,* 179.

2. Cochran, *Posie; or, From Reveille to Retreat, An Army Story,* unnumbered.

3. Watson, "Developing 'Republican Machines'," 154–56.

4. Shepperd, *Sandhurst,* 9, 24, 27; "The British Army," http://www.army.mod.uk/training_education/24487.aspx; Thomas, *Story of Sandhurst,* 15, 21–23; Le Marchant, *Memoirs of the Late Major-General Le Marchant,* 63, 65; Guggisburg, "The Shop," 42–43, 88. General Jarry headed the Prussian Kriegsschule in the mid-eighteenth century, and having commanded a French division during the Revolutionary war, he would be acquainted with practices at the French École Royale Militaire, established by Louis XV in 1750. The French military officer school, originally called École des Cadets-gentilshommes (School of Young Gentlemen), offered training for young cadets from impoverished backgrounds. Located in Addiscombe, the East India Company Military Seminary began admitting pupils in 1810. As a sister school to the Royal Military Academy at Woolwich, it trained company officers to serve in India. After the Mutiny of 1857 and the nationalization of the British East India Company in 1858, Addiscombe amalgamated with the Queen's Army, merging cadets at Sandhurst.

5. Shepperd, *Sandhurst,* 26, 54. Sébastien Le Prestre, Seigneur de Vauban, was a seventeenth-century French military engineer, famous for the design, defense, and capture of fortifications.

6. Mockler-Ferryman, *Annals of Sandhurst,* 274–92; Hodson, Biographical Index of Indian Army Officers, Box 23, 40, 42; Hart, *The New Annual Army List for 1850,* 241; Great Britain War Office, *Manual of Military Law,* 2.

7. Great Britain War Office, *The Queen's Regulations and Orders for the Army,* v, 128–29, 315–16. Emphasis is in the original.

8. *The United Service Journal and Naval and Military Magazine*, 1830, Part 2, 79–82; Hodson, Biographical Index of Indian Army Officers, Box 23, 40, 42; Matthews, Harrison, et al., *Oxford Dictionary of National Biography, from the Earliest Times to the Year 2000*, 42:347–48, 53:904–5.
9. *The United Service Journal and Naval and Military Magazine*, 1830, Part Two, 83, 85–88. Emphasis is in the original.
10. Thomas, *Story of Sandhurst*, 21–23, 65–66, 89, 91, 94; Shepperd, *Sandhurst*, 56; Busteed, *Echoes from Old Calcutta*, 17, 31–32, 390. The "Black Hole (of Calcutta)" refers to an ill-ventilated guard-room measuring fourteen feet by eighteen feet where, according to surgeon and East India Company civil servant John Z. Holwell (who held military command of Fort William during an attack in 1756 by the *nawab* of Bengal, Siraj ud-Daulah), 146 men were imprisoned, and 123 subsequently died. Bullying at Sandhurst included "ventilating"—the tying of a cadet to a ventilator and poking him with dining forks; "shovelling" forced a John to lay spread-eagled on a table and be beaten with shovels and racquets; a student who was "Adamised" would be stripped naked and lowered to the parade ground, thus having to re-enter the building via a manned guard-room.
11. Strange, *Gunner Jingo's Jubilee*, 22–23; *Dictionary of Canadian Biography Online*, s.v. "Thomas Bland Strange," http://www.biographi.ca/009004-119.01-e.php?BioId=42107; Dickens, *Dealings with the Firm of Dombey and Son*, 120 (page citations are to the reprint edition).
12. Mason, *English Gentleman*, 12; Burn, *Age of Equipoise*, 258–60; Strachan, *Wellington's Legacy*, 110–11. Mason was an administrator in India.
13. Harries-Jenkins, *The Army in Victorian Society*, 279–80; *Times*, 29 October 1840, issue 17501, 5; *The United Service Journal and Naval and Military Magazine*, 1840, Part 3, 423; Hervey, *A Soldier of the Company*, 28–29; Matthews, *Oxford Dictionary of National Biography*, 35:246–47.
14. Strachan, *Wellington's Legacy*, 110–11; Stanley, *White Mutiny*, 22–25, 28; Addison, Oakes, et al., *Who's Who, 1907*, 954, 1924. Author's emphasis.
15. Wolseley, *Story of a Soldier*, 5, 8, 10–11.
16. Jones-Parry, *An Old Soldier's Memories*, 19, 255.
17. Ibid., 33; Blane, *From Minnie with Love*, 77; Buckland, *Dictionary of Indian Biography*, 354; Baillie, *Indian Biographical Index*, 4:1527.
18. Marryat, *"Gup," Sketches of Anglo-Indian Life and Character*, 60–61; Hodson, Biographical Index of Indian Army Officers, Box 9. Emphasis is in the original. The nineteenth-century Indian Presidential Native Infantries resulted from three major factors related to the founding of the British, or Honourable, East India Company (BEIC) in 1599: European rivalry for silk, spices, and indigo, an increased naval supremacy, and the need for new markets for woolen goods. The first trade factory (station) at Surat was established in 1612. By 1717, many new trading posts were established along the east and west coasts of India. A fortified trading station was constructed at Surat (Bombay Presidency) in 1612, a second at Fort St. George in 1640 (Madras Presidency), and a third at Fort William (Bengal Presidency) in 1665, to protect trade. The first English recruits

(a company of thirty men) arrived at Madras in 1644, and Sir Fortescue remarked that these "were the first soldiers, native or European, enlisted in its service." The Company also invited freemen and gentlemen to serve for "honour and repute" alongside the soldiers. By involving themselves in local disputes between Mughal overlords and the local Indian princes, company officials courted favor with the indigenous rulers by creating a private army and selling military protection. The raison d'être of the company shifted from a purely trading venture to one that involved itself in local affairs, often via military muscle. According to historian John Keegan, manpower provided the vital component for British success in India, and the Battle of Plassey in 1757 proved the efficacy of utilizing indigenous troops. A victorious Robert Clive subdued the disgruntled *nawab*, which led to the Mughal emperor granting the BEIC vassalage status with the right to garrison army units to provide protection, among other benefits. An army of nine hundred regulars, aided and assisted by two thousand sepoys (indigenous regular soldiers), had won a convincing victory against a host of fifty thousand Indian combatants. In 1796 the troop units became known as "Native Infantries," and battalions consisted of a native rank and file, commanded by European officers, all employed by the Company. The three presidencies, Bengal, Madras, and Bombay, each with its own administration and army, became collectively known as the Indian Army. In addition, a small contingent of British Regular companies, found themselves ordered on tours of imperial duty in India. The British East India Company acted as the agent of British rule and sole military authority until the Sepoy Mutiny of 1857. See Heathcote, *Mutiny and Insurgency in India 1857–1858*, 6–8, 21–28; Fortescue, *History of the British Army*, 2:170; Chauduri, *Emergence of International Business 1200–1800*, 4:10, 226; Parsons, *British Imperial Century, 1815–1914*, 35–36; Cain and Hopkins, *British Imperialism, 1688–2000*, 93–94; Keegan, *World Armies*, 258–59; Mason, *A Matter of Honour*, 533.

19. Parkes, *Wanderings of a Pilgrim in Search of the Picturesque*, 1:409; Buckland, *Dictionary of Indian Biography*, 159, 329: Baillie, *Indian Biographical Index*, 1:303; Roberts, *Scenes and Characteristics of Hindostan*, 2:316–17. Roberts joined her sister and brother-in-law, Captain Robert McNaughton (Sixty-first Bengal Infantry), stationed in India.

20. Muter, *Travels and Adventures of an Officer's Wife in India, China, and New Zealand*, 2:1–3; Hart, *The New Annual Army List, and Militia List for 1862*, 328. The ancient festival of Saturnalia included role-reversal, with the slave population enacting the social/cultural roles of their masters.

21. Duberly, *Campaigning Experiences in Central India and the Rajputana during the Suppression of the Mutiny*, 69, 109, 178–79; Duberly, *Mrs Duberly's War*, xxxvi.

22. Fane, *Miss Fane in India*, 30, 43, 46. Emphasis is in the original. During the eighteenth and nineteenth centuries, Almack's Assembly Rooms, an exclusive London club, admitted both sexes. Membership to this elite club was not determined on wealth, but on background and behavior. Catering to fashionable society, attendees used this venue to create and sustain an image, and to network among like company. The term "nautch" is an English representation of the Hindi word "naach" whose direct translation means "dance," but often acted as a euphemism for a courtesan.

23. Sherwood, *Life and Times of Mrs. Sherwood*, 289, 293; Buckland, *Dictionary of Indian Biography*, 387. The title *nawab* ("nawaab") indicated the status of a provincial governor or viceroy of a region. During the time of Mrs. Sherwood's visit Babur Ali was the ruling Nawab of Bengal. Moorshedabad (Murshidabad) is located on the River Ganga. Published in 1604, Don Quixote was a fictional character from the pen of Miguel de Cervantes Saavedra. In the novel the protagonist set out on a doomed chivalric adventure that questions contemporary social identity and codes of conduct. Sancho Panza was Quixote's obedient and loyal servant.

24. Sherwood, *Life and Times of Mrs. Sherwood*, 332–33.

25. Weigley, *History of the United States Army*, 27–28; Washington, *The Writings of George Washington*, 5:103. Author's emphasis.

26. Coffman, *Old Army*, 3–4; Utley, *Frontiersmen in Blue*, 348–49.

27. Crackel, "The Military Academy in the Context of Jeffersonian Reform," 100, 111–12; Wagoner and McDonald, "Mr. Jefferson's Academy: An Educational Interpretation," 135, 137, 141, 146.

28. Watson, "Developing 'Republican Machines'," 154–56, 163, 167,170, 176; Vidal, "West Point," 325; Heitman, *Historical Register*, 1:952.

29. Ellis and Moore, *School for Soldiers*, 12, 32–34,160; Morrison, *"The Best School in the World,"* ix, 3–4, 61, 152–53; Weigley, *History of the United States Army*, 150; Galloway and Johnson, *West Point*, 106, 109, 123–24, 144–45.

30. Utley, *Frontiersmen*, 348–49; Coffman, *Old Army*, 3–4, 6–7, 8; Rowland, "Letters of a Virginian Cadet at West Point," 201, 208. Emphasis is in the original.

31. Boyd, *Cavalry Life in Tent and Field*, 6–7, 10–12, 14–15, 17; Heitman, *Historical Register*, 1:236; 1:343.

32. Skelton, *American Profession of Arms*, 154–55, 158–60, 165; Parks, *General Edmund Kirby Smith, C.S.A.*, 77; Heitman, *Historical Register*, 1:896. Skelton provides a table of paternal occupations and defines "professional status" as including: lawyer/judge, medical doctor, clergyman, college professor, and teacher. The commercial/manufacturing classification included merchant/shopkeeper, banker, manufacturer/founder, company employee/agent, sea captain/pilot, contractor, civil engineer/surveyor, artisan/machinist, and laborer/seaman. See Skelton, *American Profession of Arms*, 159.

33. Knight, *Life and Manners in the Frontier Army* , 3–6, 12; Schaff, *Spirit of Old West Point*, 138, 174; Heitman, *Historical Register*, 1:599; Cunliffe, *Soldiers and Civilians*, 169.

34. McKay, *Little Pills*, 7–8, 17–18, 126–27.

35. Stallard, *Glittering Misery*, 117–21; Heitman, *Historical Register*, 1:451, 760. For a full discussion of the Geddes affair, see Barnett, *Ungentlemanly Acts*. In attempting to escape charges during his second court-martial (1880), Geddes advised that he simply wished to protect a well-connected woman's reputation. This presumptive attempt of gallantry did not save his career, and Captain Geddes was cashiered from the service.

36. Custer, *Boots and Saddles*, 264 (page citations to the reprint edition); Leckie, *Elizabeth Bacon Custer and the Making of a Myth*, xviii, xx, xxii–xxiii, 256–314.

37. Summerhayes, *Vanished Arizona*, 7, 303; Heitman, *Historical Register*, 1:936; Barnett, "Introduction," v–xi, xv, xviii–xix. For a discussion of chivalric imagery utilized by

the American officers' wives in the U.S. West, see McInnis, "'Ladies' of the Frontier Forts," 35–56.

38. Baldwin, *Memoirs of Major General Frank D. Baldwin*, 121, 126, 168, 190; Heitman, *Historical Register*, 1:185; Scott, *Marmion*, 121; Vielé, *Following the Drum*, 120–21; Heitman, *Historical Register*, 1:348, 987; Dyer, *Fort Reno*, 24, 27.

39. Hooker, *Child of the Fighting Tenth*, 135; Utley, *Life in Custer's Cavalry*, 30: Heitman, *Historical Register*, 1:193, 325.

40. Skelton, *American Profession of Arms*, 177; MacKenzie, *Storms and Sunshine in a Soldier's Life*, 36–37; Hodson, Biographical Index of Indian Army Officers, Box 29; Rowland, "Letters of a Virginian Cadet at West Point," 201, 208. Emphasis is in the original.

41. Heathcote, *Mutiny and Insurgency*, 30–36.

42. Adams, *Class and Race in the Frontier Army*, 8, 17–18, 21–23, 46, 75. Adams provides a full discussion of how officers understood their middle-class status; see pages 30–46.

43. Forbes, "The United States Army," 128–29, 135; Roth, *Historical Dictionary of War Journalism*, 106–7, 134–35. Born in Scotland, Forbes served in the Royal Dragoons and after leaving the army became a front-line journalist in several British war zones. Forbes argued that American ranks held by enlisted promotion were "one lieutenant-colonel, five majors, one chaplain, seventy-two captains, and thirty-nine lieutenants. . . . In the American cavalry there are no riding masters, who, in the British cavalry, are invariably 'rankers,' while all of the adjutants and quartermasters in the American cavalry commenced their military career as commissioned officers, in contradistinction to the British custom of filling these appointments with officers promoted from the ranks."

44. Forbes, "The United States Army," 135, 139.

45. Ibid., 139, 141.

46. Ibid., 144–45. Forbes referred to an inspection of a cavalry unit at Camp Cumming. This appears to have been a visit to Fort Cummings, New Mexico. The Fourth U. S. Cavalry utilized the fort in the early 1880s as a base of operations against the Apaches.

47. Burton, *City of Saints*, 1, 8, 444–46; *Aesop's Fables*, "The Frogs Desiring a King," http://www.aesopfables.com/cgi/aesop1.cgi?sel&TheFrogsDesiringaKing. Burton's companion appears to be James Jackson Dana of the Fourth Artillery. Heitman, *Historical Register*, 1:352.

Chapter 3. Imperial Journeys and Arrivals

Epigraph: Bird, *A Lady's Life in the Rocky Mountains*, 285–86. Houstoun, *Texas and the Gulf of Mexico*, 271–73; Schneller, "Matilda Houstoun," Matthews, *Oxford Dictionary of National Biography*, 28:303–4. Both Bird and Houstoun are British women who published travelogues of their American explorations. Although not an officer's wife, Bird travelled in the U.S. West and provides a British view of the American pioneer woman. She describes the importance of middle-class female values of quietness, refinement, and self-respect in constructing female power. Adding to this view, the authoritative and assertive Matilda, the wife of Captain William Houstoun of the Tenth Hussars, recorded her view of male public behavior whilst visiting the Republic of Texas. During a stopover in Galveston she mixed with "the fashionable portions of the society," only to witness "frightful act[s] of uncleanliness [spitting and smoking] . . . which, and I do not exaggerate, is mentioned with disgust in all civilized societies, whenever the manners and habits of our transatlantic brethren chance to come under discussion." She then issued a call to the delicate, educated, and refined Texan women to exert their undoubted influence to create gentlemanly "sons of the soil."

1. Lawrence, *The Journals of Honoria Lawrence*, 14, 21–22, 25. Hodson, Biographical Index of Indian Army Officers, Box 27. Henry Lawrence's civil secondment provided for a temporary transfer from the British Army to a Civil Government Department—the Revenue Services. Emphasis is in the original.

2. Roe, *Army Letters from an Officer's Wife*, viii, 3; Heitman, *Historical Register*, 1:842.

3. Bammer, "Mother Tongues and Other Strangers," 92, 93, 95. In determining "distinctions between "the Orient" and "the Occident," Edward Said concludes that the idea of the "other" evolved as "European culture gained its strength and identity by setting itself off against the Orient as a sort of surrogate and even underground self." He qualifies Orientalism as "a Western style for dominating, restructuring, and having authority over the Orient," and positions the "Orientalist" as one who teaches, "writes about, or researches the Orient." See Said, *Orientalism*, 2–3.

4. Duncan and Gregory, "Introduction," 4–5; Said, *Orientalism*, 16, 95, 211; Iser, "Coda to the Discussion," 297; Blunt, "The Flight from Lucknow," 94. Indeed, Alison Blunt argued that "interconnections between imperialism, domestic space, and gender power . . . cannot be understood without a focus on travel, and representations of travel."

5. Comer, "Fictions of Empire," 3–4, 6, 16–17, 24, 33, 60; Raza, *British Women Writers and India, 1740–1857*, xi, xv, 67; Myres, "Frontier Historians," 37. Comer analyzes the writings of four British women writers, Eliza Fay, Bessie Fenton, Emma Roberts, and Mary Sherwood. "The definition of a nation," according to Benedict Anderson, "is an imagined political community—and imagined as both inherently limited and sovereign." He advises "communities are to be distinguished . . . by the style in which they are imagined." See Anderson, *Imagined Communities*, 6.

6. Carrington, *AB-SA-RA-KA, Land of Massacre*, dedication, 36, 40–41; Carrington, *My Army Life and the Fort Phil Kearney Massacre*, 61–62; Heitman, *Historical Register*, 1:286, 482. Emphasis is in the original. Grummond served under Carrington in the Eighteenth U.S. Infantry, and was killed in the Fetterman fight of 1866. Margaret Carrington died in 1870, and Frances Grummond subsequently married the widowed Henry in 1871.

7. Smith, *Give Me Eighty Men*, xxii, 160, 191, 198–99; Fahs, "The Feminized Civil War," 1461–94. Military officers' reputations were judged on a code of honor, courage, and confidence.

8. Graham, *Journal of a Residence in India*, lvi, viii–ix; Buckland, *Dictionary of Indian Biography*, 67.

9. MacKenzie, *Six Years in India*, iii, v, vii. Emphasis is in the original.

10. Ibid., 149.

11. At this time the term "Anglo-Indian" refers to a British subject stationed/resident in India. For those born in India of mixed race the term "Eurasian" was used.

12. Saunier, *Transnational History*, 2, 37–38. As an example of women operating transnationally, he suggests, "The travels of women missionaries, whether they stay put or criss-cross the globe, thus unveil their capacity to mediate between America and the places they tried to place under its 'moral empire.'"

13. Saunier, *Transnational History*, 41, 45; Khagram and Levitt, *The Transnational Studies Reader*, 20–21. See White, *The Middle Ground*; Pratt, *Imperial Eyes*; Bhabha, *The Location of Culture*.

14. Saunier, *Transnational History*, 57, 62, 65, 69.

15. Schiller, "Transmigrants and Nation-States," 96; Vertovec, "Conceiving and Researching Transnationalism," 447, 450–51, 455; Lima, "Transnational Families," 91, For a discussion of "the ways the world has always been transnational," see "Historical Perspectives," in Khagram and Levitt, *The Transnational Studies Reader*, 175–211. Schiller usefully separates "globalism" from "transnationalism" by advising: "Global is best reserved for processes that are not located in a single state but happen throughout the entire globe. . . . I employ the word transnational to discuss political, economic, social, and cultural processes that extend beyond the borders of a particular state, include actors that are not states, but are shaped by the policies and institutional practices of states."

16. Mahler and Pessar, "Gendered Geographies of Power," 442; Boyle, "Population Geography," 535; Itzigsohn, and Giorguli-Saucedo, "Incorporation, Transnationalism, and Gender," 897; Goldring, "The Gender and Geography of Citizenship in Mexico-U.S. Transnational Spaces," 501, 504, 524, 526. For scholarship on transnational comparative histories of gender, see Jacobs, *White Mother to a Dark Race*. For a full discussion of intimacies of empire, see Stoler, *Carnal Knowledge and Imperial Power.*.

17. Rouse, "Making Sense of Settlement," 27, 42, 45–46. Elizabeth Burt advised she spent forty-four years in the U.S. West, Martha Summerhayes twenty-four years, and Lydia Lane sixteen years.

18. Bammer, "Mother Tongues," 92, 93, 95.

19. Murison, "Memoir;" Baillie, *Indian Biographical Index*, 3:922; Myres, *Cavalry Wife*, 29; Heitman, *Historical Register*, 1:156.

20. Fougera, *With Custer's Cavalry*, 14–15; Heitman, *Historical Register*, 1:453, 669.

21. Ashmore, *Narrative of a Three Months' March*, 2–5; Hart, *The New Annual Army List for 1850*, 167.

22. Eden, *Letters from India*, 2:9–11, 22; Buckland, *Dictionary of Indian Biography*, 131.

23. Postans, *Cutch*, 4–6; Hodson, Biographical Index of Indian Army Officers, Box 37. Cutch (Kuchchh) is a North East Province of India that today borders Pakistan.

24. Baldwin, *Memoirs of Major General Frank D. Baldwin*, 121–22; Heitman, *Historical Register*, 1:185.

25. Mattes, *Indians, Infants, and Infantry*, 1, 5, 7, 11, 13, 20, 23; Myres, *Cavalry Wife*, 29, 31; Heitman, *Historical Register*, 1:156, 267.

26. Fougera, *Custer's Cavalry*, 20, 22–24, 29–31.

27. Alt and Stone, *Campfollowing*, 46; Fougera, *Custer's Cavalry*, 48–49, 52, 60, 62–64.

28. Monkland, *Life in India*, 2: 116, 125; Eden, *Letters from India*, 1:98.

29. Clemons, *Manners and Customs*, 10–12.

30. Sherwood, *Life and Times of Mrs. Sherwood*, x; Vielé, *Following the Drum*, 104–5, 109, 111, 156, 158.

31. Fane, *Miss Fane in India*, 5, 146, 155.

32. Stallard, *Glittering Misery*, 26; Godfrey, "Housewives, Hussies, and Heroines, or the Women of Johnston's Army," 161; Knight, *Life and Manners*, 112–14; Great Britain War Office, *The Queen's Regulations*, 247. "The Regulation for Troops in Barracks," Item 60, specifies, "that seniority of rank gives priority of selection of Quarters: but the selection, however, is restricted to those Quarters especially constructed and marked for the Respective Ranks of Officers, and to those only. When an Officer shall have been put in possession of Quarters by proper authority, he is not to be dispossessed by an Officer of corresponding Rank . . . but in all cases a Captain may claim a priority of choice over a Subaltern, notwithstanding such Subaltern shall have been in previous possession of the better Quarters. The Quarters for Field Officers are to be lettered F. O. Quarters—and those for Captains and Subalterns, Officers' Quarters."

33. Davies, *Splendours of the Raj*, 78, 80, 103–5; Nilsson, *European Architecture in India 1750–1850*, 21, 161; King, *The Bungalow*, 1, 7. Roberts, *Scenes*, 294–96; Parkes, *Wanderings of a Pilgrim in Search of the Picturesque*, 61–63. King asserts that "the most significant fact about the bungalow is that the term, the ideology it represents and the reality in which that ideology is expressed can be found in many quarters of the globe. It is a physical, but also an economic, social, and cultural phenomenon."

34. Myres, "Romance and Reality on the American Frontier, 421; Wooster, *Soldiers, Sutlers, and Settlers*, 37; Alt and Stone, *Campfollowing*, 51; Custer, *Boots and Saddles*, 98; Roe, *Army Letters*, 66; Utley, *Life in Custer's Cavalry*, 131; Heitman, *Historical Register*, 1:842.

35. Stanley, *My Early Travels and Adventures in America and Asia*, 1:4; Utley, *Life in Custer's Cavalry*, 18, 59, 119–20; "The Search for Livingston: Progress of the Englishman Stanley—Fierce Encounter with Arabs—Arrival at the Coast—The Great Explorer Remains Two Years More in Africa," *New York Times*, 2 July 1872. Welsh-born Henry M. Stanley became famous following his expedition to find the Scottish explorer David Livingston in the African Congo, when he "noticed in the center of a group of Arabs, strongly contrasting their sun-burned faces, a hale-looking, grey-bearded white man . . . preserving a demeanor of calmness . . . I inquired 'Dr. Livingston, I presume?'" The authenticity of this greeting is doubted, but the anecdote remains an enduring cultural legend.

36. Stanford, *Ladies in the Sun*, 73; Stallard, *Glittering Misery*, 15–66; Utley, *Frontier Regulars*, xiv; Wooster, *Soldiers, Sutlers, and Settlers*, 82, 216; Baker, "Daughters of Mars," 22–23; Nacy, *Members of the Regiment*, 10, 12, 104–5,107; *Calcutta Review*, July–December 1845.

37. Custer, *Boots and Saddles*, 126, 130; Fougera, *With Custer's Cavalry*, 116–25, 133–34, 137, 200; Summerhayes, *Vanished Arizona*, 1, 3, 100.

38. Mattes, *Indians, Infants, and Infantry*, 23.

Chapter 4. Imperial Women

Epigraph: Army and Navy Journal, 30 December 1893.

1. Custer, *Boots and Saddles*, 129–30.
2. Allen, *Plain Tales*, 79–81, 181, 269–70, 272. Kenneth Warren was a tea planter in India and served during World War I. Emphasis is in the original.
3. Showers-Stirling, "Notes on Her Life," Box 6, Envelope D, 21–22; Ellen Drummond to Minnie Thornhill, 22 February 1868, and 19 June 1868, "Letters from Ellen Drummond in Allahabad and Sialkot"; Hart, *The New Annual Army List, and Militia List for 1869*, 501, http://www.archive.org/stream/newannualarmylis1869hart#page/n9/mode/2up.
4. Roberts, *Scenes*, 25, 30–31; Coontz, "'A Heaving Volcano': Beneath the Surface of Victorian Marriage," 177–95.
5. Great Britain War Office, *The Queen's Regulations*, 315–16; Farwell, *Armies of the Raj*, 101–2.
6. Mason, *A Matter of Honour*, 367–69; Hyam, *Empire and Sexuality*, 121; Bamfield, *On the Strength*, 20; Procida, *Married to the Empire*, 30–6; Kipling, *Plain Tales*, 174, 177.
7. Procida, *Married to the Empire*, 47–48, 50–51.
8. Hood, *Advance and Retreat*, 7–8; Sherman to Ord, 23 July 1875, http://collections.mohistory.org/resource/175438.html; Heitman, *Historical Register*, 1:759, 882, 934, 961, 999.
9. Glisan, *Journal of Army Life*, 451–53; Heitman, *Historical Register*, 1:460, 540, 625.
10. Roe, *Army Letters*, 59–61, 81; Cullum, *Biographical Register*, 3:169; Heitman, *Historical Register*, 1:461. Mrs. Roe rode with a cavalry officer whom she called Lieutenant Golden, a West Point "classmate" of her husband's. No such person, however, resided at Camp Supply in 1872. The officer she refers to is in fact a Lt. Vinton A. Goddard of the Sixth Cavalry, who ranked sixth in the graduating class of 1871, with Fayette Roe passing in an unremarkable fortieth (out of forty-one) place.
11. Allen, *Plain Tales*, 82–83; "Lt.-Col. Christopher Bromhead Birdwood, 2nd Baron Birdwood," *The Peerage*, http://thepeerage.com/p14257.htm#i142570; Marryat, *"Gup,"* 62–63. Emphasis is in the original.
12. Myres, "Romance and Reality," 417–18; Custer, *Tenting on the Plains*, 400–401.
13. Parkes, *Wanderings of a Pilgrim*, 2:335; Eden, *Letters from India*, 1:311, 314; Sherwood, *A Widow's Reminiscences*, 258, 274; Nye, *Carbine and Lance*, 280; King, *Marion T. Brown*, xiii; Baldwin, *Memoirs*, 113; Custer, *Tenting on the Plains*, 447, 580, 675, 698; Baker, "Brown, John Henry," *Handbook of Texas Online*, http://www.tshaonline.org/handbook/online/articles/fbr94. Maj. John Brown commanded and served with the Third Texas Frontier District militia unit.
14. MacKenzie, *Life in the Mission, the Camp, and the Zenáná*, 267–8.
15. Mattison, "An Army Wife on the Upper Missouri," 192–93, 197, 217. Emphasis is in the original. For a discussion of the captivity narrative as a genre, see, Kolodny, *The Land Before Her*; Namias, *White Captives*; and Riley, *Confronting Race*, 38–40, 203–7.
16. Stallard, *Glittering Misery*, viii, 15–16; Utley, *Frontier Regulars*, xiv; Wooster, *Soldiers, Sutlers, and Settlers*, 82, 216; Margaret C. Hannay, Journal, 1829, 16; Baillie, *Indian*

Biographical Index, 2:518. Photographs are located in Roe, *Army Letters*, frontispiece; Fougera, *With Custer's Cavalry*, 149; "Elizabeth Custer," *Custerwest.org*, http://custer. over-blog.com/article-10579099.html; "Elizabeth Bacon Custer," Kansapedia, Kansas Historical Society, http://www.kshs.org/kansapedia/elizabeth-bacon-custer/12030; Ross, *Clothing: a Global History*, 75; A Lady Resident, *The Englishwoman in India*, 4. Although the officers' wives often wore the "solah topee," and it evolved from military wear, it became the ultimate symbol of Britishness in India, and worn by men, women, and children alike. Its function, according to Robert Ross, was "to provide a sign of difference and superiority." The lightweight pith helmet made from the Indian sola plant was first used by British soldiers in the Sikh Wars of 1840. It became officially incorporated into regulation dress in the mid-century. See Horse Guards War Office, *Dress Regulations for the Officers of the Army*, xxi.

17. Sale, *A Journal of the Disasters in Affghanistan, 1841–1842*, 3, 285; Hodson, Biographical Index of Indian Army Officers, Box 40; Glisan, *Journal of Army Life*, 52, 178, 453.

18. Coffman, *Old Army*, 105, 289; Sherwood, *Life and Times of Mrs. Sherwood*, 257, 438; Churcher, "Indian Impressions or Diary of Our Indian Trip," 71; Hart, *The New Annual Army List, Militia List, and Yeoman Cavalry List for 1903*, 78, https://archive.org/details/ hartsannualarmyl1903lond; Custer, *Boots and Saddles*, 104–5.

19. Frances J. Wells, Letters to her Father, 1853–1858, Berners Papers, 54–55, 60; Baillie, *Indian Biographical Index*, 4:1515.

20. Marryat, *"Gup,"* 16–17, 61. Emphasis is in the original. Tuft-hunting is the practice of creating social connections with people of a higher class.

21. Sherwood, *Life and Times of Mrs. Sherwood*, 227.

22. Myres, *Cavalry Wife*, 36; Heitman, *Historical Register*, 1: 937. Alexander misspells Mrs. Sutoris's last name. She was the wife of Bvt. 1st Lt. Alexander Sutorius, an immigrant from Switzerland, who joined the American army as a chief bugler.

23. Stallard, *Glittering Misery*, 2; Coffman, *Old Army*, 289; Ogden, "Queen or Camp Follower," 11, 15; Glisan, *Journal of Army Life*, 453.

24. Custer, *Tenting on the Plains*, 414–15.

25. Laurence, *Daughter of the Regiment*, 73; Heitman, *Historical Register*, 1:626; Custer, *Boots and Saddles*, 11, 103; McInnis, "'Ladies' of the Frontier Forts," 51.

26. Emma Wonnacott to Father and Mother, 6 January 1871, and Mrs. E. Swain to Emma Wonnacott, 12 January 1871, Wonnacott Collection.

27. Cott, *Bonds of Womanhood*, 1–2, 22, 64, 159, 189; Custer, *Boots and Saddles*, 125.

28. Clemons, *Manners and Customs*, 345–46, 348.

29. MacKenzie, *Scenes*, 19; Fenton, *Journal of Mrs Fenton*, 149–50, 166–67; Matthews, *Oxford Dictionary of National Biography*, 19:307–8.

30. Marryat, *"Gup,"* 1–2, 17–18. Emphasis is in the original.

31. Ibid., 58–59, Roberts, *Scenes*, 56–57,260–62 Fenton, *Journal of Mrs Fenton*, 149–50, 166–67.

32. Fougera, *With Custer's Cavalry*, 116–17, 121, 124. Patricia Spacks defines gossip as a cultural oral artifact, ranging from malicious (seeks to damage) to serious (function of intimacy). She claims "It plays with reputations, circulating truths and half-truths

and falsehoods about the activities, sometimes about the motives and feelings of others. Often it serves serious (possibly unconscious) purposes for the gossipers, whose manipulations of reputation can further political or social ambitions by damaging competitors or enemies, gratify envy and rage by diminishing another, [and] generate an immediately satisfying sense of power, although the talkers acknowledge no such intent. Supplying a powerful weapon in the politics of large groups and small, gossip can affect incalculable harm." For a full discussion see Spacks, *Gossip*.

33. Biddle, *Reminiscences*, 47; Heitman, *Historical Register*, 1:178, 799.

34. Baldwin, *Memoirs*, 13–17.

35. Totten, *The Button Box*, 98–101. Beatrice Patton was the daughter of the prosperous textile industrialist Frederick Ayer.

36. Allen, *Plain Tales*, 181–82, 268–69; Stocqueler, *The Oriental Interpreter*, 44; Blane, *From Minnie*, 151, 155. Stocqueler defined the *Burra Mem* as "a great lady; the appellation bestowed upon the female head of a house, or the wife of the principal personage at a station or presidency of India."

37. Fane, *Miss Fane in India*, 152, 155. Emphasis is in the original.

38. Lawrence, *Journals of Honoria Lawrence*, 215, 224, 226. Emphasis is in the original.

39. Hannay, Journal, 1829, 18, 30. Emphasis is in the original.

40. Knight, *Life and Manners*, 13, 16, 43; Heitman, *Historical Register*, 1:599; Custer, *Boots and Saddles*, 141; King, *Marion T. Brown*, 7, 8, 10, 37. Knight synthesized the 1882–1909 literary works of Charles King, a captain of the Fifth U.S. Cavalry during the period 1871–79. A grenadier is a soldier, generally of a powerful physique, who leads battlefield assaults.

41. Lane, *I Married a Soldier*, 15, 18, 97, 100–101; Heitman, *Historical Register*, 1:614. Lydia married Lt. William B. Lane of the U.S. Mounted Rifles on 18 May 1854. Emphasis is in the original.

42. Myres, *Westering Women*, 180, 186, 197, 211–12, 269; Williams, "Ladies of the Regiment," 161; Flipper, *Negro Frontiersman*, 3–4; Smith, *View from Officers' Row*, 4, 27; Heitman, *Historical Register*, 1:355, 425.

Chapter 5. Imperial Pageantry

Epigraph: Curzon, *Lady Curzon's India*, 139.

1. *Army and Navy Journal*, 14 April 1883.

2. Trotter, *History of India under Queen Victoria, 1836–1880*, 1:366; Buckland, *Dictionary of Indian Biography*, 252. Trotter, a prolific writer on nineteenth-century India, was a captain in the Second Bengal Fusiliers. Author's emphasis.

3. Buckland, *Sketches of Social Life in India*, 10–11. Buckland was a member of the Indian Civil Service.

4. Maunier, *The Sociology of Colonies*, 31; Greenberger, *The British Image of India*, 11, 13, 15, 19.

5. Procida, *Married to the Empire*, 16–17, 40–41, 48.

6. Ibid., 29; Stoddard and Cabanillas, "The Army Officer's Wife," 153–57. For a discussion of the traditional "companionate marriage" model in England, see Stone, *The Family, Sex, and Marriage in England, 1500–1800*, 325–404; and in America, see Lebsock, *The Free Women of Petersburg*, 17; and Degler, *At Odds*. For a discussion of the "incorporated wife," see Callan and Ardener, *The Incorporated Wife*; Finch, *Married to the Job*, especially 88–89, 150–69; and Procida, *Married to the Empire*, 42–43. Procida describes the incorporated wife as sharing her husband's work, and work environment, as a public figure who "personified the Empire," and her actions calculated to "elicit the subservience" of the indigenous population. Such women, she asserts, "not only represented imperial authority when their husbands were absent, but often acted in their stead when quick decisions and rapid action were necessary." She recognizes, however, that imperial wives moved beyond an incorporated model to "become junior partners with their husbands in their work, and to exercise autonomy as imperial actors."

7. Procida, *Married to the Empire*, 61; Myres, "Romance and Reality," 411, 425–26.

8. MacMillan, *Women of the Raj*, 41; Paget, *Camp and Cantonment*, 102; Sherwood, *Life and Times of Mrs. Sherwood*, 313; A Lady Resident, *The Englishwoman in India*, 40. The *Warrant of Precedence*, a reflection of the *Orders of Precedence*, minutely details the rigid etiquette to be observed. See Burke, *The Book of Precedence*. For military officers, see pages 78, 81–82. The revised Warrant of Precedence in India announced by Queen Victoria on 18 October 1876 (pages 85–87) demarcated brigadiers-general as First Class, lieutenant colonels as Third Class, and placed majors (along with civilians aged twelve to seventeen years!) within the lowest Fourth Class group. An addendum advised, "All ladies to take place according to the rank here'n assigned to their respective husbands, with the exception of wives of Peers, and of ladies having precedence in England independently of their husbands, and who are not in rank below the daughters of Barons; such ladies to take place according to their several ranks with reference to such precedence in England, immediately after the wives of Members of Council at the Presidencies in India." Updated regularly in some Indian states, it is still in existence today. See "Warrant of Precedence," http://rajyasabha.nic.in/rsnew/guidline_govt_mp/chap11.pdf.

9. Fane, *Miss Fane in India*, 80–81. Lord Auckland may have been correct in taking Miss Fane's arm. She, as the representative of her father General Sir Henry Fane, commander-in-chief of the Indian Army, could have been the highest-ranked woman at the dinner. Emphasis is in the original.

10. Jones, *Enchanted Journey*, 7, 57, 89, 91–93, 431. The "maneater" and "Tiger-ji" was Kitchener of Khartoum, Field Marshal Horatio Herbert, 1st Earl, P.C., K.G., O.M., G.C.S.I., K.C.I.E., commander-in-chief in India, 1902–1909. Wanamaker's Grand Depot was Philadelphia's first department store and began carrying ladies' wear in 1877.

11. Jones, *Enchanted Journey*, 92, 157.

12. Nicolson, *Mary Curzon*, 158; Fane, *Miss Fane in India*, 133; Sherwood, *Life and Times*, 290–92, 294; Matthews, *Oxford Dictionary of National Biography*, 14: 792–804. The

nawab of Bengal, Baber Ali Khan, hosted the soirée attended by the Sherwoods. General Sir Henry Fane was the commander-in-chief in India, 1835–1840.

13. Paget, *Camp and Cantonment*, 102; "Reverend John Fitz Moore-Halsey," *The Peerage*, http://www.thepeerage.com/p7241.htm#i72402; "Richard Moore," *The Peerage*, http://www.thepeerage.com/p47708.htm#i477072; "Colonel Leopold Grimston Paget," *The Peerage*, http://www.thepeerage.com/p2000.htm#i19996. Georgiana's father was the Rev. John Moore-Halsey, son of Richard Moore, an intimate of the royal family who was awarded accommodations at Hampton Court Palace. Paget's husband Leopold was the third son of the Honorable Berkeley Thomas Paget, and grandson of Sir Henry Paget, 1st Earl of Uxbridge. Emphasis is in the original.

14. Hammersley-Smith, "A Great Grandmother Remembers," 49–51; Hart, *Army List for 1903*, 367. Hammersley-Smith drew her description of the evening from Byron's poem *Childe Harold's Pilgrimage*, canto 3, st. 21. See Moore, Jeffrey, et al., *Poetical Works of Lord Byron*, 40.

15. Kerber, "Separate Spheres," 24; Welter, "The Cult of True Womanhood," 151–74; Baker, "Daughters of Mars," 22–23; Nacy, *Members of the Regiment*, 10, 12, 104–5, 107. For a full discussion of nineteenth-century northern womanhood, see Welter, "The Cult of True Womanhood;" Cott, *Bonds of Womanhood*; and Smith-Rosenberg, "Female World of Love and Ritual," 1–29. For southern womanhood, see Fox-Genovese, *Within the Plantation Household*, 44, 47, 66–67, 81, 99. Fox-Genovese argues that "the figure of the lady, especially the plantation mistress, dominated southern ideals of womanhood." For a discussion of the western female role, see Brown, *Gentle Tamers*; Faragher, *Women and Men on the Overland Trail*; Riley, *Female Frontier*; and Jeffrey, *Frontier Women*. For a discussion of officers' wives' roles in the U.S. West, see Coffman, *Old Army*, 104–36, 287–327; Stallard, *Glittering Misery*; Nacy, *Members of the Regiment*; and McInnis, "Expanding Horizons."

16. Carrington, *AB-SA-RA-KA*, 51–53. The emphases are in the originals. In writing of the Eighteenth Infantry Regiment's "last reunion," Carrington noted that a new congressional bill reorganized regiments. Indeed, the Congressional Act of 28 July 1866 ordered: "*Be it enacted by the Senate and House of Representatives of the United States of America in Congress assembled*, That the military peace establishment of the United States shall hereafter consist of five regiments of artillery, ten regiments of cavalry, forty-five regiments of infantry, the professors and corps of cadets of the United States Military Academy, and such other forces as shall be provided by this act, to be known as the Army of the United States." See U.S. Congress, Statutes at Large, *An Act to Increase and Fix the Military Peace Establishment of the United States*, 39th Cong., 1st sess., vol. 14, chapter 299, 1866, 332, http://memory.loc.gov/cgi-bin/ampage?collId=llsb&fileName=039/llsb039.db&recNum=1059.

17. Biddle, *Reminiscences*, 49–50, Heitman, *Historical Register*, 1:162, 335, 752. Emphasis is in the original. A nineteenth-century American etiquette manual codified middle-class behavior with the following advice: "A regard for appearances is . . . a leading consideration when ordering one's conduct in public. . . . [It] should be character-ized by reserve. . . . [T]he general public is our observant critic. Greetings between

acquaintances casually meeting in such places should be quiet and conventional. . . . [A]nd the manner should be perfectly open and above board. . . . But if a man meets a lady, and wishes to chat with her, he should, after greeting her, ask permission to join her, and walk with her for a short distance; he should by no means . . . prolong such a casual conversation beyond a few moments." For the full instructions on recommended public behavior, see Morton, *Etiquette*, 151–54.

18. Lane, *I Married a Soldier*, 84–86; Mattes, *Indians, Infants, and Infantry*, 30, 168; Baldwin, *Memoirs*, 14.

19. Roe, *Army Letters*, 2, 5–6.

20. Mickelson, "British Women in India 1757–1857," 239; Blane, *From Minnie*, 165. Emphasis is in the original.

21. Wells, Letters to her Father, 71, 75. For a discussion of Victorian female stereotypes, see Gilbert and Gubar, *Madwoman in the Attic*. Author's emphasis.

22. Buffum to Swaine, 19 January 1877, Steelhammer to Swaine, 28 December 1876, and Steelhammer to Blair, 6 January 1877, Records of U.S. Army Continental Commands, rolls 30, 31; Heitman, *Historical Register*, 1:260, 884, 919.

23. Steelhammer to Swaine, 4 December 1876, Swaine to Blair 20 Jan 1877, Swaine to Steelhammer, 19 Dec 1876, and Buffum to Swaine, 19 January 1877, Records of U.S. Army Continental Commands, roll 31; Heitman, *Historical Register*, 1:222, 919, 938; Wooster, *Soldiers, Sutlers, and Settlers*, 73–75.

24. Swaine to Steelhammer, 19 December 1876, and Blair to Steelhammer, 2 January 1877, Letters Sent (LS) by Headquarters, District of New Mexico, Sept. 1865–Aug. 1890, RG 393, M-1088, roll 30, National Archives and Records Administration, Washington D.C.; Steelhammer to Blair, 6 January 1877, Cover Sheet, 6 January 1877, William Buffum Sworn Deposition, 20 November 1876, Vanstan to Charlotta Buffum, 10 November 1876, Dist. NM, Letters received (LR), RG 393, M-1088, roll 30; Buffum to Swaine, 19 January 1877, Charlotta Buffum Sworn Affidavit 18 January 1877, Dist. NM, Letters received (LR), RG 393, M-1088, roll 31. Author's emphasis.

25. Captain Edward Whittemore to Swaine Acting Assistant Adjutant General, New Mexico, 19 February 1877, Dist. NM, LR, RG 393, M-1088, roll 31, Shorkley to Swaine, 22 January 1877, Dist. NM, LR, RG 393, M-1088, roll 29; Heitman, *Historical Register*, 1:321, 884, 1008, 1031.

26. Cannadine, *Rituals of Royalty*, 1, 3, 17, 19. Anthropological studies that interpret ceremonial artifacts and rituals as displays of political power include Firth, *Symbols, Public and Private*; Turner, *Dramas, Fields, and Metaphors*; and Feeley-Harnick, "Issues in Divine Kingship," 273–313.

27. Allen, *Plain Tales*, 79–81; Wells, Letters to her Father, 1853–1858, 56. The Sepoy Mutiny in India began in Meerut on 10 May 1857 and officially ended by a peace agreement in July 1858. For published and unpublished accounts of experiences and escapes written by officers' wives, see Haldane, *The Story of Our Escape from Delhi in 1857*; Wagontreiber, *The Story of Our Escape from Delhi in May, etc.*; Huxham, "Diary of the Mutiny, 1857–1858"; Jackson, "A Personal Narrative of the Indian Mutiny, 1857"; Mill, "Diary of the Mutiny, 1857–1858"; Stock, Papers, 1854–1870; Duberly, *Suppression*

of Mutiny, 1857–1858; Bartrum, *A Widow's Reminiscences of Lucknow*; Sinha, *Colonial Masculinity*, 1–24. Sinha's analysis of masculinity in India argues that the construction of the "manly Englishman" and the "effeminate Bengali" from 1880 to 1890 sought to find a common denominator in an increasingly diverse climate. This opposition assisted to ameliorate tensions in power negotiations between the colonizer and colonized, as a response to "economic, political, and cultural shifts in the imperial social formation" during this period. For a discussion of masculinity, see Mangan and Walvin, *Manliness and Morality*, and Roper and Tosh, *Manful Assertions*.

28. Paget, *Camp and Cantonment*, 175, 187. For illustrated plates of the nineteenth-century British military uniforms, see Herrington and Tomasek, *Queen Victoria's Army in Color*. For the Highlander uniforms, see pages 86–87. The Highland Regiments of the British Army originated in Scotland, were known for exceptional courage in battle, and incorporated kilts, sporrans, and tartan trousers as part of their uniform. For descriptions of both the British and American military apparel, see Knötel and Sieg, *Uniforms of the World*, 255–77, 434–42. The full dress uniforms, worn for ceremonial functions, offered the most elaborate and imposing outfits of the British Army. Adorned with medals, sashes, order insignias, and gold epaulettes, they most certainly provided a prestigious textual representation of imperial authority. U.S. uniforms appear equally imposing with gold shoulder straps, chevrons, and collars complimented with a shako-style helmet complete with a plume or cockade. See Rankin, *Uniforms of the Army*, 19–31, 33–57. Cole, "Survey of U.S. Army Uniforms, Weapons and Accoutrements." http://www.history.army.mil/html/museums/uniforms/survey_uwa.pdf. For definitions of full, dress, and undress uniforms, see Carman, *A Dictionary of Military Uniforms*, 61, 90, 131.

29. Churcher, "Indian Impressions," 109–11. Oliver Villiers Russell, 2nd Baron of Ampthill, governed as viceroy of India from April to December 1904. He married Lady Margaret Lygon in 1894.

30. Showers-Stirling, Notes on Her Life, 23–24; Adams, *Balfour*, 192–94. Lord Curzon organized the Great Durbar of 1903 (there were three such events, 1877, 1903, and 1911) to celebrate the roles of Edward VII and Queen Alexandra as emperor and empress of India. For a detailed account written by a *Times of India* journalist, see Fraser, *At Delhi*.

31. Curzon, *Lady Curzon's India*, 58; Matthews, *Oxford Dictionary of National Biography*, 34:256–57; Duberly, *Mrs Duberly's War*, xxviii.

32. Curzon, *Lady Curzon's India*, 58; Jones, *Enchanted Journey*, 107. Emphasis is in the original.

33. Allen, *Plain Tales*, 182; Gray, Unpublished Memoirs, 151–52; Matthews, *Oxford Dictionary of National Biography*, 5:829–31, 11:57–59. Ruby Gray's father was an American who lived and worked in Constantinople.

34. Carrington, *My Army Life*, 113–15.

35. Ibid., 112, 113–17. Emphasis is in the original.

36. Biddle, *Reminiscences*, 236; Cochran, *Posie*, 162–63.

37. Boyd, *Cavalry Life*, 228–29.

38. Utley, *Life in Custer's Cavalry*, 103–16. Utley advises that in July 1867 an act enabled a commission to be formed to find a peaceful solution to the escalating western conflicts. The commissioners who traveled to Medicine Lodge included politicians and high-ranking military officers.

39. Custer, *Tenting on the Plains*, 97, 99, 100, 104–5. Teresa Vielé also recorded a "drumming out." See Vielé, *Following the Flag*, 117–18. Elizabeth Custer does not name the "hated" officer in her book. The nineteenth-century British Army's portfolio of military punishment included death, transportation, flogging, and imprisonment. For desertion a soldier could be branded with the letter "D" and discharged. Henry Colburn, who witnessed a ceremony following a death sentence, noted, "A military execution is truly a terrible sight. Great military show is purposely displayed for the purpose of rendering it as impressive as possible to the troops who are to witness it." For a discussion of the British military punishment policies and practices, see Henry Colburn, *Colburn's United Service Magazine and Naval and Military Journal, 1844 Part One*, 242–56.

40. Carrington, *AB-SA-RA-KA*, dedication; Carrington, *My Army Life*, 61; Fougera, *With Custer's Cavalry*, 137. For a discussion on the rhetorical protection of the widowed Elizabeth Custer, see Leckie, *Elizabeth Bacon Custer and the Making of a Myth*, 256–314.

41. Baldwin, *Memoirs*, 154–55, 159.

42. Summerhayes, *Vanished Arizona*, 107–8.

43. Ibid., 93–95, 108.

44. Roe, *Army Letters*, 91; Twitchell, "Camp Robinson Letters of Angeline Johnson, 1876–1879," 92–93; Heitman, *Historical Register*, 1:574.

45. Mattes, *Indians, Infants, and Infantry*, 154–57.

46. Custer, *Following the Guidon*, 80, 89, 99, 100, 102; Leckie, *Elizabeth Bacon Custer and the Making of a Myth*, 256–314.

47. Fane, *Miss Fane in India*, 146–7; Lane, *I Married a Soldier*, 86.

48. Elizabeth Custer quoted in Fougera, *With Custer's Cavalry*, 137.

Chapter 6. Imperial Gender Crossings

Epigraph: Diver, *Englishwoman in India*, 48–49.

1. Forster, *A Passage to India*, 49–50.

2. Adams, *Class and Race*, 106, 120, 131.

3. Spain, *Gendered Spaces*, 2, 29.

4. Longford, *Queen Victoria*, 36, 113; Thompson, *English Landed Society in the Nineteenth Century*, 16, 184, 188. For a discussion on the American experience, see Blumin, *Emergence of the Middle Class*.

5. Johnson, "Conspicuous Consumption and Working Class Culture in Late Victorian and Edwardian Britain," 27, 29–30, 39, 41; Veblen, *Theory of the Leisure Class*, 35,70; Gunn, *Public Culture of the Victorian Middle Class*, 8–9, 69–70; Gillis, *A World of Their Own Making*, 76, 80; Sweet, *Inventing the Victorians*, 105, 114–15; Whitlock, *Crime, Gender, and Consumer Culture in Nineteenth-Century England*, 8, 12; Beeton, *Book of*

Household Management, title and contents pages, 13; Rappaport, *Shopping for Pleasure*, 114; Branca, *Silent Sisterhood*, 13–14; Halttunen, *Confidence Men and Painted Women*, xiv–xv, xvii, 91; Beecher, *A Treatise on Domestic Economy*, 116; Aimed at the developing middle class, the 1861 edition of Mrs. Beeton's domestic manual sold over 600,000 copies in its first year of publication with sales reaching two million in England by 1868. See Humble, "Introduction," in *Mrs Beeton's Book of Household Management*, viii. The principles of social courtesy provided the foundation for sentimental gentility. Kathryn Kish Sklar reports that the popularity of Beecher's *Treatise*, reprinted almost annually during the period 1841–1856, greatly influenced nineteenth-century America. See Sklar, *Catharine Beecher, A Study in American Domesticity*, 151, 305–6. Mrs. Beecher and her sister, Harriet Beecher Stowe, revised the work in 1869 as *The American Woman's Home*, selling fifty thousand copies.

6. Matthews, *"Just A Housewife"*, 6, 96; Beecher, *A Treatise on Domestic Economy*, 6, 116, 145–47; Halttunen, *Confidence Men and Painted Women*, xiv–xv, xvii, 91.

7. Montgomery, *Displaying Women*, 11, 21, 167; Sweet, *Inventing the Victorians*, 105, 114–15; Calder, *Victorian Home*, 115; Halttunen, *Confidence Men and Painted Women*, 72–73; Howe, "Victorian Culture in America," 3–26. Howe defines American Victorianism as an Anglo-American, transatlantic phenomenon that identified an evolving "bourgeois culture of industrializing Western civilization." Its diverse and contradictory culture was defined by general values of modernization, Protestantism, gentility, conscientious work ethic, self-improvement, sobriety, sexual repressiveness, competitiveness, orderliness, thrift, time-consciousness, and moral urgency. Howe argues that female domesticity, as a subculture of security and sentiment, complimented Victorian patriarchy.

8. Schlereth, "Material Culture Studies in America, 1876–1976," 2, 62; Tarlo, *Clothing Matters*, xx, 1, 5, 45, 318, 320; Wilson, *Adorned in Dreams*, 2–3, 6, 13–14. Barnes and Eicher, "Introduction," in *Dress and Gender*, 1, 7; Lurie, *Language of Clothes*, 115, 134; Cohn, "Cloth, Clothes, and Colonialism," 114–15; Chaudhuri, *Culture in the Vanity Bag*, 57–58.

9. Anonymous, *How to Behave*, 31–32, 34–35; Leith-Ross, *Stepping Stones*, 69; Callaway, "Dressing for Dinner in the Bush: Rituals of Self-Definition and British Imperial Authority," in *Dress and Gender*, eds. Barnes and Eicher, 235, 242, 246.

10. A Lady Resident, *The Englishwoman in India*, 17.

11. Steel and Gardiner, *The Complete Indian Housekeeper and Cook*, 175, 179 (page citations are to the reprint edition); Dickens, *Household Words*, 242–43. Dickens indicated that a red wax sealed envelope denoted the sanctity of, and confidence in, the missive enclosed. Emphasis is in the original.

12. Macmillan, *Women of the Raj*, 71; Steel, *Complete Indian Housekeeper*, 173; Lawrence, *Journals*, 87.

13. Wallace-Dunlap, *The Timely Retreat; or, A Year in Bengal before the Mutinies*, 230–31. Emphasis is in the original.

14. Ellen Drummond to Minnie Thornhill, 8 January 1868; Fay, *Original Letters from India*, 123–24; Buckland, *Dictionary of Indian Biography*, 144.

15. Beeton, *Book of Household Management*, 1453; Fane, *Miss Fane in India*, 88–89; Eden, *Up the Country*, 138. Author's emphasis.

16. Ashmore, *Narrative of a Three Month's March*, 344–45; Marryat, *"Gup,"* 42.

17. Roberts, *Scenes*, 2:58–59. First emphasis the author's, second is in the original. A furbelow is a superfluous gathered or pleated border added to a skirt.

18. Ibid., 59; Buck, *Simla Past and Present*, 164.

19. Clemons, *Manners and Customs*, 325–26.

20. Fane, *Miss Fane in India*, 96–97.

21. Vielé, *Following the Drum*, 14, 81; Riley, *Female Frontier*, 13, 62, 93, 99, 176, 195–96; Baker, "Daughters of Mars," 22–23; Nacy, *Members of the Regiment*, 10, 12, 104–5, 107; Riley, *Taking Land, Breaking Land*, 2, 4–5, 14; Shea, *Army Wife*, 281. The nursery poem Vielé refers to is called "The Monkey's Wedding," in which a monkey marries the baboon's sister. In the 1860s a ballad version of this West African tale appeared in American popular culture. See Anonymous, *Shilling Song Book*, 16–17; Felleman, *Best Loved Poems of the American People*, 463–64; Parsons, *Folk Tales of Andros Island, Bahamas*, ix, 166–67; Chatelain, *Folk Tales of Angola*, 127–28.

22. Knapman, *White Women of Fiji*; Collingham, *Imperial Bodies*, 2–3, 33–35; Huggins, *Sketches in India*, 3, 29–30, 60–61; Procida, *Married to the Empire*, 16. In Collingham's investigation of the transformation of the Anglo-Indian nabob to sahib during the period 1650–1900, she argues, "[T]he body was central to the colonial experience . . . as the site where structures are experienced, transmuted, and projected back on to society. Social structures include bodily techniques and activities, including clothing and consumption." She usefully defines the nabob as a "flamboyant, effeminate, and wealthy East India Company servant," and the sahib as "a sober, bureaucratic representative of the Crown." The relationship between the Queen's and Indian Army is discussed in chapter 2.

23. Johnson, *Influence of Tropical Climate*, 426; Collingham, *Imperial Bodies*, 6–40. Emphasis is in the original.

24. Williamson, *East India Vade-Mecum*, 1:501. Emphasis is in the original.

25. Ibid., 501–2. Emphasis is in the original.

26. Roberts, *Scenes*, 1:186; Fenton, *Journal of Mrs Fenton*, 82. The Victorian phrase "on the tapis" means under consideration. Fenton mentioned "Dacca muslin": this is a misspelling of a traditional lightweight textile manufactured in the Bengali city of Dhaka. The Queen of Sheba appears in Hebrew, Ethiopian, and Islamic religious texts. Modern-day scholars suggest she ruled over the Kingdom of Southern Arabia three thousand years ago. Emphasis is in the original.

27. Lane, *I Married a Soldier*, 143–44; Vielé, *Following the Drum*, 14.

28. Summerhayes, *Vanishing Arizona*, 158,192; Lane, *I Married a Soldier*, 144; Vielé, *Following the Drum*, 14. Emphasis is in the original.

29. Raugh, *Victorians at War*, 255–56; Cohn, "Cloth, Clothes, and Colonialism," 124–25; Callaway, "Dress and Gender," 242.

30. Huhndorf, *Going Native*, 2, 5, 55–57; Hardorff, *Indian Views of the Custer Fight*, 73; Custer, *My Life on the Plains*, 33, 95. See Paterek, *Encyclopedia of American Indian Costume*.

31. Ricketts, "English Society in India," 683; Diver, *Englishwoman in India*, 48–49; Procida, *Married to the Empire*, 56.

32. Ibid., 64–65; Showers-Stirling, "Notes on Her Life," 21–22; A Lady Resident, *The Englishwoman in India*, 36–39. Edwards and Ponsonby, "Desirable Commodity or Practical Necessity?," 118; Ponsonby, *Stories from Home*, 57–59. Ponsonby argues that renting a home and furniture occurred within the middle classes only as a temporary stopgap when moving. The lower-middle classes, she posits, hired furniture only until funds became available to purchase necessary items. Minimalism, a style of architecture, décor, and art, portrayed less as more, and became stylish in early twentieth-century Europe. The waler, bred in and shipped from Australia, proved a highly mobile, thus popular, military mount for the Indian Army.

33. Gray, Unpublished Memoirs, 61.

34. Lucy Elinor Lyall Grant (nèe Harvey), Notes Papers, 1906–1909, 10. The Grants' final destination of Gilgit lay in the North-West Frontier (now Pakistan). The Gilgit-Baltistan range boasts five of the Earth's "eight-thousander" mountains, including K2 and one of the world's most menacing mountains—Nanga Parbat. The fact that Lucy Grant accompanied the Mountain Battery across the Komri and Borzil (at ten thousand feet) Passes with two infants is quite remarkable. Emphasis is in the original.

35. Lawrence, *The Journals*, 35, 36–37. Kuss-kuss grass, indigenous to India, has tall, thin, and rigid stems ideal for window blinds.

36. Surgeon General's Office, *Circular Number 4*, 89, 203–4.

37. Grier, *Culture and Comfort*, vii–ix, 6, 10, 143.

38. Biddle, *Reminiscences*, 14–15; Fry, *Military Miscellanies*, 35–36.

39. Boyd, *Cavalry Life*, viii, 216–18. Mrs. Biddle referred to "W. J. Sloane Interior Decorator and Home Furnishers," New York, established in 1843. This company catered to the decorating needs of America's wealthy elite, thus setting national design trends for the nascent middle class. See Sloane, *The Story of Sloane's*.

40. Carrington, *My Army Life*, 53–54.

41. Brown, *The Army Called It Home*, 17–18, 20–21, 23, 32–34, 36–38, 41, 54, 57, 61, 210, Figs., 1:7, 8, 10, 11, 12, 23–26, 28–31, 34–35, 50–51, 54–56, 7:11; Heitman, *Historical Register*, 1:204, 493, 495, 617, 730, 804; Baldwin, *Memoirs of Major General Frank D. Baldwin*, 189. Photographic locations included western forts: Leavenworth, Mackenzie, Union (New Mexico), Bowie, Mackinac, Robinson, Sill, and Wallace. The Americans' quarters featured those of Lts. Benjamin Morse, Twenty-Third Infantry, Edward Pratt, Twenty-Third Infantry, and George Hamilton, Ninth Cavalry, Chaplains James La Tourette and Brant Hammond, Maj. Frank Baldwin, Fifth Infantry, and Lt. Cols. George Custer, Seventh Cavalry, and Eugene Beaumont, Third Cavalry. Most of the images, unfortunately, do not give the name of the photographer. George Custer, however, posed for many sittings by David F. Barry, and the British photojournalist William H. Illingworth accompanied the Seventh Cavalry on two campaigns in the 1870s. Both these men are probable candidates for the domestic prints. Mrs. Baldwin left a memoir of her experiences in the West, but with regard to the images of her home in Fort Keogh, she simply noted in 1877 (the photograph, allegedly taken in

the late 1880s, suggests refurbishments must have been made in the interim) that the quarters consisted of log houses, the chinks filled with mud. She added, however, "the ladies of the regiment had all arrived, and homes and family circles were once more established."

42. Brown, *The Army Called It Home*, 17, 212, Figs. 1:5, 7:12; Heitman, *Historical Register*, 1:819; Coffman, *Old Army*, 218.

43. Brown, *The Army Called It Home*, 24–25, 27, 40, Figs. 1:14–18, 32–33; Heitman, *Historical Register*, 1:336, 420, 475, 564; Dawson, *The Late Nineteenth-Century U.S. Army*, *1865–1898*, 80, 99. The quarters featured: Lts. Robert Irvine of the Eleventh U.S. Infantry and Lewis D. Greene of the Seventh U.S. Infantry, Lt. Leighton Finley of the Tenth U.S. Cavalry, and Capt. Emmet Crawford of the Third U.S. Cavalry.

44. Dinges, "Leighton Finley: A Forgotten Soldier of the Apache Wars," 163, 171–72, 174; Davis, *The Truth about Geronimo*, 31–32; *Army and Navy Journal*, 20 July 1889, 973–74; Wooster, *Frontier Crossroads*, 84; Heitman, *Historical Register*, 1:360. Men and women, traditionally, contributed to the internal decoration of their home. In the mid-nineteenth century, however, this duty appeared to shift to the female realm. For a discussion, see Thornton, *Authentic Décor*, 8–9. This shift became "Woman's Aesthetic Mission" as a "promoter of the beautiful." Jacob von Falke dedicated a complete chapter to this subject in von Falke, *Art in the House*, 311–36. My thanks to Jennifer Heth and R. J. Q. Adams for sharing their thoughtful insights regarding the feminization of bachelor quarters.

45. Haggis, "Gendering Colonialism or Colonising Gender?," 47, 50; Woollacott, *Gender and Empire*, 1, 3; Perry, *On the Edge of Empire*, 1, 4, 20, 25–28, 79. The latest gender scholarship confronts the problems of writing a nonrecuperative history of women that seamlessly blends within histories of empire. Although women have gained visibility as "insertions" in traditional accounts, Angela Woollacott argues that imperialism cannot be understood without establishing "the systematic operation of gender." Thus she argues that gender played a central role "in the imperial enterprise, both as one of the forces driving and shaping the empire, and as a set of ideologies produced at once in the colonies and the metropole that constituted shifting and pervasive imperial culture."

46. Khan, *From Kashmir to Kabul*, 175. A lotas jar is usually made of marble and richly decorated with Indian motifs.

47. Worswick, and Embree, *The Last Empire*, 56–57; Khan, *From Kashmir to Kabul*, 11, 175; Falconer, "Willoughby Wallace Hooper: A Craze about Photography," 258–59. Photograph in Worswick and Embree. Khan and Falconer consulted to establish Hooper's military credentials. Author's emphasis.

48. Bellew, *Memoirs of a Griffin*, 170, 172–75; Hodson, Biographical Index of Indian Army Officers, Box 4; Allen, *Plain Tales*, 73–75. Of the ten single-male oral histories regarding the "chummeries" recorded by Allen, only one military man, Brigadier and Right Honorable Sir John (Jackie) Smith, V.C., contributed to this topic. Most others held appointments with the Indian Civil Service, and Radclyffe Sidebottom was in the Bengal Pilot Service.

49. Bourke, *On the Border with Crook*, 159–60.
50. Procida, *Married to the Empire*, 64–65.
51. Myres, *Cavalry Wife*, 37, 41, 43, 45, 68, 78; Heitman, *Historical Register*, 1:882.
52. Myres, *Cavalry Wife*, 86–88.
53. Procida, *Married to the Empire*, 56.

Chapter 7. Imperial Gatekeepers

Epigraph 1: Ellis, *The Prose Work of Mrs. Ellis*, 1:17.
Epigraph 2: Buck, *Simla Past and Present*, 162.

1. *Calcutta Review*, vol. 4, no. 7; emphasis is in the original. Parkes, *Wanderings*, 1:140; Lee, *Jean, Lady Hamilton*, xvi, 29–30, 56–57.
2. Lee, *Jean, Lady Hamilton*, 57–58, 63, 356.
3. Summerhayes, *Vanished Arizona*, 266–69.
4. Leckie, *The Colonel's Lady on the Western Frontier*, 11–13, 124–26; Heitman, *Historical Register*, 1:204, 478.
5. Steel, *Complete Indian Housekeeper*, 11; Riley, *Taking Land, Breaking Land*, 14; Shea, *Army Wife*, 281.
6. Adams, *Class and Race*, 75, 78–79.
7. Davidoff, *The Best Circles*, 37, 41–42; Sherwood, *Manners and Social Usage*, 15–16, 44; Anonymous, *How to Behave*, 63–64. Emphasis is in the original.
8. Allgor, *Parlor Politics*, 4, 149–57; Halttunen, *Confidence Men and Painted Women*, xiii–xiv, 92. Allgor describes the personal calling card as measuring two inches by three inches. The contents, handwritten or embossed, often proffered gilt edging, mottoes, and images. The card, she argues, provided a buffer zone and by "using cards as proxies made the system more flexible and less personally hurtful." John Kasson examines the American social ritual of calling to agree with Davidoff (thus underscoring the similarity in the British and American practices) that by folding the card in a predetermined fashion a caller signaled a distinct message to the receiver—a sort of origami protocol. Turning down the upper-right corner indicated a personal call; the upper-left designated congratulations; the lower-left—condolences, and the lower-right announced an imminent departure. See Davidoff, *Best Circles*, 43; Allgor, *Parlor Politics*, 121, and Kasson, *Rudeness and Civility*.
9. Wells, Letters to her Father, 93; Beeton, *Book of Household Management*, 10; Beecher, *Treatise on Domestic Economy*, 144; Halttunen, *Confidence Men and Painted Women*, 222. Protocol dictated that ceremonial calls (such as marriage, childbirth) must be made between 3:00 and 5.00 P.M., semi-ceremonial calls between 5:00 and 6:00 P.M., and intimate calls may be undertaken from 6:00 to 7:00 P.M. See Davidoff, *Best Circles*, 43.
10. Allgor, *Parlor Politics*, 120–21. For a discussion on the American calling card protocol, see Lombardo, "Calling Cards used for Social Reasons, A Look Back," *Amherst Bulletin* 27 (28 April 1995): 4.
11. Barr, *Memsahibs*, 173–74; MacMillan, *Women of the Raj*, 180–81; Procida, *Married to the Empire*, 58–59. Author's emphasis.

12. Ruby Gray, Unpublished Memoir, 60.

13. A Lady Resident, *The Englishwoman in India*, 40; Jones-Parry, *An Old Soldier's Memories*, 19.

14. Paget, *Camp and Cantonment*, 93; Ellen Drummond to Minnie Thornhill, 29 March 1868; Showers-Stirling, "Notes on Her Life," 22. Emphasis is in the original.

15. Churcher, "Indian Impressions," 6–7; Hannay, Journal, 1829, 1–2; Christian Showers-Stirling, "Notes on Her Life," 58.

16. McKay, *Little Pills*, 122–23; Kinevan, *Frontier Cavalryman*, 152, 185, 191, 287; Heitman, *Historical Register*, 1:166, 311. The dinner party mentioned was hosted by Capt. John Clous and his wife. Kinevan suggests Bigelow's dancing partner was the sister of Ranald Mackenzie. Emphasis is in the original.

17. Stallard, *Glittering Misery*, 43; Sherwood, *Etiquette, the American Code of Manners*, iv–v, 182, 184, 186–87, 191.

18. Paulding, "My Army Life," 1, 4, 90; Heitman, *Historical Register*, 1:1019.

19. Utley, *Life in Custer's Cavalry*, 15; Summerhayes, *Vanished Arizona*, 165–66.

20. King, *Letters from Fort Sill*, 4, 6, 9; Biddle, *Reminiscences*, 222–23.

21. Custer, *Tenting on the Plains*, 406; Heitman, *Historical Register*, 1:452. Unfortunately, Mrs. Custer does not provide the "new arrival's" name, rank, or regiment. It is probable that, as an "appointee," he did not graduate from the U.S. Military Academy at West Point.

22. Russell, *My Diary in India in the Year 1858–1859*, 2:145; Dawson, "Woman in India," 346.

23. Beeton, *Book of Household Management*, 13. Russell was a war correspondent for the London *Times* during the Crimean War, and his dispatches included an eye-witness account of the Charge of the Light Brigade.

24. Trevelyan, *Competition Wallah*, 234; Strobel, *European Women and the Second British Empire*, 13, 15; MacMillan, *Women of the Raj*, 41, 46.

25. Ibid., 35, 41; Paget, *Camp and Cantonment*, 102; Sherwood, *Life and Times of Mrs. Sherwood*, 313; Fane, *Miss Fane in India*, 80–81.

26. Roberts, *Scenes*, 2:264–67. Emphasis is in the original. For other examples of obligatory and dull dinner parties, see Parkes, *Wanderings*, 306; Eden, *Up the Country*, 17; Fane, *Miss Fane in India*, 79, 182.

27. Roberts, *Scenes*, 2:268.

28. Ibid., 268–69.

29. Wells, Letters to her Father, 118–19.

30. Stierstorfer, *Women Writing Home*, 4:51; Duberly, *Mrs Duberly's War*, 212, 214, 216, 300. Annie was the wife of Captain William Forrest of the 11th Light Dragoons. According to Christine Kelly, Frances's dislike centered on William's strong personality and promotion prospects. Emphasis in the original.

31. Coffman, *Old Army*, 294, 327; Wooster, *Soldiers, Sutlers, and Settlers*, 182; Myres, *Westering Women*, 186, 211–12, 269; Evans, *Born for Liberty*, 67; Welter, "The Cult of True Womanhood," 151–74; Kerber, "Separate Spheres," 10–11, 28, 31, 38–39.

32. Extract from "A Lady's Account of Army Life in the Far West," *Frank Leslie's Popular Monthly* 25 (Jan. to June 1888): 187; Biddle, *Reminiscences*, 222–24. Emphasis is in the original.

33. Fougera, *With Custer's Cavalry*, 220; Stallard, *Glittering Misery*, 64; Tytler, *An Englishwoman in India*, 32–33. For a report of the ladies' Christmas entertainments, see *Army and Navy Journal*, 7 January 1888. Three officers' wives included details of their participation in a buffalo hunt; see Fougera, *With Custer's Cavalry*, 144–57, Roe, *Army Letters*, 13–15, and Pohanka, "A Summer on the Plains, 1870: From the Diary of Annie Gibson Roberts," 22, 34; Heitman, *Historical Register*, 1:1065. Elizabeth Custer attended a Cheyenne Indian Council by invitation, see Custer, *Following the Guidon*, 100–102, and Caroline Winne sat with the officers as they negotiated with Sitting Bull and other Lakota Sioux chieftains. Mrs. Winne gave her opinion of the proceedings as, "I do pity these poor wretches, for they are all deceitful." She added, however, "[T]here is no doubt they are dreadfully imposed upon and cheated by the Indian agents and traders. They don't get half that the Govt. sends them, and they are as poor as poverty itself." See Buecker, "Letters of Caroline Frey Winne," 9–10. Frances Boyd and Lydia Lane both found Mexican bullfights tiresome. Mrs. Boyd expressed her disapproval with: "To American onlookers it seemed a cruel sport, unworthy of its historic greatness." See Boyd, *Cavalry Life*, 157, 288–89, and Lane, *I Married a Soldier*, 23–24, 102, 120. On the day she recorded her complaint Mrs. Lane described offering the hospitality of her home at Fort Inge to three ungrateful "citizens," a "young German baron," and "a Texas Ranger, Captain Walker . . . who was employed by the government to look after the Indians on the Western frontier." It is possible that Mrs. Lane entertained Capt. Samuel Walker, who collaborated with Samuel Colt to produce the Colt Walker revolver. Emphasis is in the original.

34. Carrington, *My Army Life*, 239, 236, 238–39; Coker, *News from Brownsville*, xviii, 9, 13–14, 26; Heitman, *Historical Register*, 1:355, 557. Following Taylor's military successes in the Mexican American War, Col. William Davenport commanded an occupying force that remained in Matamoros to enforce martial law. Captain Chapman acted as the assistant quartermaster in this Mexican city. Although Mrs. Chapman described Major Hunter as completely feminized, he was commander of the Department of the South during the American Civil War. His General Order No. 11, issued in 1862, freed the slaves in Florida, Georgia, and South Carolina. President Abraham Lincoln, fearing a political backlash from the border states, quickly rescinded the order. See Miller, *Lincoln's Abolitionist General*. Emphasis is in the original.

35. Haggis, "Gendering Colonialism or Colonising Gender," 105.

36. Ricketts, "English Society in India," 684–85, 688. For an officer's wife's comments on returning children to England to attend boarding school, see Tytler, *An Englishwoman in India*, 21. Ricketts flags an important point. The military community in India was an artificial society as children, on reaching a certain age, returned to attend boarding schools in England, and most men upon retirement also returned home.

37. Duncan, *The Simple Adventures of a Memsahib*, vii, 112–14; Allen, *Plain Tales*, 212–14. In the introduction to Duncan's novel, Tausky catalogues the works that cast the *memsahib*

in her three roles. With regard to typecasting as a villain, see Kipling, *Plain Tales from the Hills*, 14–18, 53–59, 92–97, 118–23, 148–54, 163–67, 224–29; Forster, *A Passage to India*, 11, 214. According to David Cannadine, critics consisted of "non-official British inhabitants of Calcutta, Madras, and other commercial centers, who resented the power and snobbery" of the official imperial set. For a discussion on scholarly critics, see Chaudhuri and Strobel, "Introduction," in *Western Women and Imperialism*, 3–4. Interpretations of the *memsahibs'* attitudes as racist and frivolous include: Spear, *The Nabobs*; Stanford, *Ladies in the Sun*; Nadis, "Evolution of the Sahibs." Accounts that temper this stereotype includes: Kennedy, *The Magic Mountains*, 125–29; Edwardes, *Bound to Exile*, 173–85; Moorhouse, *India Britannica*, 121–23; Ghose, "The Memsahib Myth,", 107–28; Callaway, *Gender, Culture and Empire*, 3–30; Strobel, *European Women and the Second British Empire*, 1–15; Knapman, *White Women of Fiji*, 4–18, 175. In her analysis of the hero and villain *memsahib* stereotypes, Knapman asserts that such categorizing reveals "more about the values of the authors, and the pervasive values of our society, than about the attitudes and behavior of men and women in multi-racial societies."

38. Ricketts, "English Society in India," 683; Prinsep, *Imperial India*, 262, 267. Prinsep was a nineteenth-century Royal Academy artist touring India. The term "muffin" is Canadian slang for a woman who accompanies the same male to all social occasions. Emphasis is in the original.

39. Edwardes, *Bound to Exile*, 173; Francis Adams, "Rudyard Kipling," *Fortnightly Review* 56 (January–December 1891): 692; Buck, *Simla Past and Present*, 174. The *Fortnightly Review*, a highly popular and influential British magazine, ran during the years 1865–1954. It reacted to partisan journalism and was the first journal to use contributors' names instead of pseudonyms. See Turner, "Hybrid Journalism," 72–90.

40. Marryat, *"Gup,"* 38–39. Procida, *Married to the Empire*, 81. Procida offers the following observation regarding the character assassination of military wives in India: "The problem with the memsahib, according to her many critics, was that she was both spoiled and lazy . . . and revelled in her status as the 'Colonel's lady.'"

41. Miller, "Foragers, Army Women, and Prostitutes," 142; Greene, *Ladies and Officers of the United States Army, or American Aristocracy*, 4, 16, 27–28; Heitman, *Historical Register*, 1:474. Greene, according to Edward Coffman, was forced to resign on 31 December 1877 following several instances of questionable behavior. Charges included an alleged seduction of, and adultery with, a fellow officer's spouse. See Coffman, *Old Army*, 284–85.

42. Greene, *American Aristocracy*, 31–32, 34, 38–39, 61–63. Emphasis is in the original.

43. Custer, *Tenting on the Plains*, 176–77.

44. Annie Getty to Anna (last name unknown), 4 October 1868, Gibson-Getty-McClure Family Papers, Box 5; Greene, *American Aristocracy*, 76, 80; Heitman, *Historical Register*, 1:452, 657. The lady who "held court" in her bedroom probably remained at her husband's permanent post while he was on detached duty. Greene likens the unconventional officer's spouse to the French Enlightenment salon host Madame de Staël, who actively engaged in supposed subversive political and philosophical discourse, so much so that Napoleon Bonaparte ordered her to be kept under surveillance.

45. Allgor, *Parlor Politics*, 120–21.

46. Callaway, *Gender, Culture, and Empire*, 3–29, 227–41; Allen, *Raj: A Scrapbook of British India, 1877–1947*, 18. Callaway examines the enduring claim that white women, as racists and isolationists, caused the ruin of the British empire. This representation evolved from novels and popular media as confirmed by Allen, who reports, "It has often been said that all the worst faults of the Raj—its petty intolerance, its prejudices and snobberies, its cold-hearted arrogance—stemmed from the memsahib."

Chapter 8. Imperial Intimacy

Epigraph: Marryat, *"Gup," Sketches of Anglo-Indian Life and Character*, 35.

1. Diver, *Honoria Lawrence*, 119; Russell, *My Diary*, 59; Aitken, *Behind the Bungalow*, 5–6; Graham, *Journal*, 139. Edward Aitken served as a customs and salt duties collector in Bombay. John Bull, a jolly, rotund, middle-aged country farmer, wearing a waistcoat, breeches, and frockcoat, is a personification of the English nation. First created by Dr. John Arbuthnot in 1712, this symbolic middle-class male is still visible in twenty-first century popular culture.
2. Roe, *Army Letters*, 3646–6.
3. Patterson, *The Cult of Imperial Honor in British India*, 167–207.
4. López, "The Making of Race, Sex, and Empire,", 52, 54–55; Procida, *Married to the Empire*, 87, 91. Procida examines imperialism through the female experience within the home, while Patterson's focus analyzes issues of honor and masculinity.
5. Procida, *Married to the Empire*, 82, 84, 90; Davidoff, Doolittle, et al., *The Family Story*, 28; Usami, "Change in the Workforce in British India, 1881–1921," http://www .helsinki.fi/iehc2006/papers1/usami.pdf. Imperial governance in India rested on gaining the respect of the indigenous peoples through cooperation, order, and discipline. This prohibited interference in social and cultural customs, thus women could not participate in formal philanthropic efforts. Charitable aid could only be offered to female staff, female relatives, and children.
6. Steel, *Complete Indian Housekeeping*, 2, 3, 31–82; Starr, *The Colonel's Lady*, 24; Chota Mem, *The English Bride in India*, 54–86, 96–97; Farwell, *Armies of the Raj*, 98; Forster, *Passage to India*, 42.
7. Steel, *Complete Indian Housekeeping*, 3; Marryat, *"Gup,"* 55. Emphasis is in the original. Urdu and Hindi are both Indic languages and mutually intelligible. They share grammar and phonology and are often considered one language.
8. Procida, *Married to the Empire*, 84–85; Fane, *Miss Fane in India*, 101. For complete listings of servant titles, pay scales, and duties, see Steel, *Complete Indian Housekeeping*, 31–32. The caste system is a vast and extremely intricate subject, with its origins in the civilizations of ancient India. In brief, status relies on the Hindu concept of karma (a belief that acts and deeds performed in a previous life determined one's current caste placement). The ancient Hindu epic *The Mahabharata* contains an explanation of the origins of the caste system. Essentially, there are four *Varnas* with color, occupation, and power associations: *Brahmin*, white (priests), prestige; *Kshatriyas*, red (kings, warriors), political; *Vaishyas*, brown (farmers, merchants), economic; and *Shudras*,

black (artisans, laborers), service. A fifth group, the *Dalits* (untouchables), deals with tasks associated with the dead, such as human funerals, working with leather, and other "unclean" occupations. The *Mlechcha*, a sixth caste, is comprised of foreigners, whose occupation defines admission into one of the *Varnas*. Belonging to a certain caste is further divided along professional, cultural, locational, and linguistic lines as sub-castes (*jatis*). Intermarriage is forbidden, but flexibility exists if a *jati* introduces an economic diversity that places it within another category. Some districts reporting in the 1891 Census included caste classification. One researcher estimated that if each presidency, princely state, and province accurately recorded this information, the number of *jatis* would range from 300,000 to 500,000. For a discussion of caste as sacred law, see Müller, *The Sacred Books of the East*, vol. 25, *The Laws of Manu*. For a discussion on number of castes and *jatis*, see "Census of India 1881–1931," http://www.samanvaya.com/main/contentframes/knowledge/articles/census1881.html.

9. Fenton, *Journal of Mrs Fenton*, 70; Parkes, *Wanderings*, 35. Emphasis is in the original. For further examples of officers' wives' lengthy reports of their household servants, see Fane, *Miss Fane in India*, 101–2; Roberts, *Scenes*, 1:62–71; Graham, *Journal*, 29–31; Guthrie, *My Years in an Indian Fort*, 1:242–52.

10. Fay, *Original Letters*, 144–45.

11. Guthrie, *My Year in an Indian Fort*, 11, 243–44; Fenton, *Journal of Mrs Fenton*, 15–16. Emphasis is in the original.

12. Roberts, *Scenes*, 1:69–70.

13. Ashmore, *Narrative of a Three Month's March*, 47; Blackwood, *Our Viceregal Life in India*, 2:8, 15–16.

14. Fougera, *With Custer's Cavalry*, 67, 145–46; Heitman, *Historical Register*, 1:669. Fougera joined her sister Mollie, the wife of Lt. Donald McIntosh of the Seventh U.S. Cavalry, at Fort Abraham Lincoln, in 1875. Katherine married Lt. Frank Gibson within weeks of her arrival. Emphasis is in the original.

15. Smith, *View from Officers' Row*, 4, 27; Myres, "Army Women's Narratives," 197; Myres, *Westering Women*, 80, 85; Butler, *Daughters of Joy, Sisters of Misery*, 125; Eales, *Army Wives on the Frontier*, 56, 129.

16. Custer, *Following the Guidon*, 227–28; Vielé, *Following the Drum*, 130–2. All emphases are in the original.

17. Buecker, "Letters of Caroline Frey Winne," 5: Stallard, *Fanny Dunbar Corbusier*, 135–36.

18. Boyd, *Cavalry Life*, 255–60.

19. Carrington, *My Army Life*, 159.

20. For an example of northern prejudice held against African Americans, see Taylor, *The Forging of a Black Community*.

21. Myres, "Army Women's Narratives," 197; Stallard, *Glittering Misery*, 61; Myres, *Westering Women*, 80, 85; Foote, *Women of the New Mexico Frontier 1846–1912*, xvi, xviii, 30–32, 46–48; Eales, *Army Wives on the Frontier*, 1363–67; Vielé, *Following the Drum*, 155, 180–82, 187; Summerhayes, *Vanished Arizona*, 106–7, 111–12, 157–58; Kimball, *My Eighty Years*, 23, 40. For additional examples of the women's attitudes toward their Mexican servants, see Boyd, *Cavalry Life*, 223–24; Lane, *I Married a Soldier*, 47, 82–83, 157–58, 163.

22. Custer, *Boots and Saddles*, 197–204. Mrs. Custer advised that the laundress retained her first husband's surname of Nash.

23. Fougera, *With Custer's Cavalry*, 190–93, 222–24; Custer, *Boots and Saddles*, 198, 202.

24. Custer, *Boots and Saddles*, 198, 200; Heitman, *Historical Register*, 1:348; Boag, *Re-Dressing America's Frontier Past*, 144, 146–47, 157. For a full discussion of the national association of male-to-female cross-dressers with nonwhite/non Anglo races, see pages 130–58.

25. Lane, *I Married a Soldier*, 13, 74, 193.

26. Biddle, *A Soldier's Wife*, 82–83; Dyer, *Fort Reno*, 106.

27. Russell, *Land of Enchantment*, 120–21, 154. Mrs. Russell indicated that the Mexican government encouraged the enslavement of the Navajo Indians.

28. Mattes, *Indians, Infants, and Infantry*, 2, 3, 228; Summerhayes, *Vanished Arizona*, 162. Southern California vineyards produced (and are still manufacturing today) Cucamonga table and dessert wines.

29. McKay, *Little Pills*, 47, 50–51; Heitman, *Historical Register*, 1:911. The McKays were stationed at Fort Sill, 1870–71. Mrs. Spencer's husband was Lt. Thomas J. Spencer of the Tenth U.S. Cavalry.

30. Baldwin, *Memoirs*, 20, 165, 167. Mrs. Baldwin came into contact with the Lakota Sioux and Crow Indians at Fort Keogh, and the Navajo at Fort Wingate. Scholars have argued that officers' wives' views reflected the army's categorization of American Indians as either hostile or friendly. The Lakota Sioux for whom Mrs. Baldwin expressed sympathy, however, boasted leaders such as Sitting Bull, Red Cloud, and Crazy Horse, warriors who played active roles in the Great Sioux War of 1876–77. Her encounter with Largho and the Navajo women occurred shortly after her daughter Juanita's birth in 1867. The Navajo tribe, under the leadership of Barboncito, had recently agreed to relocate to the Bosque Redondo reservation. Fort Wingate, located on the south edge of the Navajo territory, acted as a staging point for the "Long Walk [450 miles]." In neither encounter did Alice Baldwin express disdain, fear, or even discomfort in her interactions with the "hostile" Lakota Sioux, or the "friendly" Navajo.

31. Smith, *View from Officers' Row*, 4, 6, 12, 182–84; Riley, *Confronting Race*, 173–211.

32. Biddle, *Reminiscences*, 174, 176–79.

33. Roe, *Army Letters*, 108–9, 128; Heitman, *Historical Register*, 1:322. Mrs. Conrad's husband, although Roe has not provided his first name or his company, appears to be Capt. Casper H. Conrad of the Fifteenth U.S. Infantry. In her narrative Roe attempted to phonetically record the Chinese servants' comments.

34. Roe, *Army Letters*, 132, 135–36. Boston brown bread was made with rye flour and raisins and normally steamed in a coffee can.

35. Ibid., 138, 152, 162, 164, 184. The term "highbinder" referred to a dangerous criminal or assassin in the immigrant Chinese community.

36. Roberts, *Scenes*, 1:70–71. Griselda is a character of great patience, sincerity, and loyalty in "The Tenth Day, Novel Ten" in Giovanni Boccaccio's *The Decameron*, 783–97. Written in the fourteenth century, this collection of tales, told by a group of seven young women and three men, has provided structure and inspiration to authors from

the fifteenth-century protofeminist Christine de Pizan to controversial American magazine publisher Hugh Hefner.

37. Williams, *Three Years and a Half*, 3, 7–8, 19; Heitman, *Historical Register*, 1:279. Captain Battles is not listed in Heitman.

38. Shields, "Army Life on the Wyoming Frontier," 332, 336–38.

39. Spear, *Nabobs*, 53; Williamson, *East India Vade-Mecum*, 334–36; Kerr, *The Dispossessed*, 203.

40. Sherwood, *Life and Times of Mrs. Sherwood*, 235, 255–56; Great Britain War Office, *The Queen's Regulations*, 142–44, 315–39. Six wives of noncommissioned officers and privates for every one hundred men were "allowed to proceed with their husbands" on foreign service. For further details of the British Army practice of employing a batman (from bât-horse man, *bât* meaning packsaddle in French) as a personal servant, see Vivian, *The British Army from Within*, 155–56.

41. Sherwood, *Life and Times of Mrs. Sherwood*, 243–44.

42. Paget, *Camp and Cantonment*, 2, 188, 376–77. Emphasis is in the original.

43. Blane, *From Minnie*, 69–75; Cuthell, *My Garden in the City of Gardens*, 209–10. Verification of Mrs. Cuthell's marriage to Lieutenant Colonel Thomas G. Cuthell was included in her obituary featured in the (London) *Times*, 2 February 1929. Emphasis is in the original.

44. Ashmore, *Narrative of a Three Month's March*, 101, 164–65, 270–71. Muharram is the first month of the Islamic year. Festive sherbet provided travelers with nonalcoholic refreshment made with roseships, cherries, and spices.

45. Fenton, *Journal of Mrs Fenton*, 58–59. Emphasis is in the original.

46. Blackburn, "Army Families in Frontier Forts," 22; Custer, *Boots and Saddles*, 195.

47. Ibid., 197; Boyd, *Cavalry Life*, 190, 192–94; Lane, *I Married a Soldier*, 154–55.

48. Fougera, *With Custer's Cavalry*, 96; Carrington, *My Army Life*, 198–99.

49. Buecker, "Letters of Caroline Frey Winne," 13, 18–19, 36; Heitman, *Historical Register*, 1:150.

50. Kimball, *My Eighty Years*, 27, 38–39, 51–57; Heitman, *Historical Register*, 1:598. Transvaal, a province of South Africa, existed during the period 1910–94. Marjorie Duncombe's English husband was a baker who enlisted in the American army, thus he satisfied her penchant for a tradesman as a marriage partner.

51. Anderson, "An Army Wife Among the Sioux," 73–75; Williams, "Servants at Military Posts," 145–46, 152–53; Heitman, *Historical Register*, 1:835; Wooster, *Soldiers, Sutlers, and Settlers*, 75. Williams advises that the etymology of the term "striker" "appears lost in antiquity," but suggests the moniker originated with "to strike a tent," a routine duty for an enlisted man.

52. Coffman, *Old Army*, 347; Stallard, *Glittering Misery*, 29; Mattes, *Indians, Infants, and Infantry*, 142; Mattison, "An Army Wife on the Upper Missouri," 214; Fisher, "Forrestine Cooper Hooker's Notes and Memoirs on Army Life in the West, 1871–1876," 10, 38, 41–42, 107–10; Baldwin, *Memoirs of the Late Frank D. Baldwin*, 122–23, 128–29.

53. Fougera, *With Custer's Cavalry*, 75; McConnell, *Five Years a Cavalryman*, 12; Stallard, *Glittering Misery*, 29; Custer, *Following the Guidon*, 286–7; Stallard, *Fanny Dunbar*

Corbusier, 83; Spring, "An Army Wife Comes West," 266; Heitman, *Historical Register*, 2:90.

54. Utley, *Life in Custer's Cavalry*, 132, 134; Boyd, *Cavalry Life*, vii, 47–49, 76; Summerhayes, *Vanished Arizona*, 100, 108–9,163, 201–2; Heitman, *Historical Register*, 1:193.

55. Myres, *Cavalry Wife*, 353–56, 38–39, 56–57; Roe, *Army Letters*, 285–88: Roe's Chinese cook had every reason to fear for his mistress's life. Volmer had allegedly shot and killed an army deserter.

56. Wooster, *Soldiers, Sutlers, and Settlers*, 64, 82; Butler, *Daughters of Joy*, 125–26; Coffman, "Women and Children in the Army, 1784–1812," 38; Nye, *Carbine and Lance*, 277, 281.

57. Strobel, *European Women*, 25–27. For a discussion of the British Ladies Female Emigrant Society, see Olson and Shadle et al., *Historical Dictionary of the British Empire*, 189–90. Working in the sex industry has also been offered as an alternative means of survival for a working-class female. Prostitution in India and the U.S. West, however, falls outside the remit of this project. For a discussion of the family role of British soldiers' wives who traveled with their husbands, their employment opportunities, and the connection between marriage regulations and prostitution, see Trustram, *Women of the Regiment*, 68–137. For a discussion of Victorian prostitution, see Walkowitz, *Prostitution and Victorian Society*.

Chapter 9. Conclusion

Epigraph: Greene, *American Aristocracy*, 61, 75. Egeria, a Celtic woman, who in 381–84 C.E. pilgrimaged from Galicia to the Holy Land, recorded her journey in a letter. This is possibly the first formal writing of its kind in the known Western world. "Oracles" in this statement indicates sage authoritative opinions.

1. Eden, *Letters*, 2:247–48, 260–61.

2. Kramer, "Power and Connection," 1381.

3. Summerhayes, *Vanished Arizona*, 270.

4. *Calcutta Review*, July–December 1845; Ashmore, *Narrative of a Three Months' March*, 2–5.

5. Custer, *Boots and Saddles*, 129–30; Mattison, "An Army Wife on the Upper Missouri," 192–93, 197, 217; Lawrence, *Journals*, 224, 226.

6. Nicolson, *Mary Curzon*, 158; Greenberger, *The British Image of India*, 11, 13, 15, 19; Strobel, *European Women*, 13, 15; Stoddard, "The Army Officer's Wife," 153–57.

7. Summerhayes, *Vanishing Arizona*, 158, 192.

8. Patterson, *Cult of Imperial Honor*, 173.

9. Reeder, *Born at Reveille*, 15.

Bibliography

Manuscript Collections

Asia, Pacific, and Africa Collections, British Library, UK

Chota Mem (Mrs. C. Lang). *The English Bride in India, Being Hints on Indian House-keeping.* London: Luzac and Co., 1909. Rich Papers, Mss Eur C403/ T35558.

Clemons, Mrs. Major. *The Manners and Customs of Society in India.* London: Smith, Elder and Company, 1841. Oriental Collections T 35687.

Drummond, Ellen Thornhill. "Letters from Ellen Drummond in Allahabad and Sialkot." Mss Eur B298/15.

Gray, Ruby. Untitled. Undated. Unpublished Memoir. Mss Eur D1037/11.

Haldane, Julia. *The Story of Our Escape from Delhi in 1857.* Agra: Brown and Sons, 1888. 10602.c.26(3.)

Wagontreiber, Miss. *The Story of Our Escape from Delhi in May, etc.* Delhi: Imperial Medical Hall Press, 1857. 9008.c.33(3.)

Wonnacott Collection. Mss Eur 376/3.

Centre of South Asian Studies, Cambridge, UK

Churcher, Mrs. Madeleine Amy. Papers, 1904–1905.

Grant (née Harvey), Lucy Elinor Lyall. Papers, 1906–1909.

Hammersley-Smith, Magda. "A Great Grandmother Remembers."

Hannay, Margaret Campbell. Journal, 1829; Papers, 1839.

Huxham, Mrs. A. E. "Diary of the Mutiny." 1857–1858.

Jackson, Anna Madeline. "A Personal Narrative of the Indian Mutiny, 1857."

Mill, Maria. "Diary of the Mutiny, 1857–1858."

Murison, Margaret. "Memoir: For Lucinda and Susanna by their Great Grandmother."

Showers-Stirling, Mrs. Christian. "Notes on her Life."

Stock, Catherine Ann. Papers, 1854–1870.

Wells, Frances Janet. Berners Papers, 1853–1858.

Library of Congress, Washington, D.C.

Gibson-Getty-McClure Family Papers.

Missouri Historical Society Archives, St. Louis
    William T. Sherman Collection.
National Archives and Records Administration, Washington, D.C.
    Records of U.S. Army Continental Commands, 1821–1920. Letters Received by
        Headquarters, District of New Mexico, Sept. 1865–Aug. 1890. RG 393, M-1088,
        rolls 29, 30, and 31.
National Army Museum, Templer Study Centre, London, UK
    Clowes, William. *A List of the Officers of the Army and Royal Marines, on Full, Retired,
        and Half Pay.* London: War Office, 1945.
    Hodson, Major V. C. P. Biographical Index of Indian Army Officers. Card index
    compiled by Major Hodson consisting of biographical and service data (typescript
    and manuscript notes and extracts) on the origins and services of military, naval,
    and civilian personnel in India, 1758–1947. Archives: 1964-04-69.
U. S. Military History Institute, U.S. Army War College, Carlisle Barracks, Pennsylvania
    Paulding, Grace. "My Army Life." Paulding Papers.

Periodicals

Amherst Bulletin
Calcutta Review
Frank Leslie's Popular Monthly
Household Words. A Weekly Journal conducted by Charles Dickens
Journal of the Bombay Branch of the Royal Asiatic Society
New York Times
The Fortnightly Review
The Telegraph, Calcutta
The United Service Journal and Naval and Military Magazine
Times (London)

United Kingdom Government Publications

Great Britain War Office. *Manual of Military Law.* London: Her Majesty's Stationery
    Office (HMSO), 1894.
———. *The Queen's Regulations and Orders for the Army.* London: Adjutant-General's
    Office, Horse Guards, 1844.
Parliamentary Debates. 3rd ser., vol. 180 (1865).
*Report of the Commissioners Appointed to Inquire into the Sanitary State of the Army in
    India.* Vol. 21. London: HMSO, 1863.
*Report of the Commissioners Appointed to Inquire into the Sanitary State of the Army in
    India.* Vol. 20. London: HMSO, 1864.
Army Medical Department Reports for the Year 1871. Vol. 13. London: HMSO, 1873.
Horse Guards War Office. *Dress Regulations for the Officers of the Army.* London: HMSO, 1883.

United States Government Publications

Heitman, Francis. *Historical Register and Dictionary of the United States Army.* 2 vols. Washington, D.C.: Government Printing Office, 1903.

Surgeon General's Office. *Circular Number 4, A Report of Barracks and Hospitals with Descriptions of Military Posts, 1870.* Washington: Government Printing Office, 1870.

U.S. Congress. Statutes at Large. *An Act to Increase and Fix the Military Peace Establishment of the United States.* 39th Congress, 1st sess., Vol. 14, Chapter 299, 1866. http://memory.loc.gov/cgi-bin/ampage?collId=llsb&fileName=039/llsb039.db&recNum=1059

Contemporary Works

Adams, Francis. "Rudyard Kipling." *Fortnightly Review* 56 (January–December 1891): 686–700.

Aitken, Edward H. *Behind the Bungalow.* Calcutta: Thacker, Spink, 1920.

Allen, Charles, ed. *Plain Tales from the Raj.* London: Futura Publications, 1975.

———. *Raj: A Scrapbook of British India, 1877–1947.* New York: St. Martin's Press, 1877.

Anderson, Harry H. "An Army Wife among the Sioux: The Experiences of Mrs. Cyrus S. Roberts at Cheyenne River Autonomy, Dakota Territory, 1872–73." *The Westerners Brand Book* 10 (December 1949): 73–80.

Anonymous. *Anglo India: Social, Moral, and Political, Being a Collection of Papers from the Asiatic Journal.* Vol. 1. London: William H. Allen, 1838.

Anonymous. *How to Behave: A Pocket Manual of Etiquette and Guide to Correct Personal Habits.* Glasgow: John S. Marr, 1904.

Anonymous. *The Shilling Song Book: A Collection of 175 of the Most Favorite National, Patriotic, Sentimental, and Comic Ballads of the Day.* Niagara Falls: W. E. Tunis, 1860.

Ashmore, Harriette. *A Narrative of a Three Months' March in India; and a Residence in the Doob.* London: R. Hastings, 1841.

Baldwin, Alice Blackwood. *Memoirs of Major General Frank D. Baldwin.* Los Angeles: Wetzel, 1929.

Bartrum, Katherine M. *A Widow's Reminiscences of Lucknow.* London: James Nisbet, 1918.

Beecher, Catharine E. *A Treatise on Domestic Economy: For the Use of Young Ladies at Home and at School.* New York: Harper and Brothers, 1849.

Beecher, Catharine E., and Harriet B. Stowe. *The American Woman's Home: Or, Principles of Domestic Science.* New York: J. B. Ford, 1869.

Beeton, Isabella M. *The Book of Household Management.* London: S. O. Beeton, 1863.

Bellew, Captain Francis J. *Memoirs of a Griffin; or, A Cadet's First Year in India.* London: Woodfall and Kinder, 1843. Reprint, London: William H. Allen, 1880.

Biddle, Ellen McGowan. *Reminiscences of a Soldier's Wife.* Philadelphia: J. B. Lippincott, 1907.

Bird, Isabella Lucy. *A Lady's Life in the Rocky Mountains.* New York: G. P. Putnam's Sons, 1879.

Blackwood, Harriot Georgina Rowan-Hamilton, Lady Dufferin. *Our Viceregal Life in India: Selections from My Journal.* Vol. 2. London: John Murray, 1889.

Blane, Minnie. *From Minnie with Love: The Letters of a Victorian Lady 1849–1861.* Edited by Jane Vansittart. London: Peter Davies, 1973.

Boccaccio, Giovanni. *The Decameron.* Translated by G. H. McWilliam. 2nd ed. London: Penguin Books, 1995.

Bourke, John G. *On the Border with Crook.* 2nd ed. New York: Scribner's Sons, 1892.

Boyd, Mrs. Frances Anne Mullen. *Cavalry Life in Tent and Field.* New York: J. Selwin Tait and Sons, 1894.

Buchan, John. *A Lodge in the Wilderness.* London: Blackwood and Sons, 1906.

Buck, Sir Edward J. *Simla Past and Present.* Calcutta: Thacker, Spink, 1904.

Buckland, Charles E. *Sketches of Social Life in India.* London: W. H. Allen, 1884.

Buecker, Thomas R., ed. "Letters of Caroline Frey Winne from Sidney Barracks and Fort McPherson, Nebraska, 1874–1878." *Nebraska History* 62 (Spring 1981): 1–46.

Burke, Bernard. *The Book of Precedence.* London: Harrison, 1881.

Burton, Sir Richard F. *The City of Saints and across the Rocky Mountains to California.* New York: Harper and Brothers, 1892. Reprint, Niwot: University of Colorado Press, 1990.

Busteed, Henry E. *Echoes from Old Calcutta, Being Chiefly Reminiscences of the Days of Warren Hasting, Francis, and Impey.* London: Thacker, Spink, 1908.

Carrington, Frances C. *My Army Life and the Fort Phil Kearney Massacre.* Philadelphia: J. B. Lippincott, 1911.

Carrington, Margaret. *AB-SA-RA-KA, Land of Massacre: Being the Experience of an Officer's Wife on the Plains. With an Outline of Indian Operations and Conferences from 1865 to 1879.* Philadelphia: J. B. Lippincott, 1879.

Chatelain, Heli, ed. *Folk Tales of Angola.* New York: American Folk Lore Society, 1894.

Clemons, Mrs. Major. *The Manners and Customs of Society in India.* London: Smith, Elder, 1841.

Cochran, Mrs. M. A. *Posie; or, From Reveille to Retreat, An Army Story.* Cincinnati: Tobert Clarke, 1896.

Coker, Caleb, ed. *The News from Brownsville: Helen Chapman's Letters from the Texas Military Frontier, 1848–1852.* Austin: Texas State Historical Association, 1992.

Colburn, Henry. *Colburn's United Service Magazine and Naval and Military Journal, 1844.* Part One. London, 1844.

Curzon, Mary. *Lady Curzon's India: Letters of a Vicereine.* Edited by John Bradley. New York: Beaufort Books, 1985.

Custer, Elizabeth B. *Boots and Saddles.* New York: Harper and Brothers, 1885. Reprint, Williamstown, Mass.: Corner House Publishers, 1969.

———. *Following the Guidon.* 1869. Reprint, Norman: University of Oklahoma Press, 1966.

———. *Tenting on the Plains.* 3 vols. 1887. Reprint, Norman: University of Oklahoma Press, 1966.

Custer, George Armstrong. *My Life on the Plains; or, Personal Experiences with Indians.* Norman: University of Oklahoma Press, 1976.

Cuthell, Edith E. *My Garden in the City of Gardens: A Memory with Illustrations.* London: John Lane, 1905.

Davis, Britton. *The Truth about Geronimo.* New Haven: Yale University Press, 1929.

Dawson, J. E. "Woman in India: Her Influence and Position." *Calcutta Review* 83 (July 1886): 346–370.

Dickens, Charles. *Dealings with the Firm of Dombey and Son, Wholesale, Retail and for Exportation.* London: Bradbury and Evans, 1848. Reprint, London: Macmillan, 1900.

Diver, Maud. *The Englishwoman in India.* London: William Blackwood and Sons, 1909.

———. *Honoria Lawrence: A Fragment of Indian History.* Boston: Houghton and Mifflin, 1936.

Duberly, Frances I. L. *Campaigning Experiences in Central India and the Rajputana during the Suppression of the Mutiny.* London: Smith, Elder, 1859.

———. *Mrs Duberly's War: Journal and Letters from the Crimea.* Edited by Christine Kelly. Oxford: Oxford University Press, 2011.

———. *Suppression of Mutiny, 1857–1858.* New Delhi: Sirjana Press, 1974.

Duncan, Sarah J. *The Simple Adventures of a Memsahib.* Edited by Thomas E. Tausky. Ottawa: Tecumseh Press, 1986.

Dyer, Mrs. D. B. *"Fort Reno"; or, Picturesque "Cheyenne and Arrapahoe Army Life," before the Opening of Oklahoma.* New York: G. W. Dillingham, 1896.

Eden, Emily. *Letters from India.* Vols. 1 and 2. Edited by Eleanor Eden. London: Richard Bentley and Son, 1872.

———. *Up the Country: Letters Written to her Sister from the Upper Provinces of India.* London: Richard Bentley and Son, 1866.

Ellis, Sarah S. *The Prose Work of Mrs. Ellis.* Vol. 1. New York: Henry G. Langley, 1844.

Fane, Isabella. *Miss Fane in India.* Edited by John Pemble. Gloucester: Alan Sutton Publishing, 1985.

Fay, Mrs. Eliza. *Original Letters from India, 1779–1815.* Calcutta: Thacker, Spink, 1908.

Fenton, Bessie. *The Journal of Mrs Fenton, 1826–1830.* London: Edward Arnold, 1901.

Flipper, Henry O. *Negro Frontiersman: The Western Memoirs of Henry O. Flipper, First Negro Graduate of West Point.* Edited by Theodore D. Harris. El Paso: Western Press, 1963.

Forbes, Archibald. "The United States Army." *North American Review* 135 (August 1882): 127–45.

Forster, Edward M. *A Passage to India.* New York: Harcourt, Brace and World, 1924.

Fortescue, John W. *A History of the British Army.* Vol. 11. London: Macmillan, 1910.

Fougera, Katherine Gibson. *With Custer's Cavalry.* Idaho: Caxton Printers, 1940. Reprint, Lincoln: University of Nebraska Press, 1986.

Fraser, Lovat. *At Delhi.* Bombay: The Times of India Press, 1903. http://www.archive.org/stream/atdelhifrasoofras#page/178/mode/2up.

Fry, Colonel James B. *Military Miscellanies.* New York: Brentano's, 1889.

Glisan, Rodney. *Journal of Army Life.* San Francisco: A. L. Bancroft, 1874.

Graham, Mrs. Maria. *Journal of a Residence in India.* Edinburgh: Archibald Constable, 1812.

Greene, Duane M. *Ladies and Officers of the United States Army, or American Aristocracy, a Sketch of the Social Life and Character of the Army.* Chicago: Central Publishing, 1880.

Guggisburg, Captain F. G. *"The Shop," the Story of the Royal Military Academy.* 2nd ed. London: Cassell, 1902.

Guthrie, Katherine B. *My Years in an Indian Fort.* Vol. 1. London: Hurst and Blackett, 1877.

Hart, Major H. G. *The New Annual Army List for 1850.* Vol. 11. London: John Murray, 1850.

———. *The New Annual Army List, and Militia List for 1862.* Vol. 23. London: John Murray, 1862.

Hart, Colonel H. G. *The New Annual Army List, and Militia List for 1869.* Vol. 30. London: John Murray, 1869. http://www.archive.org/stream/newannualarmylis1869hart#page/n9/mode/2up.

Hart, Lieutenant-Colonel H. G. *The New Annual Army List, Militia List, and Yeoman Cavalry List for 1903.* Vol. 64. London: John Murray, 1903. https://archive.org/details/hartsannualarmyl1903lond.

Hervey, Albert. *A Soldier of the Company: Life of an Indian Ensign, 1833–1843.* Edited by Charles Allen. London: Michael Joseph, 1988.

Hood, John Bell. *Advance and Retreat: Personal Experiences of Life in the United States and Confederate States Army.* New Orleans: Hood Orphan Fund, 1880.

Hooker, Forrestine C. *Child of the Fighting Tenth.* Edited by S. Wilson. Oxford: Oxford University Press, 2003.

Houstoun, Matilda C. *Texas and the Gulf of Mexico; or Yachting in the New World.* Vol. 1. London: John Murray, 1844.

Huggins, William. *Sketches in India.* London: John Letts, 1824.

Johnson, James. *The Influence of Tropical Climates; More Especially, the Climate of India.* London: J. Callow, 1815.

Jones, Alan, ed. *An Enchanted Journey: The Letters of the Philadelphian Wife of a British Officer of the Indian Cavalry.* Durham, UK: The Pentland Press, 1994.

Jones-Parry, Sydney H. *An Old Soldier's Memories.* London: Hurst and Blackett, 1897.

Kimball, Maria Brace. *My Eighty Years.* Boston: Thomas Todd, 1934.

Kinevan, Marcos E., ed. *Frontier Cavalryman: Lieutenant John Bigelow with the Buffalo Soldiers in Texas.* El Paso: Texas Western Press, 1998.

King, C. Richard, ed. *Marion T. Brown: Letters from Fort Sill 1886–1887.* Austin, Tex.: The Encino Press, 1970.

Kipling, Rudyard. *Plain Tales from the Hills.* New York: John W. Lovell, 1889.

Lady Resident, A. *The Englishwoman in India.* London: Smith, Elder, 1864.

Lane, Lydia Spencer. *I Married a Soldier; or, Old Days in the Old Army.* 1893. Reprint, Albuquerque: Horn and Wallace, 1964.

Laurence, Mary L. *Daughter of the Regiment: Memoirs of a Childhood in the Frontier Army, 1878–1898.* Edited by Thomas T. Smith. Lincoln: University of Nebraska Press: 1966.

Lawrence, Honoria. *The Journals of Honoria Lawrence.* Edited by J. Lawrence and A. Woodiwiss. London: Hodder and Stroughton, 1980.

Leckie, Shirley Anne, ed. *The Colonel's Lady on the Western Frontier: The Correspondence of Alice Kirk Grierson.* Lincoln: University of Nebraska Press, 1989.

Lee, Celia. *Jean, Lady Hamilton, 1861–1941: A Soldier's Wife.* London: Celia Lee, 2001.

Leith-Ross, Sylvia. *Stepping Stones: Memoirs of Colonial Nigeria, 1907–1960.* Edited by Michael Crowther. London: Peter Owen, 1983.

Le Marchant, Denis. *Memoirs of the Late Major-General Le Marchant.* London: Samuel Bentley, 1841.

MacKenzie, Helen. *Life in the Mission, the Camp, and the Zenáná.* London: Richard Bentley and Son, 1854.

———. *Six Years in India. Delhi: the City of the Great Mogul.* London: Richard Bentley, 1857.

———. *Storms and Sunshine in a Soldier's Life: Lt-General Sir Colin MacKenzie, C.B., 1825–1881.* Edinburgh: David Douglas, 1884.

Mahan, Dennis H. *An Elementary Course of Civil Engineering, for the Use of Cadets of the United States' Military Academy.* New York: John Wiley and Son, 1864.

Marryat, Florence *"Gup." Sketches of Anglo-Indian Life and Character.* London: Richard Bentley and Son, 1868.

Mattes, Merrill J., ed. *Indians, Infants, and Infantry: Andrew and Elizabeth Burt on the Frontier.* Denver: Old West Publishing, 1960.

Mattison, Ray, ed. "An Army Wife on the Upper Missouri: The Diary of Sarah E. Canfield, 1866–1868." *North Dakota History* 20 (October 1953): 191–220.

McConnell, H. H. *Five Years a Cavalryman; or, Sketches of Regular Army Life on the Texas Frontier, Twenty Odd Years Ago.* Jacksboro, Tex.: J. N. Rogers, 1889. Reprint, Norman: University of Oklahoma Press, 1938.

McKay, Robert H. *Little Pills: An Army Story, by R. H. McKay . . . Being Some Experiences of a United States Army Medical Officer on the Frontier Nearly a Half Century Ago.* Pittsburg, Kans.: Headlight, 1918.

Mockler-Ferryman, Major A. F. *Annals of Sandhurst: A Chronicle of the Royal Military College.* London: William Heinemann, 1900.

Monkland, Mrs. *Life in India; or, The English at Calcutta.* Vol. 2. London: Henry Colburn, 1828.

Moore, Thomas, Lord Jeffrey, et al. *Poetical Works of Lord Byron.* New York: D. Appleton and Company, 1848.

Morton, Agnes H. *Etiquette: Good Manners for All People, Especially Those Who Dwell within the Broad Zone of the Average.* Philadelphia: Penn Publishing, 1892.

Müller, F. Max., ed. *The Sacred Books of the East.* Vol. 25. *The Laws of Manu.* Translated by George Bühler. Oxford: Clarendon Press, 1886.

Muter, Mrs. D. D. *Travels and Adventures of an Officer's Wife in India, China, and New Zealand.* 2 vols. London: Hurst and Blackett, 1864.

Myres, Sandra, ed. *Cavalry Wife: The Diary of Eveline M. Alexander, 1866–1867.* College Station: Texas A&M University Press, 1977.

Paget, Mrs. Leopold. *Camp and Cantonment: A Journal of Life in India in 1857–1859, with Some Account of the Way Thither.* London: Longman, Roberts, and Green, 1865. Reprint, London: Adamant Media Corporation, 2003.

Parkes, Frances. *Wanderings of a Pilgrim in Search of the Picturesque.* Vols. 1. and 2. London: Pelham Richardson, 1850.

Pohanka, Brian, ed. "A Summer on the Plains, 1870: From the Diary of Annie Gibson Roberts." In *Custer and his Times.* Edited by Paul Hutton. El Paso: Little Big Horn Associates, 1981.

Postans, Mrs. Marianne. *Cutch; or, Random Sketches, Taken during a Residence in One of the Northern Provinces of India; Interspersed with Legends and Traditions.* London: Smith, Elder, 1839.

Prinsep, Val C. *Imperial India: An Artist's Journal.* London: Chapman and Hall, 1879.

Reeder, Colonel. *Born at Reveille.* New York: Duell, Sloan and Pearce. 1966.

Roberts, Emma. *Scenes and Characteristics of Hindostan, with Sketches of Anglo-Indian Society.* 2 Vols. London: William H. Allen, 1835.

Roe, Frances M. A. *Army Letters from an Officer's Wife, 1871–1888.* New York: D. Appleton, 1909. Reprint, Lincoln: University of Nebraska Press, 1973.

Roland, Charles P., and Richard P. Robbins, eds. "The Second Cavalry Comes to Texas: The Diary of Eliza (Mrs. Albert Sidney) Johnson." *Southwestern Historical Quarterly* 60 (April 1957): 463–500.

Rowland, Thomas. "Letters of a Virginian Cadet at West Point," *South Atlantic Quarterly* 14, no. 3 (July 1915): 142–56.

Russell, Marian Sloan. *Land of Enchantment: Memoirs of Marian Russell along the Santa Fé Trail.* Dictated to Mrs. Hal Russell. Edited by Garnet M. Bayer. Evanston, Ill.: The Branding Iron Press, 1954.

Russell, Sir William H. *My Diary in India in the Year 1858–1859.* Vol. 2. London: Routledge, Warne, and Routledge, 1860.

Sale, Lady Florentia. *A Journal of the Disasters in Affghanistan, 1841–1842.* London: John Murray, 1844.

Sargent, Alice Applegate. *Following the Flag: Diary of a Soldier's Wife.* Kansas City: E. B. Barnett, n.d.

Schaff, Morris. *The Spirit of Old West Point.* Boston: Houghton, Mifflin, 1907.

Scott, Sir Walter. *Marmion: A Tale of Flodden Field.* Philadelphia: Henry Altemus, n.d.

Sherwood, Mrs. John. *Manners and Social Usage.* New York: Harper and Brothers, 1887.

Sherwood, Mary E. W. *Etiquette, the American Code of Manners.* London: Routledge, 1884.

Sherwood, Mary M. *The Life and Times of Mrs. Sherwood (1775–1851): From the Diaries of Captain and Mrs. Sherwood.* Edited by F. J. Harvey Darton. London: Wells Gardner, Darton, 1855.

Shields, Alice M., ed. "Army Life on the Wyoming Frontier." *Annals of Wyoming* 13, no. 4 (October, 1941): 331–344.

Spring, Agnes W., ed. "An Army Wife Comes West: Letters of Catherine Weaver Collins, 1863–1865." *Colorado Magazine* 31 (October 1954): 241–73.

Stallard, Patricia, ed. *Fanny Dunbar Corbusier: Recollections of Her Army Life, 1869–1908.* Norman: University of Oklahoma Press, 2003.

Stanley, Henry M. *My Early Travels and Adventures in America and Asia.* Vol. 1. New York: Scribner's Sons, 1895.

Starr, Leonora. *The Colonel's Lady.* London: Herbert Jenkins, 1943.

Steel, Flora, and Grace Gardiner. *The Complete Indian Housekeeper and Cook.* London: William Heinemann, 1890. Reprint: Cambridge: Cambridge University Press, 2010.

Stierstorfer, Klaus, ed. *Women Writing Home, 1700–1920: Female Correspondence across the British Empire.* Vol. 4. London: Pickering and Chatto, 2006.

Stocqueler, Jaochim, ed. *The Oriental Interpreter and Treasury of East India Knowledge.* London: James Madden, 1848.

Strange, [Thomas] Bland Major-General. *Gunner Jingo's Jubilee.* London: Remington, 1893.

Summerhayes, Martha D. *Vanished Arizona: Recollections of the Army Life of a New England Woman*. Philadelphia: J. B. Lippincott, 1908.

Totten, Ruth E. P. *The Button Box: A Daughter's Memoir of Mrs. George S. Patton*. Columbia: University of Missouri Press, 2005.

Trevelyan, George O. *The Competition Wallah*. London: B. Clayson and Taylor, 1864.

Trotter, Captain Lionel J. *History of India under Queen Victoria, 1836–1880*. Vol. 2. London: W. H. Allen, 1886.

Twitchell, Phillip G., ed. "Camp Robinson Letters of Angeline Johnson, 1876–1879." *Nebraska History* 77 (1996): 89–95.

Tytler, Harriet. *An Englishwoman in India: The Memoirs of Harriet Tytler*. Edited by Anthony Sattin. Oxford: Oxford University Press, 1986.

Utley, Robert M., ed. *Life in Custer's Cavalry: Diaries and Letters of Albert and Jennie Barnitz, 1867–1868*. New Haven: Yale University Press, 1977.

Veblen, Thorstein. *The Theory of the Leisure Class: An Economic Study of Institutions*. London: Macmillan, 1899. Reprint, New York: Mentor Books, 1953.

Vielé, Teresa Griffin. *Following the Drum: A Glimpse of Frontier Life*. New York: R. Craighead, Printer, 1858.

von Falke, Jacob. *Art in the House*. Translated by Charles Perkins. Boston: L. Prang, 1879.

Wallace-Dunlap, Madeline and Rosalind. *The Timely Retreat; or, A Year in Bengal before the Mutinies*. Vol. 1. London: Richard Bentley, 1858.

Washington, George. *The Writings of George Washington*. Vol. 5. Edited by Worthington C. Ford. New York: G. P. Putnam's Sons, 1890.

Whitworth, George C. *An Anglo-Indian Dictionary*. London: Kegan Paul, Trench, 1885.

Williams, Ellen. *Three Years and a Half in the Army; or, History of the Second Colorados*. New York: Fowler and Wells, 1885.

Williamson, Captain Thomas. *The East India Vade-Mecum; or Complete Guide to Gentlemen Intended for the Civil, Military or Naval Service of the Honourable East India Company*. Vol. 1. London: Black, Parry, and Kingsbury, 1810.

Wolseley, Field-Marshall Viscount Garnet. *The Story of a Soldier*. New York: Scribner's Sons, 1904.

Secondary Sources

Adams, Kevin. *Class and Race in the Frontier Army: Military Life in the West, 1870–1890*. Norman: University of Oklahoma Press, 2009.

Adams, R. J. Q. *Balfour: The Last Grandee*. London: John Murray, 2007.

Addison, Henry R., Charles H. Oakes, et al. *Who's Who, 1907: An Annual Biographic Dictionary*. London: Adam and Charles Black, 1907.

Allgor, Catherine. *Parlor Politics: In Which the Ladies of Washington Help Build a City and a Government*. Charlottesville: University Press of Virginia, 2000.

Alt, Betty S., and Bonnie D. Stone. *Campfollowing: A History of the Military Wife*. New York: Praeger Publishers, 1991.

Anderson, Benedict. *Imagined Communities: Reflections on the Origin and Spread of Nationalism*. London: Verso, 1983.

Anderson, Fred, and Andrew Clayton. *Dominion of War: Empire and Liberty in North America, 1500–2000*. New York: Penguin Books, 2005.

Baillie, Laureen. *Indian Biographical Index, India, Pakistan, Bangladesh, and Sri Lanka*. München: K. G. Sour, 2001.

Baker, Anni P. "Daughters of Mars: Army Officers' Wives and Military Culture on the American Frontier." *The Historian* 67 (March 2005): 20–42.

Bamfield, Veronica. *On the Strength: The Story of the British Army Wife*. London: Knight, 1974.

Bammer, Angelika. "Mother Tongues and Other Strangers: Writing 'Family' across Cultural Divides." In *Displacements: Cultural Identities in Question*. Bloomington: Indiana University Press, 1994.

Barnes, Ruth, and Joanne B. Eicher. "Introduction." In *Dress and Gender: Making and Meaning in Cultural Contexts*, edited by Ruth Barnes and Joanne Eicher, 1–7. Oxford: Berg Publishers, 1992.

Barnett, Louise. *Ungentlemanly Acts: The Army's Notorious Incest Trial*. New York: Hill and Wang, 2001.

———. "Introduction." In *Vanished Arizona: Recollections of the Army Life of a New England Woman*. Martha Summerhayes, v–xxiii. 2nd ed. Lincoln: University of Nebraska Press, 2014.

Bhabha, Homi K. *The Location of Culture*. New York: Routledge, 1994.

Blackburn, Forrest R. "Army Families in Frontier Forts." *Military Review* 49 (October 1969): 17–28.

Blumin, Stuart M. *The Emergence of the Middle Class: Social Experience in the American City, 1760–1900*. Cambridge: Cambridge University Press, 1989.

Blunt, Alison. "The Flight from Lucknow: British Women Travelling and Writing Home, 1857–8." In *Writes of Passage: Reading Travel Writing*, edited by James S. Duncan and Derek Gregory, 93–113. London: Routledge, 1998.

Boag, Peter. *Re-Dressing America's Frontier Past*. Berkeley: University of California Press, 2011.

Boyle, Paul. "Population Geography: Transnational Women on the Move." *Progress in Human Geography* 26, no. 4 (2002): 531–43.

Branca, Patricia. *Silent Sisterhood: Middle Class Women in the Victorian Home*. London: Croom Helm, 1975.

Brauer, Kinley. "The United States and British Imperial Expansion, 1815–1860," *Diplomatic History* 12 (1988): 19–38.

Brown, Dee. *The Gentle Tamers: Women of the Old Wild West*. New York: Bantam Books, 1974.

Brown, William L. III. *The Army Called It Home: Military Interiors of the Nineteenth Century*. Gettysburg: Thomas Publications, 1992.

Buckland, C. E. *Dictionary of Indian Biography*. London: Swan Sonnenschein, 1906.

Burn, William L. *The Age of Equipoise: A Study of the Mid-Victorian Generation*. London: Gregg Revivals, 1964.

Burton, Antoinette. "The White Woman's Burden: British Feminists and the 'Indian Woman,' 1865–1915." In *Western Women and Imperialism: Complicity and Resistance*, edited by Nupur Chaudhuri and Margaret Strobel. Bloomington: Indiana University Press, 1992.

Butler, Anne M. *Daughters of Joy, Sisters of Misery: Prostitutes in the U.S. West, 1865–90.* Urbana: University of Illinois Press, 1987.

Cain, P. J., and A. G. Hopkins, *British Imperialism, 1688–2000.* 2nd ed. Harlow: Longman, 2002.

Calder, Jenni. *The Victorian Home.* London: Batsford, 1977.

Callan, Hilary, and Shirley Ardener, eds. *The Incorporated Wife.* London: Croom Helm, 1984.

Callaway, Helen. "Dressing for Dinner in the Bush: Rituals of Self-Definition and British Imperial Authority." In *Dress and Gender: Making and Meaning in Cultural Contexts,* edited by Ruth Barnes and Joanne Eicher, 232–47. Oxford: Berg Publishers, 1992.

———. *Gender, Culture and Empire: European Women in Colonial Nigeria.* Urbana: University of Illinois Press, 1987.

Cannadine, David, and Simon Price. *Rituals of Royalty: Power and Ceremonial in Traditional Societies.* Cambridge: University of Cambridge, 1987.

Carman, W. Y. *A Dictionary of Military Uniforms.* New York: Scribner's Sons, 1977.

Chaudhuri, K. N. *The Emergence of International Business 1200–1800.* Vol. 4. *The East India Company.* London: Routledge, 1999.

Chaudhuri, Nirad. *Culture in the Vanity Bag.* Bombay: Jaico Press, 1976.

Chaudhuri, Nupur, and Margaret Strobel. "Introduction." In *Western Women and Imperialism,* edited by Nupur Chaudhuri and Margaret Strobel, 1–15. Bloomington: Indiana University Press, 1992.

Coffman, Edward M. *The Old Army: A Portrait of the American Army in Peacetime, 1784–1898.* Oxford: Oxford University Press, 1986.

———. "Women and Children in the Army, 1784–1812." *Journal of the Council on America's Military Past* 12 (May 1982): 31–39.

Cohn, Bernard S. "Cloth, Clothes, and Colonialism: India in the Nineteenth Century." In *Colonialism and Its Forms of Knowledge: The British in India.* Washington, D.C.: Smithsonian Institution Press, 1989.

Colley, Linda. "What Is Imperial History Now?" In *What Is History Now?,* edited by David Cannadine, 152–47. London: Macmillan, 2002.

———. "The Difficulties of Empire: Present, Past and Future," *Historical Research* 79 no. 205 (August 2006): 367–82.

Collingham, Elizabeth M. *Imperial Bodies: The Physical Experience of the Raj, 1800–1947.* Cambridge: Polity Press, 2001.

Comer, Denise K. "Fictions of Empire: British Women's Travel Narratives in India, 1799–1854." PhD diss., University of South Carolina, 1999.

Coontz, Stephanie. "'A Heaving Volcano': Beneath the Surface of Victorian Marriage." In *Marriage, a History: From Obedience to Intimacy or How Love Conquered Marriage.* London: Viking Penguin, 2005.

Cott, Nancy F. *The Bonds of Womanhood.* 2nd ed. New Haven: Yale University Press, 1997.

Crackel, Theodore J. "The Military Academy in the Context of Jeffersonian Reform." In *Thomas Jefferson's Military Academy: Founding West Point.* Charlottesville: University of Virginia Press, 2004.

Cullum, George W. *Biographical Register of the Officers and Graduates of the U.S. Military Academy.* Vol. 3. 3rd ed. New York: Houghton, Mifflin, 1891.

Cunliffe, Marcus. *Soldiers and Civilians: The Martial Spirit in America, 1775–1865.* New York: The Free Press, 1968.

Davidoff, Leonore. *The Best Circles: Society Etiquette and the Season.* London: Croom Helm, 1973.

Davidoff, Leonore, Megan Doolittle, et al. *The Family Story: Blood, Contract, and Intimacy, 1830–1960.* London: Longman, 1999.

Davies, Philip. *Splendours of the Raj: British Architecture in India, 1660–1947.* London: John Murray, 1985.

Dawson, Joseph G., III. *The Late Nineteenth-Century U.S. Army, 1865–1898: A Research Guide.* Westport, Conn.: Greenwood Press, 1990.

Degler, Carl N. *At Odds: Women and the Family in America from the Revolution to the Present.* Oxford: Oxford University Press, 1980.

Dinges, Bruce J. "Leighton Finley: A Forgotten Soldier of the Apache Wars." *Journal of Arizona History* 29 (Summer 1998): 163–284.

Doyle, Michael W. *Empires.* Ithaca: Cornell University Press, 1986.

Duncan, James S., and Derek Gregory. "Introduction." In *Writes of Passage: Reading Travel Writing,* edited by James S. Duncan and Derek Gregory, 1–13. London: Routledge, 1998.

Eales, Anne B. *Army Wives on the Frontier: Living by the Bugles.* Boulder: Johnson Books, 1996.

Eblen, Jack E. *The First and Second United States Empires: Governors and Territorial Government, 1784–1912.* Pittsburgh: University of Pittsburgh Press, 1968.

Edwardes, Michael. *Bound to Exile: The Victorians in Indian.* New York: Praeger Publishers, 1970.

Edwards, Clive, and Margaret Ponsonby. "Desirable Commodity or Practical Necessity? The Sale and Consumption of Second-Hand Furniture, 1750–1900." In *Buying for the Home: Shopping for the Domestic from the Seventeenth Century to the Present,* edited by David Hussey and Margaret Ponsonby, 117–38. Aldershot, UK: Ashgate Publishing, 2008.

Ellis, Joseph, and Robert Moore. *School for Soldiers: West Point and the Profession of Arms.* Oxford: Oxford University Press, 1974.

Evans, Sara M. *Born for Liberty: A History of Women in America.* New York: Free Press, 1989.

Fahs, Alice. "The Feminized Civil War: Gender, Northern Popular Literature, and the Memory of War, 1861–1900." *Journal of American History* 84, no. 4 (March 1999): 1461–94.

Falconer, Stuart. "Willoughby Wallace Hooper: A Craze about Photography." *The Photographic Collector* 4 (1984): 258–86.

Faragher, John Mack. *Women and Men on the Overland Trail.* New Haven: Yale University Press, 1979.

Farwell, Byron. *Armies of the Raj: From the Great Indian Mutiny to Independence, 1858–1947.* New York: W. W. Norton, 1989.

Feeley-Harnick, Gillian. "Issues in Divine Kingship." *Annual Review of Anthropology* 14 (1984): 273–313.

Felleman, Hazel, ed. *The Best Loved Poems of the American People.* New York: Doubleday, 1936.

Fields, Barbara J. "Slavery, Race, and Ideology in the United States of America." *New Left Review* (May–June, 1991): 95–118.

Finch, Janet. *Married to the Job: Wives' Incorporation in Men's Work.* London: Allen and Unwin, 1983.

Firth, Raymond W. *Symbols, Public and Private: Symbol, Myth, and Ritual.* Ithaca: Cornell University Press, 1975.

Fisher, Barbara. "Forrestine Cooper Hooker's Notes and Memoirs on Army Life in the West, 1871–1876." MA thesis, University of Arizona, 1963.

Foote, Cheryl J. *Women of the New Mexico Frontier 1846–1912.* Colorado: University Press of Colorado, 1990.

Fox-Genovese, Elizabeth. *Within the Plantation Household: Black and White Women of the Old South.* Chapel Hill: University of North Carolina Press, 1988,

Galloway, K. Bruce, and Robert B. Johnson Jr. *West Point: America's Power Fraternity.* New York: Simon and Schuster, 1973.

Ghose, Indira. "The Memsahib Myth: Englishwomen in Colonial India." In *Women and Others: Perspectives on Race, Gender, and Empire,* edited by Celia Daileader et al., 107–28. New York: Palgrave Macmillan, 2007.

Gilbert, Sandra, and Susan Gubar. *The Madwoman in the Attic: The Woman Writer and the Nineteenth-Century Literary Imagination.* 2nd ed. New Haven: Yale University Press, 2000.

Gillis, John. *A World of Their Own Making: A History of Myth and Ritual in Family Life.* Oxford: Oxford University Press, 1997.

Go, Julian. *Patterns of Empire: The British and American Empires, 1688 to the Present.* Cambridge: Cambridge University Press, 2011.

Godfrey, Audrey M. "Housewives, Hussies, and Heroines, or the Women of Johnston's Army." *Utah Historical Quarterly* 54 (Spring 1986): 157–78.

Goldring, Luin. "The Gender and Geography of Citizenship in Mexico-U.S. Transnational Spaces." *Identities* 7, no. 4 (January 2001): 501–25.

Graebner, Norman A. *Empire on the Pacific: A Study in American Continental Expansion.* New York: The Ronald Press Company, 1955.

Greenberger, Allen J. *The British Image of India: A Study in the Literature of Imperialism, 1880–1960.* Oxford: Oxford University Press, 1969.

Grier, Katherine C. *Culture and Comfort: Parlor Making and Middle-Class Identity, 1850–1930.* Washington, D.C.: Smithsonian Institution Press, 1997.

Guha, Ranajit. "Not at Home in Empire." *Critical Inquiry* 23 (Spring 1997): 482–93.

Gunn, Simon. *The Public Culture of the Victorian Middle Class: Ritual and Authority and the English Industrial City, 1840–1914.* Manchester, UK: Manchester University Press, 2000.

Haggis, Jane. "Gendering Colonialism or Colonising Gender? Recent Women's Studies Approaches to White Women and the History of British Colonialism." *Women's Studies International Forum* 13, nos. 1–2 (1990): 105–15.

Halttunen, Karen. *Confidence Men and Painted Women: A Study of Middle-Class Culture in America, 1830–1870.* New Haven: Yale University Press, 1982.

Hardorff, Richard G. *Indian Views of the Custer Fight: A Source Book.* Norman: University of Oklahoma Press, 2005.

Harries-Jenkins, Gwyn. *The Army in Victorian Society.* London: Routledge and Kegan Paul, 1977.

Heathcote, T. A. *Mutiny and Insurgency in India 1857–1858.* Barnsley, UK: Pen and Sword Military, 2007.

Herrington, Peter, and Michel Tomasek. *Queen Victoria's Army in Color: The British Military Paintings of Orlando Norie.* Atglen, Pa.: Schiffer Publishing, 2003.

Hietala, Thomas R. *Manifest Design: Anxious Aggrandizement in Late Jacksonian America.* Ithaca: Cornell University Press, 1985.

Hixson, Walter L. *American Settler Colonialism: A History.* New York: Palgrave Macmillan, 2013.

Howe, Daniel W. "Victorian Culture in America." In *Victorian America.* Philadelphia: University of Pennsylvania Press, 1976.

Huhndorf, Shari M. *Going Native: Indians in the American Cultural Imagination.* Ithaca: Cornell University Press, 2001.

Humble, Nicola, ed. "Introduction." In *Mrs Beeton's Book of Household Management.* Abridged edition, vii–xxx. Oxford: Oxford University Press, 2000.

Hyam, Bertram. *Empire and Sexuality: The British Experience.* Manchester, UK: Manchester University Press, 1990.

Immerman, Richard H. *Empire for Liberty: A History of American Imperialism from Benjamin Franklin to Paul Wolfowitz.* Princeton: Princeton University Press, 2010.

Iser, Wolfgang. "Coda to the Discussion." In *The Translatability of Cultures: Figurations of the Space Between,* edited by S. Budick and Wolfgang Iser, 95–302. Palo Alto: Stanford University Press, 1996.

Itzigsohn, José, and Silvia Giorguli-Saucedo. "Incorporation, Transnationalism, and Gender: Immigrant Incorporation and Transnational Participation as Gendered Processes." *International Migrant Review* 39, no. 4 (Winter 2005): 895–920.

Jacobs, Margaret. *White Mother to a Dark Race: Settler Colonialism, Maternalism, and the Removal of Indigenous Children in the U.S. West and Australia, 1880–1940.* Lincoln: University of Nebraska Press, 2009.

Jeffrey, Julie Roy. *Frontier Women: "Civilizing" the West? 1840–1880.* 1979. Reprint, New York: Hill and Wang, 1998.

Johnson, Paul. *The Birth of the Modern World Society 1815–1830.* New York: Harper Collins, 1991.

———. "Conspicuous Consumption and Working Class Culture in late Victorian and Edwardian Britain." *London: Transactions of the Royal Historical Society* 5th Series no. 38 (1998): 27–42.

Joseph, Betty. *Reading the East Indian Company: Colonial Currencies of Gender.* Chicago: University of Chicago Press, 2004.

Kakel III, Carroll P. *The U.S. West and the Nazi East: A Comparative and Interpretive Perspective*. New York: Palgrave Macmillan, 2011.

Kaplan, Amy. "Left Alone with America: The Absence of Empire in the Study of American Culture." In *Cultures of United States Imperialism*, edited by Amy Kaplan and Donald E. Pease, 3–21. Durham: Duke University Press, 1993.

Kasson, John F. *Rudeness and Civility: Manners in Nineteenth-Century Urban America*. New York: Hill and Wang, 1990.

Keegan, John. *World Armies*. 2nd edition. London: Palgrave Macmillan, 1983.

Kennedy, Dane. *The Magic Mountains: Hill Stations and the British Raj*. Berkeley: University of California Press, 1996.

Kerber, Linda K. "Separate Spheres, Female Worlds, Woman's Place: The Rhetoric of Women's History." *Journal of American History* 75 (June, 1988): 9–39.

Kerr, Barbara. *The Dispossessed: An Aspect of Victorian Social History*. London: John Baker, 1974.

Khagram, Sanjeev, and Peggy Levitt. "Constructing Transnational Studies." In *The Transnational Studies Reader: Intersections and Innovations*, edited by Sanjeev Khagram and Peggy Levitt, 1–22. London: Routledge, 2008.

Khan, Omar. *From Kashmir to Kabul: The Photographs of John Burke and William Baker, 1860–1900*. Ahmedabad, India: Mapin Publishing, 2002.

King, Anthony D. *The Bungalow: The Production of a Global Culture*. London: Routledge and Kegan Paul, 1984.

Knapman, Claudia. *White Women of Fiji, 1835–1930: The Ruin of Empire?* London: Allen and Unwin, 1987.

Knight, Oliver. *Life and Manners in the Frontier Army*. Norman: University of Oklahoma Press, 1978.

Knötel, Herbert, and Herbert Sieg. *Uniforms of the World: A Compendium of the Army, Navy, and Air Force Uniforms, 1700–1937*. Translated by Ronald G. Ball. New York: Scribner's Sons, 1937.

Kolodny, Annette. *The Land Before Her: Fantasy and Experience of the American Frontiers, 1630–1860*. Chapel Hill: University of North Carolina Press, 1884.

Kramer, Paul. "Power and Connection: Imperial Histories of the United States in the World." *American Historical Review* (December 2011): 1348–91.

LaFeber, Walter. *The New Empire: An Interpretation of American Expansionism, 1860–1898*. Ithaca: Cornell University Press, 1963.

Lebsock, Suzanne. *The Free Women of Petersburg: Status and Culture in a Southern Town, 1784–1860*. New York: W. W. Norton, 1984.

Leckie, Shirley A. *Elizabeth Bacon Custer and the Making of a Myth*. Norman: University of Oklahoma Press 1993.

Lima, Fernando H. "Transnational Families: Institutions of Transnational Social Space." In *New Transnational Social Spaces: International Migration and Transnational Companies in the Early Twenty-First Century*, edited by Ludger Pries, 77–93. London: Routledge, 2001.

Limerick, Patricia N. *The Legacy of Conquest: The Unbroken Past of the American West.* 2nd ed. New York: W. W. Norton, 2006.

———. "Going West and Ending Up Global." *Western Historical Quarterly* 32 (Spring 2001): 5–23.

Lombardo, Daniel. "Calling Cards Used for Social Reasons, A Look Back." *Amherst Bulletin* 27 (28 April 1995): 4.

Longford, Elizabeth. *Queen Victoria.* Phoenix Mill, UK: Sutton Publishing, 1999.

López, Ian F. Haney. "The Making of Race, Sex, and Empire." In *An Introduction to Women's Studies: Gender in a Transnational World*, edited by Inderpal Grewal and Caren Kaplan, 52–56. New York: McGraw Hill, 2002.

Lurie, Alison. *The Language of Clothes.* London: Bloomsbury Press, 1981.

MacMillan, Margaret. *Women of the Raj: The Mothers, Wives, and Daughters of the British Empire in India.* New York: Thames and Hudson, 1988. Reprint, Random House, 2007.

Mahler, Sarah J., and Patricia R. Pessar. "Gendered Geographies of Power: Analyzing Gender across Transnational Spaces." *Identities* 7, no. 4 (2001): 441–49.

Mangan, J. A., and James Walvin, eds. *Manliness and Morality: Middle-Class Masculinity in Britain and America, 1800–1940.* Manchester, UK: Manchester University Press, 1987.

Marcus, Sharon. *Apartment Stories: City and Home in Nineteenth-Century Paris and London.* Berkeley: University of California Press, 1999.

Mason, Philip. *A Matter of Honour: An Account of the Indian Army, its Officers and Men.* New York: Holt, Rinehart and Winston, 1974.

———. *The English Gentleman: The Rise and Fall of an Ideal.* New York: William Morrow, 1982.

Matthews, Glenna. *"Just a Housewife": The Rise and Fall of Domesticity in America.* New York: Oxford University Press, 1987.

Matthews, H. C. G., Brian Harrison, et al., eds. *Oxford Dictionary of National Biography, from the Earliest Times to the Year 2000.* Vols. 1–60. Oxford: Oxford University Press, 2004.

Mattison, Ray H. "The Army Post on the Northern Plains, 1865–1895." *Nebraska History* 35 (1954): 1–27.

Maunier, René. *The Sociology of Colonies: An Introduction to the Study of Race Contact.* Vol. 1. Edited and translated by E. O. Lorimer. London: Routledge and Kegan Paul, 1949.

McInnis, Verity. "Expanding Horizons: Officers' Wives on the Military Frontiers, 1846–1903." MA thesis, Texas A&M University–Corpus Christi, 2006.

———. "'Ladies' of the Frontier Forts." *Military History of the West* 35 (2005): 35–56.

Mickelson, Joan M. "British Women in India 1757–1857." Ph D diss., University of Michigan, 1978.

"Military Times Hall of Valor: Colonel Forrest E. Williford." http://valor.militarytimes.com/recipient.php?recipientid=18367.

Miller, Darlis A. "Foragers, Army Women, and Prostitutes." In *New Mexico Women: Intercultural Perspectives.* Albuquerque: University of New Mexico Press, 1986.

Miller, Edward A. *Lincoln's Abolitionist General: The Biography of David Hunter.* Columbia: University of South Carolina, 1997.

Montgomery, Maureen. *Displaying Women: Spectacles of Leisure in Edith Wharton's New York*. London: Routledge, 1998.

Moorhouse, Geoffrey. *India Britannica*. New York: Harper and Row, 1983.

Morrison, James L. *"The Best School in the World": West Point, the Pre–Civil War Years, 1833–1866*. Kent, Ohio: Kent State University Press, 1986.

Myres, Sandra. "Army Women's Narratives as Documents of Social History: Some Examples from the Western Frontier, 1840–1900." *New Mexico Historical Review* 65 (April, 1990): 175–98.

———. "Frontier Historians, Women, and the 'New' Military History." *Military History of the Southwest* 19, no.1 (Spring 1989): 26–37.

———. "Romance and Reality on the American Frontier: Views of Army Wives." *Western Historical Quarterly* 13 (October, 1982): 409–27.

———. *Westering Women and the Frontier Experience 1800–1915*. Albuquerque: University of New Mexico Press, 1982.

Nacy, Michele J. *Members of the Regiment: Army Officers' Wives on the Western Frontier, 1865–1890*. Westport, Conn.: Greenwood Press, 2000.

Nadis, Mark. "Evolution of the Sahibs." *The Historian* 19 (1975): 425–35.

Namias, June. *White Captives: Gender and Ethnicity on the American Frontier*. Chapel Hill: University of North Carolina Press, 1993.

Nicolson, Nigel. *Mary Curzon: The Story of an Heiress from Chicago Who Married Lord Curzon Viceroy of India*. London: Futura Press, 1978.

Nilsson, Sten. *European Architecture in India 1750–1850*. New York: Taplinger Publishing, 1969.

Nye, Colonel W. S. *Carbine and Lance: The Story of Old Fort Sill*. Norman: Oklahoma Press, 1974.

Ogden, Annegret. "Queen or Camp Follower? The Life of the Military Wife in Early California." *Californian* 2 (March–April 1984): 11–16.

Olson, James S., and Robert Shadle, et al., eds. *Historical Dictionary of the British Empire*. Westport, Conn.: Greenwood Press, 1996.

Parks, Joseph H. *General Edmund Kirby Smith, C.S.A.* Baton Rouge: Louisiana State University Press, 1954.

Parsons, Elsie C., ed. *Folk Tales of Andros Island, Bahamas*. New York: American Folk Lore Society, 1918.

Parsons, Timothy. *The British Imperial Century, 1815–1914: A World History Perspective*. London: Rowman and Littlefield, 1999.

Paterek, Josephine. *Encyclopedia of American Indian Costume*. New York: W. W. Norton, 1994.

Patterson, Steven. *The Cult of Imperial Honor in British India*. London: Macmillan, 2009.

Pease, Donald. "New Perspectives on U.S. Culture and Imperialism." In *Cultures of United States Imperialism*, edited by Amy Kaplan and Donald E. Pease, 22–40. Durham: Duke University Press, 1993.

Perry, Adele. *On the Edge of Empire: Gender, Race, and the Making of British Columbia, 1849–1871*. Toronto: University of Toronto Press, 2001.

Ponsonby, Margaret. *Stories from Home: English Domestic Interiors, 1750–1850.* Aldershot, UK: Ashgate Publishing Company, 2007.

Pratt, Mary Louise. *Imperial Eyes: Travel Writing and Transculturation.* London: Routledge, 1992.

Procida, Mary. *Married to the Empire: Gender, Politics and Imperialism in India, 1883–1947.* Manchester, UK: Manchester University Press, 2002.

Rankin, Colonel Robert H. *Uniforms of the Army.* New York: G. P. Putnam's Sons, 1967.

Rappaport, Erika. *Shopping for Pleasure: Women and the Making of London's West End.* Princeton: Princeton University Press, 2000.

Raugh, Harold E. *The Victorians at War, 1815–191; An Encyclopedia of British Military History.* Santa Barbara: ABC-CLIO, 2004.

Raza, Rosemary. *British Women Writers and India, 1740–1857.* Oxford: Oxford University Press, 2006.

Ricketts, Mrs. L. C. "English Society in India." *Contemporary Review* 101 (January/June 1912): 681–88.

Riley, Glenda. *Confronting Race: Women and Indians on the Frontier, 1815–1915.* Albuquerque: University of New Mexico Press, 2001.

——. *Divorce: An American Affair.* Oxford: Oxford University Press, 1991.

——. *Taking Land, Breaking Land: Women Colonizing the American and Kenyan Frontiers, 1840–1940.* Albuquerque: University of New Mexico Press, 2003.

——. *The Female Frontier: A Comparative View of Women on the Prairies and the Plains.* Lawrence: University Press of Kansas, 1988

Roper, Michael, and John Tosh, eds. *Manful Assertions: Masculinities in Britain since 1800.* London: Routledge, 1991.

Rosier, Paul. *Serving Their Country: American Indian Politics and Patriotism in the Twentieth Century.* Cambridge, Mass.: Harvard University Press, 2009.

Ross, Robert. *Clothing: A Global History; or, The Imperialists' New Clothes.* Cambridge: Polity Press, 2008.

Roth, Michael P. *Historical Dictionary of War Journalism.* Westport, Conn.: Greenwood Press, 2001.

Rouse, Roger. "Making Sense of Settlement: Class Transformation, Cultural Struggle, and Transnationalism among Mexican Migrants in the United States." In *Towards a Transnational Perspective on Migration*, edited by Nina Glick Schiller, Linda Basch, and Cristina Blanc-Szanton, 25–52. New York: New York Academy of Sciences, 1992.

Said, Edward W. *Culture and Imperialism.* New York: Vintage Books, 1994.

——. *Orientalism.* London: Routledge and Kegan Paul, 1978. Reprint, London: Penguin Books, 2003.

Saunier, Pierre-Yves. *Transnational History.* New York: Palgrave Macmillan, 2013.

Schiller, Nina Glick. "Transmigrants and Nation-States: Something Old and Something New in the U.S. Immigrant Experience." In *The Handbook of International Migration*, edited by C. Hirschman, J. Dewind, and P. Kasinitz, 94–119. New York: Russell Sage Foundation, 1999.

Schlereth, Thomas. "Material Culture Studies in America, 1876–1976." In *Material Culture Studies in America*, edited by Thomas Schlereth, 1–78. Lanham, Md.: AltaMira Press, 1999.

Schueller, Malani J., and Edward Watts, eds. *Messy Beginnings: Postcoloniality and Early American Studies*. New Brunswick: Rutgers University Press, 2003.

Shea, Nancy. *The Army Wife*. 4th ed. New York: Harper and Row, 1966.

Shepperd, Alan. *Sandhurst: The Royal Military Academy and Its Predecessors*. London: Country Life Books, 1980.

Sinha, Mrinalina. *Colonial Masculinity: The 'Manly Englishman' and the 'Effeminate Bengali' in the late Nineteenth Century*. Manchester, UK: Manchester University Press, 1995.

Skelton, William B. *An American Profession of Arms: The Officer Corps, 1784–1861*. Topeka: University of Kansas Press, 1992.

Sklar, Kathryn K. *Catharine Beecher, A Study in American Domesticity*. New Haven: Yale University Press, 1973.

Sloane, W. and J. *The Story of Sloane's*. New York: W. J. Sloane, 1950.

Smith, Shannon D. *Give Me Eighty Men: Women and the Myth of the Fetterman Fight*. Lincoln: University of Nebraska Press, 2008.

Smith, Sherry L. *The View from Officers' Row: Army Perceptions of Western Indians*. Tucson: University of Arizona Press, 1990.

Smith, Thomas T. *The Old Army in Texas: A Research Guide to the U.S. Army in Nineteenth-Century Texas*. Austin: Texas State Historical Association, 2000.

———. "West Point and the Indian Wars 1802–1891." *Military History of the West* 24 (Spring 1994): 24–56.

Smith-Rosenberg, Carroll. "The Female World of Love and Ritual: Relations between Women in Nineteenth-Century America." *Signs* 1 (Autumn 1975): 1–29.

———. *This Violent Empire: The Birth of an American National Identity*. Chapel Hill: University of North Carolina Press, 2010.

Spacks, Patricia M. *Gossip*. New York: Alfred A. Knopf, 1985.

Spain, Daphne. *Gendered Spaces*. Chapel Hill: University of North Carolina Press, 1992.

Spear, Percival. *The Nabobs: A Study of the Social Life of the English in Eighteenth-Century India*. Oxford: Oxford University Press, 1963.

Stallard, Patricia Y. *Glittering Misery: Dependents of the Indian Fighting Army*. Fort Collins and San Rafael, Colo.: Old Army Press and Presidio Press, 1978.

Stanford, John K. *Ladies in the Sun: The Memsahibs' India 1760–1860*. London: Galley Press, 1962.

Stanley, Peter. *White Mutiny: British Military Culture in India*. New York: New York University Press, 1998.

Stoddard, Ellwyn R., and Claude E. Cabanillas. "The Army Officer's Wife: Social Stresses in a Complementary Role." In *The Social Psychology of Military Service*, edited by Nancy L. Goldman and David R. Segal, 151–71. Beverly Hills: Sage Publications, 1976.

Stoler, Ann L. *Carnal Knowledge and Imperial Power: Race and the Intimate in Colonial Rule*. Berkeley: University of California Press, 2002.

Stone, Lawrence. *The Family, Sex, and Marriage in England, 1500–1800*. London: Weidenfeld and Nicolson, 1977.

Strachan, Hew. *Wellington's Legacy: The Reform of the British Army, 1830–1854*. Manchester, UK: Manchester University Press, 1984.

Strobel, Margaret. *European Women and the Second British Empire*. Bloomington: Indiana University Press, 1991.

Sweet, Matthew. *Inventing the Victorians*. London: Faber, 2001.

Tarlo, Emma. *Clothing Matters: Dress and Identity in India*. Chicago: University of Chicago Press, 1996.

Tate, James P., ed. *The American Military on the Frontier*. Washington, D.C.: Office of Air Force History, 1978.

Tate, Michael L. *The Frontier Army in the Settlement of the West*. Norman: University of Oklahoma Press, 1999.

Taylor, Quintard. *The Forging of a Black Community: Seattle's Central District from 1870 through the Civil Rights Era*. Seattle: University of Washington Press, 1994.

Thomas, Hugh. *The Story of Sandhurst*. London: Hutchinson, 1961.

Thompson, F. M. L. *English Landed Society in the Nineteenth Century*. London: Routledge and Kegan Paul, 1963.

Thornton, Peter. *Authentic Décor: The Domestic Interior, 1620–1920*. New York: Viking Penguin, 1984.

Trustram, Myna. *Women of the Regiment: Marriage and the Victorian Army*. Cambridge: Cambridge University Press, 1984.

Turner, Mark W. "Hybrid Journalism: Women and the Progressive Fortnightly." In *Journalism, Literature and Modernity: From Hazlitt to Modernism*, edited by Kate Campbell, 72–90. Edinburgh: Edinburgh University Press, 2000.

Turner, Victor W. *Dramas, Fields, and Metaphors: Symbolic Action in Human Society*. Ithaca: Cornell University Press, 1975.

Utley, Robert M. *Frontiersmen in Blue: The United States Army and the Indian, 1848–1865*. New York: Macmillan, 1967. Reprint, Lincoln: University of Nebraska Press, 1981.

———. *Frontier Regulars: The United States Army and the Indian, 1866–1891*. London: Macmillan, 1973.

Van Alstyne, Richard W. *The Rising American Empire*. New York: W. W. Norton, 1974.

Venning, Annabel. *Following the Drum: The Lives of Army Wives and Daughters*. London: Headline Book Publishing, 2005.

Vertovec, Steven. "Conceiving and Researching Transnationalism." *Ethnic and Racial Studies* 22 (1999): 447–62.

Vidal, Gore. "West Point." In *American Identities: Contemporary Multicultural Voices*. Hanover: Middlebury College Press, 1994.

Vivian, Evelyn C. *The British Army from Within*. London: Hodder and Stroughton, 1914.

Wagoner, Jennings L. Jr., and Christine C. McDonald. "Mr. Jefferson's Academy: An Educational Interpretation." In *Thomas Jefferson's Military Academy: Founding West Point*. Charlottesville: University of Virginia Press, 2004.

Walkowitz, Judith R. *Prostitution and Victorian Society: Women, Class and the State.* Cambridge: Cambridge University Press, 1980.

Watson, Samuel J. "Developing 'Republican Machines': West Point and the Struggle to Render the Officer Corps Safe for America, 1802–33." In *Thomas Jefferson's Military Academy: Founding West Point.* Charlottesville: University of Virginia Press, 2004.

Weeks, William E. *Building the Continental Empire: American Expansion from Revolution to the Civil War.* Chicago: Ivan R. Dee, 1996.

Weigley, Russell F. *History of the United States Army.* London: Macmillan, 1967.

Welter, Barbara. "The Cult of True Womanhood: 1820–1860." *American Quarterly* 18 (Summer 1966): 151–74.

White, Richard. *"It's Your Misfortune and None of My Own." A New History of the American West.* Norman: University of Oklahoma Press, 1991.

———. *The Middle Ground: Indians, Empires, and Republics in the Great Lakes Region, 1650–1815.* Cambridge: Cambridge University Press, 1991.

Whitlock, Tammy C. *Crime, Gender, and Consumer Culture in Nineteenth-Century England.* Aldershot, UK: Ashgate Publishing Limited, 2005.

Williams, Mary L. "Ladies of the Regiment: Their Influence on the Frontier Army." *Nebraska History* 78, no. 4 (Winter 1997):159–164.

———. "Servants at Military Posts: A Glimpse at 'Domesticity' through the Letters of Alice Kirk Grierson." *Journal of Big Bend Studies* 11 (1999): 145–58.

Wilson, Elizabeth. *Adorned in Dreams: Fashion and Modernity.* 2nd ed. New Brunswick: Rutgers University Press, 2003.

Woollacott, Angela. *Gender and Empire.* London: Macmillan, 2006.

Wooster, Robert. *Frontier Crossroads: Fort Davis and the West.* College Station: Texas A&M University Press, 2006.

———. *Soldiers, Sutlers, and Settlers: Garrison Life on the Texas Frontier.* College Station: Texas A&M University Press, 1987.

Worswick, Clark, and Ainslie Embree. *The Last Empire: Photography in British India, 1855–1911.* New York: Aperture, 1976.

Websites

Baker, Erma. "Brown, John Henry." *Handbook of Texas Online,* http://www.tshaonline.org/handbook/online/articles/fbr94.

"The British Army." http://www.army.mod.uk/training_education/24487.aspx.

"Census of India 1881–1931." http://www.samanvaya.com/main/contentframes/knowledge/articles/census1881.html.

Cole, David. "Survey of U.S. Army Uniforms, Weapons and Accoutrements." http://www.history.army.mil/html/museums/uniforms/survey_uwa.pdf.

Dictionary of Canadian Biography, vol. 15. "Thomas Bland Strange," by Roderick C. Macleod. Toronto: University of Toronto, 2005; online ed., 2015. http://www.biographi.ca/009004-119.01-e.php?BioId=42107.

"Elizabeth Bacon Custer." *Kansapedia, Kansas Historical Society.* http://www.kshs.org/kansapedia/elizabeth-bacon-custer/12030.

"Elizabeth Custer." *Custerwest.org.* http://custer.over-blog.com/article-10579099.html.

"Letters from W. T. Sherman, Headquarters of the United States Army, St. Louis, Missouri." William T. Sherman Collection, Missouri Historical Society Archives. http://collections.mohistory.org/resource/175438.html.

Oxford Dictionary of National Biography. http://www.oxforddnb.com.

The Peerage. www.thepeerage.com.

Usami, Yoshifumi. "Change in the Workforce in British India, 1881–1921." Paper presented at XIV International Economic History Congress, Helsinki, Finland, 21–25 August 2006. http://www.helsinki.fi/iehc2006/papers1/Usami.pdf.

"Warrant of Precedence." http://rajyasabha.nic.in/rsnew/guidline_govt_mp/chap11.pdf.

Index

Page numbers in *italics* indicate photographs.